LYLE

1,001 More Antiques
Worth a Fortune

LYLE

1,001 More Antiques Worth a Fortune

Anthony Curtis

A PERIGEE BOOK

A Perigee Book
Published by The Berkley Publishing Group
A division of Penguin Putnam Inc.
375 Hudson Street
New York, New York 10014

Copyright © 1999 by Lyle Publications
Cover design by Jack Ribik

Published simultaneously in Canada.

The Penguin Putnam Inc. World Wide Web site address is
http://www.penguinputnam.com

Library of Congress Cataloging-in-Publication Data

Curtis, Tony, 1939–
Lyle : 1,001 more antiques worth a fortune / Anthony Curtis.
       p.   cm.
"Published simultaneously in Canada."
Includes index.
ISBN 0-399-52507-6
1. Antiques—Catalogs.   I. Title.
NK1125.C886   1999   99-12453
745.1'075—dc21   CIP

Printed in the United States of America

10   9   8   7   6   5   4   3   2   1

Acknowledgments

Academy Auctioneers, Northcote House, Northcote Avenue, Ealing, London W5 3UR
Auction Team Köln, Postfach 50 11 68, D-5000 Köln 50, Germany
Bearne's, St Edmunds Court, Okehampton Street, Exeter EX4 1DU
Bonhams, Montpelier Street, Knightsbridge, London SW7 1HH
Bonhams Chelsea, 65–69 Lots Road, London SW10 0RN
Bonhams West Country, Dowell Street, Honiton, Devon
Bosleys, 42 West Street, Marlow, Bucks SL7 1NB
Bristol Auction Rooms, St John Place, Apsley Road, Clifton, Bristol BS8 2ST
Butterfield & Butterfield, 220 San Bruno Avenue , San Francisco CA 94103, USA
Butterfield & Butterfield, 7601 Sunset Boulevard, Los Angeles CA 90046, USA
Canterbury Auction Galleries, 40 Station Road West, Canterbury CT2 8AN
Cheffins Grain & Comins, 2 Clifton Road, Cambridge
Christie's (International) SA, 8 place de la Taconnerie, 1204 Genève, Switzerland
Christie's Monaco, S.A.M, Park Palace 98000 Monte Carlo, Monaco
Christie's Scotland, 164–166 Bath Street, Glasgow G2 4TG
Christie's South Kensington Ltd., 85 Old Brompton Road, London SW7 3LD
Christie's, 8 King Street, London SW1Y 6QT
Christie's East, 219 East 67th Street, New York, NY 10021, USA
Christie's, 502 Park Avenue, New York, NY10022, USA
Christie's, Cornelis Schuytstraat 57, 1071 JG Amsterdam, Netherlands
Christie's SA Roma, 114 Piazza Navona, 00186 Rome, Italy
Christie's Swire, 2804–6 Alexandra House, 16–20 Chater Road, Hong Kong
Christie's Australia Pty Ltd., 1 Darling Street, South Yarra, Victoria 3141, Australia
Dee & Atkinson & Harrison, The Exchange Saleroom, Driffield, Nth Humberside YO25 7LJ
William Doyle Galleries, 175 East 87th Street, New York, NY 10128, USA
Dreweatt Neate, Donnington Priory, Newbury, Berks.
Dreweatt Neate, Holloways, 49 Parsons Street, Banbury
Du Mouchelles Art Galleries Co., 409 E. Jefferson Avenue, Detroit, Michigan 48226, USA
Eldred's, Box 796, E. Dennis, MA 02641, USA
Ewbanks, Burnt Common Auction Rooms, London Road, Send, Woking GU23 7LN
Finarte, 20121 Milano, Piazzetta Bossi 4, Italy
Galerie Koller, Rämistr. 8, CH 8024 Zürich, Switzerland
Andrew Hartley Fine Arts, Victoria Hall, Little Lane, Ilkley
George Kidner, The Old School, The Square, Pennington, Lymington, Hants SO41 8GN
Lawrence's Fine Art Auctioneers, Norfolk House, 80 High Street, Bletchingley, Surrey
David Lay, The Penzance Auction House, Alverton, Penzance, Cornwall TA18 4KE
Dave Lewis, 20 The Avenue, Starbeck, Harrogate, North Yorkshire HG1 4QD
Onslow's, The Depot, 2 Michael Road, London, SW6 2AD
Phillips Manchester, Trinity House, 114 Northenden Road, Sale, Manchester M33 3HD
Phillips Son & Neale SA, 10 rue des Chaudronniers, 1204 Genève, Switzerland
Phillips West Two, 10 Salem Road, London W2 4BL
Phillips, 11 Bayle Parade, Folkestone, Kent CT20 1SQ
Phillips, 49 London Road, Sevenoaks, Kent TN13 1UU
Phillips, 65 George Street, Edinburgh EH2 2JL
Phillips, Blenstock House, 7 Blenheim Street, New Bond Street, London W1Y 0AS
Phillips Marleybone, Hayes Place, Lisson Grove, London NW1 6UA
Phillips, New House, 150 Christleton Road, Chester CH3 5TD
Pieces of Time, 1–7 Davies Mews, Unit 17–19, London W1Y 1AR
Derek Roberts Antiques, 24–25 Shipbourne Road, Tonbridge, Kent TN10 3DN
Russell, Baldwin & Bright, The Fine Art Saleroom, Ryelands Road, Leominster HR6 8JG
Skinner Inc., Bolton Gallery, Route 117, Bolton MA, USA
Sotheby's, 34–35 New Bond Street, London W1A 2AA
Sotheby's, 1334 York Avenue, New York NY 10021
Sotheby's, 112 George Street, Edinburgh EH2 2LH
Sotheby's, Summers Place, Billingshurst, West Sussex RH14 9AD
Sotheby's, Monaco, BP 45, 98001 Monte Carlo
Street Jewellery, 5 Runnymede Road, Ponteland, Northumbria NE20 9HE
G E Sworder & Son, 14 Cambridge Road, Stansted Mountfitchet, Essex CM24 8BZ
Tennants, Harmby Road, Leyburn, Yorkshire
Tool Shop Auctions, 78 High Street, Needham Market, Suffolk IP6 8AW
T Vennett Smith, 11 Nottingham Road, Gotham, Nottingham NG11 0HE
Wallis & Wallis, West Street Auction Galleries, West Street, Lewes, E. Sussex BN7 2NJ
Wintertons Ltd., Lichfield Auction Centre, Fradley Park, Lichfield, Staffs WS13 8NF

While every care has been taken in the compiling of information contained in this volume, the publisher cannot accept liability for loss, financial of otherwise, incurred by reliance placed on the information herein.

All prices quoted in this book are obtained from a variety of auctions in various countries and are converted to dollars at the rate of exchange prevalent at the time of sale. The images and the accompanying text remain the copyright of the contributing auction houses.

The publishers wish to express their sincere thanks to the following for their involvement and assistance in the production of this volume.

TONY CURTIS (Editor)

EELIN McIVOR (Sub Editor)

ANNETTE CURTIS (Editorial)

CATRIONA DAY (Art Production)

ANGIE DEMARCO (Art Production)

NICKY FAIRBURN (Art Production)

PHILIP SPRINGTHORPE (Photography)

Contents

7

CONTENTS

Introduction

Almost every week there are headlines in the newspapers. Someone, somewhere, has discovered that a piece of apparent junk in their attic or garage or at the local flea market is, in fact, a really hot collectable which they have gone on to sell for a fortune. And so more and more people are joining in the treasure hunt, becoming aware of the possibilities of that humdrum old golf club (one sold recently for over $160,000) sewing machine, toaster, games board or whatever.

A French or German ivory comb, 15th century, one side carved with two jousting knights, the other side with bathing scene, 4⅞in. *(Sotheby's)*   **$28,750**

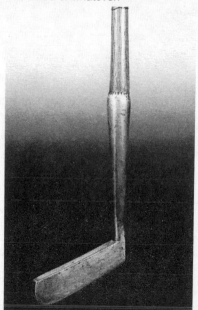

A rare metal-headed blade putter, late 18th/early 19th century, with fruitwood shaft and well-knopped hozel, with suede grip and listing, the hozel 6¼. long. *(Christie's)*   **$155,800**

Sometimes it can just be a tidy little sum, like the humble iron washboard which fetched over $2,000, or $3,400 plus for a piece of chalkware (not bad, considering it was reckoned to be the 'poor man's pottery'). Then there's over $8,000 paid for a piece of sewer pipe art - now hugely collectable, incidentally. $8,405 was also the price paid for a television and radio combination, while a metal tea trolley can fetch $27,180 and an ivory comb $28,750.

A Martin Brothers stoneware bird vase and cover, standing, the wise old bird casting an upwards, knowing glance, 1902, 26cm. high. *(Christie's)*   **$13,800**

A rather unlikely pine and gesso carving of a poodle (though the Canine Club wouldn't necessarily recognise it as such) holding a basket in its mouth could net you $35,650.

On the other hand it could be enough to keep you in comfort for the rest of your life. Consider the young scientist who managed to grab the ball hit into the crowd by Mark McGwire of the St. Louis Cardinals when he notched up his record 70 home runs in September 1998. He managed to pick it up as it bounced under a metal bench, and, having already turned down an offer of $1 million for it, sent it to Christie's for auction, where it fetched $3.2 million. If you'd happened to be sitting in that seat, it could have been you!

A façon de Venise polychrome armorial goblet, first third of the 16th century, Venice or South Germany, 5³/₈in. high. *(Christie's)* **$75,000**

A George I walnut ratchet-back wing armchair, the slightly arched top, outscrolled arms, bowed seat and squab cushion covered in contemporary florally-patterned petit and gros point needlework. *(Christie's)* **$166,830**

Of course, it helps to have some sort of inkling of what you should be looking for. A souvenir copy of, say, a newspaper issued on the day of a royal wedding or the first moon landing isn't likely to fetch much in the foreseeable future simply because so many people kept them as souvenirs. On the other hand, anything carrying Princess Diana's signature already commands a premium. And that's where this book comes in. It gives you invaluable information on just which often unlikely items, the very kind you might inadvertently throw away, are fetching even more unlikely sums, and, wherever possible, it also tells you why. Perhaps most importantly of all, every item is illustrated, with a description of its distinguishing features and its current market value. After all, you're hardly going to make that fortune if you don't recognise your money spinner when you see it. This book will give you a head start in the recognition and awareness stakes which in turn can seriously improve your chances of becoming the next person to find that they have their hands on one of the 1,001 Antiques which really are Worth a Fortune.

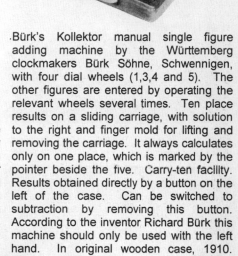

An Answer Game working adding machine in the form of a tinplate toy robot, by Ischida, Japan. Battery powered, with gearwheel mechanism, two-row number keyboard, the answer button to the left and the light button above right. With plus/minus lever, a plus sign lighting up in the left eye and a minus sign in the right, and with spiral plate rotating on the head, circa 1963, 36.5cm. high.
(Lyle) **$2,160**

·Bürk's Kollektor manual single figure adding machine by the Württemberg clockmakers Bürk Söhne, Schwennigen, with four dial wheels (1,3,4 and 5). The other figures are entered by operating the relevant wheels several times. Ten place results on a sliding carriage, with solution to the right and finger mold for lifting and removing the carriage. It always calculates only on one place, which is marked by the pointer beside the five. Carry-ten faclilty. Results obtained directly by a button on the left of the case. Can be switched to subtraction by removing this button. According to the inventor Richard Bürk this machine should only be used with the left hand. In original wooden case, 1910. *(Auction Team Köln)* **$4,581**

The Millionaire, 1895, an early export model with nine insertion bars and results to 16 places, serial no. 2,707, in original wooden case.

A large, well-known, four-function adding machine, made by Otto Steiger, St. Gallen, after Louis Bollé's 1888 invention, and produced by Hans W. Egli of Zürich. This model with distributor's plate of *Otto Hess & Cia, Florida 667, Buenos Aires*.
(Auction Team Köln) **$3,903**

Peek, Frean Biscuits, framed advertisement. *(Lyle)* **$480**

Enamel sign for Komo Metal Frame, 24 x 30in. *(Dave Lewis)* **$240**

Printed card counter display sign for Vesta Paints for Every Home, 21in. high. *(Lyle)* **$55**

Bovril, 'Oh Mamma don't forget to order Bovril', 1896. *(Street Jewellery)* **$800**

Zebra Grate Polish, enamel sign, circa 1900, 24 x 24in. *(Street Jewellery)* **$480**

Shop window display figure for Askeys 'The name for Wafer Biscuits of Good Taste', produced by Pytram Ltd, New Malden, Surrey, of papier-mâché construction, 1930s. 29in. high. *(Dave Lewis)* **$400**

Hudson's Soap, enamel sign indicating closing times, 18 x 10½in. *(Dave Lewis)* **$240**

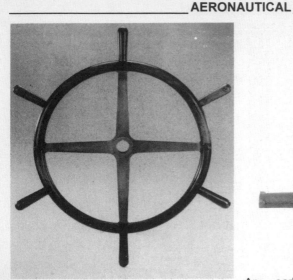

A wheel believed to be from H.M. Airship No.1, 'The Mayfly', circa 1911, in mahogany with cast metal spokes and frame, 28in. wide overall.

In 1908, in response to the developments in Germany's Zeppelin program, the Admiralty ordered Britain's first rigid airship to be built by Vickers in Barrow. Work began in 1909 but was delayed when it was found that the craft was too heavy to fly. The Mayfly, as it was most commonly known, was larger than any Zeppelin at the time and was the first airship to incorporate duralumin.

Shed trials took place in February 1911 and on 22nd May, she was towed out and became the first airship to be moored to a mast. Further lightening took place over the next few months, including the removal of the keel, and on 24th September she emerged from the shed once more. Unfortunately, a sudden wind pushed her onto her side and she then broke in two. A Court of Inquiry was subsequently convened but concluded that no blame could be attached: Winston Churchill, then the First Lord, prevented the findings being published.

Thus, the Mayfly never actually flew, other than to a few feet during shed trials. The naval airship section was disbanded and the ill-fated craft was left to rot.
(Sotheby's) **$9,218**

An early bomb-release mechanism, possibly from a small airship or WW1 period aircraft, with small fabric label inscribed *Zeppelin Bomb Release*, 12in. high.
(Sotheby's) **$956**

After E. Montaut 'En Reconnaissance' Clement-Bayard; a rare early poster depicting airship, aeroplane and four-seater tourer, in military usage, full color lithograph, linen backed, 62 x 45in.
(Christie's) **$2,185**

Important Grueby Pottery vase, globular form with rolled rim, seven broad leaf-forms with negative space in relief, exceptional leathery glaze at shoulder transitioning to a smooth glaze at base, circular impressed Grueby mark, incised Inltlals *E.P.*, 11in. high.
(Skinner) **$25,300**

Exceptional Grueby Pottery lamp with Tiffany Studios crocus shade, base with five leaf-forms under a rich, leathery, matte green glaze, original fittings with good patina, shade with unusual shading and glass texture in two colors of green, yellow, opalescent on a deep red background, 20in. high.
(Skinner) **$37,950**

Rare Rookwood Pottery ale set, tankard and five mugs, decorated by Sturgis Lawrence in 1898, each with a portrait of a different Native American, Rookwood logo, date, shape 656, tankard decorated with Chief 'Hollow-Horn-Bear', Sioux, 9¾in. high, mugs decorated with Chief 'Mountain', Blackfeet; Chief 'White Man', Kiowa; Kichn Woman 'Nasuteas', Wichita; Chief 'Wolf Robe', Cheyenne; Chief 'Goes-To-War', Sioux, 5in. high.
(Skinner) **$6,900**

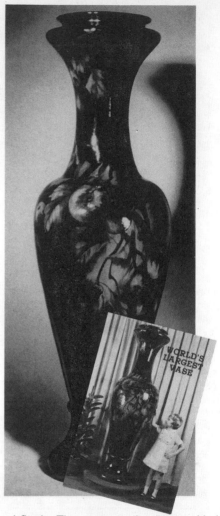

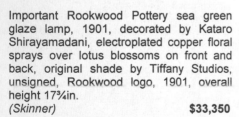

Important Rookwood Pottery sea green glaze lamp, 1901, decorated by Kataro Shirayamadani, electroplated copper floral sprays over lotus blossoms on front and back, original shade by Tiffany Studios, unsigned, Rookwood logo, 1901, overall height 17¾in.
(Skinner)   **$33,350**

Important and monumental Weller Pottery vase, decorated by Frank Ferrell, accompanied by the 'Gold Medal' award from the St. Louis Louisiana Purchase Exposition in 1904, large apple tree boughs with leaves and branches in colors of green, reddish-brown, yellow, dark brown, on a standard glaze ground, signed by Frank Ferrell, impressed Weller mark, 5ft.8in. high.

Many problems were encountered in its production, and eight attempts were made before the vase was successfully molded and fired. The upper portion was molded in two parts and joined together in a special firing before it was decorated by Frank Ferrell. A special kiln was constructed to accommodate the huge vase; and including labor, materials and expenditures from the seven previous failures, the manufacturing cost was estimated at $2,000.

Weller's perseverance was rewarded; his magnificent entry was selected by the International Jury of Awards to receive the Gold Medal in the Arts Category.
(Skinner)   **$112,500**

A Sioux beaded hide child's vest, sinew sewn, decorated with alternating cross motifs, a pair of American flags, and American flag crests flanked by cross motifs on the front panels and on the reverse side lazy stitched in two shades of blue, white, translucent red and green beads against a white ground, translucent red beaded narrow band border, 14¾in. long. (Christie's)   **$5,750**

A Southern Cheyenne girl's beaded hide dress, open sided yoke painted in yellow with red and green bands at the sleeves, a row of dentalia pendants accented with red and orange basket beads, across the skirts midsection also decorated with a row of dentalia pendants accented with red and orange basket beads and a second row of basket beads in similar colors, 50½in. long.

Accompanied by a letter from June 13, 1934 written by the owner of the dress. It reads in part:

My darling Mary Eleanor,
....I always intended to leave my Indian dress to your dearly-loved Grandma, who was my closest friend in the Indian service, but she went home first, and it seemed as if the one who was so very precious to her would be the one to have to have it. The little girl who owned it was in my schoolroom. Her father's name was Roman Nose, and I understood they were Southern Cheyennes.
(Christie's)   **$36,800**

A northern Northwest Coast bent corner storage box, probably Tlingit, with corner oriented design painted in black and red formlines, ovoids, circles, U forms and eye forms on all four sides with two bilaterally symmetrical designs one showing a frontal face at the top with joint designs at the bottom, 14¼ x 11in.
(Christie's)   **$10,925**

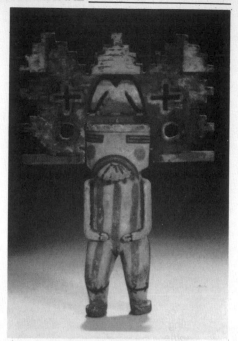

A pair of woman's Apache beaded hide boots, sinew and thread sewn, with a blue, white yellow and translucent red beaded medallion on top of the upper, a narrow beaded band border around the foot and along the top decorated with linked diamond and cross motifs in translucent red and green beads against light blue beaded ground, 17¾in. long.
(Christie's) **$9,200**

An important early Hopi polychrome cottonwood kachina doll, representing a dancing Shalako Mana, finely carved, both stout legs bent at the knees, her arms modeled in low relief and hugging the torso, decorated overall with orange and white striped body paint, and wearing a classic sack mask with a hatched rainbow at the chin, surmounted by an elaborate openwork tableta headdress, 11¼in. high.

A charming 19th century (circa 1870-1890) Hopi sculpted depiction of a Palhik/Poli Mana. This female supernatural being figures prominently in the ceremonial traditions of the ancient Hopi culture still surviving in the rugged mesa country of northeastern Arizona. Commonly referred to as the little 'Corn Maiden', 'Butterfly', or 'Water Drinking Girl', formally she is part of the supernatural order known as the Momoyam or the Katsina Women.

A Tlingit ceremonial dancing blanket, Chilkat, woven in black, ivory, yellow and blue green commercial wool and cedarbark fiber in a crest pattern perhaps based on the diving whale motif in center with side panels representing stylized raven figures in cedarbark and wool fringe, corner ties in yellow and blue green squares, hide tie straps, 69in. long.
(Christie's) **$18,975**

As a collective the Katsinum, a body of semi-divine beings who regulate the forces of nature and life, direct their energies toward assisting the Hopi and other pueblo people.
(Christie's) **$107,000**

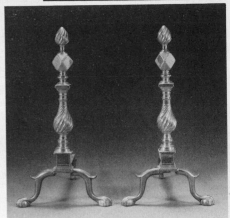

A pair of polychrome-decorated cast iron Hessian soldier fireplace andirons, 19th/20th century, each figure looking left and holding a sword in mid-stride, 19½in. high. *(Sotheby's)* **$575**

A pair of Federal brass andirons, Philadelphia, 1760-1780, each with a spiral flame and diamond finial above a spiral baluster-shaped shaft over a plinth, on spurred cabriole legs with ball-and-claw feet; together with a firetool holder, 24½in. high. *(Christie's)* **$51,750**

A pair of Chippendale engraved bell-metal andirons, Massachusetts, probably Boston, circa 1795, each with a lemon form finial above a bright-cut decorated wafer and columnar standard, the bright cut decorated plinth on spurred, arched supports ending in claw-and-ball feet, a wrought-iron log guard behind, 20in. high. *(Sotheby's)* **$8,625**

A pair of painted cast iron baseball player andirons, American, late 19th/early 20th century, each modeled in the half-round depicting a baseball player in profile with black-painted cap, white uniform with black and yellow-painted trim, a black-painted belt and black socks and shoes, one holding a beige-painted bat, the other holding a white-painted baseball, 19¼in. high. *(Christie's)* **$23,000**

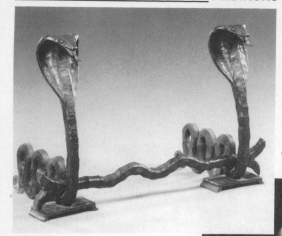

Edgar Brandt, cobra fire irons, circa 1925, black patinated wrought iron, fashioned as rearing serpents with spread hoods, with waved cross bar, both serpents stamped *Edgar Brandt,* one further stamped *France,* the cross bar stamped *E. Brandt,* 41in. wide.
(Sotheby's) **$61,289**

◄

A set of brass and iron firestools, American, 1800-1820, comprising a pair of andirons, each with double-lemon top finial over a molded hexagonal plinth on a circular base with pierced billet bar, on double spurred legs and ball feet and similar tools comprising a shovel, poker and tongs, together with a bowed brass rail and iron wire fire fender with scrolling wire decoration, the andirons 25½in. high, the fender 18in. high.
(Christie's) **$19,550**

Gilbert Poillerat, pair of fire irons, circa 1930, wrought iron, each with a design of intertwined loops surmounted by a highly stylized crest, 13in. high.
(Sotheby's) **$23,046**

A Roman stucco painted fresco fragment in two registers, the lower in bright red with a hound chasing a deer, circa 1st century A.D., 7½ x 8in.
(Bonhams) **$2,258**

A Roman aubergine mold-blown glass flask, styled as a bunch of grapes, with short tubular neck and infolded disk rim, circa 1st century A.D., 3½in.
(Bonhams) **$7,950**

A Roman mosaic glass patella cup, composed of opaque red, yellow and white floral canes set in an amethyst matrix, 1st century B.C./A.D., 1¾in. high.
(Bonhams) **$6,360**

An Egyptian limestone relief fragment, inscribed in raised relief with the hieroglyphic titles of Alexander the Great, after 332 B.C., 28 x 16in. *(Bonhams)* **$7,418**

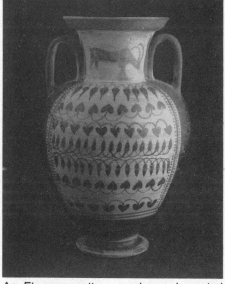

An Egyptian polychrome painted cartonnage mummy mask of a female, with central frontal uraeus, Late Period, after 500 B.C., 17in. high.
(Bonhams) **$2,988**

An Etruscan pottery amphora, decorated on both sides of the neck with a grazing stag, the body on one side decorated with linked ivy leaves framed on either side by a vertical band with a double row of dots, similar scene on the other side with a register of palmettes, circa 6th century B.C., 14¾in. high.
(Bonham's) **$6,773**

A Hispano-Moresque marble capital, 10th century, elaborately carved with various chain-like openwork motifs, losses and wear, 7¾in. high.

This capital relates directly to another probably commissioned for a structure in Madinat al-Zahara, northwest of Córdoba. *(Sotheby's)* **$24,150**

A Roman marble monumental carving of a bull's head with carved eyes and pupils and flared deeply carved snout, the lower jaw missing and some damage to the snout area, circa 2nd-3rd century A.D., 19½in. long. 11in. high. *(Bonhams)* **$9,858**

A Roman marble relief fragment, carved in the late Archaic style, with naked Apollo on the right of the scene, holding a lyre in the crook of his left arm, ?Zeus standing centrally, his left hand resting on his hip, his right hand held to his side, naked to the waist, a rolled diadem in his hair, the head of a third figure on the left of the scene, all within a molded frame, circa 2nd century A.D., 21½ x 10¾in. *(Bonhams)* **$5,406**

Cast iron and glass aquarium, probably J.W. Fiske & Co., New York, last quarter 19th century, the shell and foliate decorated octagonal tank centering a rockery-form fountain above a figural heron form standard on a molded, circular base, 47¾in. high. *(Skinner)* **$3,335**

◄

A George III mahogany goldfish bowl stand of triangular outline, the top with raised circular center and gadrooned border, 22¼in. wide.
(Christie's) **$17,900**

◄

Cast iron and glass aquarium, J.W. Fiske & Co., New York, circa 1875, signed on interior of bowl *J.W. Fiske 41...Place N.Y. pat'd Feby... 1875,* foliate decorated octagonal form tank with shaped skirt centers a baluster form fountain, above a pierced baluster form foliate and scroll decorated standard on a shaped tripod base, 48in. high. *(Skinner)* **$2,070**

24

Porcelain first appeared in Japan when the discovery of kaolin nearby in 1616 led to the establishment of a ceramic center in Saga prefecture, Hizen, which came to be known as Arita. Early Arita was painted in grayish underglaze blue and primitive red and green enamels. Enameled and blue wares with paneled decoration in the later Ming style were brought to the West by the Dutch from the 17th century onwards, often through the port of Imari. Kakiemon and Nabeshima wares were also made at Arita, and production continues there to the present day.

A pair of Arita blue and white models of seated horses, late 17th century, their saddle cloths with flowers and foliage, the irregularly shaped bases with scrolling karakusa, each 7¹/16in. long. *(Christie's)* **$11,835**

A rare Arita model of a cat, 17th century, decorated in iron-red and black enamel, seated with its tail curled about its back, 8½in. high.

Many of the animals, birds and fish were used to decorate grand banqueting tables in the early 18th century. When not in use on the table, such figures served to embellish the mantelshelf, cabinet or secrétaire. Really precious porcelain would be kept in the cabinet of curiosities in the lady's dressing room or closet, where such rarities served for entertainment to while away the evenings.
(Christie's) **$51,540**

A pair of Arita blue and white vases with covers, 17th century, decorated with chrysanthemums in three panels separated by stylized flower motifs, the neck decorated in bands of repeating patterns, the covers similarly decorated, 11¼in. high. *(Christie's)* **$8,590**

A rare huanghuali folding horseshoeback armchair, Jiaoyi, late 16th/early 17th century, the U-shaped toprail continuing in a wide arc to the arms with out-curved ends, above bracket-shaped spandrels, supported by hooked extensions of the front legs and plain dowel struts, the S-curved backsplat divided into three pierced panels, the top carved as a stylized shou character above a central lattice finely carved as a qilin amidst cloud scrolls, itself above a narrow shaped panel, the front seat stretcher carved with confronted dragons separated by interlocking tendrils extending from the wide beading, the hinged circular legs terminating in base stretchers with baitong mounts and a central baitong openwork plaque, the front base stretcher supporting the fixed footrest, 39½in. high, 27½in. wide.
(Christie's) **$200,500**

A turned and joined cherrywood and hickory armchair, Coastal South Carolina, 1680–1700, the compressed-ball turned finials above incised cylindrical stiles centering eight ring and reel-turned spindles framed above and below by rectangular rails surmounted by nine ring-and-reel turned finials over flaring-turned and incised arms above a splint-woven trapezoidal seat, on ball and cylindrical-turned legs joined by ring and reel-turned double box stretchers with tapering feet, 41in. high.

With its vigorous turnings, early construction techniques, and commanding presence, this great chair is a remarkable survival of seventeenth century South Carolina craftmanship. The only known armchair of its kind, it is a rare document of the aesthetic preferences, craft traditions, and cultural nuances that shaped the earliest material culture of the region.

This armchair was probably made by an emigré Huguenot joiner. One third of the joiners documented in seventeenth century South Carolina were Huguenots and by 1700, there were approximately 325 people of French origin in the region.
(Christie's) **$288,500**

Alvar Aalto for Oy. Huonekalu-ja-Rakkennustyötehdas AB, Turku, Finland, lounge chair 'Paimio', model No. 41, designed 1931–32, manufactured after 1932, retailed by Artek OY. AB, Helsinki, distributed in the U.K. by Finmar Ltd., bent laminated and solid birch frame, stained black and lacquered seat in bent plywood, the underside with Finmar Ltd label, 25³/₈in. wide.
(Sotheby's) **$8,998**
◀

Painted William and Mary maple and pine ▶ chair table, southeastern New England, early 18th century, the oval two board top tilts on a base of two horizontal supports ending in scrolled hand holds joining four block vase and ring turned legs with medial seat and box stretchers all resting on turned feet, 26in. high.
(Skinner) **$20,700**

◀
A Louis XV beechwood fauteuil pliant by Antoine Migeon, the ratcheted arched padded back, squab-cushion, arms and bowed seat covered in close-nailed floral yellow silk damask, the arms carved with acanthus finials above the folding seat-rail conformingly carved and the cabriole legs headed by a leaf and a flower and terminating in a foliate scroll, stamped to the left back leg *MIGEON*.
(Christie's) **$16,560**

An inlaid birch armchair, designed by Mackay Hugh Baillie Scott, manufactured by the Dresdener Werkstätten für Handwerkskunst, circa 1903.

The triangular cane seat with deep apron, gently concave tapering slat back inlaid with mother-of-pearl and bone, tapering square-section uprights forming the front legs.

The production of this design by the Dresdener Werkstätten für Handwerkskunst is recorded in the photo archives of the DWH, dated *1903*.
(Christie's)   **$7,123** ▶

Ludwig Mies van der Rohe for the Berliner Metallgewerbe Joseph Müller, Berlin, cantilever armchair 'MR20', 1927 chromium-plated tubular steel, stained cane seat and arms, 32¾ high.
(Sotheby's)   **$16,871**
◀

A Venetian giltwood gondola chair, 19th ▶ century, the curved and arched back with beaded edge headed by a flowerhead and a shell-motif, above the padded lower section, arms and bowed seat covered in pink striped silk, the arms terminating in foliate masks above the seat-rail centered by a male mask, the back decorated with St. Mark's lion above a shield flanked by two dragons, on four upturned dolphin supports. *(Christie's)*   **$5,083**

A classical carved mahogany bergère, New York, 1815–1820, the reeded crest above an upholstered barrel back and seat continuing to reeded downswept arms terminating in scrolled handholds over reeded downswept arm supports with foliate-carved rectangular panel bases, on saber legs waterleaf-carved and with paw feet, 32in. high.

Essentially a Grecian throne form, this chair reflects a variety of influences while remaining a distinctive example of New York Classical cabinetmaking. Its low back and covered sides are both reminiscent of the French fauteuil girandole and its anglicized Regency version, while its ultimate source in antiquity cannot be overlooked.

Acanthus-carved legs and animal paw feet similar to those on this chair are Greco-Roman features that were assimilated by many New York cabinetmakers. The hairy leg carving and forward-facing orientation is a particular characteristic of Duncan Phyfe's work. *(Christie's)* **$222,500**

A very fine turned maple rush-seat ladder-back armchair, Delaware River Valley, possibly by the Ware family of Roadstown, New Jersey, 1740–80 of generous proportion, the ball and steeple finials above flaring stiles centering six graduated serpentine backrests and a yellow painted rush seat flanked by line-incised arms on baluster form supports and turned legs centering a bold ball and reel turned frontal stretcher ending in flattened ball feet.

Maskell Ware, born December 13, 1766, was the patriarch of a chair-making dynasty that lasted well into the 20th century, with Wilmon Ware still turning chairs in Newport, New Jersey as late as 1942. Maskell was born near Roadstown and apprenticed to John Lanning, of Greenwich, Cumberland County, New Jersey. He married his wife, Hannah, in 1790 and together welcomed the first of eleven children, Thomas, in 1792. In this year, he returned to Roadstown founding the Ware Chair Works which employed many of his seven boys. *(Sotheby's)* **$24,140**

by Friske Kinball in 1929 for the Philadelphia Museum of Art. A single chair with harp-shaped splat was sold at Sotheby's New York, January 23, 1982. A group of four armchairs were sold in October 19, 1991, of which one is in the Mabel Brady Garvan Collection, Yale University Art Gallery; one is in the collection of Bayou Bend, The Museum of Fine Arts, Houston; one is at Winterthur and one is in a private collection. Another chair, acquired in 1960, is also in the collection at Winterthur. According to tradition, an additional settee and matching eight chairs, from which the previously enumerated are alleged to have come, also exist; the location of that last chair and settee are unknown.
(Christie's) **$81,700**

A painted and gilded cabriole armchair, Philadelphia, 1790–1810, the arched crest above an upholstered tablet back with carved and gilded surround flanked by reeded baluster stiles issuing carved and gilded arms with upholstered rests over gilded reeded baluster-turned supports centering a trapezoidal half-over upholstered seat above carved and gilded seat rails punctuated by carved and gilded reserves, on tapering cylindrical gilded ring-turned and reeded front legs, outside back appears to retain original paper insert, 36½in. high.

The chair illustrated here adds an additional clue to the growing number of identified French-inspired Philadelphia-made white painted and gilt-decorated seating forms. A set of 12 chairs and a settee are recorded in the Winterthur Library as having belonged to Edward Burd of Philadelphia. Called the 'Marie Antoinette Suite', these chairs and settee were sold from the Shippen Burd Collection at American Art Galleries, March 7 & 8, 1921, and were subsequently purchased

An Irish George II mahogany and oak open armchair, the pierced arched toprail centered by a scallop-shell and scrolled patera with waved secondary toprail, above a foliate-carved vase-shaped splat, flanked by outscrolled arms with paper-scroll terminals, above a padded drop-in seat covered in red velvet, on cabriole legs capped with scallop-shells and acanthus claw feet, with molded ankle.
(Christie's) **$42,500**

A rare elbow-gauntlet for an Officer of Harquebusiers, English, circa 1630-40, possibly Greenwich, with long open cuff of shot-proof weight unusually drawn-up to a standing flange extending from the point of the elbow to around the inside joint, strongly incised with broad bands of very narrow linear fluting, retaining some of its original crimson velvet and brocade pickadils and almost all of its original lining, 16¾in. long.
(Sotheby's)   **$3,450**

A full armor in German Maximilian style, 19th century, finely constructed throughout, comprising close helmet with one piece skull embossed with convex ribs over the rear and a boldly roped comb, hinged bevor, hinged visor embossed with a grotesque mask in the manner of Konrad Seusenhofer of Innsbruck, breast-plate of strongly pronounced globose form with boldly cabled flanged turns across the top and at the gussets, en suite with matching back-plate with skirt, a pair of full arm defenses including asymmetrical spaulders with haute-pieces, large couters and pair of mitten gauntlets, full leg defenses with cuisses cabled, probably made by Winkelmeier of Vienna.
(Sotheby's)   **$13,800**

An extremely rare early parrying manifer, an exchange-piece for the German Foot Tournament, circa 1500-30, made in one piece for carrying over the left forearm, extending from around the point of the elbow and covering the full upper surface of the hand, drawn-up to a prominent ridge over the knuckle and embossed with three low diagonal ridges over the upper half.

The raised shape over the forearm is of sufficient breadth to suggest that this piece was intended to be worn over a gauntlet and lower-cannon.

This piece is possibly unique as a surviving example of the period.
(Sotheby's)   **$17,250**

A German cuirassier armor of blackened steel, circa 1620-30, comprising closed burgonet with two-piece skull embossed with v-shaped flutes radiating in an oval from a rearward point applied with a ring finial on a stellate washer, fitted with plume-holder at the base, pivoted peak, flat upper-bevor with deep vision aperture divided centrally and pierced with a small mouth-like hole between symmetrical arrangements of breaths.

The full arm defenses, including large multi-lame pauldrons with ogival subsidiary edges matching both those of the burgonet's peak and the lames of the couters.

(Sotheby's) **$19,550**

A fine kon ito odoshi do-maru (an armor with dark blue laced cuirass wrapping round the body without hinges), Edo period, mid 19th century, the very fine armor of hon kozane laced in dark blue, comprising a richly mounted twenty-four plate o-boshi kabuto (a low rounded helmet), eighteen of the plates with standing flanges and eight large rivet heads (hoshi), the remaining plates overlaid by two decorative plates in gilded copper and shakudo, engraved with a design of flowers and having three shinodare to the front in the same metal, at the base of the bowl a row of rivets, the four lame kebiki laced plates for the o manyo jikoro (large rounded neckguard) with a copper gilt kanamono on the last two plates, a six stage tehen kanamono, the bowl signed *Miochin*.

(Christie's) **$83,000**

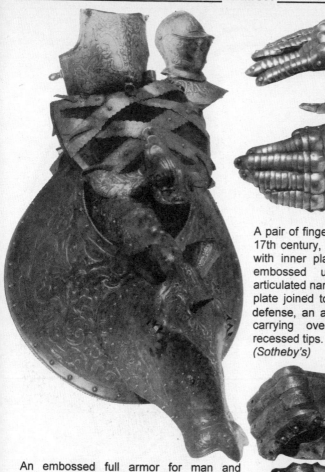

A pair of fingered gauntlets, late 16th/early 17th century, each with flared pointed cuff with inner plate, turned roped edge and embossed ulna, metacarpus of five articulated narrow plates and a larger fluted plate joined to a fluted prominent knuckle defense, an additional articulation in front carrying overlapping finger-plates with recessed tips.
(Sotheby's) **$6,900**

An embossed full armor for man and horse in the style of the second half of the 16th century, the armor for the man comprising close helmet with two-piece skull, pierced visor of duck's bill shape, pivoted pierced upper- and lower-bevors, and neck-guard front and rear, hinged gorget of three plates front and rear, breast-plate of late globose form with strong roped turns at the neck and moveable gussets and fitted with skirt of three articulations.

The horse armor comprising full shaffron with applied sides, muzzle ear defenses, central spike and ocular guards, the latter formed as domed pierced sun masks, crinet of eleven lames each with an embossed nodule on the top.
(Sotheby's) **$28,750**

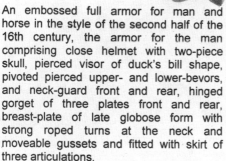

A rare pair of late Gothic mitten gauntlets, South German or Austrian (Innsbruck), circa 1490-1500, each with flared gutter-shaped short cuff with medial ridge and recessed border with angular outward turn at the edge, four articulated metacarpal plates each with a central cusp and ogival corners, the rear plate embossed with three bold v-shaped flutes radiating from the rear cusp.
(Sotheby's) **$8,050**

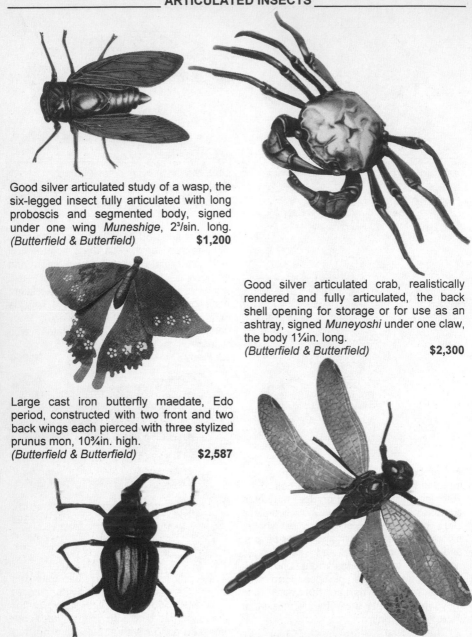

Good silver articulated study of a wasp, the six-legged insect fully articulated with long proboscis and segmented body, signed under one wing *Muneshige*, 2³/₈in. long. *(Butterfield & Butterfield)* **$1,200**

Large cast iron butterfly maedate, Edo period, constructed with two front and two back wings each pierced with three stylized prunus mon, 10¾in. high. *(Butterfield & Butterfield)* **$2,587**

Good silver articulated crab, realistically rendered and fully articulated, the back shell opening for storage or for use as an ashtray, signed *Muneyoshi* under one claw, the body 1¼in. long. *(Butterfield & Butterfield)* **$2,300**

Good articulated study of a beetle, the shakudo arachnid with six legs and articulated wings, expertly modeled and signed *Muneyoshi* under one wing, 2in. long. *(Butterfield & Butterfield)* **$1,200**

Silver and shakudo articulated study of a dragonfly, elegantly rendered with silver wings and shakudo body, the six-legged insect signed under one wing *Muneyoshi*, 3³/₈in. long. *(Butterfield & Butterfield)* **$2,875**

Joe Colombo for Arnolfo di Cambio 'Biglia' ashtray, designed 1968-69, yellow painted metal over pink tinted glass, moveable clear glass top element labels to glass *designer Joe Colombo* and manufacturer's label with logo, approximately 4¾in. high. *(Sotheby's)* **$596**

Metal ashtray mounted with an Alfa Romeo 158 made by Alfa to celebrate their victory in the world championships, 1950. *(Finarte)* **$1,070**

Scratch my Back matchstriker and ashtray. *(Lyle)* **$240**

Chairman matchstriker and ashtray. *(Lyle)* **$280**

Caleys Table Waters matchstriker and ashtray. *(Lyle)* **$240**

Royal Doulton John Barleycorn ashtray designed by C.J. Noke, 1936. *(Lyle)* **$128**

▶

A rare signed menu from a banquet celebrating Louis Blériot's Cross-Channel Flight, held by La Colonie Française, London on 16th September 1909, the four-page card signed in pencil by the aviator on the front, 5½ x 8½in.
(Sotheby's) **$922**

▲

Adolf Hitler, large signed 9½ x 14½in. photograph, to lower white border, head and shoulders with chin resting on hand, photo by Kleine of Hanover, circa 1934-7, extremely rare in this size.
(Vennett Smith) **$2,722**

▶

Princess Diana, a very fine signed and inscribed 7 x 5½in. photo, to mount, in original green leather frame, with gilt crown and initial *D* at head, contained in original green presentation box, by Andrew Soos of London, rare in this form.
(Vennett Smith) **$1,518**

THE SALE

Diana

18/250

Diana Princess of Wales, leather hardback limited edition of the catalog of the sale of dresses from the collection of Diana Princess of Wales, by Christie's of Park Avenue, signed by Diana and numbered by her *18/250* on the front title page, showing each of the 80 lots, in color, many from famous photos taken of the Princess wearing the garments, together with an admission to view card, with original package and box. *(Vennett-Smith)* **$14,080**

Marilyn Monroe, an 8 x 10in. black and white photograph signed and dedicated to *David, Marilyn Monroe.* *(Bonhams)* **$4,480**

Harry Houdini, signed and inscribed sepia 6 x 8in. photograph in green, *To Jack Hanson, all kinds of good luck are the wishes of Houdini, June 2/20*, in original white oval mount, 10 x 12. *(Vennett-Smith)* **$1,312**

Diana Princess of Wales, a souvenir program for the Wales Festival of Remembrance, St. David's Hall, Cardiff, 5th November 1994, signed by Diana beneath her full page portrait inside and dated in her hand, *1994.* *(Vennett-Smith)* **$3,097**

THE RT. HON. WINSTON S. CHURCHILL, C.H., M.P.
(as First Lord of the Admiralty)

Winston S. Churchill, signed bookplate photo, as First Lord of the Admiralty, removed from The World Crisis, 1911-1918, 5½ x 8in. *(Vennett Smith)* **$1,360**

One of the most fascinating autographs of all is that of William Shakespeare, not least because of the continuing speculation as to whether in fact the man of that name really composed all these amazing works. Certainly, given his prodigious output and undoubted literacy, one would have expected to find more than the half dozen or so examples that are known to exist. If you can find any more, and get them authenticated, you will find yourself with an asset worth several million dollars.

A musical automaton of a tightrope walker, attributed to Jean Phalibois, French, circa 1870, the stage consisting of ornately carved and gold leaf painted wood in oriental style hung with pink silk and supporting a stand with tightrope on which an articulated painted wooden lady in cut and painted paper skirt applied with gold circles, gold and blue bodice and white turban, jumps on the rope lifting her arms holding a garland, 22in. high without dome. *(Sotheby's)* **$48,000**

◀

A shop display automaton, probably French 1920s, the electrically operated movement operating the mechanical figure of a man in evening suit who answers the telephone while moving his head and arm, standing in front of a cloth covered screen with illuminated panel.
(Sotheby's) **$5,704**

▶

◀

A musician and clown automaton, French, late 19th century, probably made by Gustave Vichy, the standing figure of the Negro musician with composition head, moving mouth and neck, playing a banjo while tapping his foot, the white faced Negro clown standing along side jumping through a hoop held in front of him, on rectangular wooden base, 33 x 28in.
(Sotheby's) **$24,000**

A fine and rare Gustav and Henri Vichy musical automaton of 'Sonnette de l'entracte' the sleeping clown banjo player, French, circa 1890, the papier mâché headed clown with articulated lower lip and eyelids, brown glass eyes and a painted telegraph wire symbol on his forehead, cream and orange hair, holding a banjo and seated on a burgundy and dark green painted high solid stool which houses the keywound stop-start musical mechanism, 29½in. high. *(Sotheby's)* **$56,000**

▶

Clown Equilibriste, a composition headed musical automaton, by Vichy, 35in. high. *(Christie's)* **$34,000**

Musical automaton, with five tunes and two mechanical dolls, circa 1890. *(Auction Team Köln)* **$25,500**

Pope Pius XII, a large processional motorcade pennant, double sided silk with leather reinforced edges, heavily embroidered with crossed keys motif of St. Peter and the Vatican, with silver and gold woven threads and raised-work on divided yellow and white ground, 12 x 13in. *(Christie's)* **$1,687**

◄

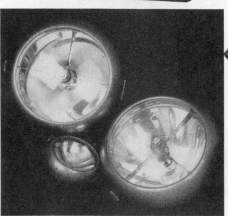

A good pair of electric headlamps; includes original nickel-plated with etched curved glass lens inscribed *Stephen Grebel*; together with a matching scuttle-mounting spotlamp, circa 1928, headlamps: diameter:11in., depth: 7in.
(Christie's) **$3,450**

A running board mounted spare-wheel security carrier trunk with three straps to affix to spare tyre stamped *S.C. Simon & Co. Luggage, Phila; U.S.A.*, circa 1912, diameter: 25in.
(Christie's) **$2,070**

After Franco Guibara, Bugatti T57 Atalante, a good bronze model of the famous machine, well sculpted and detailed and surmounted upon polished black marble base and polished wood plinth. *(Christie's)* **$6,325**

The postcard was introduced in Britain by the GPO in 1870 and was so designed to take the address only on one side with the message alongside the illustration on the other. The form was given a boost by the Paris Exhibition of 1889 and the first picture postcards were permitted in Britain in 1894. Then, in 1902 an Act of Parliament decreed that the message and address could be written on the same side, leaving the other free for a picture, and after this postcards became very much more popular as other countries quickly followed Britain's lead. One phenomenon of the time was the 'Lifeboat Saturday' card, which was delivered by Balloon Post.

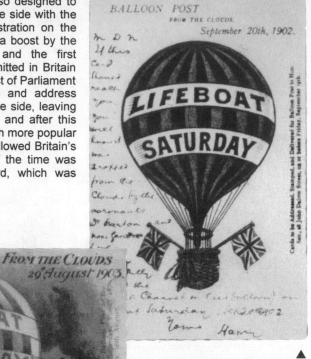

▲

Lifeboat Saturday Balloon Post, 20th September 1902, the flight was from Manchester to Haslingden, *If this card should reach you, you will know it was dropped from the clouds by the aeronauts who recently, successfully crossed the English Channel in their balloon on Lifeboat Saturday Sept. 20th 1902. (Vennett-Smith)* **$3,600**

◄

Lifeboat Saturday, Balloon Post, 29th August 1903, sold on behalf of the Lifeboat Saturday in Manchester, the flight was canceled and then flown in September from London, dropped from the balloon and postally used Epping September 7th 1903. *(Vennett-Smith)* **$2,500**

42

Baseball cards were issued by manufacturers of cigarettes, bubble gum, sweets and even sausages, and featured the great players of the day, such as Babe Ruth, Eddie Planck and Nap Lajoie.

Honus Wagner was not perhaps the greatest in the baseball hall of fame, but his card has become the rarest and the most valuable ever. It was included in cigarette packets, but without Wagner's permission, and, as a non-smoker, he took exception to his image gracing a cigarette card. He complained, the cards were withdrawn, and only 20 are believed still to be in circulation. Of these, the only one in mint condition and backed by an advertisement for Piedmont cigarettes, rather than the more usual sweet Caporal, sold at Sotheby's in 1992 for $451,000 (£300,000), to the top American hockey star, Wayne Gretsky. It turned up next as a prize on the CNN Larry King television talk show, where it was won by a Miami postal worker, Patricia Gibbs. Ms Gibbs wasted no time in offering it for sale at Christie's.

Other rare baseball cards include one from Sweet Caporal of the pitcher Eddie Planck. Issued in 1910, 30 are known still to exist. Of the Goudey Gum Co's Nap Lajoie card of 1933, 50 are believed still to be circulating.

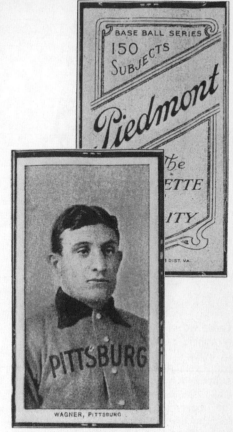

Honus Wagner's baseball card from America's No 1 game.
(Christie's) **$640,000**

A cushioned cork center RON baseball hit by Mark McGwire for his record 70 home runs at the Busch Stadium in St. Louis, September 1998. Thought to be a record price for a piece of sporting memorabilia. *(Christie's)* **$3,200,000**

In September 1998, Mark McGwire of the St Louis Cardinals made history when he notched up a record 70 home runs at the Busch Stadium in St. Louis. (The previous record of 60 was set by Babe Ruth in 1927, and remained unsurpassed until 1961, when it was upped to 61.) As the McGwire ball sailed into the crowd, a 26 year old research scientist, Philip Ozersky, managed to pick it up as it ricocheted off the back wall and bounced under a metal bench. Having already turned down an offer of $1 million for it, Ozersky put it up for auction at Christie's, where it flew again, this time to a record $3.2 million (£2 million).

Nantucket lightship basket, dated 1891, paper label on base *made on board South Shoal Lightship by William Sandsbury sold... George R. Folger Main Street, Nantucket Mass.*, with illegible ink inscription, 4in. high, diameter 8¾in. *(Skinner)* **$1,495**

Large woven bamboo square sided flower arranging basket, Meiji period, composed of strips of bamboo of varied sizes, with wide vertical sections forming the sides supported by a fine tightly woven interior lining and twisted ropes of bamboo along the upper rim, base and mid-section, and forming the raised handle above, 28½in. high. *(Butterfield & Butterfield)*

$2,587

Eastern Woodland Indian paint decorated covered splint basket, 19th century, with salmon and black swab decoration, 10¾in. high, diameter 15¾in.
(Skinner) **$4,312**

Large woven bamboo flower basket, Meiji/Taisho period, signed *Chikuunsai*, fashioned with an irregular but tight weave of bamboo strips rising to a wrapped rim and a wide, irregularly curved bamboo stalk handle, signed to the underside. 17¼in. high. *(Butterfield & Butterfield)*
$2,875

A fully beaded Creek sash, central strap and suspended tabs loom woven, the warp and weft composed of brown and black cotton twill, and beaded with white and translucent blue pony beads, strap consisting of twenty one columns enclosing alternating patterns of four or five square designs, 107in. long.

This was acquired from the family of Abner Smith, missionary, in Goshen, N.Y., during the 19th century. Form and decoration of the bandoleer bag and sash indicate an origin from the Southeastern U.S.
(Christie's) **$57,500**

A Creek beaded cloth bandoleer bag, of small proportions, composed of narrow shoulder strap made from blue wool, finely beaded in white, lavender, two shades of blue, clear and translucent red and blue glass seed beads in two sizes, with a column of linked curvilinear designs on the proper left side, changing at the shoulder to a pattern of diamonds enclosing cross motifs alternating with foliate designs, 28¼in. long.

Having lost their provenance, many bandoleer bags of the Southeastern type are assumed to be of Seminole origin, but one very similar example was found with a reliable documentation, indicating its origin from the Creek Indians circa 1830s.
(Christie's) **$48,300**

An early Victorian beadwork model of a parrot, circa 1845, with inset eyes, on an ebonized wood stand, 13in. long.
(Christie's) **$1,965**

A late George III polychrome-painted four-post bed, with baluster front posts joined by a square stretcher to the front and a three piece cornice painted in yellow, orange, green and brown floral designs, comprising a pair of pale-blue lined curtains; pelmet bed-cover and padded bedstead, 6ft. wide.
(Christie's)   **$30,544**

A fine and extremely rare Huanghuali four-poster canopy bed, Jiazichuang, late 16th/early 17th century, the soft-mat top set within the thick rectangular frame above the slightly recessed, cusped plain apron with beaded edge continuing along each of the two center surfaces of the slender legs to the leaf-shaped flange above the shaped, tapered feet, the railings on three sides of simple, wide pingzi lattice-pattern and the upper frieze a series of plain panels pierced with cusped narrow openings separated by short, pillar-shaped struts, 75in. high.

The design of this example, where the canopy is supported on only the four corner posts, is rare. Other categories include: those with two additional posts rising from a narrower 'entrance' at the front making the better-known six-poster bed; four-poster beds with a large circular 'full moon' opening at the front; or the corridor beds with a separate antechamber on one side.
(Christie's)   **$354,500**

Jacques Adnet, bed, circa 1925, black lacquered wooden frame, veneered with galuchat, the bed with long rectangular back panel, with short side section with two cupboard doors on outer side and two small cabinets on front short side.
(Sotheby's) **$30,728**

A George III oak metamorphic bureau-bed, the rectangular top above a hinged slope and four simulated long drawers enclosing a folding bed, on shaped bracket feet, 43½in. wide.

A design for a deal bureau-bedstead with five sham drawers and corded canvas frame features in the 1788 Gillows 'Estimate Sketch Book'. *(Christie's)* **$12,825**

A rare Chippendale carved and ▶
inlaid mahogany four post
bedstead, Charleston, South
Carolina, circa 1780, the waterleaf-
carved reeded flaring footposts on
rice-carved and fluted urn-form
supports with waterleaf-carved urns
below on line and oval-inlaid
square tapering legs, the
headposts of square form centering
a shaped mahogany headboard,
overall width 5ft.8in.

Although Lowcountry beds
made during the colonial period are
very rare, a relatively large sample
of Charleston Neoclassical beds
survives, most of them dating from
the late 1780s to about 1810.

The original owner of the
bedstead was Thomas Bourke who
was born in Dublin, Ireland, married
Jane Smith in June 1783 and who
died in South Carolina in 1804.
(Sotheby's)   **$42,550**

◀
A George II mahogany four-poster bed,
attributed to Giles Grendey, the egg-and-
dart molded cavetto cornice hung with an
orange-tasseled fringe and framing two
waved rectangular chamfered panels with
an egg-and-dart molded frame hung with
red-silk curtains, the twin-paneled back
with further waved rectangular chamfered
panels divided by three stop-fluted
composite pilasters and above a molded
dado and two molded rectangular panels,
65in. wide.

The Knebworth bed is likely to have
been commissioned by John Robinson-
Lytton (d.1762) at the time of his marriage
in 1744 to Leonora Brereton of Borras,
Denbighshire. Its canopy, with enriched
compartments in the Tudor style,
harmonized with the manor's ancient
architecture, while its Bacchic lion-paw feet
emerging from Roman foliage corresponds
with the Falkland bedroom mantelpiece
that is richly carved with an echinous egg-
and-dart banding.

This bed can be attributed to the
celebrated Clerkenwell cabinet-maker and
upholsterer Giles Grendey (d.1780).
(Christie's)   **$108,398**

Berlin ceramics date back to the late 17th century, when from 1678 faience and red earthenware were produced. In 1763 the factory came under royal patronage when Frederick the Great purchased it to become the Königliche Porzellan Manufaktur, and production turned to hard-paste porcelain. From the end of the First World War it became known as the Staatliche Porzellan Manufaktur in Berlin.

Important Berlin porcelain ormolu mounted presentation vase, Germany, mid-19th century, of Munchner form, blue ground with gilt foliate and paneled borders, polychrome enamel decorated with a half-portrait to one side, flanked by ascending promotions in rank to the one side and victories in the Napoleonic War to the other, 31in. high.
(Skinner)   **$41,400**

A Berlin K.P.M. ruby luster 'Veduta' vase (Amphora mit Greifenkopfhenkeln), late 19th/20th century, blue scepter mark, with gilt scrolling arched griffin head handles, the amphora form vase finely painted after 'The Connoisseur' by Hendrik Siemiradzky with a naked concubine standing on a leopard skin rug clinging to a yellow drape, being shown by two slave traders to a Roman Emperor and a young onlooker, the background filled with worldly artifacts, 21⅝in. high.
(Christie's)   **$16,100**

One of a pair of German rectangular plaques, Berlin (K.P.M.), late 19th/20th century, impressed scepter and monogram marks, paper label for Julius Greiner Sohn, Dresden, one finely painted with the 'Kiss of the Wave', the other with 'The Storm's End' of a shipwrecked Norse warrior clinging to a rock, a water nymph at his side, 10½ x 12⅞in.
(Christie's)   **$16,100**

While most people tend to think of Beswick as a product of the 1950s, it was in fact in 1894 that James Wright Beswick established his pottery at Longton, Stoke on Trent. By the 1920s they were producing tableware, glazed ornaments and a whole range of figurines and animals. In the 1930s, they decided to recruit a resident modeling team, and it is from this time that their move away from tableware to purely decorative items dates. Throughout the succeeding four decades they produced well modeled, bright and affordable ornaments. Their range of horses are particularly well-known as are the legendary flying duck wall plaques, which have come to epitomize the style of the 50s. Almost from the beginning, Beswick was a collector's dream, appealing to adults and children alike, as they introduced ranges such as Beatrix Potter and Disney characters. In 1969, the company were taken over by Royal Doulton, and under Doulton's subsidiary Royal Albert, they are still in production today.

Beswick Beatrix Potter figure of Tommy Brock, introduced 1955, gold oval back stamp, 3½in. high.
(Ewbank)   **$365**

Beswick Beatrix Potter figure of Benjamin Bunny, introduced 1948, gold oval back stamp, the first version with left arm and slipper held away from the body, 4in. high.
(Ewbank)   **$460**

Beswick Beatrix Potter figure 'Duchess', (first version), 3¾in. high introduced 1955, gold oval back stamp.
(Ewbank)   **$2,905**

A Victorian paint-decorated pine birdcage, third quarter 19th century, the demilune-shaped top fitted with a hanging ring, one side with sliding door, the interior fitted with two paint-decorated carved wood birds, 16in. high.
(Sotheby's) **$1,380**

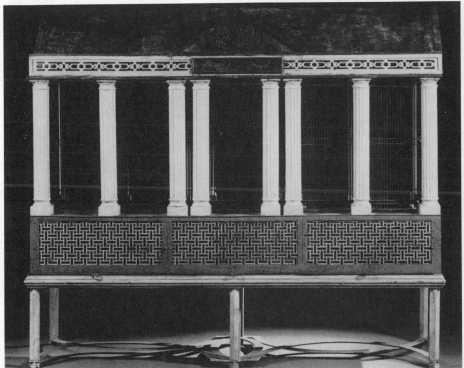

A fine cast iron and copper bird cage, English, in the form of an orangery, the pitched roof centered by the Royal arms above a pierced frieze on sixteen fluted doric columns, enclosing brass grills, the lower section with Chinese pierced fretwork panels above sliding trays, on six hexagonal legs, 230cm. wide. *(Sotheby's)* **$28,118**

Victorian Gothic Revival carved and painted wood and wire birdcage, 19th century, with removable carved acanthus leaf base, 20¼in. wide.
(Skinner) **$1,380**

A fine and rare carved panbone birdcage, from New London, Connecticut, late 19th century, constructed in the form of an octagonal building with four double columned portals, the sides and dome constructed of pierced and incised sawtooth fretworks, the whole centering a parquet floor and mounted on a plinth base, has a movable sliding trap door, 25in. high. *(Sotheby's)* **$10,350**

An unusual painted and parcel-gilt bird cage, probably French, circa 1860, of octagonal, architectural form with a balustrade and copper roof above brass grills, interposed by outset pilasters, painted with foliage and husks, on scrolled feet carved with foliage, 135cm. wide. *(Sotheby's)* **$22,568**

Candlestands became popular in France as early as the mid 17th century, and many were made in the form of a negro figure holding up a circular tray. Because of this, they became known as guéridons, guéridon being the term applied to young Moors brought over from Africa as pages. The fashion quickly caught on in England also, and spread particularly fast after the Restoration. Blackamoor figures continued to form a popular decorative feature, especially for such stands, until well into the 19th century.

A North Italian polychrome wood standing blackamoor figure, possibly late 19th/early 20th century, shown holding a mahogany tray with molded border, the underside applied with a paper label *Massa! Take a programme of the music please*, the figure partially clad and with various jewelry to the arms and neck, with inset glass eyes and simulated pearl earrings, on a rectangular plinth with castors, 60in. high. *(Christie's)* **$8,538**

A pair of Italian ebonised and parcel-gilt blackamoor torchères, 18th/early 19th century, each with a blackamoor wearing a part-feathered robe and a turban supporting on his head a gadrooned and a part-fluted dish, on a rocky surface and a waisted turned spreading base with cabochon edge and foliate clasps, 52in. high. *(Christie's)* **$17,595**

A pair of Venetian blackamoors on pedestals, circa 1880, each figure upholding a cornucopia and holding an oar in the other hand, painted with brocade tunics, standing on the top of a gondola, on hexagonal painted and gilded pedestals, 242cm. high.
(Sotheby's) **$20,620**

◄

▲

A Venetian fruitwood and ebonised blackamoor torchère, 19th century, the circular dished top supported by a blackamoor doing a handstand, on a tasseled and foliate-patterned cushion, on a later platform, 32in. high. *(Christie's)* **$5,083**

◄

A pair of polychrome and giltwood blackamoor figures, 20th century, each shown holding a dish to the front, on waisted octagonal plinths, 73in. high.
(Christie's) **$26,560**

A rare blue-painted pine chest-on-legs, possibly Pueblo, Taos, New Mexico, circa 1800, the hinged rectangular top opening to a well, the paneled sides carved with geometric motifs, the stiles continuing to form the feet. Has undergone various native updates including leather strap hinges and iron hasp. Blue paint of 19th century origin, 29¼in.

The earliest examples of chests-on-legs made in New Mexico date from the end of the 18th century. *(Sotheby's)* **$26,450**

A paint-decorated pine diminutive blanket chest, New York State, dated *1829*, the rectangular molded hinged lid opening to a well with a till, the interior of the lid with attached watercolor on paper, decorated with a wing-spread American Eagle and shield, trumpeting angels, and an inscription entitled *Glory be to God on high*, the front of the case painted with a pot filled with tulips and flowers in yellow, red, white and black, centering the initials *A.N.* 1829, all on a blue ground. 43in. long.

A second chest, bearing the initials *E.N.* and dated *1829*, with the same design of potted tulips and four petal flowers, is known to exist. It has been suggested that the painted decoration may have been carried out by an itinerant artist, who traveled around using this standard composition in various communities. Alternatively, the chests could have been made by one artist, who painted the chests for members of the same family.

It is interesting to note that labels, or Fraktur, such as appear on this chest, were often awarded by country schoolteachers to star pupils as a kind of prize. Whether for this purpose or simply as a greeting, a record or just a note of ownership, the inscription was almost always an individual possession. *(Sotheby's)* **$67,400**

A fine and very rare blue-green and white-painted pine blanket chest, attributed to Johannes Spitler, Shenandoah County, Virginia, circa 1800, the hinged rectangular top opening to a well and a till, the case sides decorated with white hex signs, the front with geometric tulips above inverted hearts, centering a hex sign, a smaller inverted heart and the initials *N.R.*, the molded base below on tall bracket feet. 4ft. wide.

Johannes Spitler (1774-1837) lived in Massanutten, Shenandoah County, Virginia, where he established himself as a furniture decorator. Massanutten was a small, isolated town which had been settled by Swiss and German settlers from Lancaster County, Pennsylvania.

Johannes Spitler was one of the few German Swiss artists working in Virginia, and while his work exhibits great diversity in design, he most commonly decorated blanket chests with geometric motifs in polychrome over a blue field. *(Sotheby's)* **$74,000**

An important carved pine blanket chest, New Mexico, 18th century, the rectangular top opening to a well, the case sides with unusually deep carving, carved with large rosettes and pomegranates spandrels, the front divided in seven panels, the central panel carved with a rosette and stylized vines, flanked by rosettes with pomegranates, and birds below, centering rampant lions, all within molded surrounds, retains its original patina. In original unrestored condition. Lacking hinges and hasp, case fitted with sheet metal patches, chips and cracks to moldings, left side of case missing all moldings, right sides missing three moldings, all consistent with native usage.
(Sotheby's) **$118,000**

Bluejohn is a remarkable material, a purple and yellow crystalline fluorspar which was first discovered by the Romans and in all the world is found only in small quantities at Castleton in Derbyshire. The mine was reopened in the late 18th century, and bluejohn quickly became highly prized by connoisseurs as a decorative material for vases, table tops, etc., often with ormolu mounting. The name derives from the French bleu-jaune, or blue-yellow.

A pair of bluejohn and black and white marble obelisks, late 18th or early 19th century, each on a molded plinth base, restorations, 17in. high.
(Christie's) **$26,726**

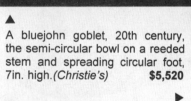

▲

A bluejohn goblet, 20th century, the semi-circular bowl on a reeded stem and spreading circular foot, 7in. high.*(Christie's)* **$5,520**

▶

A large bluejohn veneered circular table top, 20th century, 40in. diameter.
(Christie's) **$23,920**

A gilt bronze and mahogany bookcase in Empire style, French, 19th century, of inverted breakfront form, the molded top surmounted by a ribbon-tied floral garland, above a frieze centered by a winged female mask with foliage and anthemions at each corner, above a paneled glazed door enclosing five shelves flanked by sphinxes, 152cm. wide.
(Sotheby's)   **$31,860**
◀

An oak bookcase, designed by E.W. Godwin for Dromore Castle, Ireland, manufactured by William Watt, circa 1869/70. Three open shelves surmounted by pierced triangular console finials and supported above the base by arched brackets with central turned columns, the lower part with twin paneled doors mounted with typical riveted brass handles/lockplates, square section legs with scrolled feet, 49in. maximum width.

This bookcase is one of several examples produced for Dromore Castle by William Watt to Godwin's design of 1869. Dromore Castle was commissioned by William Hale James Charles Perry, 3rd Earl of Limerick, in 1865, Godwin being responsible for both the exterior and interior designs. The furniture for Dromore was manufactured to Godwin's designs by William Watt, whose exceptional skill as a cabinet-maker met Godwin's own exacting standards.
(Christie's)   **$28,117** ▶

A Böttger silver-gilt mounted chinoiserie baluster coffee-pot and a domed cover, circa 1725, gilder's *69*, the Augsburg mounts with maker's mark of Elias Adam, with a short curved spout and scroll handle, painted by J.G. Höroldt with two Orientals embracing beneath a parasol and flanked by a crane and a table with vases, and with an Oriental kneeling in prayer before a sacrificial altar and an attendant with a tray of flasks, within gilt and lobed Böttger luster paneled cartouches with iron-red scrolling foliage, and with loose bouquets of indianische Blumen beneath a gilt interlocking scrollwork border, the domed cover decorated at Augsburg with a trailing flowering branch, 8⁵/8in. high overall.
(Christie's) **$13,827**
▶

A Böttger silver-mounted white porcelain Augustus Rex tankard, modeled by J.J. Irminger, of cylindrical form with a plain handle, applied with three crowned AR monograms within baroque scrolling foliage and strapwork cartouches, the footrim with a later silver band of stylized foliage, after 1713, 7⁷/8in. high overall.
(Christie's) **$47,880**

A Böttger brown stoneware copper-gilt-mounted coffee-pot and cover, modeled by Johann Jakob Irminger and most probably enameled by Johann Martin Meyer, of square section, the molded scroll handle with polished ribs and facets, the curved spout of square section with polished panels, issuing from a sea-monster's jaws and joined to the body by a yellow S-shaped foliage scroll, 1710-1712, impressed Ruyi lappet mark, 5⁷/8in. high.
(Christie's) **$280,440**

A leather bottle, 17th century, of globular outline, with flat arched panels to the ends, one side indistinctly punched with the owner's initials and date, further punched to both sides with rosettes, the arched top with suspension holes to the buttressed neck, with later associated stopper and leather strap, 8in. high.
(Christie's) **$1,325**

William Burges, a remarkable jeweled and decorated bottle, 1868, conceived around a shouldered ovoid Chinese crackle-glazed ceramic vase, probably Ching dynasty, 17th or 18th century, the vase contained within a cage of three horizontal and eight vertical bands, the majority of the intersections set with a wide variety of semi-precious stones mounted as oval cabochons, the vertical stems spreading at the collar into oak leaf motifs, at the base wrought as scrolling roots, enameled foot ring with inscription *WILLIAM. BURGES.ME.FF.MDCCC LXVIII*, reserved against a rich blue ground, tall waisted neck incorporating frieze of variegated semi-precious stone cabochons, frieze of eight grotesque mythological beasts within alternating blue and green panels, 6¼in. high.
(Sotheby's) **$75,000**

A 'marqueterie-de-verre' glass bottle and stopper, by Gallé, circa 1900, flattened rectangular body in milky amber glass, internally colored with deep amber/green at the base, overlaid with swirling trails of lemon yellow and inlaid in marqueterie-de-verre technique with three flowering anemones in rich brown, green and yellow, the flowerheads, stamens and leaves finely carved, 4¼in. high.
(Christie's) **$20,620**

An Italian pietra dura and ebony jewelry box, circa 1800, the raised top and sides with molded, wavy ebony panels of Baroque type and inset with multiple rectangular and chevron-form hardstone panels incorporating birds and flowers, also with bands of specimen marbles, the interior fitted with later glass on lid and covered in red velvet, a drawer below, upon bun feet. 11¼ x 16 x 13in.
(Sotheby's) **$23,000**

◀

A Neapolitan tortoiseshell gold and mother-of-pearl inlaid piqué box, mid-18th century, the rounded rectangular hinged top inlaid with a scene of courtly figures meeting with attendants carrying canopies, the angles and the frieze inlaid with foliate scrolls and sprays, 9¼in. wide.

The technique of inlaying tortoiseshell with mother-of-pearl, gold and silver probably originated in Naples towards the end of the 16th century. Judging by the number of contemporary references to the Neapolitan piqué work and the surviving pieces which bear the signatures of Neapolitan craftsmen, Naples would seem to have been the center of production, certainly for those pieces made in the eighteenth century.
(Christie's) **$27,000**

◀

An Italian ebonized wood and pietre dure inlaid games box, second half 19th century, of rectangular outline with molded borders, the cover inlaid with pietre dure playing cards and hardstone specimens, with recessed circular panels to the sides representing suits of cards, the compartmented interior with lift-out trays, 12¼in. wide.
(Christie's) **$7,383**

▶

Polychrome decorated pine lift top box, attributed to John Colvin, Scituate, Rhode Island, early 19th century, red, black, white, and salmon pinwheels, overlapping circles and other geometric motifs with black borders, the interior lined with various wallpapers, trade advertisements, and pages from a farmer's almanac dated 1874, 17in. wide. *(Skinner)* **$17,250**

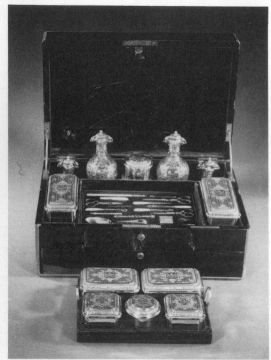

A Victorian parcel-gilt lady's traveling dressing table service, maker's mark of Robert Garrard, London, 1844. Comprising four silver-gilt mounted glass scent bottles with gilt painted decoration, a similarly decorated silver-gilt mounted glass jar, four oblong boxes, two square boxes and two circular boxes, the exterior inset with a plaque engraved with a coat-of-arms with Duke's coronet above, 106oz.

The arms are those of Spencer quartering Churchill accollé with Stewart for George, 6th Duke of Marlborough (1793-1857) and his wife Jane (d.1844), daughter of George, 8th Earl of Galloway (1768-1834), whom he married in 1819. Jane, Duchess of Marlborough was her husband's first cousin. She died on 12 October 1844, very shortly after the present dressing service had been commissioned.
(Christie's) **$32,649**

▶

A north Italian certosina bone and ebony-inlaid coffer, from the Embriachi workshop, circa 1500, of sarcophagus form, inlaid with a variety of geometric patterns, with molded base, 6¾ x 13⁷/8 x 8⁵/8in. *(Sotheby's)* **$13,800**

Pair of red painted alms boxes, 19th century, the dovetail constructed boxes with gilt lettering shaded in black reading *Orphans Fund* and *Widows Fund* centering black foliate decoration, 6in. wide.
(Skinner) **$6,325**

A Victorian memento mori of the 17th Lancers, circa 1870, in the form of a cigar cutter, the cutter modeled as a mortar, flanked by another mortar forming the vesta, centered by an automaton ivory model of a human skeleton, with articulated jaw and eyes, operated by a button to the reverse, mounted on an ebony stand with match strike, fitted in an oak case modeled as a sentry box, with doors to the front and sides, the front inset with a canvas panel, painted in oils with the standing figure of a Lancer in full uniform holding a spear, the gabled front applied with the silver Lancers insignia badge of skull and cross-bones with the cartouche inscribed *OR GLORY.*, 18in. high.

This very unusual cigar was almost certainly a special commission for the 17th Lancer Regiment in commemoration of the Charge of the Light Brigade at the battle of Balaclava on the 25th of October 1854, during the Crimean War. The British troops of the Light Dragoons under General Lord Cardigan were known as the 17th Lancers from 1876 onwards.
(Christie's) **$15,180**

A French Gothic iron-mounted cuir ciselé wood coffer, 15th century, of sarcophagus-form, the whole worked with various panels of floral designs and mounted with hinged straps, the lid with handle and iron hasp, the base with pierced lockplate, 13½in. wide.
(Sotheby's) **$12,650**

Thomas Tompion No. 375. A particularly fine example of the work of England's most eminent clockmaker, circa 1700. It is numbered at the bottom of the backplate and on the case in three places and has hour strike and pull quarter repeat on one bell, 14in. high.
(Derek Roberts) **$156,750**

A William and Mary tortoiseshell striking bracket clock, John Eagle, London, circa 1695, the case with large double-S scroll handle to the cushion-molded top applied with foliate cast gilt mounts, similar sound frets to the front door and sides, the molded base on block feet, the 17.5cm. square dial with silvered chapter ring and later blued steel hands, matted center with mock pendulum aperture, winged cherub spandrels, the massive seven ringed pillar movement with pull quarter repeat on three bells and hour strike on further bell, 14¼in. high.

John Eagle 1669-circa 1710, was apprenticed to Stephen Wilmot and transferred several times until free in 1690. He is listed as supplying a clock for the Earl of Salisbury.
(Christie's) **$28,290**
◀

Joseph Knibb, London circa 1685. A very rare grande sonnerie striking spring clock with numbered external count-wheels for the hours and quarters, split-plates and skeletonized chapter ring. 12½in. high.
(Derek Roberts) **$165,000**

A 19th century brass slave's neck-lock inscribed *John Jones Esq. Clapham.*
(Bearne's) **$1,023**

▶

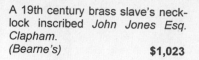

A Regency brass cutlery tray, of rectangular bombé form and on claw feet, with pierced geometric banding, with interior division, 14in. wide. *(Christie's)* **$2,981**

◀

An Edwardian brass coal scuttle, the hinged cover embossed with a foliate patera, with turned handle and waisted foot, with conforming hand shovel fitted to the rear, 18½in. high.
(Christie's) **$3,167**

▶

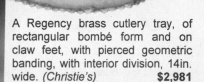

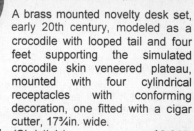

A brass mounted novelty desk set, early 20th century, modeled as a crocodile with looped tail and four feet supporting the simulated crocodile skin veneered plateau, mounted with four cylindrical receptacles with conforming decoration, one fitted with a cigar cutter, 17¾in. wide.
◀ *(Christie's)* **$2,215**

A pierced gilt brass jardinière, early 20th century, of cylindrical form with pierced lattice frieze and molded base on paw feet, with liner, 14in. high. *(Christie's)* **$7,383**

Pair of brass trumpet based candlesticks, probably England, second half 17th century, with sausage turnings, 7⁹/₁₆in. high. *(Skinner)* **$13,800**

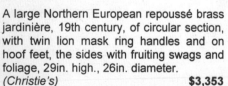

A large Northern European repoussé brass jardinière, 19th century, of circular section, with twin lion mask ring handles and on hoof feet, the sides with fruiting swags and foliage, 29in. high., 26in. diameter. *(Christie's)* **$3,353**

A set of fifteen brass ball weights, by R.B. Bate of London, dated *1824*, for the County of Argyleshire, fitted in three iron bound deal cases, one with the paper label of R.B. Bate of London, the others with the labels of Doyle & Son. *(Christie's)* **$6,640**

Federal mahogany inlaid breakfast table, attributed to William Whitehead, New York City, 1792–1800, the line inlaid top with hinged leaves and stringing banding the edge above the oval inlaid frieze one with working and one with false drawer above the square tapering inlaid legs which begin with twelve-point paterae and continue with V-shaped and looped stringing in conjunction with the three-point bellflowers, and terminate in cuff inlays, 32in. wide. *(Skinner)* **$134,500**

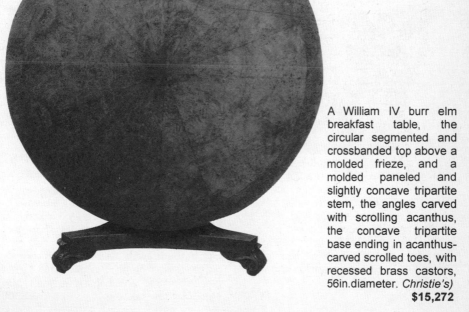

A William IV burr elm breakfast table, the circular segmented and crossbanded top above a molded frieze, and a molded paneled and slightly concave tripartite stem, the angles carved with scrolling acanthus, the concave tripartite base ending in acanthus-carved scrolled toes, with recessed brass castors, 56in. diameter. *Christie's)* **$15,272**

A Maling Edward VIII Coronation plaque, designed by Lucien Boullemier, with relief molded central portrait within double ribbon tied wreath edging divided by a wide blue ground border decorated with Royal and union symbols and flags, 32in. diameter. *(Tennants)* **$2,816**

A Maling vase and cover, of baluster shape, decorated with a green dragon amidst peonies and other Oriental flowers on a purple luster ground, printed castle mark, 1930s, 46cm. high. *(Tennants)* **$8,168**

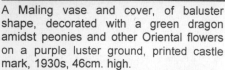

A Wrotham slipware dated puzzle-jug by John Livermore, 1642, molded with the initials *IL*, of squat baluster form with hollow loop handle and short straight spout, the hollow rim applied with four spotted animals above a pierced band, the brown body applied with cream slip flowerheads flanking two square and rectangular cartouches with raised initials and date *1642*, 4¼in. high. *(Christie's)* **$14,404**

A Royal Doulton Chang stoneware vase by Charles Noke and Harry Nixon, of shouldered cylindrical form, the short neck applied with a dragon in high relief, on a blue ground with white running crackle glaze under green, yellow and flambé glazes, printed and painted marks, 7¾in. high. *(Andrew Hartley)* **$3,300**

68

A Royal Worcester vase, 11¾in. high, decorated by Harry Davis, in colored enamels with a flock of sheep in a misty Highland landscape.
(Canterbury) **$7,755**
▶

A large William de Morgan Iznik vase, ovoid with knopped cylindrical neck, applied with strap handles, decorated in the 'Damascus' manner with peacocks amongst stylized foliage, in shades of blue, purple and green on a white ground, late Chelsea/early Merton Abbey period, 49cm. high.
(Christie's) **$11,212**

▶

A large Royal Worcester figure of the Bather Surprised, modeled by Sir Thomas Brock, the scantily clad maiden stands with outstretched arms beside a tree trunk, date code for 1894, 64cm. high.
(Tennants) **$2,381**

A French bronze erotic figure of a maiden, late 19th century, the partially draped figure shown seated on a wicker basket, 7¼in. high. *(Christie's)* **$4,950**

A gilt-bronze vase by Antonin Larroux (1859-1937), of squat form, cast with reapers, signed *A.Larroux,* 45cm. high.

Antonin Larroux exhibited at the Salon des Artistes Français. He was awarded bronze medals at the Expositions of 1889 and 1900. He is best known for his allegorical works.
(Sotheby's) **$13,541**

Cast bronze clad hands of Abraham Lincoln, each hand is inscribed *This cast of the hand of Abraham Lincoln was made from the first replica of the original made at Springfield, Ill. the Sunday following his nomination to the Presidency in 1860*, originals by Leonard Wells Volk (American, 1828–95), 6½in. long. *(Eldred's)* **$440**

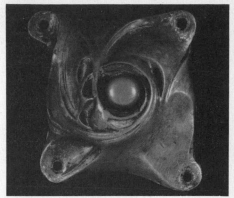

A bronze bell plate designed by Hector Guimard, circa 1904, cast with typically formalized swirls, 2⁷/₈in. wide. Formally part of the interior fittings in a Guimard apartment in Paris.
(Christie's) **$1,885**

'Butterfly Girls', a bronze and ivory group, cast from the model by Otto Poertzel, 1930s, the two dancers standing 'en arabesque', each reaching to touch the flowing hem of the other, creating the outline of a butterfly, green onyx base, 16¾in. high, base engraved *Prof. O. Poertzel.*
(Christie's) **$38,640**

A gilt-bronze ewer, by Vibert, Paris, circa 1890, cast with a handle in the form of a tree, with a nymph seated to the side, hauling a net full of fish, cast in relief with water plants and fish, indistinctly signed and with the Siot/Paris foundry mark, 42cm. high.

The maker of this gilt-bronze ewer very much in the French Art Nouveau style could be Alexandre Vibert (died 1909). He exhibited in several 'Salons des sculptures'. For his high quality sculpture and works of art he worked mostly in bronze or in pewter and sandstone.

The foundry Siot-Decauville was located in Paris on 8 to 10 rue Villehardoin, the exhibition salon of the firm was in 24 boulevard des Italiens. After 1920 they were situated on 63 Avenue Victor-Emmanuel III. Among the many artists who placed their sculpture with the Siot-Decauville foundry were Gérôme, Gardet and Daumier.
(Sotheby's) **$13,892**

A North German bronze lion-form aquamanile 'of Hildescheim type,' 13th century, standing and gazing forward, the spout in his mouth, a hinge at the top of the head and the handle in the form of a serpent, the full mane chased, 9^{15}/16in. high. *(Sotheby's)* **$233,500**

Danseuse à la pomme, by Jean Léon Gérôme, French (1824-1904) the patinated, gilded bronze and tinted marble figure in Grecian dress, her left arm raised, her right hand clasping an apple, on an onyx socle, the circular bronze base, signed *J.L Gérôme* and stamped *Siot Paris*, 67cm. high.

Gérôme's early career was entirely devoted to painting and he is best known for his orientalist work. But he also had a fascination for the classical world, in particular the arts of Greece. He had a good classical grounding from his father and understood both Latin and Greek. Greek itself, newly independent from the Ottoman empire, still had something of the aura of the orient about it and at the time an interest in classically inspired subjects did not seem remotely incompatible with the lure of the east. The bronze reflects this dichotomy with its sinuous exotic allure, its movement evocative of the dance of Isadora Duncan and the flowing robes echoing the work of Fortuny.

Gérôme did not take up sculpture until late in his career, his first work dating from 1868, and his first major success was at the Paris Exposition Universelle of 1878. *(Sotheby's)* **$93,225**

The gentlemen scholars of late Imperial China lived lives of ease and elegance, surrounded by classical Chinese furniture and many distinctive artefacts. In particular, their studios would be equipped with items to enable the scholar to pursue the four arts, calligraphy, painting, poetry and music. An essential accessory for at least two of these was the brush pot, a straight sided vessel, often of the finest porcelain and itself beautifully decorated, which he would use to store his painting and calligraphy brushes. Examples of these can be found in most sales of oriental wares, and the finest will now fetch many thousands of dollars.

An engraved molded gourd cylindrical brushpot, four-character molded hallmark, Xing You Hen Tang, the sides molded into six vertical panels and decorated with a finely detailed horse shown rolling on its back with its legs kicking and mane and tail flying, of rich amber color, the interior and base covered in black lacquer, 4½in. high, The hallmark, Xing you Heng tang, may be translated, 'made for the hall of constancy', the residence of Zhai Quan, a grandson of the emperor Qianlong, and famous collector of the Daoguang period.
(Christie's) **$3,680**

A well-carved dark green jade cylindrical brushpot, Qianlong, the thick sides carved in high relief with boys at play within a pavilion compound, three riding hobby horses and several playing instruments, the scene interrupted on the reverse by a bridge spanning a river surrounded by pine trees and rocks, raised on four shallow bracket supports and with a slightly rounded mouth rim, the stone of dark mottled green tone.
(Christie's) **$30,000**

A huanghuali brushpot, Bitong, 17th/18th century, with subtly waisted sides and upward-tilting mouth rim, the grain with gently wavy patterning and dense whorls, 7in. diameter.
(Christie's) **$5,750**

A fine paint decorated pine bucket, Joseph Long Lehn, Elizabeth Township, Lancaster County, 1880-92, the tapering cylindrical body composed of pine staves encircled by sheet metal bands with a turned top, the whole with freehand painting of pussy willows in black, yellow, green over a striped and white ground, 8in. high. (Sotheby's) $4,600

A pair of mahogany plate buckets early 19th century, of coopered brass brand form with brass carrying handles. (Sotheby's) $13,443

A matched pair of Irish George III mahogany brass-bound buckets, each with handle, scrolling attachment, inset metal liner and ribbed tapering sides, and underside with paper label and indistinguishable ink stamp ...KAHN..., one 16¾in. the other 16½in. high. (Christie's) $17,181

An inlaid and decorated chair by Bugatti, circa 1900, circular back slung between turned uprights, the seat in tooled vellum attached with ropes, the whole applied with strips of hammered metal, the back with pewter and brass inlay.
(Christie's) **$3,427**

Carlo Bugatti, one of a pair of asymmetric chairs, circa 1900, each with square vellum seat, hung with silk tassels, the drum back rests with painted vellum centers strung from slender turned uprights, one extending to stepped dish finial hung with silk tassels, the whole decorated throughout with beaten copper banding and ebonized wood, 60in. high.
(Christie's) (Two) **$16,324**

An applied and decorated table by Bugatti, circa 1900, circular vellum-covered top above lower square shelf, four turned legs, X-shaped base, the whole inlaid with brass and copper and applied with beaten metal strips, the lower shelf vellum-covered, 25½in. diameter, 28½in. high.
(Christie's) **$4,284** ▶

Emile-Jaques Ruhlmann, meuble rasson, amboyna, with ivory stringing and ivory and brass mounts, the slightly bombé front with two doors joined by a circular lock plate cast as a crouched female nude, the front two feet with ivory sabots, the reverse with branded mark *Ruhlmann* and *B* in a circle, 55^7/8in. wide. *(Sotheby's)*   **$66,800**

A George III painted breakfront side cabinet, decorated with 'd'Handcarville' style cut-out part-painted paper panels, the arcaded floral frieze above four doors centered with oval fan medallions and Etruscan figures, on outswept bracket feet, re-decorated, 63in. wide x 37½in. high x 18½in. deep.   *(Christie's)*   **$29,808**

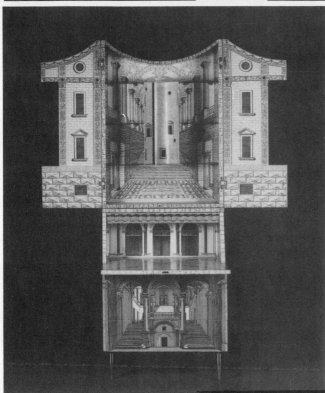

'Architettura', a decorative bureau/cabinet, designed by Piero Fornasetti and Gio Ponti in 1951, the upper part opening to reveal architectural interior with central painted metal alcove flanked by clear glass shelves, the lower section with fall-front bureau above three long drawers, the whole decorated in monochrome with architectural details, 86½in. high. *(Christie's)*

$16,278

A pair of gilt bronze and mahogany side cabinets by Victor Raulin, Paris, circa 1880, each with a shaped brêche violet marble top within a leaf-cast border above a paneled kingwood crossbanded door surmounted by a mask of a putto and flanked by leaf-cast scrolls headed by masks, 100cm. wide.

Victor Raulin took over his father's business in 1878 and stayed in the original premises on 93, rue de Turenne until he moved in 1882 to 110, rue de Vieille-du-Temple and later to 209, boulevard Saint-Germain, where he remained until circa 1925. He is particularly well known for his furniture in the 18th century French styles as well as for the use of lacquer panels in his furniture.
(Sotheby's) **$46,860**

Leica I(c) Luxus no. 48417 non-standardized, with gilt top and baseplate and fittings, skin-covered body, a matched Leitz gilt-barrel Elmar f/3.5 50mm. lens, the barrel engraved *417* and cap.

According to information from Leica Camera GmbH Leica 48417 was purchased or loaned by Dölz on 8-11-1932. Serial number information indicates that the camera was part of a batch numbered 48417-48419 produced in 1931.

(Christie's) **$38,000**

◄
Nikon I no. 609118, chrome, 24 x 32mm., the base plate engraved *Made in Occupied Japan* and *609118* and with a Nippon Kogaku Nikkor-QC f/3.5 5cm. lens no. 7051585 and lens cap, in maker's early-type ever ready case. This example dates to October 1948.

(Christie's) **$29,911**

Nikon S3M no. 6600046 18 x 24mm., black, rear sliding viewfinder frame adjustment, the exposure counter with 72/40 window and a Nippon Kogaku Nikkor-S f/1.4 5cm. lens no. 401735.

The Nikon S3M was launched in April 1960 and was the only Nikon half-frame camera made. According to production records 195 examples of the camera were made in the serial number range 6600000-6699999.

(Christie's) **$28,460**

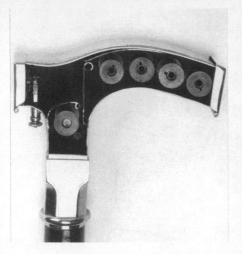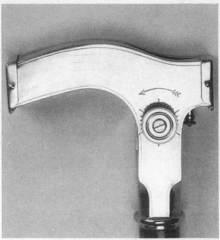

Ben Akiba walking stick camera, the nickel-plated metal body with shutter, lens, five film spools and wood cane holding ten film spools. *(Christie's)* **$7,360**

A daguerreian outfit, comprising an 18 x 20cm. walnut-body, sliding-box camera with brass fittings and removable focusing screen; a lacquered-brass rack and pinion focusing lens, the barrel engraved *Photographie À Verres Combines, Inventé par Charles Chevalier, Palais Royal 158, Paris*, with brass lens cap and two metal rings, one stamped *Portraits et Paysages*, the other *Portraits*, in fitted walnut box; two walnut single plate holders with spare doors; reducing back; a 12 x 15cm. daguerreian plate holder; three 12 x 16cm. silvered copper daguerreotype plates, one exposed, each stamped *30EIH**, in a twelve-section plate box; all contained in a fitted walnut box ink-stamped *Charles Chevalier, Deux Médailles D'Or en 1834. Palais Royal 158, À Paris, Fabrique Cour des Fontaines, N I Bis. (Christie's)* **$37,490**

Eastman Kodak Co., Rochester NY, a 120 rollfilm cardboard body George Washington Kodak camera. *(Christie's)* **$23,000**

A very rare decoratively engraved spy camera, reputedly used by the Russian K.G.B.
(Christie's) **$19,700**

A 35mm walnut bodied Cinematographic camera with brass body direct vision finder by Lumiere.
(Christie's) **$20,250**

A very rare 2¼ x 3¼ rollfilm No.2 Cone Pocket Kodak camera with Morocco leather covered body.
◄ *(Christie's)* **$5,630**

A Chippendale carved and figured mahogany birdcage candlestand, Philadelphia, circa 1795, the circular dished top tilting and rotating above a birdcage support, the ring-turned and urn-form standard above three downswept legs ending in snake feet. Appears to retain an old and possibly original surface on the underside of the top and birdcage, 23¾in. diameter. *(Sotheby's)* **$28,750**
▶

▲
A fine and rare red-painted and turned tripod candlestand, northeastern New England, 1750-1775, the octagonal molded top above a tapered urn-form and ring-turned standard on delicate faceted cabriole legs ending in snake feet. 25½in. high. *(Sotheby's)* **$24,150**
▶

A very fine and rare Chippendale carved and figured walnut bird-cage candlestand, Philadelphia, circa 1770, the dished circular top tilting and revolving above a birdcage support and a ring-turned compressed-ball standard, on cabriole legs ending in well-articulated claw-and-ball feet. Appears to retain its original finish, iron 'spider' and cast brass spring lock.

Philadelphia bird-cage candlestands with claw-and-ball feet are exceedingly rare. *(Sotheby's)* **$173,000**

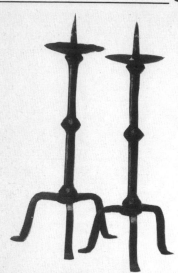

A French Gothic wrought-iron candlestick, 14th century, the faceted and knobbed stem resting on square pan with pierced apron on all sides, upon four feet, 10⅝in. high. *(Sotheby's)* **$10,350**

A pair of Continental Gothic wrought-iron pricket candlesticks, 15th century, each with circular drip-pan upon stem with three knobs supported by a tripod base, 13⅞in. high. *(Sotheby's)* **$3,450**

Brass capstan candlestick, Europe, 17th century, 13in. high.

This candlestick purportedly belonged to Governor John Endicott of the Massachusetts Bay Colony and was brought by him from England in 1628. It was exhibited at a centennial celebration in Bath, Maine and written up in the Boston Globe in the 1920s.

A pair of turned panbone candlesticks, probably 20th century, the baluster-turned standards with shaped candle cup and turned and incised bases, 10½in. high. *(Sotheby's)* **$1,380**

(Skinner) **$16,100**

82

A pair of brass candlesticks, 18th century, each with a petal-form flared candlecup and baluster stem, on a domed petal-shaped base, 7¾in. high.
(Sotheby's)   **$5,462**

A pair of George III Staffordshire enamel candlesticks, circa 1780, the knopped and waisted stems on shaped domed bases, the white ground with gilt heightened blue reserves and trailing foliage overall, 9¼in. high. (Christie's)   **$4,658**

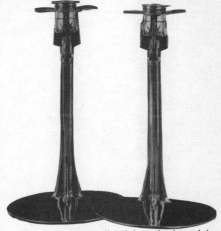

A pair of large Italian or Flemish brass altar candlesticks, circa 1600, each with broad drip pan and brass pricket, the haft of baluster-form, with domed base and resting on three ball feet, 54½in. high.
(Sotheby's)   **$10,350**

A pair of silver candlesticks, designed by Rex Silver, manufactured by Liberty & Co., Birmingham, 1906, each with slender stems applied with delicate square-section branches angled below the nozzle and terminating in finely hammered formalized leaves, undulating drip pans, hammered circular base, 9⁷/₈in. high.
(Sotheby's)   **$37,490**

A classical figured maple canterbury, New York, mid/late 19th century, the rectangular frame headed by ring-turned ball finials enclosing two conforming shaped dividers above ring turned corner supports and slat supports over a conforming apron fitted with a drawer, on ring and baluster-turned supports, with socket castors.
(Christie's) **$6,900**
▶

A George IV ormolu-mounted and brass-inlaid rosewood whatnot, the rectangular top with waved foliate three-quarter gallery and with lappeted border, above a foliate-inlaid frieze and two tiers, each with ring-turned baluster supports and X-shaped filled sides, on ring-turned pinched and tapering feet, brass caps and ceramic castors, 25¼in. wide.
(Christie's) **$11,693**

▶

A William IV rosewood canterbury, after a design by John C. Loudon, with four X-shaped divides joined at the top by ring-turned spindles, the front and reverse each with a ribbon tied laurel wreath, above a mahogany lined frieze drawer, on ring-turned baluster legs by turned finials, brass caps and castors, 19in. wide.

This canterbury derives from a design by John C. Loudon published in 1833 in his Encyclopedia of Cottage, Farm and Villa Architecture and Furniture, 1833.
(Christie's) **$8,487**

CAPO DI MONTE

The Capodimonte factory near Naples was established by King Charles III in 1742 to make soft-paste porcelain of the French type.

It was not until 1744, however, after numerous failed attempts, that Gaetano Schepers managed to produce a paste which was suitably 'white and diaphanous' and which achieved a brilliance to rival Meissen.

The most famous modeler at the Capodimonte factory was Giovanni Caselli, a former gem engraver and miniature painter. Figurines were among the earliest output of the factory, but snuff boxes, tea services and scent bottles were also made.

In 1759 Charles acceded to the throne of Spain, and the factory closed. He set up again at Buen Retiro, but the quality of products produced there is generally inferior to their Capodimonte antecedents.

Pair of Capo di Monte covered covered two-handled vases, Italy, 19th century, each with a nautical theme in high relief above dolphin molded plinths, 18in. high. *(Skinner)* **$2,875**

A Capodimonte (Carlo III) figure of a lady, circa 1750, modeled by Guiseppe Gricci, standing before a tree stump in white headdress, red-edged white bodice tied with a blue ribbon, 5¾in. high. *(Christie's)* **$76,000**

A Capodimonte (Carlo III) group of a lady and her artist companion, circa 1755, blue fleur-de-lys mark, modeled by Guiseppe Gricci, she standing in a white lace cap with gilt-edged white ruff, blue-patterned, yellow underskirt and red and gilt shoes, holding a gilt-edged fan, her companion seated on a waisted stool to her left in a long sleeved puce-patterned jacket, black breeches and gilt-buckled shoes, on a plain rectangular base, 5¾in. high. *(Christie's)* **$25,000**

René Lalique, a scarce 'Perche' mascot; amber tinted glass, with etched *R. Lalique* to base, French, circa 1930, 6in. long. *(Christie's)* **$2,875**

'Tete de Paon', a frosted blue glass car mascot by René Lalique, 17.5cm. high. *(Christie's)* **$60,000**

'Longchamps', a Lalique car mascot, the clear and satin-finished glass molded as a stylized head of a horse, 12cm. high. *(Christie's)* **$13,500**

German Officer's mascot of chrome plated brass, reputed to have originally been the property of one Richter Kurler, an officer attached to Rommel's personal staff in the North African Campaign during World War II, very rare. *(Lyle)* **$1,225**

'The Dummy Teat', nickel plated mascot manufactured by J. Grose & Co., in the 1920s for attaching to the Austin 7, fondly known as the Baby Austin, hence the dummy teat. *(Lyle)* **$245**

An important Federal satinwood-inlaid and figured mahogany demilune games table, labelled *John Seymour & Son, Creek Square, Boston, Massachusettts,* 1794–96, the hinged D-shaped lozenge and dot inlaid top opening to a figured playing surface with crossbanded edge, the conformingly-shaped frieze inlaid with swags of graduated husks suspended from inlaid bowknots on square tapering legs similarly-inlaid with graduated husks terminating in shaped term feet, 36in. wide.

Claire Beckmann (nee Wiegand), an elementary school teacher and yard sale enthusiast, purchased this extraordinary games table at a yard sale in Bergen County, approximately thirty years ago. Mrs Beckmann came upon the table one Friday afternoon and went home to think about whether or not it would be suitable for her new home. She returned late the next day with a friend and the $25.00 required to make the purchase and luckily the table was still there. She recalls that her friend strongly advised against buying the table as it was "wobbly and would not even hold a lamp.' Because of the table's condition Ms. Beckmann decided to leave it on the lady's porch over the weekend and pick it up on Monday, which was a much more suitable time to tighten the legs before presenting the table to her family. Upon returning home on Monday afternoon she turned the table upside down to tighten the legs at which time she discovered the Seymour label. Having never heard of

John Seymour, she immediately went to the local library to do research and found Vernon Stoneman's 1959 book entitled John and Thomas Seymour, Cabinet makers in Boston. It was then that she realized that she owned an authentic table. A dealer had offered to buy the table in the late 1970s but she turned down the offer. *(Sotheby's)* **$541,500**

The Van Vechten family Chippendale carved and figured mahogany serpentine-front five-leg card table, New York, circa 1770, the oblong top with serpentine sides and squared outset corners opening to a leather-lined playing surface with oval counters, counterwell and square candlestick pockets, the conformingly-shaped frieze below with gadrooned skirt continuing to C-scroll and acanthus-leaf and flowerhead-carved cabriole legs ending in claw-and-ball feet, height with leaf closed, 27¾in.

This card table one of a small group of related serpentine-front, claw-and-ball foot, five-legged mahogany gaming tables considered to be masterpieces of American eighteenth century furniture design. These serpentine-front card tables are products of the best New York cabinetmaking workshops of the 1760s through the 1780s and many, including this example, have descended in prominent New York families. *(Sotheby's)* **$266,500**

A carved and painted carousel jumper, attributed to Charles I.D. Looff (active 1875-1918), Brooklyn, New York.

Carved in the Country Fair Style the full-bodied olive-painted horse with articulated head, ears, mouth, glass eyes, and a red, black and yellow-painted buckled bridle above a shallow-carved articulated mane over a brown, red and black-painted saddle and green and yellow-paint detailing on articulated legs with black-painted hooves and horse-hair tail, 58in. wide.
(Christie's)   **$14,950**

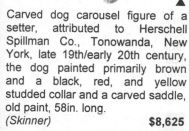

▲

Carved dog carousel figure of a setter, attributed to Herschell Spillman Co., Tonowanda, New York, late 19th/early 20th century, the dog painted primarily brown and a black, red, and yellow studded collar and a carved saddle, old paint, 58in. long.
(Skinner)   **$8,625**

A carved and painted carousel prancer, possibly Stein and Goldstein (active 1912-1925), Brooklyn, New York, early 20th century, carved in the Coney Island style, the full bodied brown painted horse with articulated head, ears, mouth, glass eyes, and green, yellow and maroon-painted buckled bridle above an articulated mane over an ocher, yellow, red and salmon-painted saddle with yellow and green-painted detailing, on articulated legs with black-painted hooves and horse-hair tail, 59in. high. *(Christie's)*   **$8,050**

Da Silva Bruhns, carpet, circa 1930, wool, woven in shades of chocolate, coffee, caramel and cream with decorative linear motifs, signed in the weave *da Silva Bruhns*, 105¾ x 72½in.
(Sotheby's) **$27,680**

Edouard Bénédictus, floral carpet, circa 1925, wool, woven in polychrome decoration of highly stylized flowers and leaves, against a trellis ground scattered with flowers, 121¼ x 78¾in.
(Sotheby's) **$24,966**

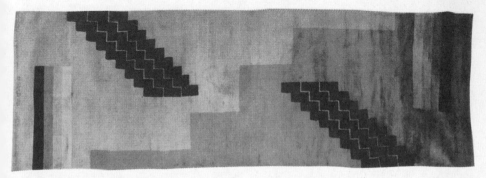

Da Silva Bruhns, abstract carpet, circa 1930, wool, woven in shades of salmon pink, black, gray, mushroom and fawn with geometric motifs, signed in the weave *da Silva Bruhns*, and monogramed *MS*, the reverse with two indistinct labels, one apparently marked *for the Reception Room,* 188 x 65in.
(Sotheby's) **$34,360**

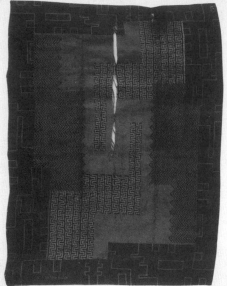

Da Silva Bruhns, geometric carpet, circa 1930, wool, woven in shades of brown, sienna and cream with geometric designs, signed in the weave *da Silva Bruhns* and monogramed MS, 148½in. x 105¼in. *(Sotheby's)* **$18,245**

a border of stylized tulips, in shades of pale blue, pale greens and ivory, 160½ x 131½in.

Voysey was a prolific designer of wallpapers, textiles, tiles and other decorative media for domestic use, and carpets were no exception. On the advice of his friend, A.H. Mackmurdo, he created designs whilst waiting for architectural commissions and the influence for his naturalistic flowing designs probably owes more to Mackmurdo, founder of the Century Guild, than to William Morris.

The 'Duleek' was manufactured in Alexander Morton's Donegal range, and retailed at Liberty's, where it was included in their 'Irish Carpet Exhibition', held at the Grafton Gallery, in Bond Street, London, in 1903. *(Christie's)* **$75,985**

'Duleek', a hand-knotted carpet, designed by C.F.A. Voysey and woven by Alexander Morton & Co., circa 1903, the moss green ground patterned with a river running through a stylized wooded landscape, deer and swans below, birds in flight above, with

A Donegal carpet, designed by Gavin Morton and G.K. Robertson, the dark blue field woven with a trelliswork of pink and ocher stylized flowers, divided by similar purple flowerheads, between flowering sprays, the ocher ground similarly woven with stylized flowerheads and scrolling foliage, between coral floral guard stripes, 20ft x 15ft 9in. *(Christie's)* **$43,844**

A Victorian gilt brass quarter chiming giant chronometer carriage clock of exhibition quality with flat-rim balance, Victor Kullberg, London. No. 6037, movement stamped *JM 8158*, circa 1895. The case with foliate cast bracket feet to the molded plinth, deeply chamfered angles flanking large beveled glasses, the molded top inset with a similar glass and mounted with a large scrolling handle, hinged door to the arched silvered dial signed *Victor Kullberg London. (Christie's)* **$157,600**

A Swiss engraved gilt-brass and Limoges enamel-mounted mignonnette striking and repeating carriage clock, circa 1890, the anglaise style case with Limoges enamel panels to sides and rear door depicting Renaissance hunting scenes, a youth with his dog blowing a hunting horn to left side, a lady on horseback with falcon to the rear, a lady standing beside a tree with a falcon to right side, the dial with gilt Roman chapter ring above scene of two squires carrying a deer on a pole, with a castle behind them, silvered lever platform to bimetallic balance, 3in. high.

The panels are typical of the high quality Limoges enamels being used on carriage clocks at the end of the 19th century. Renaissance figures - especially in the guise of the hunt - were particularly popular. *(Christie's)* **$19,320**

◀

A Victorian ebonized striking four glass traveling clock, E.J. Dent London No. 15051, second quarter 19th century, the case of typical proportions with beveled glass to the sides and top with foliate cast gilt-metal handle, white enamel Roman dial signed *E.J.Dent* London with blued spade hands, within a gilt foliate engraved mask, the twin chain fusee movement with maintaining power and large gilt platform for the underslung lever escapement, 9¼in. high. (Christie's) **$19,800**

1930 Duesenberg Model J Dual Cowl Phaeton, Coachwork by La Grande, engine no. J-436, black with red wheels and striping and brown leather interior. Engine: straight-eight with twin overhead camshafts and four valves per cylinder, 420 cu. in., 320bhp at 4,200rpm; Gearbox: three-speed; Suspension: beam axle to front, live axle to rear, half elliptic leaf springs all round; Brakes: servo assisted hydraulically operated drums on all wheels. Left hand drive.

The late automotive writer, Ken Purdy, once wrote, *The man who had really arrived drove a Duesenberg. It cost him from 6,500 to 25,000 one-hundred-cent-dollars and it looked it. What is more, it acted like it. Nobody driving a stock anything made in America passed a Duesenberg if the Duesenberg was earnest about it.*
As well as the 150mph speedometer, the combined clock and stop-watch altimeter, barometer and brake pressure dials, there was the famous engine-driven timing box of planetary gears controlling lights to warn the driver to change the engine oil every 700 miles, check the battery water every 1400 miles, together with other functions.

Duesenberg exercised firm control over the bodies fitted to their chassis encouraging clients to order coachwork directly from the factory. During the time when this car was going through the shops, the great Gordon Buehrig, stylist of the model 810 Cord, was chief designer. La Grande was the name used by Duesenberg for bodies built by outside companies but trimmed and fitted by Duesenberg itself. With its everlasting hood, sidemounts, sweeping fender line and separate trunk the La Grande Dual Cowl 'sweep panel' phaeton marks a high point in classic American auto styling. Notable fittings on J-436 are the glass side and quarter curtains with their chromed metal frames.
(Christie's) **$618,500**

Jaguar XKSS Sports two-seater, British Racing Green with tan leather upholstery, Engine: six cylinders, twin overhead camshaft, 3,442cc, 275bhp at 6,000 rpm; Gearbox: 4-speed manual; Suspension: independent front by unequal length wishbones, live rear axle with trailing links, torsion bars all round; Brakes: four wheel disc. Right hand drive.

During the 1950s, it was toward the Le Mans GP d'Endurance 24-hours race that high performance automobile manufacturers eager for reputation directed the attention of their most gifted engineers. Well-organized, often richly endowed factory teams battled for supremacy in a series of epic races. The Jaguar D-Type, built very much with the demands of that circuit in mind, created an enduring legend and consolidated its maker's reputation in a manner that few other sports-racing models have ever done. Jaguar's first Le Mans victories, in 1951 and 1953, had been gained with the aerodynamic C-Type. At Le Mans that year, the leading Jaguar factory team car of Rolt and Hamilton ran a gallant second behind the mighty 4.9 litre Ferrari V12 of Gonzales and Trintignant, but the factory returned to claim first and third in 1955. There was victory again in the 1956 race and a remarkable clean sweep in 1957 by Ecurie Ecosse and private entrants, when D-Types took the first four places.

(Christie's) **$1,014,500**

1931 Alfa Romeo Tipo 6C-1750 Supercharged Gran Sport Spyder, coachwork by Zagato, red leather interior, Engine: six-cylinder, twin overhead camshafts, 1,750cc, 85bhp at 4,500rpm; Gearbox: four-speed manual; Suspension: semi-elliptic leaf springs front and rear; Brakes: four wheel mechanical drum. Right hand drive.

The 6C series had been founded as early as 1924 when Alfa Romeo engineer, Vittorio Jano, was detailed to develop a medium capacity light car with brilliant performance.

This desirable example from the 5th series of production carries the highly striking Zagato coachwork. It appears that this car has an interesting early provenance and in 1934 was owned by the famous English racing driver, Charlie Martin. *(Christie's)* **$398, 500**

1938/40 Duesenberg Model SJ Long Wheelbase Convertible, coachwork by Rollson, black with violet leather interior. Engine: Straight eight with twin overhead camshafts and four valves per cylinder with centrifugal supercharger, 420 cu. in., 320bhp at 4,750 rpm; Gearbox: three-speed; Suspension: beam axle to front, live axle to rear, half elliptic leaf springs all round; Brakes: servo assisted, hydraulically operated drums on all wheels. Left hand drive.

Frederick Samuel Duesenberg was a visionary engineer and an outstanding craftsman who earned his reputation as a racing car designer, making history when one of his cars won the 1921 French Grand Prix. His eight-cylinder racers went on to win at Indianapolis in 1924, 1925 and 1927 and set records at tracks across the USA. In 1921 he introduced the road-going Model A Duesenberg, built without compromise – the first production car made in the USA to have a straight eight engine and hydraulic brakes. Despite its undoubted merits, sales were sluggish and in 1926 the company passed into the control of E.L. Cord. He decreed that a new Duesenberg should be created – more powerful, faster and more glamorous than any competitor. The result was the breathtaking Model J that was unveiled late in 1928 at the New York Salon, the aristocrat of motor shows. With 265bhp available and a claimed 116mph maximum, it was engineered to the highest standards and was clad with coachwork of lavish ostentation. The new Duesenberg was, and still is, to many observers the crowning achievement of a brilliant era in automotive design. But it was not well timed. Within twelve months, Wall Street crashed and the market for costly automobiles dwindled. Determined to survive, the great motor car manufacturers launched ever more splendid designs. In 1932 Fred Duesenberg's response was the SJ, a supercharged version of the Model J that produced a remarkable 320bhp at 4,750rpm from its great-hearted engine. It was installed in a massive chassis that offered superb handling, stability and braking power. Upon demonstration, a factory production SJ four-passenger phaeton could reach 104mph in second gear, and an astonishing 129mph in top! Unfortunately, by August 1937, Auburn, Cord and Duesenberg were unable to survive the depths of the Great Depression. *(Christie's)* **$1,267,500**

1967 AC Cobra MK III Twin-Turbo Roadster 'Cob 1', Engine no. HM201, metallic midnight blue with blue/gray leather interior, Engine: V8, 427cu in., 6997cc, twin Garrett turbochargers, Holley 'double-pumper' carburettor, c.750bhp at 6000rpm; clutch: triple dry plate; gearbox: manual four-speed with synchromesh, limited-slip differential; suspension: independent all-round by wishbones and heavy-duty coil springs. Right hand drive.

Ford Motor Company of Detroit had a very fine small block V8 powerplant they wanted to use in International Championship racing; AC Cars of Surrey had a much admired all-independent two-liter roadster for which the engine supply had just dried up; retired racing driver Carroll Shelby very much wanted to drop an American V8 engine into a British-style sports chassis and market the result in the US. Those three threads came together in 1961 and produced the 4.7 liter, 289cu in. Cobra, first shown at the New York Auto Show in 1962.
(Christie's) **$307,255**

A large inlaid mahogany table, designed by Philip Webb and made by Morris, Marshall, Faulkner and Co., 1860s, the oval top with inlaid edge, the hexagonal base with turned and inlaid legs and stretchers, 66¾in. maximum width.

This table was designed by the architect Philip Webb who was responsible for most of the early furniture made by the Morris firm, of which he was a partner from its foundation in 1861.
(Christie's) **$34,570**

An Irish George II mahogany and Chinese black and gold-lacquer center table, the molded rectangular top with black and gilt japanned border and re-entrant corners, and decorated with a Chinese landscape with figures and birds, above a frieze drawer and a simulated frieze drawer to the reverse, on cabriole legs and scrolled feet, 26½in. wide.

This rare Irish center table has a Chinese lacquer top. Japanned and lacquered furniture was certainly being produced in Dublin during the 18th century, as can be seen from the study of contemporary advertisements and inventories.
(Christie's) **$84,660**

A mahogany table, designed by Adolf Loos, circa 1903, the scalloped top banded in bronze, above a lower shelf with looping frieze, the walnut cabriole legs with bronze sabots, 25¾in. high, 31½in. maximum width.
(Christie's) **$16,871**

Chalkware, 'the poor man's pottery', referred to items made of gypsum, the main ingredient of plaster of Paris. It was a medium particularly popular in America, though the first pieces were imported from Europe, probably brought by Italian and German immigrants. Indigenous manufacture began around 1768. Chalkware was used mainly to create ornaments such as figures of animals, birds, contemporary personalities and lamps in the form of cottages. These would be slip-molded in plaster of Paris, then coated inside with heavier plaster to add weight. While they were mass-produced from the molds, they would then be individually painted in bright oils or watercolors, so no two pieces are really identical.

Pennsylvania was a major center of output, but the first real mass-producer of chalkware was John Rogers of New York, a railroad mechanic who became a sculptor, and who produced some 80,000 chalkware pieces between 1860 and 1893.

A molded and painted chalkware still life with fruit, American, 19th century, the cluster of fruits and leaves issuing from a red, green, yellow and black with indecipherable inscription on verso, 14¼in. high. *(Sotheby's)* **$3,450**

A molded and painted chalkware compote of fruit, American, 19th century, the circular bowl with a flaring ruffled rim on a circular foot, filled with grapes, pears, oranges and bananas, painted yellow, green and orange, 15in. high.
(Sotheby's) **$1,265**

A molded and painted chalkware bust of Ulysses S. Grant, American, 19th century, the brown-haired gentleman with a mustache dressed in full uniform, on a footed pedestal, painted brown, blue, green and gold, 9¼in. high.
(Sotheby's) **$2,500**

René Lalique, A magnificent luster 'serpents et cameleons', after 1902, patinated bronze and blown glass, the sides cast with a frieze of chameleons, the underside with interlocking serpents, with hanging chains and ceiling rose, 30¾in. diameter. This luster is a larger variant of that designed for the interior of Lalique's premises at 40 cours la Reine, Paris. *(Sotheby's)* **$82,000**

One of a pair of antler chandeliers, last quarter 20th century, the branches mounted with six brass sconces, below a stem of entwined antlers to the corona, 55in. high. *(Christie's)* **$27,686**

A rare wrought iron mounted cameo glass 'bat' chandelier, by Daum, circa 1900, the shade mottled with yellow, amber and purple, overlaid in deep purple/black and etched with bats in flight, and a background of clouds, mounted at the rim with a wrought iron ring of branches and leaves and with three angled supports with foliate finials, hanging from three double rod arms cast in the form of branches connected to hammered wrought iron and brass ceiling fitment cast in the form of four bats with open wings, 15¾in. diameter of glass shade. *(Christie's)* **$29,129**

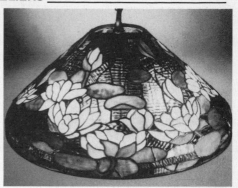

Tiffany flowering water lily chandelier, conical hanging shade composed of favrile glass segments leaded as pastel pink, rose, and opalescent white pond lily blossoms on green pads against rippled glass as blue water, rim impressed *Tiffany Studios New York 149–17*, 20in. diameter. *(Skinner)* **$75,100**

A gilt-bronze and cut-glass chandelier, French, circa 1890, in Louis XV style, with twelve branches, on a scroll framework cast with foliage and enclosing a central finial, adorned with further finials and hung with shaped drops, 137cm. high. *(Sotheby's)* **$11,245**

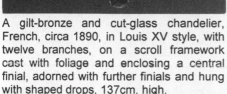

A rare lacquered brass chandelier, Victorian, circa 1855, with a central double-baluster stem, above a fluted column intertwined with ivy, flanked by four female heads supported on a fluted leaf-cast baluster, approximately 1135cm. high. *(Sotheby's)* **$48,730**

A Louis XV style ormolu eighteen-light chandelier, late 19th/early 20th century, in the manner of Jacques Caffieri, the foliate cast corona above a similarly cast cage-form support issuing two tiers of scrolling candlearms ending in leaf-tip cast drip-pans and similarly cast bobèches above a tripartite foliate scrolled finial, 41¼in. high. *(Christie's)* **$13,800**

It was the great Doulton designer Charles Noke who first saw the possibilities for a 20th century revival of the old Staffordshire Toby jug tradition and developed it with a completely new approach to the old 'face jug' concept.

He had in mind the creation of a series of characters from English legend, history and literature, which would be much more colorful than their prototypes but would, like them, have an immediate appeal for his own and future generations.

Though Noke joined Doulton in 1889, it was not until the early 1930s that he had the time and opportunity to put his concept into production. The first such jug to appear was John Barleycorn, which was an instant success. It was soon followed by Old Charley, the Night Watchman, Dickens' Sairey Gamp, Parson Brown and Dick Turpin.

Other leading Doulton designers joined Noke in the production of these jugs, such as Leslie Harradine and Harry Fenton. Harradine was responsible for many Dickens' characters, while Fenton contributed in addition such figures as John Peel, Old King Cole and the Vicar of Bray. Later names associated with the genre are Max Henk (Long John Silver, Lord Nelson etc.) and David Biggs (Town Crier, Veteran Motorist, and many others.)

The range has also been extended to include modern personalities from all walks of life from politicians to stars of stage and screen, pop stars, as well as contemporary types such as Golfer and Fireman.

Given the basic high quality of design and production, the value of each jug is often determined by its rarity, for many have a colorful history attached to their launch. Small variations in color and design can also make an enormous difference.

The Maori was a pilot jug which never went into production. It was made circa 1939 in two forms, one of which was more of a caricature than the other. Some examples did escape however and either version will fetch up to £19,000.
(Phillips) **$30,400** ▶

Doulton was involved with the beer and spirit trade from the beginning of the 19th century and they produced all manner of promotional items for these industries ranging from public house tiled or terracotta frontages and ceramic beer pump handles to ashtrays and spittoons for public bars. The large Kingsware character jug, 'The McCallum', was made for D. & J. McCallum Whisky Distillers, circa 1930 and is worth £1,000.
(Lyle) **$1,600**

were in any case superseded after the Second World War by the White haired clown which was manufactured between 1951–55. The Red and Brown haired versions will fetch £1,650 while the White haired clown will fetch around £650. Only one Black haired clown D5610 has turned up at auction so far, where it fetched £12,000. This dates from the Red haired period of the late 1930s and seems to have been a one-off commission to Doulton by a family in memory of their grandfather, who had in fact been himself a black-haired clown. *(Lyle)*   **$18,750**

▲

The normal Old King Cole character jug, D6036, designed by H. Fenton and issued 1939–1960 has reddish brown crown and handle and as such is worth £165. With a yellow crown and a greenish colored handle, issued 1939–1940, it is worth £1,450 and if it comes complete with a musical movement, D6014, issued in 1939, it is worth over £1,750.
(Lyle)   **$2,800**

The Clark Gable character jug D6709 was conceived as the first in a series of six celebrity jugs in 1983 (the others are Louis Armstrong, Mae West, Groucho Marx, W.C. Fields and Jimmy Durante). They were commissioned for the American market by American Express. About 150–200 were sent to the US as a trial, and immediately fell foul of the Clark Gable Association who informed the Retailers Association of America that they were issuing a writ against Doulton for copyright reasons. Doulton didn't argue, but immediately withdrew the jugs. Most were pulled back, leaving about 50 in circulation. For this reason, while others in the series fetch only £75–£100, Clark Gable will fetch a cool £2,000. *(Lyle)*   **$3,200**

The first Doulton clown jug was the red-haired version with a multi-colored handle which was produced in the late 1930s. There is a visible difference in coloration between early examples and those produced during the war years when the supply of materials was restricted, so much so that the later ones have become known more or less unofficially as Brown haired clowns. The Red/Brown haired versions

101

The Churchill character jug, made during the Battle of Britain was one of the first jugs to be withdrawn. The first version was cream colored with two black handles and bears the inscription 'Winston Spencer Churchill Prime Minister of Britain 1940'. It was withdrawn after only eighteen months however because, it is said, Churchill himself was not pleased with the likeness. Because so few were produced this jug is an extremely rare and desirable item, coveted by collectors throughout the world. The second version had natural coloring and bears the number D6170. The cream version, which was rather longer on the market before withdrawal, has fetched over £5,000, while one with natural coloring, which is even rarer, would be worth about £12,500. *(Lyle)* **$18,750**

Harry Fenton's 'Drake' jug was introduced in 1940. In the first version the rim is the character's hair, but in later versions it became his hat. The earlier jug, known as 'The Hatless Drake' D6115 carries the inscription 'Drake he was a Devon Man' and was produced only in limited numbers. Today, a 'hatless' Drake will sell for around £1,650, while the hatted version will fetch only about £85. *(Lyle)* **$2,640**

'Arry and 'Arriet are favorite Doulton jugs designed by Harry Fenton, with somewhat complicated variations. These figures of a Cockney costermonger and his wife were introduced in the mid 1940s and withdrawn by 1960. 'Arry is predominantly brown in color. In some variations however he is embellished by having brown or white buttons on his hat (a reference to the costermongers' custom of dressing up on high days and holidays as Pearly Kings and Queens) when he becomes Brown Pearly Boy, and can be worth £950. Even more rare is the version with pinkish white buttons on a brown hat with blue peak, when he becomes Blue Pearly Boy and fetches £3,000! *(Lyle)* **$4,800**

Greco (Gioachino) The Royall Game of Chesse-Play. Sometimes the Recreation of the late King, with many of the Nobility. Illustrated with almost an hundred Gambetts. Being the study of Giochimo the famous Italian, first edition, engraved frontispiece portrait of King Charles, Henry Herringman, 1656.
(Sotheby's) **$2,062**

A fine and important chessboard and chessmen, Turkish/Persian, late 17th century, the elaborately adorned board folding into three sections, with two storage drawers to the center concealed within, and with inter-locking 'toothed' side sections, the central checkered board section inlaid with ivory, stained wood and mahogany foliate roundels and small birds in flight, the corners with ivory double headed eagles surmounted with crowns, the borders formed from coiling foliage and stylized blooms, 20½in. square when opened, the chessmen of ivory and black hardwood, the kings of tapering baluster form, the queen of more bulbous form, unusual stylized serpentine-shaped horse-form knights.
(Sotheby's) **$18,400** ▶

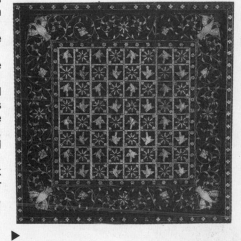

▼

Rare Roycroft bridal chest, mortise and tenons on sides, cast iron hardware, orb mark on front, original dark finish, missing interior tray, minor seam splits, 39¼in. wide. *(Skinner)* **$17,250**

◄

A Spanish Renaissance style trunk, with wrought iron mountings and red velvet lining, the domed cover with metal bands and shell ornament, with corner handles, 115cm. wide. *(Christie's)* **$10,033**

►

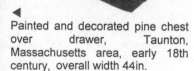

◄

Painted and decorated pine chest over drawer, Taunton, Massachusetts area, early 18th century, overall width 44in.

This chest is one of a group of about a dozen similarly decorated chests attributed to Robert Crosman (1707–1799), a drum maker of Taunton. *(Skinner)* **$31,050**

An exceptional 19th century Goanese carved padouk chest with rectangular hinged top, pulvenated frieze carved with a continuous band of fish centered by pistols and swords, the two doors below depicting carracks and galleons in confrontation, 78cm. high x 120cm. wide. *(Bearne's)* **$10,725** ►

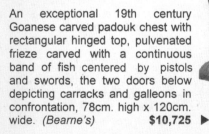

A pair of painted drawers, 20th century, each of tapering form, simulating eight stacked books with drawers fitted to each spine, on turned feet with recessed castors, each 26in. wide.
(Christie's) **$4,600**

A George III burr-yew bachelor's chest, banded overall in rosewood and boxwood, the rectangular folding top above two simulated drawers functioning as lopers and concealing two short mahogany-lined drawers, above three graduated long mahogany-lined drawers, the sides with yewwood veneer and on shaped bracket feet, 36in. wide.
(Christie's) **$102,920**

▶

A Dutch burr and figured walnut chest early 18th century, the serpentine molded quarter-veneered top inlaid with a narrow band above a bombé front and sides with four graduated long drawers and on later elm bun feet, 32¾in. wide.
(Christie's) **$47,800**

A Federal inlaid mahogany serpentine-front chest-of-drawers, Boston, 1780-1800, the rectangular top with serpentine front and banded and string-inlaid edge above a conforming case fitted with four serpentine-front and string-inlaid long drawers over a conforming molded base centering a husk-inlaid pendant, on straight bracket feet with husk inlay, appears to retain original brasses, 40⁵/₈in. wide.
(Christie's) **$85,000**

An oyster-veneered walnut chest, early 18th century, decorated with crossbanding and geometric lines, fitted with two short and three long graduated drawers, on later bun feet, restorations, 36¾in. wide.
(Christie's) **$10,246**

A Federal inlaid mahogany serpentine chest-of-drawers, attributed to Thomas Needham (1780-1858), Salem, Massachusetts, 1811-1820, the serpentine top above a conforming case with four string-inlaid and graduated drawers with cockbead surrounds over a shaped apron with a central inlaid fan pendant continuing to flared bracket feet, 36½in. high x 41¾in. wide.

This chest-of-drawers is attributed to Thomas Needham (1780-1858) of Salem on the basis of its interior construction and the bold sweep of its serpentine façade. Fitted with a full dustboard between its second and third drawers, this chest exhibits a feature common to Philadelphia-area furniture but rare in New England furniture.
(Christie's) **$14,950**

A Chinese Export 'Tobacco Leaf' pattern oval tureen stand, 1770–80, painted with a green-centered rose and yellow tobacco blossom, a gold and iron-red chrysanthemum, and sprays of smaller rose, blue, iron-red, yellow and purple flowers and green leaves superimposed on and surrounding large leaves in shades of underglaze-blue, yellow, turquoise and pink, 15¹/₁₆in. long.
(Sotheby's)   **$16,100**

A rare pair of Chinese Export stag's head wall ornaments, early 19th century, the young bucks modeled turned slightly towards each other, their ears held up in alert pose and their detachable antlers with three short branches, fur markings in underglaze blue and a collar of molded oak leaves on their shield form plaques, 15½in. high.

The very rare model represents a fascinating confluence of the European hunting trophy tradition and the Chinese reverence of deer as sacred. In China spotted deer in particular are associated with both longevity and wealth, and are typically depicted alongside the sacred fungus, which only they are able to root out.
◄ (Christie's)   **$85,000**

A fine Chinese Export porcelain hunting punch bowl, circa 1770, the exterior colorfully painted and heightened in gilding on the front with four huntsmen and their pack 'Going out in the Morning', and on the reverse with five huntsmen and the pack 'Beating and trailing for a hare', the scenes within large panels edged in grisaille and gilt scrollwork and separated at the side with a worn gilt filigree ground reserved with a floral panel above a smaller iron-red oriental landscape panel, diameter 15¹/₈in.
(Sotheby's)   **$18,400**

Of the many figurine artists who emerged during the years following the First World War one of the most important was Dimitri (Demetre is the Gallicised form) Chiparus. Chiparus was a Rumanian who came to Paris to study under A Mercié and J Boucher. He started exhibiting at the Salon des Artistes Français in 1914, when he received an Honourable Mention, and continued to do so until 1928.

His figures include realistic reproductions of nudes and women in everyday clothes, as well as columbines and pierrots, and dancers, some in amazing postures and obviously influenced by the Ballets Russes.

Much of his work was executed in chryselephantine, a medium encouraged at the time by the Belgian government who were anxious to create a European market for Congolese ivory.

▲
'Antinea', a bronze and ivory figure cast from the model by Demetre Chiparus, 1920s, the female figure in scant cold-painted costume, her arms outstretched above her head holding a richly decorated fringed drape, veined black marble base with wedges of green and red onyx, 26½in. high.
(Christie's)   **$76,440**
◄
'Persian Dance', a bronze and ivory group, cast from the model by Demetre Chiparus, 1920s, the two dancers clad in extravagant cold painted oriental costume, the male figure holding his partner in his arms, both leaning forwards, stepped marble base veined in red, beige and black, 21¼in. high. (Christie's)   **$65,200**

◄

'Finale', a bronze and ivory group, cast from the model by Demetre Chiparus, 1920s, the central male dancer in elaborate silvered, gilt and cold-painted costume flanked by female dancers in silvered, gilt and cold-painted dresses with flared skirts, the trio standing on tip-toe with arms outstretched, meeting in V-shapes, elaborate brown and white onyx base, 16¼in. high.
(Christie's) **$44,436**

'The Dolly Sisters', a bronze and ivory group cast from the model by Demetre Chiparus, 1920s, the identical sisters standing with arms upstretched holding out their skirts, brown onyx base applied with central motif incorporating colored layers of marble, 29¹/₈in. high.

Also known as The Sisters, this group is thought to represent one of the most famous dancing pairs of the 1920s, the Dolly Sisters. The popular phenomenon of duos such as the Rowe Sisters or the Dodge Twins was ultimately superceded by chorus lines during the second half of the decade. Nevertheless, so enduring was the fame of the Dolly Sisters that their story was made into a film starring Betty Grable and June Haver in 1946.
(Christie's) **$76,440**

An important Chippendale carved mahogany Gothic-back armchair, Philadelphia, circa 1760, the arched serpentine crest with scrolled ears above a pierced beaker-form splat centering a diamond, and flowerhead carved lunette, the shaped arms ending in scrolled handholds above incurvate arm supports and a trapezoidal seat, the front seat rail carved with an asymmetrical acanthus-leaf device, acanthus-leaf and strapwork-carved cabriole legs ending in claw-and-ball feet. Height of seat 16¾in.
(Sotheby's) **$508,500**

▶

An extremely fine and rare pair of early Chippendale carved walnut side chairs, Philadelphia, circa 1750, each with a serpentine rope and tassel-molded crest.

Although past scholars once suggested a Chester County, Pennsylvania or Maryland origin for these chairs, construction details such as the fluted stiles, stump rear legs, and flat arched seat rails are all typical of Philadelphia.
(Sotheby's) **$189,500**

▼

The Sarah Slocum Chippendale mahogany block-and-shell carved chest of drawers, labeled by John Townsend (1732-1809), Newport, dated 1792, the rectangular top with molded edges above a conforming case fitted with four blocked and graduated drawers with cockbeaded surrounds, the uppermost centered by a recessed carved shell flanked by convex carved shells, all over a conforming molded base, on blocked ogee bracket feet, the uppermost drawer with two labels: the first printed, *Made by John Townsend, Newport*, with inscriptions, *Sarah Slocum's* and *November 20th 1792*; the second hand inscribed, *(illeg.) give to Lydia T. Connor*, the backboards with chalk inscription, *J T*; a cross brace with the hand inscription in graphite, *J.C.S. Taber*, appears to retain original brasses, 34½in. high; 36¾in. wide.

Displaying superbly carved blocked shells and bearing the label of John Townsend, this chest of drawers represents one of the hallmarks of American design and craftsmanship. Long hailed as one of America's innovations in furniture design, the block-and-shell furniture of Newport, Rhode Island demonstrates the economic vitality and cultural confidence of the trading port city during the second half of the eighteenth century. Merchants such as the Brown family of Providence and George Champlin of Newport amassed substantial fortunes through the maritime trades and parlayed some of their earnings toward the patronage of the leading cabinetmakers of Newport, members of the Townsend and Goddard families.

(Christie's) **$4,732,500**

A Chippendale carved mahogany bombé chest of drawers, Boston or Salem, 1770–85, the molded rectangular top with cusped corners above a bombé case fitted with four conforming and graduated thumbmolded long drawers over a rectangular molded base centered by a shaped pendant drop, on ogee bracket feet, 37in. wide.

Employing a graceful curve within its structural members, the bombé chest form was the technological masterpiece of the most accomplished cabinetmakers of late eighteenth century Boston and Salem. The high level of skill required to construct the form parlayed into greater expense for the consumer. As such, the patronage of bombé chest-of-drawers, desk-and-bookcases, chests-on-chests and dressing mirrors was the exclusive prerogative of the elite. Compared to the contemporaneous options of block-front, serpentine and reverse-serpentine facades, bombé furniture was made in far fewer quantities and only about sixty examples survive today. Those that have survived with family histories indicate the prestige of their first owners. Crossing political boundaries, bombé furniture was owned by wealthy Loyalists and Patriots such as Governor Thomas Hutchinson, Sir William Pepperell, Josiah Quincy and Elias Hasket Derby.

Made soon after their English prototypes, American bombé caseforms indicate that the colonial elite were able to keep abreast of the latest fashions. In his seminal article, 'The Bombé Furniture of Boston', Gilbert T. Vincent concludes that the bombé form was introduced to America by the importation of English examples, most notably a bombé chest-on-chest with glass doors made about 1740 and brought to Boston by Charles Apthorp (1698–1758). The bombé section of this object bears strong aesthetic and structural similarities to the earliest dated American bombé example, a desk-and-bookcase signed by Benjamin Frothingham and dated 1753.

This chest is one of about seven similar examples with cusped cornered tops and closely related pendant drops, knee returns and ogee bracket feet.
(Christie's) **$827,500**

A rare Chippendale carved mahogany blockfront chest-of-drawers, Boston or Salem, 1760-80, the molded rectangular top with rounded blocking above a conforming case fitted with four cockbeaded and graduated long drawers, all similarly blocked, over a conforming molded base above a central shaped pendant drop, on cabriole legs with hairy ball-and-claw feet, the sides with brass bale handles, 36in. wide.

With rounded blocking and finely carved hairy-paw feet, this blockfront chest-of-drawers exemplifies the sophistication of Boston's late eighteenth century cabinetmakers.
(Christie's) **$607,500**

A very fine and rare Chippendale mahogany serpentine-front chest of drawers, Boston, Massachusetts, circa 1780, the oblong molded, serpentine and block-fronted top above a conformingly shaped case with four graduated drawers, on straight bracket feet, 36in. wide.
(Sotheby's) **$82,250**

A fine and rare Chippendale carved and figured mahogany reverse-serpentine blocked chest of drawers, Massachusetts, circa 1780, the oblong molded top above four graduated line-incised long drawers, the molded base below on frontal short cabriole legs ending in claw-and-ball feet. Appears to retain its original cast-brass drawer pulls and escutcheons, width at top 38½in.
(Sotheby's) **$101,500**
▶

Chippendale mahogany carved veneer serpentine chest of drawers, Boston or Salem, Massachusetts, 18th century, with molded top with canted corners above a conforming case with dressing slide above cockbeaded veneered drawers flanked by fluted and stop fluted corners on a molded base with a shell-carved central drop and broad ogee bracket feet, 41½in. wide.
(Skinner) **$74,000**

Dr Christopher Dresser was born in Glasgow in 1834. He studied at the London School of Design at Somerset House, and then trained and lectured as a botanist. Both these interests came together in the articles he wrote in the 1850s for Art Journal, in which he examined the significance to design of the relationship between structure and function, in plants.

By the 1860s he was designing silver, and his inspirations were characterized by their simplicity of form and the careful consideration of the function of each piece, for example the handling and pouring properties of jugs, teapots etc.

He was also an enthusiastic collector of Japanese art, and its influence on his work is most clearly seen in some of his designs for handles.

During his career, his name was associated with a host of different manufacturers. For the electroplaters Hukin & Heath he designed among other things, tureens, claret jugs and tea services. 'Designed by Dr. C. Dresser' sometimes appears beside the manufacturers' mark on these. For J. Dixon, around 1880, his designs include a silver tea service of round shape, with the cast metal feet held by rivets. These bear his facsimile signature in the mark. For Elkington & Co. in the mid 1880s, he produced severe, often angular designs, while for Benham & Froud he designed firedogs, kettles etc. in copper and sometimes brass. His name is also associated with wallpaper and tiles. He even produced a cast iron hall stand for the Coalbrookdale Co.

Dresser was a prime mover in the establishment of the Linthorpe Pottery in 1879, for which he supplied many designs based on Egyptian, Greek and Roman originals and a wide range of native cultures. His work for them was impressed *Chr. Dresser.* Though his active participation in the pottery stopped in 1882, during the 1890s he designed pottery for W. Ault's factory, which often incorporated animal or grotesque masks. He collaborated too on the designs of Clutha glass vases and bowls.

A rare electroplated toast rack, designed by Christopher Dresser, manufactured by James Dixon & Sons, circa 1881, the rectangular frame with seven triangular supports, on four spike feet, with 'T' shaped carrying handle, 6¼in., maximum height.

Between 1879 and 1882 Dresser supplied approximately thirty-seven designs for silver and electroplate to the Sheffield firm of James Dixon & Sons. These were among the least orthodox and most clearly Japanese-inspired designs that Dresser ever produced. The toast rack is one of a group of ten designs submitted to James Dixon in 1881 and these were produced in limited numbers only. The designs for toast racks which appeared in Dixon's catalog of 1885 were numbered models; this one bears no such number which may indicate that the design was not thought suitable for mass production and therefore only very few examples were produced.

The original design for this toastrack, illustrated in Dresser's account book for 1881, was published by Nikolaus Pevsner in his article in The Architectural Review of 1937, 'Christopher Dresser, Industrial Designer', and is recorded in the Nikolaus Pevsner Papers archived at the Getty Center for the History of Art and the Humanities, Los Angeles, California. *(Christie's)* **$17,284**

An electroplated 'crow's foot' claret jug, designed by Christopher Dresser, manufactured by Hukin and Heath, circa 1878, flat hinged cover, angular silver handle, set on three riveted feet, 9¾in. high. *(Christie's)* **$14,400**

Christopher Dresser for J.W. Hukin & J.T.Heath, tureen, cover and ladle, design registered 28th July, 1880, electroplated metal, ebony, the underside of the tureen stamped with maker's mark and *Designed by Dr C. Dresser*, numbered *2123* and with P.O.D.R. mark for 28th July 1880, 8¹/₈in. high. *(Sotheby's)* **$11,622**

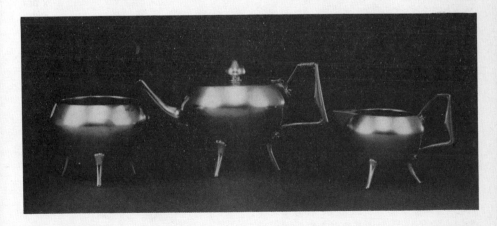

A rare three piece silver tea service, designed by Dr. Christopher Dresser, manufactured by James Dixon and Sons, Sheffield, 1882, conical teapot, cream jug and sugar basin, supported on three prong legs, angular handles on the two vessels terminating in foliate bosses, the sugar basin and cream jug with gilt interiors, teapot 4in. high. *(Sotheby's)* **$20,701**

A painted carved wood tobacconist's counter display bust, 18th century, modeled as a mustachioed Turk's head, wearing a turban, on a later associated painted wood plinth, of rectangular stepped form, 15in. high.
(Christie's) **$1,895**

A carved and painted pine cigar-store Indian, American, late 19th century, the full figured Indian squaw standing on a partial step with one raised hand holding a tin, the other holding two cigars, wearing a red and yellow-painted feathered headdress and a red-painted tunic with a green and yellow-painted sash and green and yellow-painted trim above brown-painted leggings and black-painted moccasins, standing on a stepped rectangular gray painted base, 77½in. high. *(Christie's)* **$29,900**

A painted carved wood tobacconist's shop counter display figure, circa 1700, the semi-naked native wearing a feather skirt, distressed, 20½in. high.
(Christie's) **$1,800**

A carved and painted pine cigar store Indian figure, American, 19th century, the full-length standing figure of an Indian princess wearing a feathered headdress, green gown and cloak, holding a bunch of cigars in one hand and a sheaf of tobacco leaves in the other, the figure mounted on a pine base, 69in. high.
(Sotheby's)   **$29,900**

A polychrome-painted cast metal cigar store Indian, stamped *Wm. Demuth (1835–1911) & Company, New York City,* late 19th century, modeled in the round as an Indian Chief, standing contrapposto on a rocky plinth, 70½in. high.

William Demuth (1835–1911) operated a manufactory of 'Smokers' Articles', including cigar store figures, at various addresses in lower Manhattan. The company produced and imported figures in both wood and cast metal, ranging in a variety of forms from the Indian illustrated here to medieval royalty, contemporary military, and various Chinese figures. This model of cast metal Indian was exhibited by Demuth in the Agricultural Hall of the 1893 Columbian Exposition in Chicago.
(Christie's)   **$11,500**

A yellow metal enameled cartographic cigarette-case, by Fabergé, Workmaster Henrik Wigström, St. Petersburg, 1908-1917, the cover enameled with a ship, 3¾in. long, 8.7oz. gross. *(Christie's)* **$12,317**

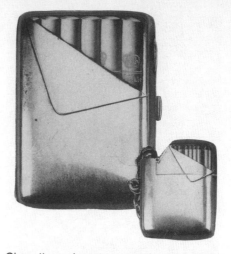

Cigarette and vesta case, the rectangular cigarette case cast to incorporate a 'flap' revealing a row of enameled cigarettes, the vesta similarly cast and incorporating a wick holder, the 'flap' revealing a row of enameled vestas, both Austro-Hungarian, late nineteenth century, 8.8cm and 4.4cm. respectively. *(Christie's)* **$1,700**

A parcel-gilt silver cigarette case, Maker's mark of Tiffany & Co., New York, 1878-1891, in the Japanese taste; shaped rectangular, the surface spot-hammered, the hinged cover applied with two shells and silver-gilt reeds, the interior gilt, 5¼in. long. 6oz. 10dwt. *(Christie's)* **$2,990**

F. Zwickl, blue Daimler racing car cigarette case, 1931, silver-colored metal, enameled panel, 8.25 x 11.5cm. *(Sotheby's)* **$3,353**

An electro-plated and enamel cigarette case, circa 1900, the hinged cover with polychrome enamel panel depicting the interior of a harem with three nude Circassian female figures seated on a Persian carpet with an attendant carrying a Turkish coffee pot on a tray, 3½ x 3¼in. *(Christie's)* **$858**

A silver combined petrol lighter and watch, Dunhill, No. 3679, 1927, 15-jewel movement with three adjustments, 54mm. high. *(Christie's)* **$1,840**

Royal Doulton table lighter depicting Rip Van Winkle, D6463, designed by G. Blower, issued 1958, 3½in. high. *(Lyle)* **$480**

A cast metal tobacconist's gypsy cigar and cigarette lighter, probably New York, late 19th century, the half length figure of gypsy girl with a cigarette in mouth, hands behind her head and arms raised, the figure wearing a coin-decorated turban, arm bracelets and a highly patterned garment; on a round base. Gas jet in rear leads to cigarette, 31in. high.
(Sotheby's) **$5,175**

An 18ct. gold combined petrol lighter and watch, Dunhill, 1938, the engine turned lighter with wind guard and signed on the extinguishing arm *Dunhill*, the base stamped *AD* and with London marks for 1938, the front with hinged rectangular panel enclosing the watch, silvered dial with gilt Arabic numerals, 15-jewel nickel plated movement with three adjustments, the watch case with Edinburgh marks for 1938, 53 x 43mm.
(Christie's) **$8,280**

The legendary Clarice Cliff was born in 1899 in, perhaps inevitably, Staffordshire where she started work at 13 in one of the local potteries, painting freehand onto pottery.

Her formal training comprised a year, when she was 16, at the Burslem School of Art, and a later year at the Royal College of Art, where she studied sculpture. At 17, she had gone to work at the firm of A.J. Wilkinson, and she remained with them, and their subsidiary the Newport Pottery, for the next two decades, ending up as Art Director and marrying the boss, Colley Shorter, when she was forty.

During the 1920s she painted Tibetan ware, large jars painted with floral designs in bright colors and gold, and she also transferred on to pottery designs by such distinguished artists as Paul Nash and Laura Knight.

In 1928, however, she painted 60 dozen pieces of her own design to test the market at a trade fair. These proved so popular that by 1929 the whole factory was switched to producing her Bizarre ware.

A superb wall plaque by Clarice Cliff painted with a scene inspired by Diaghilev's costume design for The Ballet Russe. *(Christie's)* **$13,000**

A pair of Clarice Cliff teddy bear book ends decorated in the 'Red Flower' pattern, painted in colors, 6in. high. *(Christie's)* **$6,800**

'Inspiration Caprice' a 'Bizarre' twin-handled lotus jug, painted in shades of blue, black and ocher on a turquoise ground, printed and painted marks, 30cm. high. *(Christie's)* **$3,560**

A good Clarice Cliff 'Age of Jazz' figural group, painted in black red and brown against a cream ground, 12.3cm. high. (Phillips) **$6,200**

'May Avenue' a 'Bizarre' conical sugar sifter, painted in colors between blue bands, printed factory marks, 14cm. high. (Christie's) **$9,375**

A 'House and Bridge' pattern Meiping vase, shape 14, 16¼in. high, lithograph mark Fantasque Hand Painted Bizarre by Clarice Cliff Newport Pottery England. (Bonhams) **$12,225**

'Windbells', a 'Fantasque Bizarre' Bon Jour coffee set for six, painted in colors, comprising; Bon Jour coffee pot and cover, milk-jug and sugar basin and six conical cups and saucers. Coffee pot 19.5cm. high. (Christie's) **$6,375**

121

An amusing French faience mantel clock, late 19th century, the case modeled as a gong held by a mandarin seated on a stool, with faux bamboo frame to the glazed dial with silvered chapter ring applied with Roman numerals, the clock resting on a scroll-sided hardwood plinth in the Chinese manner, twin barrel movement with strike on bell, 20¼in. high.
(Christie's) **$6,450**

A fine and rare Federal inlaid brass-mounted eglomisé and mahogany banjo clock, Daniel Munroe, Concord, Massachusetts, circa 1810, surmounted by a gilt pointed-ball finial above a diamond-shaped hood, the hinged glazed door opening to a white-painted dial painted with a red, white, and blue American shield with gilt foliate spandrels, the reeded and inlaid throat below decorated with an eglomisé panel depicting acorns and oak leaves tied with a bowknot flanked by pierced brass side arms, the eglomisé box door panel below decorated with geometric motifs in blue, gold and black and painted with the inscription *Daniel Munroe.*, above brass bracket feet, 38½in. high.
(Sotheby's) **$167,500**

Kem Weber for Lawson Time Inc., Alhambra, California, U.S.A., digital clock 'The Zephyr', model No. 304-P 40', 1934, copper, plastic, 8¹/8in. maximum width.
(Sotheby's) **$1,875**

122

lower portion of the wall board with printed face depicting a young angel watching over a calendar dial, 29in. high.

Sand clocks of this form are, by the very nature of their construction, fragile and thus rare. Most, however, were constructed with iron frames supporting the four hour-glasses which were contained in stamped brass frames, decorated with floral and other motifs, the upper and lower framework supporting a decorative frieze and separated by either 'barley-twist' or tubular brass columns. Others were decorated with baluster turned silver columns with pressed and engraved mounts. *(Christie's)* **$14,465**

A rare late 17th/early 18th century Chancel sand-clock, signed on the printed paper face of the wall board *CHRISTOPH KREM [?* * *] SANDURMACHER in Leipzig*, the four glass time piece constructed of eight white-sand filled phials bound at the center with wax and cord and supported in a carved fruitwood frame with decorative vellum upper and lower frieze, arranged to rotate on the shaped wall board, the upper portion with portrait of Augustus Rex, military trophies, the hour dial flanked by two angels above a tableau showing an hour-glass resting on a table and a putti sitting on a sphere with landscape beyond and scroll inscribed *Memento mori*; the

A rare Federal inlaid rosewood and eglomisé 'Acorn' shelf clock, Connecticut, circa 1825 attributed to the Forrestville Connecticut Clock Manufactory, the hinged eglomisé door with arched and peaked upper section opening to a white-painted dial, supported between two serpentine uprights with acorn finials, on a stepped base, 25in. high.
(Sotheby's) **$12,650**

A Japanese burr wood and gilt-wood striking lantern clock with alarm and calendar, signed *Araki Yamato No Jo Tidishi in Kyoto*; first quarter 19th century.

The movement with going barrels for the strike and alarm and Japanese style fusee for the going, foliot verge escapement, twin circular apertures above the chapter ring indicating the sixty days of the Chinese month, the rear left hand pillar signed in Japanese script *Made by Araki Yamato No Jo Tadashi in Kyoto who lived in Shijo tori Sakaimachi, Kyoto*, 9¼in. high.
(Christie's)   **$15,000**

Federal gilt gesso and mahogany veneer mirror timepiece, Joshua Wilder, Hingham, Massachusetts, circa 1815, the molded cornice with applied spherules above the eglomisé stenciled tablet enclosing a painted iron dial and brass eight-day weight driven drop strike movement above the mirror flanked by molded pilasters, 27¾in. high. *(Skinner)*   **$25,300**

Peter Behrens for AEG, Berlin, Synchron double sided electric clock, circa 1910, brass, sheet steel, black painted metal, glass, the face marked *AEG*, with affixed metal AEG label, 14³/₈in. diameter. *(Sotheby's)*   **$8,998**

In cloisonné enameling, every detail of the design is defined with narrow bands of metal, gold, silver or copper, in such a way as to cover the whole surface to be decorated. These are then filled with appropriate enamel colors, ground to a fine powder, moistened and fired. After firing, the wires remain visible and become an integral part of the design. The method differs from champlevé enameling in which depressions are cut into a metal base and filled with enamel paste before firing. It is thought that the Chinese adopted cloisonné techniques from the West, particularly from Byzantium, but it became very popular again in Europe during the 19th century when Alexis Falize, a French silversmith, began importing and selling articles of Chinese cloisonné as well as adopting the technique for his own products.

A Chinese Qing Dynasty bronze and enamel cloisonné censer, 17th century, 31.8cm. high.
(Galerie Koller) **$15,931**

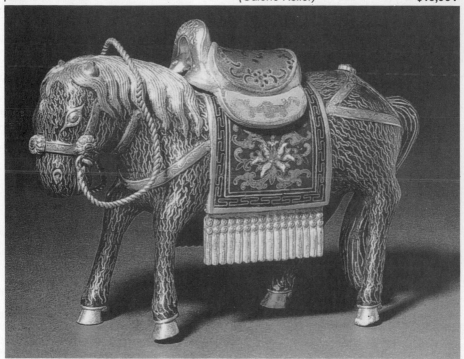

An Imperial cloisonné enamel model of a saddled horse, Qianlong, the harnessed horse colorfully enameled with elaborately decorated saddlecloth and detachable saddle, the hide finely detailed and enameled in a reddish brown, the inclined head with a twisted rope strap flung over the mane, 7^7/8in. wide. *(Christie's)* **$14,059**

A Namikawa Sosuke kidney-shaped cloisonné tray, with Namikawa Sosuke seal, Meiji period, late 19th century, decorated in various colored enamels, partly in wireless enamel and with silver wire depicting a sparrow perched on a blossoming branch covered by snow, shakudo rim, the reverse similarly decorated with scattered cherry blossom in two tones of brown on a darker brown ground, 11⁵/₈in. diameter. (Christie's) $22,494

A fine Ando moriage cloisonné vase, with Ando Jubei mark inlaid in silver wire, Meiji period, late 19th century, of baluster form decorated in various tones of colored enamels with silver wire depicting a persimmon tree branch in light beige with fruits in bright orange and yellow, the fine leaves in tones of blue and green on a pale grayish-green ground, 13¾in. high.

This is among the finest and largest examples of Ando Jubei's work in the moriage technique, in which the enamels are raised in relief within the individual cells.
(Christie's) $74,165
▶

A rare pair of cloisonné enamel square stools, early 19th century, each with a flat top above a narrow waist supported on a thick apron with scrolls, centered on a cloud head, joining square-section legs terminating in hoof feet, colorfully decorated with bats and flowers in geometric arrangements on a pale blue enamel ground within a purple frame, 19¾in. square.

Cloisonné enamel furniture is very rare. Cloisonné stools are seldom found but appear to have been more popular in the rounded barrel shape imitating porcelain.
(Christie's) $22,080

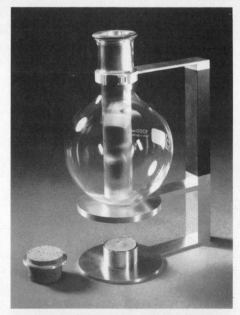

Designed and executed by Herbert Schulze, Fachhochschule, Dusseldorf, tea maker, 1990, silver-colored metal, glass, ebony, cork, the pot and the stand stamped on the underside with designer's monogram and numbered '8/8', 11¼in. high. This tea maker was produced in an edition of eight.
(Sotheby's) **$3,374**

Anon, Italian, coffee machine and coffee pot, circa 1930, brass and plastic, coffee machine 11in., coffee pot 6⁷/₈in.
(Sotheby's) **$1,030**

A cast-iron and paint-decorated coffee grinder on stand, Enterprise Manufacturing Company, Philadelphia, mid-19th century of impressive size, the eagle finial above a hinged lid and urn-form reservoir with a grinding mechanism below, bearing a plaque inscribed *No. 218* and the inscription *Pat. Oct 21,1873* also with the word *American* on the back, flanked by large fly-wheels with strapwork spokes inscribed *Enterprise Mf'g Philadelphia USA*, on a pierced arched support with paint decorated tôle bin and scoop, on pierced shaped frame, 5ft.8in. high.
(Sotheby's) **$5,000**

George Lecompte for G. Carre & Cie., Paris, Samovar, circa 1935, comprising kettle, cover and detachable water flow regulator, with integral stand, burner with detachable wick, lightly hammered silver-colored metal. The kettle stamped *G. Carre & Cie Paris*, the kettle and burner also stamped *Travail au Marteau de G. Lecomte*, 15½in. high.
(Sotheby's) **$2,812**

English silver coffee urn, globular form with quatrefoil base, gadroon rims and lion's-head mask and loose ring handles, cover lamp and two liners, marks of Wilson and Gill, London, 1923, 14in. high, 75.0 troy oz. *(Eldred's)* **$2,200**

Gerhard Marcks for Schott & Gen. Jena'er Glassworks, Jena, coffee machine 'Sintrax' and hot ring, circa 1925, clear, heat-resistant glass, chromium-plated metal, black painted wood, rubber, porous rock filter, the glass marked *Sintrax* and *RDH 1925 81*, the underside of the lower section with stenciled factory mark, the underside of the stove marked *Engel Kocher*, 15¹/₈in. high.
(Sotheby's) **$1,875**

Detective Comics No. 1, March 1937, about 30 copies known to exist. *(Lyle)* **$24,500**

Whiz Comics No. 1 featuring Captain Marvel, February 1940, about 150 copies known to exist. *(Lyle)* **$40,000**

Action Comics No. 1, the first to feature Siegel & Schuster's creation Superman, June 1938, about 100 copies known to exist. *(Lyle)* **$100,000**

Adventure Comics No. 40, first Issue to feature The Sandman, July 1939, about 55 copies known to exist. *(Lyle)* **$9,000**

Marvel Comics No. 1, November 1939, about 100 copies known to exist. *(Lyle)* **$57,000**

Batman No. 1, the Brand New Adventures of Batman and Robin the Boy Wonder, spring 1940, about 300 copies known to exist. *(Lyle)* **$32,000**

Superman No. 1, the Complete Story of the Daring Exploits of the One and Only Superman, summer 1939, about 200 copies known to exist. *(Lyle)* **$65,000**

Detective Comics No 27, Starting This Issue, the Amazing and Unique Adventures of The Batman, May 1939, about 100 copies known to exist. *(Lyle)* **$125,000**

Hans Coper (1920-1981) trained as an engineer in his native Germany, but fled to England in the late '30s. During the war, he met another refugee, Lucie Rie, and went to work in her studio. They started making ceramic buttons, then graduated to domestic ware and in the evenings Coper could experiment with his own designs.

His biggest 'break' came when Basil Spence commissioned two candlesticks from him for Coventry Cathedral.

A fine and large Hans Coper vase, dated 1972, the cylindrical body rounded at the shoulder and set with a flat disk rim covered in a brown glaze, on a short cylindrical neck, buff glazed with an inlaid brown line and a brown textured glaze around the narrowed base, impressed HC seal, inscribed underneath: *1.X.1972 HC. To Writhlington School. Thank you for Jennea the goat.* Writhlington School, 30¾in.

Hans Coper and his wife Jane, took over a derelict farm house in Frome, Somerset, in the late 1960s when the artist was at the height of his fame. To complete their rural idyll the couple adopted an unwanted kid goat, which had been born on a farm run by the pupils of nearby Writhlington School. Jane Coper said that Hans had no desire to own a goat but when one of the school's teachers told them that the kid needed a home, he changed his mind. Hans offered to pay for the animal, but the farm manager would not accept, saying 'Oh, just give me a pot.' Little did the farm manager realise that large examples of Coper's work were already much sought after by dealers and collectors.

Nevertheless, when Jennea was delivered to her new owners in the school bus - a red, converted ambulance - a full scale party was held in the garden to celebrate her arrival! Afterwards the warm-hearted Coper took the farm manager at his word, immediately starting work on an extra-special pot which he thought worthy of exchange for a living thing.

Mrs Coper said that he went rather over the top in size, making the pot plain and strong so it would fit in at the school. *(Sotheby's)* **$29,624**

A rare early stoneware shallow dish by Hans Coper, covered in matt manganese glaze, the interior with carved decoration through to a pitted translucent white glaze of abstract design with stylized fish, impressed *HC* seal, circa 1950, 37cm. diameter. *(Christie's)* **$37,202**

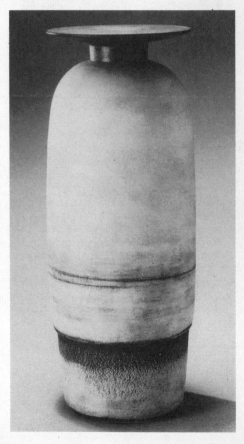

Many corner chairs, the present example included, originally served as commode chairs. Known as 'night chairs' or 'closestools', such chairs had frames for chamber pots fastened to the seat rails below the loose seat frame.

The heavy and high molded crest rail, the bulbous ring-turned supports, the heart-pierced vasiform splats, and the serpentine-shaped front seat rails exhibited on the present chair are features associated with corner chairs made in New York in the 18th century. The knees of this chair, however, are carved with an unusual lappet motif that generally appears on seating furniture manufactured in Philadelphia. This same motif is featured on several pieces of furniture documented to the Philadelphia cabinet and chairmaker William Savery (1722–1787). The fact that this motif appears on the present corner chair suggest that it was made by a New York craftsman familiar with Philadelphia chairmaking designs and shop practices. Another characteristic exhibited on this chair - the four cabriole legs terminating in claw-and-ball feet - is an exceedingly rare feature that appears on few American eighteenth century chairs of this type.
(Sotheby's)   **$27,600**

A fine and rare Chippendale carved and figured mahogany corner chair, Boston, Massachusetts, circa 1770, the shaped crest above a concave arm with outscrolled terminals.
(Sotheby's)   **$40,250**

An important Chippendale carved and figured mahogany corner chair, New York, circa 1760, the reverse scrolling concave crest above a conformingly-shaped arm with outscrolled terminals on shaped supports centering two strapwork splats.
(Sotheby's)   **$63,000**

puncheon door, hinged at right, with two rows of carved spindles and a panel below; scalloped and arched removable cornices; a framed structure with open-mortise and tenon joints and a single panel for each side. Trasteros, the Spanish term describing upright cupboards often with pierced or spindled doors, are 'often regarded as being the most 'New Mexican' of all furniture made there. Their designs can be traced directly to Spain...' *(Sotheby's)* **$81,700**

▼

A fine and rare William and Mary paneled pine and turned maple valuables chest, Massachusetts, 1700-1740, the rectangular molded top above a case centering a paneled door and opening to an arrangement of six graduated short drawers, the molded base below on turned bun feet.

Cabinets consisting of a box on feet with a single large keyed door with sliding drawers behind it, were used by both men and women for the storage of valuables. According to Robert Trent, 'The concept of concealing drawers with doors is a typical Mannerist design strategy. It is also typical of the seventeenth century mentality to have a small portable box containing important papers and cash or jewelry, which could be kept in bed chambers and easily carried of the house in case of fire'. *(Sotheby's)* **$20,700**

An important blue-green-painted turned and joined pine trastero, New Mexico, circa 1780, the arched scalloped removable cornice flanked by similarly decorated sides, the spindle-and panel inset cupboard door below opening to two shelves with shaped galleries and a removable accessories box, the stiles continue to form the feet, 5ft. 10¼in. high.

Distinctive construction characteristics of this workshop include: a single

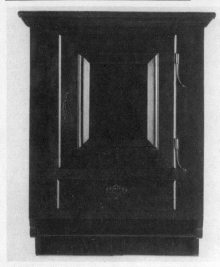

A fine and rare paneled walnut hanging wall cupboard with drawer, Pennsylvania, circa 1760, the molded cornice above a paneled molded door with wrought iron 'rat's tail' hinges opening to a shelf, a single molded drawer below, the sides with lower scroll cut-out with medial shelf below. 39in. high.

In German Protestant households, the hanging corner cupboard was used in the parlor to house religious materials such as a Bible or hymnal book.
(Sotheby's) **$28,750**

A paneled yellow pine hanging corner wall cupboard, Pennsylvania, 1750-1770, the molded cornice above a double-paneled hinged door opening to shelves, the sides continuing to form a scrolled pendant with two quarter-round shelves. Appears to retain its original wrought-iron strap hinges and the inked inscription on the inside door *from Eshelman Family Oley Vally PA.*, 4ft.8in. high. *(Sotheby's)* **$39,100 ▶**

A Chippendale blue-painted pine hutch cupboard, Pennsylvania, circa 1780, in two parts; the upper section with a dramatic dentil-molded overhanging cornice above glazed cupboard doors opening to two shelves pierced for cutlery flanked by fluted stiles and quarter-columns on shaped bracket supports; the projecting lower section with three short drawers and two field-paneled cupboard doors opening to a shelf flanked by similarly turned stiles and columns, on bracket feet, 6ft. high. *(Sotheby's)* **$33,350**

A Chelsea teabowl and trembleuse saucer, circa 1755, red anchor marks, each painted with two putti in iron-red on a grassy mound surrounded by a flock of birds and with scattered flower sprays, brown line rims. *(Christie's)* **$7,682**

A Meissen Hausmalerei teabowl and acanthus-molded saucer, circa 1720, decorated circa 1735 in Bayreuth at the J.F. Metzsch workshop.

The teabowl interior finely painted in Purpurmalerei with a woodsman in a landscape, the saucer with a naval encounter close to a shoreline, within gilt roundels and flowers below gilt Laub-und-Bandelwerk, the exterior molded with acanthus leaves enriched in green and gilt and edged in purple, the exterior of the teabowl painted with ribbon-tied bouquets. *(Christie's)* **$18,400**

A Chinese European-decorated beaker and saucer, the porcelain Kangxi circa 1700 and with a blue Lingzhi mark, the decoration circa 1730 and by Ignaz Preissler.

Incised with a ground of lotus flowers within underglaze blue bands, painted in Eisenrot and gilt, the slender beaker with two Oriental figures, one teaching a hound to jump through a hoop below a bird, the saucer with three figures in conversation, the borders gilt with a 'cracked ice' pattern. *(Christie's)* **$10,350**

A Sèvres (hard paste) cylindrical coffee-can and saucer (gobelet litron et soucoupe), 1787, gilt interlaced L marks flanked by date letters *KK* above painter's mark *VT* OF Mme. Marie-Anne Gérard. *(Christie's)* **$7,297**

▲

A Vincennes bleu lapis two-handled chocolate-cup, cover and stand (gobelet à lait et soucoupe), 1756, the stand with blue interlaced L's mark enclosing date letter D, painter's mark of Buteux, incised cS l to cup and 4 to stand.

Painted en camaieu bleu with Cupid playing a lyre and with a torch among clouds, within gilt flower and foliage scroll cartouches, the stand similarly painted with Cupid holding a posy of flowers, the cover with two kidney-shaped panels of trophies and with gilt and white carnation finial, gilt dentil rims. The stand 7¼in. diameter. (Christie's) **$21,125**

◄

A Sèvres cup and saucer, each piece painted by Charles-Nicolas Dodin, the elaborately gilded borders with tooled oval medallions, hanging garlands and scrolls on a dark blue ground, the saucer painted with an interior scene with drums, a horn and a cello, beside a music stand near a chair, the cup with three musicians at a harpsicord and the violin, interlaced L's, painter's mark K, gilder's mark for Michel-Barnabé Chauvaux, date code for 1778, the cup 7.5cm. (Tennants) **$15,200**

A small purple-splashed Junyao bowl, and a Junyao-type saucer-dish, the bowl Song dynasty, the saucer dish probably Ming dynasty, the rounded sides of the bowl covered with a thick unctuous lavender blue glaze with purple-mauve splashes to the interior and exterior thinning at the rim and pooling around the unglazed foot, some kiln adhesion to glazed base, around the foot and to interior; the shallow dish with slightly recessed base and gently outward flaring sides, covered with a mottled violet and pale blue glaze, the foot and base unglazed, the bowl 3¼in., the dish 6¼in.

(Christie's) **$83,130**

Wassily Kandinsky for the Imperial Russian Porcelain Factory, Petrograd, cup and saucer, 1921, porcelain, polychrome enamel decoration, the underside of the cup with blue enamel maker's mark and dated *1921*, cup 3in. high, saucer 6¼in. diameter.

Surviving examples of porcelain with decoration by Kandinsky are extremely rare. Sketches by Kandinsky in the museum of the Lomonossov Porcelain Manufactory, St Petersburg, show designs for decoration en-suite with this cup and saucer. This is the only recorded example decorated to this design.

(Sotheby's) **$56,235**

A set of twelve gilt-bronze curtain tie-backs, last quarter 20th century, the circular plates cast in relief with Apollo masks, 5in. diameter.
(Christie's) **$4,061**

A set of twelve ormolu curtain tiebacks, 20th century, each with lion-mask set in a concave-banded roundel, 7¼in. long.
(Christie's) **$10,436**

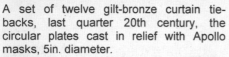

A set of twelve parcel gilt bronze curtain tie backs, of recent manufacture, the disk terminals with ram's head masks within a foliate cast border, 6¾in. diameter, 9¼in. protrudence.
(Christie's) **$3,795**

A set of twelve Empire-style gilt bronze curtain tie-backs, 20th century, the dishes with lion masks, with engine turned borders, with supports and screw threads, 5⁵⁄₈in. diameter.
(Christie's) **$6,460**

A pair of mahogany and bronze curtain poles, 20th century, the fluted poles with pierced anthemion terminals, with conforming curtain rings and mounts to the brackets, 98½in. long.
(Christie's) **$7,590**

A set of four large gilt bronze mounted curtain poles, 20th century, the terminals modeled as Persian griffins, on gilt metal cylindrical poles, with foliate cast brackets, 139½in. long.
(Christie's) **$18,458**

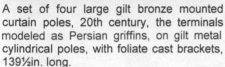

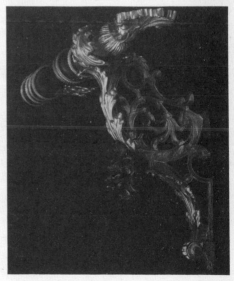

A set of four large gilt-bronze curtain poles of recent manufacture, each with rams' head terminals and boldly cast scroll brackets, 161in. overall.
(Christie's) **$8,540**

A pair of gilt bronze curtain poles and brackets, the cylindrical poles each with anthemion cast terminals, on pierced foliate brackets with protruding lion masks, 86in. wide.
(Christie's) **$8,306**

One of a pair of tapestry cushions, Aubusson early 19th century, one woven with playing children, the other with sporting dogs and a hind, in oval panels with a floral eau-de-nil surround, silk bobble fringe and old gold velvet backing, 46 x 52cm.
(Sotheby's) (Two)   **$4,048**

A pair of Brussels tapestry cushions, the tapestry 17th century, woven in wools and silks, each depicting a youth holding a ribbon and a shield, above a quiver, within a metal-thread tasseled border and on a green silk backing, minor re-weaving, panel reused from a border fragment, 20 x 15in.
(Christie's)   **$7,636**

▶

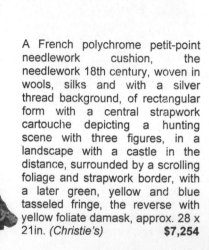

A French polychrome petit-point needlework cushion, the needlework 18th century, woven in wools, silks and with a silver thread background, of rectangular form with a central strapwork cartouche depicting a hunting scene with three figures, in a landscape with a castle in the distance, surrounded by a scrolling foliage and strapwork border, with a later green, yellow and blue tasseled fringe, the reverse with yellow foliate damask, approx. 28 x 21in. *(Christie's)*   **$7,254**

Top: A pair of Beauvais tapestry cushions, the tapestry mid-18th century, woven in wools and silks, each depicting a scene from Aesop's fables, one with a wolf and a stork with its beak down a jar, in a wooded landscape, the other with a cockerel baiting a bear tied to a tree, both in foliate borders, with later green and yellow tasseled fringe and green silk damask reverse, 20 x 21½in., 20 x 22½in. *(Christie's)* **$10,300**

Middle: A pair of Beauvais tapestry cushions, the tapestry mid-18th century, woven in wools and silks, one depicting a wolf in a wooded landscape with buildings in the distance, the other with a scene from Aesop's Fables of a toad talking to a cow in a river landscape, both with a foliate border, with later green and yellow tasseled fringe and green silk-damask reverse, 20 x 19in., 20 x 21in. *(Christie's)* **$7,500**

Bottom: A pair of Beavais tapestry cushions, the tapestry mid-18th century, woven in wools and silks, one depicting a pair of hounds in a wooded landscape with buildings in the distance, the other depicting a wounded leopard pulling an arrow out of its side, in a wooded landscape, with later green and yellow tasseled fringe and green silk-damask reverse, one cushion: 20 x 19in., the other: 23 x 24in. *(Christie's)* **$7,900**

An eighteen piece cutlery set, designed by Josef Hoffmann, manufactured by Sturm, Mayer & Söhne, circa 1900, comprising; 6 table knives, 6 table forks, 6 spoons, each with a stylized *B* stamped on the handle.

This design pre-dates the creation of the Wiener Werkstätte, when Hoffmann was producing designs for a number of Viennese manufacturers.
(Christie's) **$35,615**

A nine piece flatware service, designed by Josef Hoffmann, manufactured by the Wiener Werkstätte, 1904, each with tapering handle with four-ball finial, stamped with designer's mark, *WW*, rosemark and Viennese poinçon.

This flatware service formed part of an extensive service designed by Hoffmann in 1904 for Lily and Fritz Wärndorfer and was exhibited at Der gedeckte Tisch exhibition in October 1906, mounted to coincide with the opening of the new Wiener Werkstätte showroom in the Neustiftgasse.
(Christie's) **$64,963** ▶

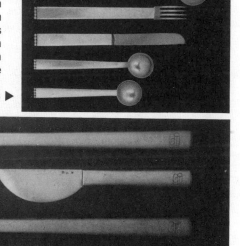

An electroplated ladle, serving fork and butter knife, designed by Joseph Hoffmann, manufactured by the Wiener Werkstätte, circa 1906, from the series 'Rundes Modell', each piece monogramed on the handle *GHB*, 12¾in. length of spoon. Butter knife and fork each stamped with designer's monogram, *WW* monogram and registration mark, the spoon apparently unmarked. This design was originally created for the Palais Stoclet in 1906 and was also used by Hoffmann himself. *(Christie's)* **$9,747**

DEDHAM

The Dedham Pottery was established in 1895, following the move of the Chelsea Keramic Art Works to Dedham, Mass. under Hugh Robertson, who had succeeded his father as master potter at Chelsea. At Dedham, Robertson produced a crackle glaze on a heavy stoneware decorated with borders of bird and animal designs. Dedham Ware was made in forty eight patterns and proved very popular. Its mark is *Dedham Pottery* over a crouching rabbit.

Dedham Pottery Fish Pattern plate, scalloped edge, blue stamp, 9in. diameter. *(Skinner)* **$4,025**

Large Dedham Pottery high glaze vase, by Hugh Robertson, frothy sea green glaze with hints of red oxide, incised *Dedham Pottery*, 8½in. high. *(Skinner)* **$3,000**

Dedham Pottery Snipe plate, blue stamp, 10in. diameter. *(Skinner)* **$4,887**

Dedham Pottery stork pattern plate, raised design, blue stamp, diameter 9in. *(Skinner)* **$5,750**

Dedham Pottery Golden Gate plate, signed *H.C.R.*, blue stamp, M. Shephard, 10in. diameter. *(Skinner)* **$2,645**

When Chinese porcelain arrived in the West, Europe was literally dazzled. Nothing of such beauty and brilliance had ever been manufactured there, and the indigenous pottery industries now had to compete with the flood of imports. Majolica had been made in small workshops throughout Holland by potters who were experienced yet open to new techniques. A result of this was delft, a decorated, tin-glazed earthenware, known elsewhere as faience. It first appeared in the early 17th century and the next 120 years were to see the steady development of both technique and quality. Majolica had been mainly multicolored, but delft was nearly all blue and white, imitating Chinese porcelain. Decoration too at first followed Chinese traditions, but later pieces saw innovative themes, such as the peacock jar, with a motif of two peacocks facing a central basket.

The finest period lasted until about 1730, when the seduction of enamel colors and the prettiness of porcelain began to sap the vitality of the medium.

A Dutch Delft small tureen, cover and stand, circa 1770, the stand and tureen modeled as overlapping green leaves with blue veins, the cover with a coiled blue, green and yellow pike with manganese markings and with a minnow in its mouth forming the finial, 7½in. wide.
(Christie's) **$4,875**

A garniture of Dutch Delft polychrome vases, circa 1770, three bells mark in blue, each painted in underglaze blue with a figure before a church in a wooded landscape within molded scroll cartouches, flanked by iron-red flowers and red and yellow scrolls, the reverses and feet with precious objects, 16in. and 11½in.
(Christie's) **$4,125**

An unrecorded documentary inscribed and dated blue and white London Delft tankard, *1638*, probably Pickleherring Quay Pottery, Southwark, of straight-sided tapering form with loop handle, the rim inscribed *Dilvcvlo Bibere Salvberrimum Est Si Mod* above a broad band of 'bird–on-a-rock' decoration with insects and birds in flight and perching on rocks on a ground of stylized flowers, foliage and scrolls, the base inscribed *M / WI / SEP: T''E 9th / ANNO DOM / 1638*, 5½in. high.

This previously unrecorded mug is a significant addition to the corpus of wares attributed to Christian Wilhelm's workshop at Pickleherring Quay at Southwark in London.

The earliest account of Christian Wilhelm in London was in 1617 in the records of St. Olave's Parish, Southwark where he is described as a 'member of the Dutch Congregation in London.'
(Christie's)   **$135,000**

A Bristol Delft polychrome water-cistern, circa 1725, red A mark to underside. Of baluster form with flat back, painted in blue, yellow, green and red with peacocks perched on rockwork and insects and birds in flight and perched in flowering shrubs, below a molded border at the rim with a band of red and green hatch ornament, the lower part molded in relief with a horned satyr's mask, the mouth formed as a pierced aperture, the upper part for suspension at the back, 12½in. high.
(Christie's)   **$52,500**

A Dublin Delft lobed plate, circa 1760, Henry Delamaine's factory, painted in manganese with two figures beneath a tree on prominent rockwork, in a shrubby mountainous stylized landscape within a border of four groups of foliage beneath drapery swags, 10¼in. wide.
(Christie's)   **$6,560 ▶**

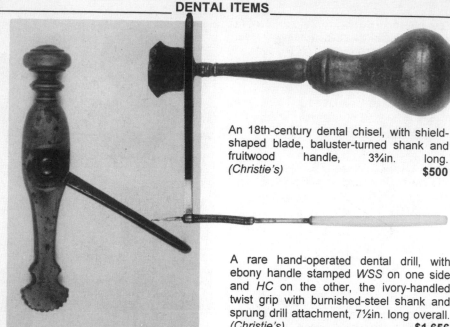

An 18th-century dental chisel, with shield-shaped blade, baluster-turned shank and fruitwood handle, 3¾in. long. *(Christie's)* **$500**

A rare hand-operated dental drill, with ebony handle stamped *WSS* on one side and *HC* on the other, the ivory-handled twist grip with burnished-steel shank and sprung drill attachment, 7½in. long overall. *(Christie's)* **$1,656**

A rare fruitwood and iron pelican, with turned handle, carved grip, the iron claw with arrow head maker's trademark, 5¼in. long. *(Christie's)* **$2,085**

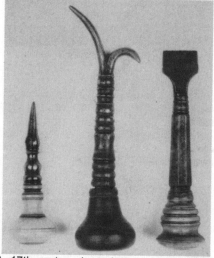

A silvered-copper model of the upper and lower sets of human teeth, mounted on an articulated frame, the top engraved *Wekabe 2 D.R.P. Ausl. Pat. Angem 7252*, mounted with simulated teeth arranged to detach, false teeth showing filling structure, the frame, 3½in. long. *(Christie's)* **$685**

A 17th-century iron dental elevator, with ebony handle, 4¼in. long, an 18th century iron dental probe, with ivory handle, 2⅝in. long, and a 17th century iron dental chisel, stamped *Joseph Gibbs* with bone handle, 3½in. long.

The company of Gibbs was established circa 1740, and Joseph was working at 137 Bond Street in 1756. *(Christie's)* **$2,944**

The pottery industry in Deruta, Umbria, dates from the late 15th century. At that time wares in the usual high temperature colors were produced, together with some with metallic luster decoration. Some, too, were very distinctive in that, in order to achieve a 'near-flesh' tint, the enamel was scraped away to reveal the pinkish clay body, to which a clear lead glaze was then added.

Early 16th century Deruta luster is brassy yellow outlined in soft blue, often showing a nacreous iridescence. Later wares have a deeper tone, sometimes approaching olive green.

Large plates predominate as a form, with tin glaze on the underside.

A Deruta lusterware charger, first half of the 16th century, Saint Catherine holding the martyr's palm and spiked wheel, surrounded by a scale-pattern border, 15¹/₈in. diameter. *(Sotheby's)* **$8,050**

A Deruta tin-glazed earthenware charger, first half of the 16th century, a Turk on a charging stallion in the center, the border with green foliage on white ground, 15in. diameter. *(Sotheby's)* **$11,500**

A Deruta 'peacock feather' luster-ware charger, second quarter 16th century, decorated throughout in blue and gold luster, 15⁵/₈in. diameter. *(Sotheby's)* **$17,250**

A Deruta lusterware charger, first half of the 16th century, the painted and molded decoration consisting of joined hands with a crown above in the center, surrounded by harpies and hippocampi, the rim with flowers and trophies, 13⁷/₈in. diameter. ◄ *(Sotheby's)* **$10,925**

A William and Mary burl walnut veneered slant-front desk, Boston, 1710-1725, the rectangular top centering a veneered rectangular panel framed by double crossbanded inlay above a similarly veneered slant-lid opening to a fitted interior with a central prospect door flanked by pigeonholes and short drawers all over a case fitted with two short drawers above two graduated long drawers, on turned compressed ball feet.
(Christie's) $74,000

A Queen Anne walnut desk-on-frame, Philadelphia, 1740-1760, in two sections: the upper with a rectangular top above a thumbmolded slant-lid enclosing a compartmented interior with a central prospect door enclosing four drawers and three secret drawers all flanked by six pigeonholes over twelve drawers; the lower with a rectangular case fitted with one long thumbmolded drawer over an apron with a pendant drop, on cabriole legs and trifid feet, 33in. wide.
(Christie's) $76,200

An Irish George II mahogany library pedestal desk, the molded rectangular top above a slide and four long graduated drawers to one side and on the other side with a slide above a kneehole, flanked on each side by a paneled door enclosing two adjustable shelves, the sides with brass carrying-handles with pierced backplates, on shaped bracket feet, with sunk brass castors, 42½in. wide.

The desk, designed to stand in the center of a library, has a writing-slide above a kneehole and commodes, and is backed by a further slide above folio-drawers. With its serpentined feet, it relates to a 'bureau-table' pattern issued in Thomas Chippendale's The Gentleman and Cabinet-Maker's Director, 1754. *(Christie's)* **$56,580**

A carved pearwood desk designed by Hector Guimard, circa 1903, the back with low upper panel with shaped shelves at each end, single large drawer with original gilt bronze handle, two lower open side shelves, paneled back, the whole carved with fine whip lash motifs, 63⅞in. maximum width. *(Christie's)* **$68,786**

An early Dickin medal to the homing pigeon 'Tyke' for the Mediterranean campaign, 1943, bronze medal *P.D.S.A.*, *For Gallantry, We Also Serve*, officially engraved as above, complete with suspension ring, and with original presentation certificate. Date of award: 2nd December 1943.

For delivering a message under exceptionally difficult conditions and so contributing to the rescue of an Air Crew while serving with the RAF in the Mediterranean in June 1943.

Tyke was born in Cairo of British and South African parents and served with the Middle East Pigeon Service. In June 1943 he carried a message from a point approximately one hundred miles from a base in visibility that was never more than two miles. As a result an American air crew were rescued, who afterwards claimed that they owed their lives to the gallant pigeon.

(P.D.S.A.)

The Dickin Medal, popularly referred to as 'The Animal V.C.' was awarded on 53 occasions between 1943 and 1949. Of these 31 went to pigeons, 18 to dogs and 3 to horses. The final award, made in 1949, went to ship's cat 'Simon' who was aboard H.M.S. Amethyst when she made her legendary dash down the Yangtze in that year. *(Sotheby's)* **$5,830**

An important Charles Apthorp Queen Anne figured and carved walnut compass-seat side chair, carving attributed to John Welch, Boston, Massachusetts, circa 1735, the shaped crest centering a carved and pierced shell flanked by fish-scale-carved strapwork flanked by carved leafage, the crotch-figured veneered splat below, flanked by shaped stiles and with cupid's-bow shoe, below, the balloon-shaped seat enclosing a slip-seat cushion on shell-carved cabriole legs joined by molded stretchers ending in frontal claw-and-ball feet.

The English-born Charles Apthorp was one of the wealthiest merchants in Boston during the second quarter of the eighteenth century. He served as the American agent for Thomlinson and Trecothick, a London-based merchant house that supplied money to the British Army in the colonies. *(Sotheby's)* **$211,500**

A pair of Louis XV giltwood chaises, each with channeled shaped padded back and seat covered in green floral silk damask, the waved toprail centered by a cabochon and foliate cartouche and flanked by rocaille C-scrolls, the serpentine-fronted molded seat-rail centered by a further foliate cabochon cartouche, on channeled foliate-headed cabriole legs and scroll feet. *(Christie's)* **$18,400**

Gio Ponti, prototype 'Modello 1938' chair for a series of office chairs for the first Montecatini building, Milan, 1936, polished aluminium, the underside cast with *Modello 1938* and *Montecatini S.A.*, 31¾in. high. *(Sotheby's)* **$10,497**

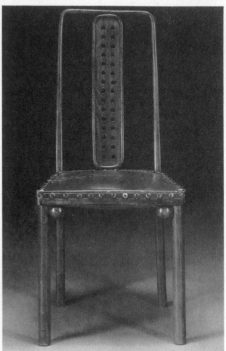

One of a pair of ebonized bentwood side chairs, designed by Josef Hoffmann for the dining room of the Purkersdorf Sanatorium, circa 1904, manufactured by J. & J. Kohn, central back panel pierced with two rows of circles, seat with original red oil-cloth upholstery, 38¾in. high.
(Christie's)   (Two)   **$64,963**

Peter Behrens, side chair for the house of the poet, Richard Dehmel, Hamburg, 1903, white painted wood, with original tapestry seat cover, 37½in. high.

This chair was designed by Behrens for the dining room of the poet Richard Dehmel, Hamburg. An identical chair from this same source is in the collection of the Kunstgewerbermuseum, Humburg. Apart form these pieces no other example, either in public or private collections, is known.
(Sotheby's)   **$4,499**

Tapio Wirkkala for Asko, chair, circa 1955, decorative laminated birch of an angular slice through the year rings of the tree, tubular nickel plated metal legs, black rubber feet, underside with braised stamp *Tapio Wirkkala Asko Made in Finland*, 31¼in. high. *(Sotheby's)* **$5,216**

▶

An important Chippendale carved walnut side chair, Philadelphia, Pennsylvania, circa 1755, the shaped leaf-carved crest with central scallop shell flanked by shell-carved ears above a volute and acanthus-leaf-carved pierced vase-form splat, fluted stiles flanking, the trapezoidal molded seat enclosing a slip-seat cushion with a shell-carved skirt below continuing to volute and acanthus-leaf carved cabriole legs ending in claw-and-ball feet.

This chair appears to be a mate with a well-known set of six side chairs and one armchair that was made for the Loockerman family of Dover, Delaware. *(Sotheby's)* **$112,500**

A carved pearwood side chair, designed by Hector Guimard, circa 1903, open back with padded top, the whole delicately carved with fine tendrils and pierced with foliate scrolls, original muslin covered upholstery. *(Christie's)* **$39,364**

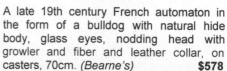

A late 19th century French automaton in the form of a bulldog with natural hide body, glass eyes, nodding head with growler and fiber and leather collar, on casters, 70cm. *(Bearne's)* **$578**

A Samson model of a dog, Edo Period (19th Century), decorated in iron red, black enamels and gilt, seated with a bell suspended from a tied collar, 15in. high. *(Christie's)* **$2,999**

A pair of Dutch delft blue and white models of seated hounds, 18th century, each with spotted markings and wearing a manganese collar, on oval mound base, 4⁷/₈in. high.
(Christie's) **$5,750**

A Victorian cast iron stick stand, registry mark for 1852, modeled as a chihuahua, holding a whip, perched on its hind legs on a naturalistic base, the underside of the drip tray with registry mark, and numbers *No. 85297* and *No. 14*, 23½in. high. *(Christie's)* **$5,690**

A fine A. Thuillier bébé with closed mouth, blue yeux fibres, shaded brows, pierced ears, blonde mohair wig and jointed wood and papier mâché fixed wrist body. dressed in blue silk ruched and pleated frock, underwear, socks and shoes, 22in. high. Circa 1879, impressed *A 11 T,* shoes marked *A La Providence 74 Rue de Rivoli.* *(Christie's)* **$27,427**

▶

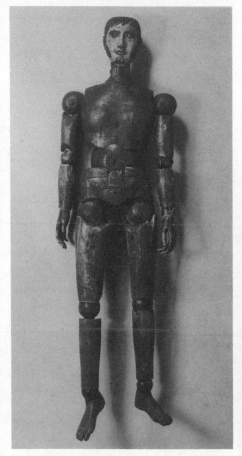

An amusing carved and painted wood articulated mannequin, late 19th/early 20th century, the full-sized fully articulated figure with carved and painted hair, sideburns and facial details, and realistically carved hands and feet, 60in. high. *(Sotheby's)* **$6,900**

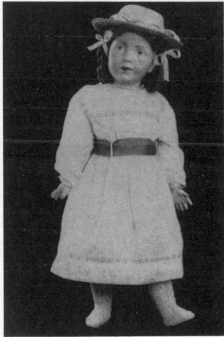

A unique Kammer & Reinhardt bisque character doll, no. 108, German, circa 1908. *(Sotheby's)* **$290,290**

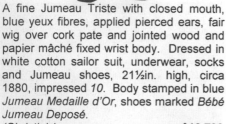

A fine Jumeau Triste with closed mouth, blue yeux fibres, applied pierced ears, fair wig over cork pate and jointed wood and papier mâché fixed wrist body. Dressed in white cotton sailor suit, underwear, socks and Jumeau shoes, 21½in. high, circa 1880, impressed *10*. Body stamped in blue *Jumeau Medaille d'Or*, shoes marked *Bébé Jumeau Deposé*.
(Christie's)   **$12,799**

A fine A. Thuillier bisque doll, French, circa 1880, impressed *A 11 T*, with fixed blue paperweight eyes with long lashed, pronounced eyebrows, closed mouth, cork pate with long blonde wig, jointed wood and composition body, in original starched muslin underwear; an apricot satin gown and cap, straw bonnet; pair of brown leather shoes, 23¾in. high.
(Sotheby's)   **$34,960**

A 1964 set of four Beatles dolls, wearing black suits with trademark bowl-style haircuts, each playing their appropriate instrument with facsimile signatures in gold, 5in.
(Christie's)   **$1,150**

156

An important English wooden dolls' house painted to simulate stucco, with Dutch gable ends and slate roof, of five bays and three stories, the windows with painted pediments, the hinged attic with variously shaped dormers, opening at the front in three hinged sections to reveal six rooms, staircase with unusual 'port hole' balustrades and landings, opening painted panelled interior doors, original papers and woolwork stair carpet, 54½in. wide.

Sir Robert Harry Inglis Palgrave married in 1859 Sarah Maria Brightwen, her father Thomas was a partner in the Yarmouth Bank, which was one of the 20 banks to form Barclays Bank in 1896. Sir Inglis became a local director of Barclays Bank and he was editor of the Economist from 1877-1883. His only child was Elizabeth, born in Great Yarmouth in 1860. The house was made for her in 1865/6, was probably modelled on an existing house in Great Yarmouth as the architectural style is indicative of the region, and most of the furnishings date from her childhood. She married the Reverand Canon Roland Vectis Barker in 1883 and they had four boys and one daughter, Alice Elizabeth. *(Christie's)* **$17,077**

A 19th century painted wood and paper covered dolls house of three-storey form, the folding front opening to reveal six rooms and stairwells, the interior with papered walls and with fireplaces, the breakfront with balconies to first floor Oriel windows and with two columns surrounding front door, 38in. wide x 40in. high, containing an extensive collection of furniture and accessories. *(Canterbury)* **$5,000**

Marianne Brandt for Ruppelwerk, Gotha, napkin holder, circa 1930, lime green painted sheet steel, the underside marked *Ruppel* and *mehrfach geschüzt*.
(Sotheby's) **$1,462**

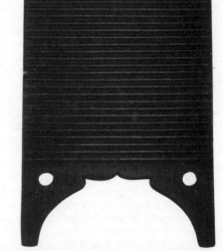

A large pair of elm bellows, 18th century, with conical brass nozzle and tapering handles, 42in. long.
(Christie's) **$1,138**

Christian Dell, tea infuser, circa 1924, electroplated brass, 5¹/₈in. long. A comparable tea infuser purchased from Christian Dell is in the collection of the Bauhaus-Archiv Berlin, inventory number 300. *(Sotheby's)* **$1,275**

Walter Gropius and Adolf Mayer for S.S. Loewy, Berlin, two door handles and lock plate, 1922, nickel-plated brass, 4¹/₈in. handle depth.
(Sotheby's) **$862**

Cast iron washboard with heart cut-out, Pennsylvania, 19th century, original surface, 22½ x 12½in.
(Skinner) **$2,415**

A French iron doorknocker, 16th century, of the oblong shape and worked in the form of addorsed sea creatures, knocker 6¾in. long.
(Sotheby's) **$1,725**

A bronze doorknocker, in Italian Renaissance style, composed of two parts, the knocker of two putti supporting the Medici shield and standing on scrolling strapwork with acanthus decoration, the upper section of grotesque mask, height of knocker 8³/8in.
(Sotheby's) **$920**

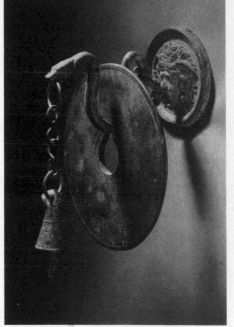

A French steel doorknocker, late 16th century, the s-shaped body of an amphisbaena with grotesque masks, knocker 7¹/8in. long.
(Sotheby's) **$1,150**

A Neapolitan bronze entrance gong, late 19th century, of disk form, supported on a serpent, suspended with a hammer from its jaws, issuing from a mask of Mercury cast to the circular backplate, 9in. protrudence.
(Christie's) **$5,300**

The first highly skilled figure maker who worked for Doulton was George Tinworth, the Lambeth sculptor, but his figure output was small.

However in 1889 Charles J. Noke left the Royal Worcester Company where he was already showing his prodigious talent as a sculptor and went to work for Doulton's at Burslem. The son of an antiques dealer who appreciated the fine vases and figures made by Derby, Bow, Chelsea, Meissen and Sèvres, he was fired with the ambition of recreating the once greatly admired Staffordshire figure making industry. For the Chicago Exhibition of 1893 he made several figures including 'Jack Point' and 'Lady Jester'.

During the next five years more figures followed, including Noke's 'Pierrot', 'Geisha' and the double figures 'Oh Law!' and 'Double Jester'.

These figures, though finely modeled, were of dull colors and did not sell well so Noke's figure making was suspended until around 1912 when he re-introduced a figure range which was released to the public in 1913 after Queen Mary, on a visit to Burslem, exclaimed "What a Darling!" at the sight of a figure called 'Bedtime' modeled by Charles Vyse.

'Bedtime' was re-christened 'Darling' and proved to be one of the most popular Doulton figures ever produced. It is still in production.

The colors of the new figures were bolder and a group of very talented sculptors worked on them.

Bather (style two) HN1227, designed by L. Harradine, 7½in., color variation, issued 1927-1938. *(Lyle)* **$2,400**

Dreamland HN1473, designed by L. Harradine, 4¾in., issued 1931-1938. *(Lyle)* **$3,200**

Sunshine Girl HN1344, designed by L. Harradine, 5in., issued 1929-1938. *(Lyle)* **$4,000**

In the stocks (style one) HN1475, designed by L. Harradine, 5¼in., color variation, issued 1931-1938. *(Lyle)* **$2,000**

Scotties HN1281, designed by L. Harradine, 5½in., issued 1928-1938. *(Lyle)* **£2,160**

Geisha (style two) HN1234, designed by C.J. Noke, 6¾in., color variation, issued 1927-1938. *(Lyle)* **$1,200**

Eve HN2466, designed by P. Davies, 9¼in., issued 1984 in a limited edition of 750. *(Lyle)* **$1,200**

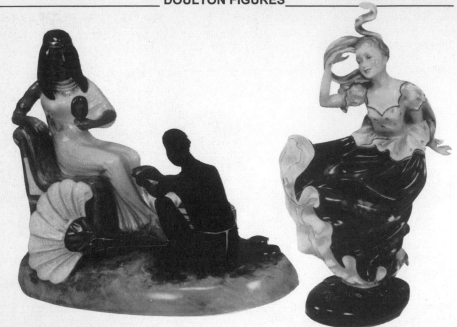

Cleopatra HN2868, designed by P. Davies, 7¼in., issued 1980 in a limited edition of 750. *(Lyle)* **$1,520**

Columbine HN3288, designed by D. Tootle, 12½in., commissioned by Harrods in 1993, USA edition. *(Lyle)* **$2,000**

Jack Point HN3920, designed by C.J. Noke, 17in., issued 1996, color variation. *(Lyle)* **$4,400**

Princess Badoura HN3921, designed by H. Tittensor, H. Stanton and F. Van Allen Phillips, 20in., issued 1996, color variation. *(Lyle)* **$21,200**

The Morris Family Chippendale carved mahogany dressing table, Philadelphia, 1760-1780, the rectangular top with molded edge and cupid's-bow front corners, 35½in. wide.
(Christie's) **$59,700**

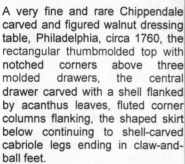

A Queen Anne carved mahogany dressing table, attributed to John Goddard (1723–85), Newport, 1750–60, the rectangular top with cove molded edge above a conforming case fitted with a thumbmolded long drawer over two thumbmolded short drawers centering a scalloped carved fan enclosing a spray of fluted petals above a shaped skirt on cabriole legs with padded disk feet, 31¾in. wide. *(Christie's)* **$519,500**

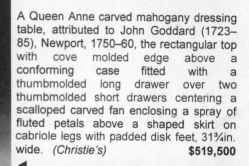

A very fine and rare Chippendale carved and figured walnut dressing table, Philadelphia, circa 1760, the rectangular thumbmolded top with notched corners above three molded drawers, the central drawer carved with a shell flanked by acanthus leaves, fluted corner columns flanking, the shaped skirt below continuing to shell-carved cabriole legs ending in claw-and-ball feet.
(Sotheby's) **$134,500**

A fine Chippendale carved and figured walnut drop-leaf dining table, Pennsylvania, circa 1760, of impressive size, the rectangular top flanked by hinged leaves with notched corners above a shaped apron, on cabriole legs ending in large claw-and-ball feet, 4ft. 9in. wide open.
(Sotheby's) **$40,250**

A small oak gate-leg table designed by Edward Barnsley, circa 1926, curved double flap on two pairs of chamfered leg supports, and pegged central stanchion, 30½in. wide. *(Christie's)* **$4,784**

▶

Queen Anne tiger maple drop-leaf table, New England, 18th century, the figured maple drop-leaf top above a base with molded skirt and cabriole legs ending in high pad feet, original surfaces with figured maple top and red painted base, 28in. high.
(Skinner) **$145,500**

A fine and rare Queen Anne figured mahogany six-leg drop-leaf dining table, New York, 1740–60, the oblong top with two hinged D-shaped leaves above a single-drawer frieze, on circular tapering legs ending in pointed slipper feet. Warm reddish brown color. Width extended 5ft.6in.
(Sotheby's)   **$18,400**

A Chippendale carved mahogany drop-leaf table, Newport, 1780–1800, the rectangular top with hinged leaves above a conforming frame, on stop-fluted Marlborough legs, 27½in. high, 40½in. wide.
   With its simple proportions, straight edges, and stop-fluted Marlborough legs, this breakfast table epitomizes the elegant simplicity of such tables produced in Newport during the third quarter of the 18th century.
(Christie's)   **$32,200**

▶

A Federal carved and figured mahogany drop-leaf library table, attributed to Duncan Phyfe, or one of his contemporaries, New York, circa 1810, the rectangular top with two hinged D-shaped drop leaves above a single cockbeaded drawer, the skirt with turned ball pendants raised on four spirally-twisted and vase-form ring-turned uprights, the fluted plinth base raised on molded down-curving legs ending in brass animal-paw feet and brass castors, extended width 50in.
(Sotheby's)   **$24,150**

Dummy boards originated in the Low Countries and became fashionable in Britain in the 17th and 18th centuries. They consisted of flat wooden boards, painted in oils with human and other figures, the boards being shaped to the contours of the figure represented. Many were designed to stand out from walls, and had suitable attachments to support them, while others, supported by a strut at the back, could stand independently.

The purpose of these boards seems to have been purely decorative. Many representations were of servants or children.

Most look out directly at the spectator, and one theory is that they were intended to deter the casual passing footpad, who at a swift glance might take them for the real inhabitants of the house.

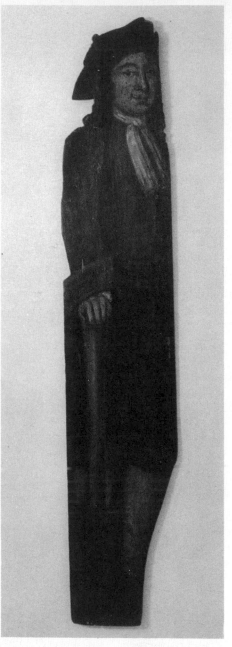

A dummy board of a young girl, the painting late 17th century, 34in. high. (Christie's) **$6,640**

An English painted wood 'Dummy Board', 18th century, painted as a young gardener resting on a shovel, height 66⅝in. (Sotheby's) **$5,750**

A pair of late 18th/early 19th century painted wood dummyboards, of young girls in period costume facing each other, German or Austrian, 41¾in. and 40in. high. (*Christie's*) **$10,805**

A polychrome-decorated dummy-board figure, 19th century, in the form of a girl in a green dress trimmed with lace, with a white veil and red satin gloves, on a spreading rectangular base, 40in. high.
(*Christie's*) **$2,640**

A pair of polychrome-painted dummyboards, 19th century, depicting a courtly couple in Elizabethan dress, the young nobleman with trellis doublet and ruff collar offering a rose to his companion, who holds an ostrich-feather fan, on block plinths, the nobleman's arm with later metal bracket support, one: 39in. high, the other: 38¼in. high.
(*Christie's*) **$5,281**

A Black Forest carved wood desk companion, late 19th century, modeled as an eagle with inset glass eyes, with hinged top opening to a recess, 13¾in. high.
(Christie's) **$1,230**

▲

An Austrian cold painted terracotta model of an eagle owl, late 19th or early 20th century, shown perched on a branch, with inset glass eyes, 25in. high.
(Christie's) **$6,520**

A rare carved and painted pine miniature billet eagle's head, American late 19th/early 20th century, the full-carved head with incised feather detail, beak open and fitted with a curved whale ivory tip, painted black, white and orange.
(Sotheby's) **$1,380**

A full carved and painted oak American eagle bowsprit billethead, John Haley Bellamy, Kittery, Maine, circa 1900, the flat figure of an eagle fashioned from a thick oak plank, the body with scrolls, with open jaws and red tongue, with details picked out in yellow polychrome, 56in. long. *(Sotheby's)* **$11,500**

A carved and painted spread-wing eagle, attributed to John Haley Bellamy (1836–1914), Kittery Point, Maine, late 19th century, the spread-wing eagle with upturned neck and articulated eyes, beak, tongue, feathers and talons, grasping an olive branch, a red, white, silver and blue-painted star and stripe-decorated shield and clutching a billowing American flag, 32in. high, 19½in. wide. *(Christie's)* **$13,800**

A black-enamelled 'London-Dome' ear trumpet, with vulcanite ear-piece and petal-pierced grille, 6in. long.
(Christie's) **$530**

A late 19th-century black-enameled brass ear trumpet, of bell shape, with tapering extension piece with vulcanite end, detachable, with suspension cord, 19in. long. *(Christie's)* **$552**

A fine silver-plated, leather mounted ear trumpet, with ivory earpiece, the turn and bell-mouth profusely engraved with flowers and foliage, the interior of the bell-mouth with gilded acoustic attachment, 8in. long.
(Christie's) **$1,328**

A 19th century simulated tortoiseshell 'beehive' ear trumpet, with ivorine earpiece, swan-neck tube, brass grille and pierced mouth, 5in. high.
(Christie's) **$665**

A glazed earthenware figure, manufactured ▶
by Essevi, circa 1920, modeled as a young
melancholic girl wearing a bonnet and
black dress printed with brightly colored
flowers, seated on a low wall, a lizard
beside her, 11in. high.
(Christie's) **$2,400**

An earthenware vase, by Amphora, circa
1900, tapering cylindrical with organic neck
and foot, green glaze decorated with
multicolored glass centered cobwebs
above a frieze of butterflies and bees, 16in.
high, stamped on the base *Amphora* in an
oval, numbered *55, 26, 35415* and with
monogram *VLAA.*
(Christie's) **$6,992**

▶

An earthenware luster glazed vase,
designed by Walter Crane, manufactured
by Maw and Co., circa 1888/9, baluster
form with everted stepped rim, the body
decorated with a full length frieze of
classical maidens, formalized motifs at foot
and neck, 12½in. high.
(Christie's) **$7,498**

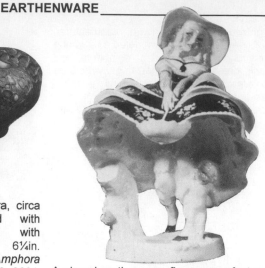

An earthenware vase, by Amphora, circa 1900, squat form decorated with 'honeycomb' design applied with multicolored glass cabochons, 6¼in. high., stamped on the base *Amphora Austria* in an oval and numbered *93, 3661, 52. (Christie's)* **$2,208**

A glazed earthenware figure manufactured by Essevi, circa 1920, modeled as a blushing young girl, her skirts caught by the wind, a cupid at her feet 13¼in. high., underglazed mark *Essevi Made in Italy Torino-Vento di Primavera-Sandro Vacchetti. (Christie's)* **$4,000**

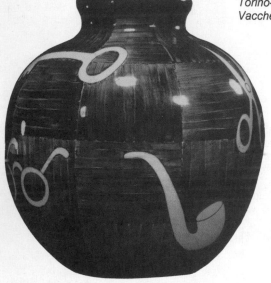

A large glazed earthenware vase, designed by Gio Ponti, manufactured by Ginori, circa 1925/30, decorated with a design of household objects - scissors, spectacles, keys and a pipe, against a squared crushed cherry ground, 10½in. high. *(Christie's)* **$9,747**

A glazed earthenware figure manufactured by Lenci, 1930s, modeled as a young woman seated coquettishly on a bookcase, 15¼in. high, painted mark *Lenci Made in Italy Torino 9.XI P.* *(Christie's)* **$4,800**

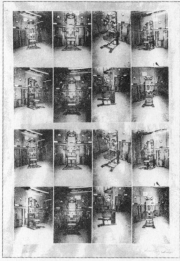

After Andy Warhol and Pietro Psaier. Color reproduction. Series of sixteen photographs of the electric chair. Bears signatures. Ltd edn. 2/20. 76x47.5cm. *(Bristol)*

A steel electric chair. Ex Dept of Penal Correction, California State, once owned by Andy Warhol then Pietro Psaier, entitled *Rest in Peace, PAX*, height 169cm.

Three are in existence: this one was previously owned by RKO Pictures from 1949 and sold off at the Warner Bros takeover. *(Bristol)* **$7,440**

Elvis Presley's Sun Record Collection, 1954–55, Elvis' personal copies of his first five Sun releases comprising Sun#209 'That's Alright (Mama)/Blue Moon of Kentucky' (sample copy), Sun #210 'Good Rockin' Tonight/I don't Care if the Sun Don't Shine', Sun #215 'Milkcow Blues Boogie/You're a Heartbreaker', Sun #217 'Baby Let's Play House/I'm Left, You're Right, She's Gone and Sun #223 'Mystery Train/I Forgot to Remember to Forget', in original sleeves, each signed by Elvis.

The most historic rock 'n' roll recordings of all time are Elvis' first five recordings for Sam Phillips 'Sun' records. This set includes the extremely rare sample copy of Blue Moon of Kentucky and is made rarer still as they are all signed and come from Elvis' personal collection.

(Bonhams) **$23,700**

Elvis Presley's Gretsch Chet Atkins country gentleman guitar, 1960s, the double cutaway stained body with painted 'f-holes', edge binding, De Armond pickups, Bigsby vibrato-unit, gold plated rotary controls and hardware, the ebony fingerboard with 'thumbnail' inlay, the headstock with Grover machine heads, in original case; together with letters of authenticity and photographs of Elvis playing the guitar.

There are many photographs of Elvis playing this guitar, and the photograph illustrated shows him playing it at his historic opening night at the International Hotel, Las Vegas in August 1969 when he returned to live performances after a nine year absence.

(Bonhams) **$56,880**

◀ Elvis Presley's unreleased acetate of 'Milkcow Blues Boogie', circa 1955, 12in. acetate stamped *Audiodisc 3291 Audiodisc - made in USA* in a red circle on both sides and *77 Elvis - Milkcow UNK (Unknown) Female Voc* written in Sam Phillips' hand on a piece of attached adhesive tape, both sides containing the same unreleased version of the song, the center with three ¼in. holes used to hold the acetate in place while cutting it.

Provenance: Given to Elvis by Sam Phillips of Sun Records. Elvis' Sun recordings changed the face of popular music forever. This early, unreleased recording is one of the rarest in rock 'n' roll history. *(Bonhams)* **$14,220**

An autographed photograph of Elvis Presley as a baby, the color photograph of two year old Elvis and signed and dedicated in black ink *To Mr & Mrs Taurog & Family - With Love & Respect - 'Little Baby Elvis' Priscilla & Lisa 1970,* in original frame.

Provenance: The estate of Norman Taurog, Elvis' friend and the director of nine of his greatest films. This is perhaps the only time that Elvis signed Priscilla and Lisa's names making this one of the most important written documents in rock 'n' roll history. *(Bonhams)* **$6,636**

A one-piece stage suit of cream wool with high collar and flared trouser legs, the flared split cuffs trimmed with two rows of covered buttons, the front decorated with metal eyelets either side of slashed opening, labeled IC Costume Co. *Hollywood, California*, made for Elvis for stage use in the early 1970s; accompanied by a corresponding black and white machine-print photograph of Presley on stage. *(Christie's)* **$14,720**

A large Chinese gilt bronze and enamel cloisonné box and cover, Qianlong period, 1736–95, 40cm. diameter.
(Galerie Koller) **$13,940**

An enameled vase, by Eugene Feuillatre, circa 1898, the copper body in midnight blue puzzled with pale lilac, decorated with a moth intricately detailed in pink and ocher with silvering, 3½in. high.
(Christie's) **$3,312**

A silver-plated brass and enamel wall bracket, possibly designed by Alexander Fisher, circa 1905, 26 x 12in.
(Christie's) **$4,311**

A pair of Chinese cloisonné enamel models of cranes, standing in mirror image, the wing feathers multi-colored, 22½in. high.
(Christie's) **$4,784**

An Attic style red figure pottery rhyton, ▶ probably late 18th century, the neck decorated with a figure of a nude male being attacked by a lion, 10¾in. high. *(Christie's)* **$760**

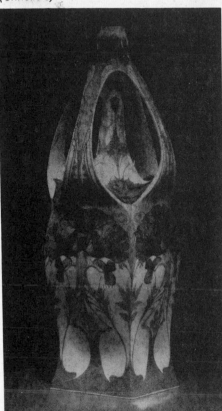

An exceptionally large eggshell vase, manufactured by Rozenburg, decorated by Sam Schellink, 1903, of square baluster form with four handles, painted in purple, green and ocher with formalized flowers and abstracted motifs, 15¹/8in. high. *(Christie's)* **$11,960**

A Kloster-Veilsdorf figure of Pantaloon, circa 1764-1765, modeled by W. Neu after the engraving by J.B. Probst, in a black snood, cape and orange suit with a white belt, modeled standing holding a candlestick, his other hand raised, 6¹/8in. high. *(Christie's)* **$27,600**

177

A gilt metal and bisque group, French, circa 1890, modeled with two sleeping children, on a canapé, 44cm. wide.
(Sotheby's) **$10,436**

A very rare 'Table Mountain' saucer dish, 18th century, enameled with a coastal view of Cape Town with the Table Mountain in the background and two merchant ships flying Dutch flags in front, taken from a print presumably depicting Cape Town as one of the most important bases for Dutch East India Company commercial activities outside Europe, 6¼in. diameter.
(Christie's) **$24,369** ▶

A fine pair of platinum ground porcelain vases, Paris, dated *1878*, each of ovoid form with a cover with a grape and leaf finial, the bodies painted with flowering cacti, exotic birds and butterflies signed with the monogram for N.V. probably N. Vivien, on key pattern scroll feet, signed for F.E. Caldwell & Co. Exposition Univ'elle Paris 1878, 58cm. high.

One pair of birds has been identified as Paradise Tanagers (Tanagra chilensis), which ranges widely over South America, the other pair has not been identified but may be hybrids bred in captivity.
(Sotheby's) **$43,642**

This was a style developed at the Wedgwood factory in the 1920s by their designer, Daisy Makeig-Jones, who worked there from 1915-32. It consisted of a luster decoration of fairy subjects painted on thinly potted vases, dishes etc., sometimes on a black or powder blue ground.

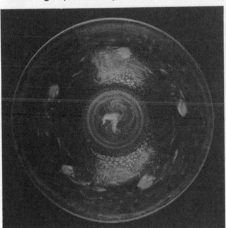

A Wedgwood Fairyland Luster malfrey pot and cover, designed by Daisy Makeig Jones, decorated in the Bubbles II pattern, 18cm. high. *(Christie's)* **$20,240**

Wedgwood Fairyland Luster vase, of baluster form, printed and painted with Candlemas pattern, in colors beneath a gilt geometric patterned neck, printed and painted marks, 8in. high. *(Doyle)* **$4,000**

Wedgwood Fairyland Luster punch bowl, designed by Daisy Makeig-Jones, the exterior decorated in the Poplar Trees pattern, the interior with a central mermaid medallion bordered by the Woodland Bridge pattern, monogramed, printed and enameled factory marks, 11¼in. diameter. *(Doyle)* **$9,000**

A rare Wedgwood Fairyland Luster malfrey pot and cover designed by Daisy Makeig-Jones, decorated in the 'Ghostly Wood' pattern, printed and painted in colors and, highlighted in gilt, on original wooden stand printed and painted marks, 38cm. *(Christie's)* **$40,480**

An unusual tortoiseshell brisé fan, lacquered in silver with figures and buildings, both recto and verso, 9in., Canton, mid-19th century. *(Christie's)* **$9,200**

A fine fan signed *Edouard Moreau*, dated *1865*, the leaf painted with a 16th century skating scene with elegant figures in a sledge and two smaller vignettes of guests arriving at a banquet with a musician and a banquet with a noblewoman holding a crown, the ivory sticks painted en grisaille with four vignettes of love and marriage in 18th century costume, two signed *Ed. Moreau*, the guardsticks carved in high relief with dolphins and masks, 12in., French.
(Christie's) **$8,538** ▶

◀

A fine brisé fan lacquered with the Seven Sages of the Bamboo Grove, with carved faces and mother of pearl headdresses, one holding a scroll inscribed *pine, bamboo and plum, the three grades of excellence,* the verso with monogram *LO* and a basket of flowers, the guardsticks with Shibayama work karako flying a kite and a vase of roses, 12in., Japanese, circa 1880.
(Christie's) **$14,230**

An Assemblage of Gods, a fan, the leaf painted with two shaped vignettes of Juno and Diana and other gods, a tilted oval vignette of Chinoiserie figures in a garden, the reserves with trompe l'oeil of a wooden wall, the verso with prunus and other flowers, the ivory sticks finely carved with hunting scenes, pierced and backed with cat-gut, 10in., English, circa 1750.
(Christie's) **$9,487**

Gibraltar, a printed commemorative fan, the leaf a hand colored etching of the rock of Gibraltar with a fleet of French and Spanish vessels in the foreground and a flag inscribed *Viva Carlos III y vincas sus armos*, to the left the Franco-Spanish camp, all with numbers and letters referring to a key in Spanish on the verso, the ivory sticks silvered, gilt and trimmed with foil with a ship, a fort and flags, the guardsticks carved, pierced and silvered with ships and drums, 11in., French for the Spanish market, mid-18th century. *(Christie's)* **$20,240**

A fine fan by Alexandre, the leaf painted with a theatrical scene of lovers and attendants, the verso of canepin painted with a border of arabesques and signed *Alexandre* in gold, the ivory sticks carved and pierced and set with carved and pierced mother of pearl plaques, the guardsticks carved in high relief with putti and trophies of love, the fore-edges also carved to form a bunch of flowers when closed, 11in., French, circa 1865, in brown leather box lined with pale blue satin by Alexandre Eventailliste de leurs Majestes l'Imperatrice des Francais, L'Imperatrice de Russie, La Reine d'Angleterre, La Reine d'Espagne, 11 Boulevard Montmartre Paris. *(Christie's)* **$18,400**

A Louis Philippe gilt and patinated bronze fender, circa 1840, the uprights with foliate mounts and recumbent lion surmounts, flanking a foliate clasped polished steel rail with molded plinth, 58¾in. wide. *(Christie's)* **$6,640**

A polished brass club fender, early 20th century, the padded seat on a tubular frame with stepped plinth, with mesh guard to the lower section, 58in. wide. *(Christie's)* **$7,360**

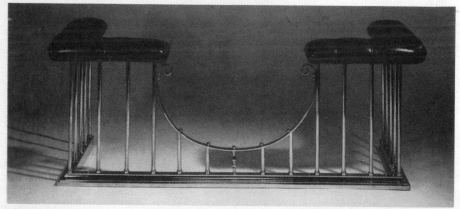

A polished brass and leather padded club fender, early 20th century, the buttoned seat on cylindrical supports and molded plinth, the rail with central U-shaped section, 63in. wide. *(Christie's)* **$6,072**

The first posters were made by wood or copper engraving, a process which was both costly and complicated. With stone lithography, a process using limestone slabs as printing plates, came radical changes. An artist would create his handpainted design in fine detail and it would then be reproduced on the slab, resulting in a poster which was both beautiful and distinctive in appearance. With the advent of sound, poster quality deteriorated, perhaps because of rising film production costs.

It is thought that, for the average picture, between 7,000 and 12,000 posters were created and distributed among cinema owners, who had to return them after the film run against credit on future posters. For a 'blockbuster' the studio might print twice or even four times as many, but as those returned posters were recycled to as many other cinemas as their condition allowed, the wear and tear of repeated use meant that very few have survived, and even fewer in good condition.

The Pilgrim, First National, 1923, six-sheet, linen backed, 81 x 81in.
(Christie's) **$10,929**

King Kong, 1933, R.K.O., U.S. three-sheet, 81 x 41in. style A, linen backed, framed.

This U.S. three-sheet style A poster is one of only four known copies and is considered one of the most important American film posters. The image of Kong on top of the Empire State Building is certainly one of the most enduring images of American popular culture. This classic image only appears on this particular style poster for the American advertising campaign.
(Christie's) **$47,438**

A Dog's Life, First National, 1918, six-sheet, linen backed, 81 x 81in. *(Christie's)* **$31,556**

▲

The Devil is a Woman, Paramount, 1935, one-sheet, linen backed, 41 x 27in. *(Christie's)* **$14,792**

◄

Das Kabinett Des Dr. Caligari/The Cabinet of Dr. Caligari, 1919, U.F.A., U.S. one-sheet, 41 x 27in. linen backed.

The cabinet of Dr. Caligari is one of the most exciting and inspired expressionist horror films ever made. Against a background which borrows from Cubist imagery, the U.S. one-sheet on offer here captures the paranoid and scheming character of Dr. Caligari. This poster is one of only three known copies.
(Christie's) **$22,770**

Blonde Venus, Paramount, 1933, original Belgian poster, linen backed, 30 x 24in. *(Christie's)* **$9,370**

Citizen Cane, R.K.O., 1941, one-sheet, linen backed, 41 x 27in. *(Christie's)* **$19,723**

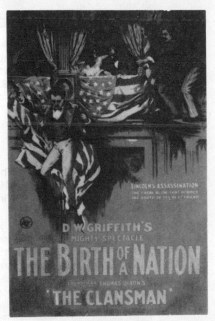

The Birth of a Nation, Epoch Producing Corp., 1915, one-sheet, linen backed, 41 x 27in. *(Christie's)* **$25,639**

The Old Dark House, Universal, 1932, one-sheet, 41 x 27in. *(Christie's)* **$43,390**

A painted leather ceremonial fire bucket, ▶
probably New England, mid-18th century,
the baluster-form bucket with molded red-
painted leather trim, painted with stylized
and elaborate scrolling devices, the banner
inscribed *Fasslictus Consolatio*, with a
leather swing handle; on a blue-green
ground, 11½in. high.
(Sotheby's)   **$5,175**

A fine painted leather ceremonial fire
bucket, attributed to John S. Blunt for
Edmund Brown, probably New Hampshire,
dated 1811, the bucket with molded rim
and leather swing handle, painted on the
front with a spread-winged American eagle
and shield, the eagle grasping a banner in
its beak, inscribed *Mechanic Fire Society*,
and at the base *Edmdm Brown*, 12¾in.
high. *(Sotheby's)*   **$9,775**

A fine and rare painted leather fire bucket,
signed *Israel Whiton, Mutual Fire Society*,
dated *1809*, the tapered bucket painted
green with a red rim and swing handle,
dated *1809* above two joined hands and
two white banners inscribed *Mutual Fire
Society* and *Israel Whiton* surrounded by
gilt scrolling foliage, the back stamped *C.
Lincoln* twice, 13¼in. high.
(Sotheby's)   **$8,050** ▶

A Regency cast-iron rectangular fireback, cast with a Baron's coronet above the coat-of-Arms of Lord Bolton and supporters and motto *Aymez Loyaute*, with screw holes and side supports, 29½ x 24¾in. *(Christie's)* **$4,500**

A cast iron fireback, American, early 19th century, the shaped, arched and molded crest above the Great Seal of the United States a spreadwing eagle clutching arrows and olive branches in its talons and centering a stars- and stripes-emblazoned shield, molded base below, 30½in. high. *(Sotheby's)* **$3,162**

A fine and very rare cast iron fireback, Pleasant Furnace, Monongehela County, Virginia, 1799-1811, emblazoned with the Great Seal of The United States, 29¾in. high. *(Sotheby's)* **$31,050**

A rare decorated cast iron fireback, Virginia, circa 1730, of arched oblong form, the crest centering a shell flanked by leafage, 30¼in. high. *(Sotheby's)* **$72,900**

A Dresden ceramic fireplace surround, late 19th/20th century, impressed *CHR. S&S,* of Rococo form, with half putti caryatid supports and S-scroll terminals flanking a shell-molded mantel and holding a black slate top, the base fenestrated with three rectangular trellis panels, 47 x 51½in.
(Christie's) **$6,325**

Thomas Jeckyll for Barnard, Bishop and Barnard, fire surround, 1873, bronze frame cast with Japanese style badges, inset with Doulton tiles decorated with apple-blossom, iris blooms and butterflies in delicate shades of yellow and green against a deep green ground, the reverse monogramed *'BBB'* and with P.O.D.R. mark, 45in. high, 45⁵/₈in. wide.
(Sotheby's) **$23,046**

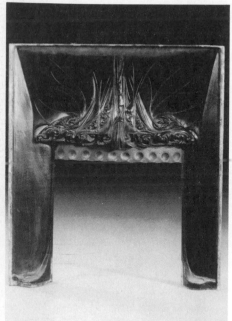

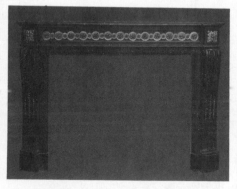

A cast-iron fire surround, designed by Hector Guimard, circa 1900, with red marble top, 31in. wide.
(Christie's) **$11,408**

A Napoleon III ormolu-mounted rouge marble chimney-piece, in the Louis XVI style, with a breakfront slightly bowed shelf, above a paneled frieze with foliate roundel mounts, flanked to each side by a square foliate-mounted end block, on scrolled fluted jambs with a circular ormolu air vent to the plain side panel, on block feet, 62½in. wide x 45¼in. high.
(Christie's) **$16,000**

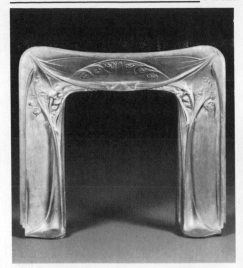

A cast-iron fire place, designed by Hector Guimard, circa 1904, cast with typically stylized floral designs and floral motifs swirling around the central recess, 35¾in. high, 39⅛in. wide. Formerly part of the interior fittings in a Guimard apartment in Paris. *(Christie's)*   **$12,851**
◄

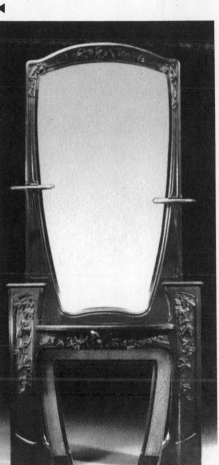

A George II white statuary and Siena marble chimneypiece, attributed to Sir Henry Cheere, the foliate molded double-breakfront rectangular shelf supported by scrolled acanthus brackets punctuated by rosettes, the dentiled stiff-leaf and egg-and-dart molded bed molded above a paneled frieze with overlaid acanthus sprays, the breakfronted sections with foliate rosettes, above a rosette trellis and bead-and-reel paneled frame and plain paneled soffitt above a ribbon and rosette reveal flanked by turned, entasised Siena marble columns with undercut acanthus carved composite capitals and ribbon-tied laurel overlay garlands, on a turned socle and square stepped plinth, restorations, two angle rosettes lacking, 84¾in. wide, 66¾in. high.
(Christie's)   **$367,690**

A carved mahogany overmantel and fireplace, designed by Louis Majorelle, circa 1900, carved with branches of pineapples, the upper section with large mirror surmounted by further carved details of pineapples supporting twin shelves, 57¼in. wide, 118in. high.
(Christie's)   **$34,040**

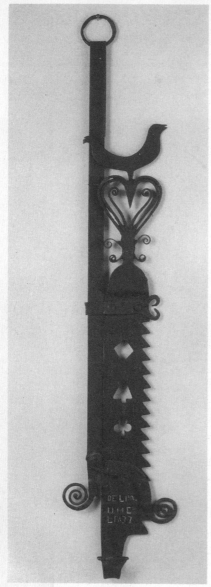

A painted metal twin division coal box, late 19th century, of tapering rectangular form, the green ground heightened with gilt foliate decoration, on paw feet, 21½in. high. *(Christie's)* **$3,225**

An important wrought-iron fireplace trammel, Pennsylvania, dated *1837*, surmounted by a ring support, the central standard decorated with a bird above a scrolled heart, the shaft pierced with a diamond, a spade, a heart, and a club, incised on the lower section of the shaft *BELPA LIME L1837*, height unextended 42in. *(Sotheby's)* **$11,500**

Set of Egyptian Revival gilt bronze fireplace equipment, comprising a pair of andirons and a set of tools. *(Skinner)* **$2,760**

Samuel Yellin cast iron fireplace screen, one hundred twelve scrolls and seven foliate pillars, splayed feet, signed *Samuel Yellin, Philadelphia*, 53¾in. wide. *(Skinner)* **$21,850**

▶

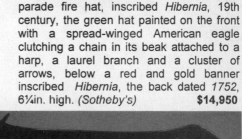

An ormolu-mounted mahogany firescreen, late 19th/early 20th century, the turned column with scrolled foliate capital, with a pair of double-hinged brown leather-lined shaped triangular screens, each with a brown leather pocket to each side and a swan's neck cresting, 42¼in. high. *(Christie's)* **$6,560**

▶

A Regency painted japanned metal plate warmer, first quarter 19th century, of curved rectangular form of four bracket feet with ring handles to the sides, the red ground decorated in gilt with Oriental scenes, within foliate borders, 33in. wide. *(Christie's)* **$1,700**

A fine and rare painted leather ceremonial parade fire hat, inscribed *Hibernia*, 19th century, the green hat painted on the front with a spread-winged American eagle clutching a chain in its beak attached to a harp, a laurel branch and a cluster of arrows, below a red and gold banner inscribed *Hibernia*, the back dated *1752*, 6¼in. high. *(Sotheby's)* **$14,950**

A rare 3¹/8-Inch tournament casting reel; grooved brass foot stamped *4HM*, black handle on counter balanced serpentine bar, sprung line guide, nickel silver adjustable knobs, on/off check, in its baize lined teak box.
(Sotheby's) **$11,661**

A scarce and rare 3-inch Silex Multiplier tournament casting reel with additional vented drum containing air resistant governors; grooved brass foot, black handle, large brake knob, on/off check and governor engagement lever, additional mounted drum with sliding vents and two resistor paddles.
(Sotheby's) **$14,576**

A carved and painted bass decoy, attributed to Hans Janner, circa 1930–40, exhibits metal fins, glass eyes and inlet weights on the underside.

Hans Janner Sr. was a tall mustached man. He owned a saloon in Adair, Michigan in the early 1900s, later moving to Mt. Clemens, Michigan. He was a popular figure in the Mt. Clemens area and was a master locksmith by the age of 12, able to make a lock and all components out of a single piece of metal. He had his own forge and made his own spears. He made some of the finest decoys ever found mainly for sculpture and construction. Most decoys remained in the family but a few were given to friends. He fished Lake St. Clair at the foot of Crocker Boulevard. Hans speared some of the largest muskies ever speared in this lake. One reason his decoys are large is, he believed the bigger the decoy the bigger the fish.
(Sotheby's) **$4,887**

The name Flambé describes the streaky, flame like effect of the deep blood red glaze which was produced by mixing copper oxide and other minerals and allowing certain amounts of oxygen to be admitted to the kiln during firing. The technique was first discovered by Bernard Moore, a chemist and innovator who worked in conjunction with Doulton at the turn of the century. After two years of experimentation the first examples of Flambé were shown at the St. Louis Exhibition of 1904 and it had a huge appeal. Although it is expensive to make, Flambé is still being produced.

Flambé tobacco jar with elephant finial, 6in. high, circa 1936. *(Lyle)* **$560**

Snarling Figure of a Panther, 9in. long, circa 1930. *(Lyle)* **$640**

A large Royal Doulton flambé elephant with trunk down, designed by C. Noke, 12in. high, circa 1930. *(Lyle)* **$1,600**

Peruvian Penguin on Rock, Model 585, designed by C. Noke, 1947, 9in. high. *(Lyle)* **$560**

A George IV mahogany coaching-table, by Hindley and Sons, with hinged X-frame support by a baluster stretcher and rounded eared folding top, stamped *C. Hindley & Sons 134 Oxford St., London*, 33½in. high, 36in. wide.
(Christie's) **$7,254**

A late Regency simulated rosewood coaching table, the oval hinged top on a collapsible X-frame support joined by ring-turned stretchers, on brass caps and castors, 49in. wide, 28½in. high.
(Christie's) **$4,614**

◄

An Austrian polychrome-painted folding table, 18th/ 19th century, the polygonal top centered by a scantily-draped cherub holding a shell within a floral wreath, the reverse with extensive foliate and floral scrolls with putti centered by a medallion depicting a queen pointing towards a kneeling maiden and flanked by two further figures, the carved baluster supports with maiden's heads, above a tripod stand conformingly decorated and terminating in reeded baluster supports, 35½in. diameter. This polygonal table-top, painted in the picturesque manner and celebrating love's triumph, depicts Cupid with Venus's shell-badge in a landscaped vignette wreathed with flowers. *(Christie's)* **$6,452**

A walnut whatnot, designed by J.P. Seddon, 1860, the four-tiered corner cabinet with finely carved upper frieze and elaborate finials, above four triangular shelves each with back-panels pierced with hexafoil roundels, slender carved and fluted capitals on either side, the whole with gilt and painted decoration, 67½in. high, 38in. wide.
(Christie's) **$27,847**

A Black Forest carved and stained pine jardinière stand, late 19th/early 20th century, the rectangular frame carved in high relief with scrolling foliage overall, on a knopped column with tripod base, 34¾in. high. *(Christie's)* **$2,422**

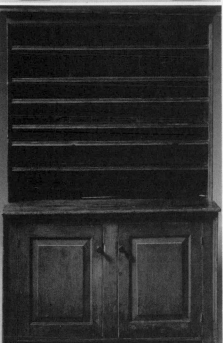

◀

A fine blue-painted pine and poplar 'Dutch' cupboard, Pennsylvania, circa 1780, in two parts; the overhanging cornice with three molded shelves, the projecting base with raised-panel cupboard doors opening to a shelf flanked by molded stiles, the sides continuing to form the feet; painted in blue over red. Label inside bottom drawer, on right side, 6ft.5in. high.
(Sotheby's) **$23,000**

A Louis XIV ormolu-mounted boulle brass-inlaid red tortoiseshell bureau mazarin, decorated en première partie, with Bérainesque scenes of birds, insects, exotic animals, foliate arabesques, strapwork and husk-trails, the rectangular top centered by a foliage medallion above seven walnut-lined drawers around the paneled kneehole with raised paneled sides with conforming decoration, on square tapering legs joined by waved stretchers and bun feet, 44in. wide. *(Christie's)* **$65,760**

A late Louis XV ormolu-mounted tulipwood and marquetry secrétaire à abattant, attributed to Roger Van Der Cruse dit Lacroix and probably supplied by the marchand-ebéniste Léonard Boudin, the molded shaped rectangular brêche d'alep marble top above a waved fall-front with a ribbon-tied floral spray enclosing a fitted interior with two tambour doors enclosing an associated mahogany and mirrored interior above four small drawers, the angles headed with Greek-key enriched satyr-masks and acanthus, the lower doors enclosing a further fitted trellis-parquetry interior with two drawers above a coffre-fort, the waved apron molded with C-scrolls and foliate sprays, on cabriole legs with C-scroll and acanthus sabots, 25½in. wide. *(Christie's)* **$310,400**

A kingwood, marquetry and gilt-bronze display cabinet, French, circa 1890, of bombé form, with a large glazed central door framed by scrolling foliate borders, with a lower cartouche filled with flower marquetry, the sides similarly divided, the red velvet inside with two glass shelves and a wooden shelf, the corners applied with ribbon tied banding, all surmounted by a scroll leaf cresting flanked by urns, on cabriole legs terminating in scroll feet, 163cm. wide.*(Sotheby's)* **$22,490** ▶

A Louis XIV ormolu-mounted boulle brass, pewter, and tortoiseshell inlaid ebony stand, inlaid overall in contre-partie with scrolling flowers and foliage, the later breakfront red, green and white marble top above three frieze drawers, on four serpentine supports, the back with four panels flanked by conforming supports, on a breakfront platform, on later toupie feet with gadrooned collars, reconstructed in the early 19th century and incorporating some later elements. 38¾in. wide.
(Christie's) **$174,880**

A Viennese ormolu-mounted mahogany and parcel-gilt secrétaire à abattant, in the manner of Franz Steindl, of oval form, the rectangular stepped top with lappeted molded edge, above the oval body with a fall-front with fruitfilled cornucopiae escutcheon enclosing an architectural amboyna-lined fitted interior, the upper shelf with a pedimented door with Egyptian herm supports enclosing a mirror-backed interior, 72½in. high.
(Christie's) **$18,750**

An important Chippendale carved and figured mahogany scroll-top spice chest, Philadelphia, Pennsylvania, circa 1765, of high chest of drawers form, in two parts; the upper section with scrolled swan's-neck crest ending in flowerhead-carved terminals centering a cabochon-carved pierced cartouche flanked by urn-and-flame finials, the tympanum carved with a pierced shell flanked by acanthus leaves, 22in. wide. *(Sotheby's)* **$123,500** ▶

Emile Gallé (1846-1904) established his glass factory in Nancy in 1874. Initially he also made earthenware and then experimented with stoneware and porcelain, decorated often with heraldic motifs and scenes reminiscent of delft ware. It is, however, for his glassware that he is chiefly remembered, as one of the chief Art Nouveau craftsmen in glass, using flowing designs of foliage, flowers, birds or female figures.

Gallé evolved many new techniques such as marqueterie de verre and experimented with the addition of metal oxides to glass melt, coloring glass in imitation of precious stones.

By 1889 he had perfected both enameled and colored glass techniques with a wide range of colors and effects. Cameo glass was another of his characteristic styles, and his designs were often inspired by Oriental influences. In 1899 this was being produced on a commercial scale at Nancy, and he also began decorating lighting glass, producing lamps in flower forms, with the light fittings concealed by the half-open petals.

All his own work as well as that of his flourishing factory (by then with 300 employees) was signed. His personal signature, however, is sometimes to be found hidden among the foliage, and naturally adds an enormous cachet to a piece. The firm continued after his death, and finally closed in 1935.

It seems that now the great painters of the 1900s have been discovered and rendered unaffordable, it may well be the turn of the great craftsmen of the period, with a noticeable increase in interest especially from the Far East. Anything by Gallé is likely to be a sound investment. A private collection which was changing hands for the first time since it left Gallé's workshops was sold recently by Habsburg Feldman in Geneva. This included a series of monumental vases, claimed to be the largest ever produced at Nancy. The tallest of them all, standing 74cm. high, with a magnificent design of overlaid and inlaid glass depicting blue hydrangeas, fetched a new Gallé world record of Sfr 929,500 ($530,000).

Two black-painted faience cats by Gallé, circa 1895, each with creamy white detailed snout, each cat approx. 12⅝in., with underglaze mark *Gallé*. *(Christie's)* **$9,600**

Emile Gallé, flowerform lamp, circa 1900, patinated bronze base cast as a leafy stem, gray glass shade overlaid with mauve and green, with etched detail, the shade with cameo mark *Gallé*, 20⅝in. high. *(Sotheby's)* **$28,808**

A mold blown cameo glass 'elephant' vase by Gallé, circa 1920, in amber-tinted glass, overlaid in clear green and brown and etched and mold-blown with a frieze of elephants amidst palm trees, the ground between acid-textured, 15¹/₈in. high.
(Christie's) **$56,235**

Emile Gallé, 'Blow Out' cherries lamp, circa 1900, gray glass internally decorated with yellow, overlaid with red and etched with profusely fruiting cherry boughs, the fruits mold-blown, base and shade with cameo mark *Gallé,* 18½in. high.
(Sotheby's) **$96,000**

◄

A cameo glass 'polar bear' vase, by Gallé, circa 1920, ovoid form, aquamarine-tinted glass overlaid in creamy white and finely etched with an arctic scene of three polar bears standing on ice-floes before snow-capped mountains and glaciers, 14¼in. high.
(Christie's) **$52,486**

A fine carved and painted parcheesi game board, American, late 19th century/early 20th century, the square board with molded edge painted red, yellow, brown and black, the reverse with a gray and black checkerboard, 27 x 37in.
(Sotheby's) **$7,475**

Paint decorated wood game board, America, late 19th/early 20th century, in red and black paint, branded *D. Clark* on the reverse, 14½ x 14½in.
(Skinner) **$1,380**

A north Italian bone, ivory and ebony-inlaid gamesboard of Embriachi type, circa 1500, the elaborate intarsia designs inlaid alla certosina, with a checkerboard on the exterior, and backgammon on the interior, when closed 21¼ x 13^1/8in.
(Sotheby's) **$16,100**

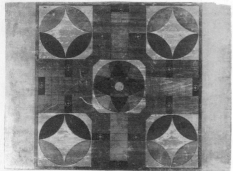

A painted pine game board, American, 19th century, the parcheesi board painted in shades of red, yellow and black, 24in. x 24in. *(Sotheby's)* **$3,737**

Two paint-decorated pine gameboards, probably Pennsylvania, early 20th century, the first of rectangular form painted with a checkerboard in green and white, the borders with an Amish farmer and his wife flanked by two large green-roofed barns; the second of rectangular form with beaded edge centering a checker and parcheesi board painted red and black. 2 pieces. 26¼ in. high x 17¼in. long.
(Sotheby's) **$2,875**

A pair of ormolu-mounted siena marble wall fountains, second half 19th century, each with shaped back, headed by a scallop shell, centered by a sun-mask with water spout, above the scallop-shaped bowl, supported on a treble scrolled volute base cast with laurel and husk pendants, on stepped block plinth, 53¼in. wide x 73in. high. *(Christie's)* **$45,000**
◄

A mid Victorian sculpted white marble throne, the back carved in relief with spires flanking stylized foliate roundels above two niches with soldiers, the scroll arms surmounted by mythical beasts, the base with conforming foliate frieze and square section legs, 62in. high x 28½in. wide. *(Christie's)* **$9,315**

An Italian white marble well-head, possibly by Cesare Lapini, late 19th/early 20th century, the green-patinated bronze overthrow with scrolled supports and entwined vine ornament, the well head carved in the round in high relief with a Bacchic procession of cherubs and a panther-drawn chariot, on a stepped naturalistic base, on a six-piece stepped marble foot, 36½in. high, excluding the overthrow, 46in. diameter. The overthrow
◄62in. high. *(Christie's)* **$110,000**

A Coalbrookdale medallion pattern cast iron seat, circa 1870, with iron front rail, the back centered with a panel of a reclining classical maiden, 65in. wide.
(Andrew Hartley)   **$13,188**

A pair of George III lead urns, each with open circular top and the tapering sides with grotesque masks linked by swags of palm fronds, on molded base, 14½in. diameter.

The early provenance of these urns is unknown but the crossed palm-fronds seem related to the palm and bullrush ornament that John Vardy (died 1765) used repeatedly on mirrors for Hackwood. *(Christie's)*   **$34,960**

A terracotta figure of a gnome, modeled lying to one side, stamped on the underside *J M O,* 28½in. long. *(Christie's)* **$1,640**

A terracotta figure of gnome wearing a red hat and holding a broom, 35in. high. *(Russell, Baldwin & Bright)* **$2,480**

An Austrian polychrome terracotta figure of a gnome, early 20th century, the bearded figure shown standing and holding a naturalistic bowl with both hands, mounted on a wooden rectangular plinth, 26¾in. high. *(Christie's)* **$2,475**

GERRIT RIETVELD

Gerrit Rietveld (1888-1964) sprang to prominence as an architect and cabinet maker in the early years of the 20th century. He was a member of the influential de Stijl group, and departed from conventional furniture forms, using cuboid, circular or rectangular shapes. He used bright colors, and made no attempt to conceal the way his pieces were constructed. One of his most distinctive designs was his Zig-Zag chair of 1934, which consisted of four boards in zig-zag shape.

The 'Berlin' chair, designed for the Dutch pavilion at the Juryfreie Kunstschau Exhibition, Berlin, was Rietveld's first asymmetrical chair and both right and left-hand versions are known to have been made. *(Sotheby's)* **$66,993**

Gerrit Rietveld, executed by G.A. van de Groenekan, 'Militar' chair, designed 1923, executed circa 1930, gray, black, white and yellow painted wood, the underside stamped *H.G.M G.A.v.d. Groenekan de bilt Nederland* and signed in ink *G.A.v.d. Groenekan*, 35³/8in. high.

The 'Militar' chair was originally made for the Catholic Military Home in Utrecht and was produced in several colors. Examples of this chair can be found in the collection of the Stedelijk Museum, Amsterdam and in the Schröder-Huis, Utrecht. *(Sotheby's)* **$10,497**

The original dark-stained wood model of this chair together with a table and washstand were made for the children of the Schelling family in 1921. Their whereabouts are no longer known. *(Sotheby's)* **$22,494**

Daum Fuchsia plafonnier, circa 1905, gray glass internally streaked with white and royal blue and etched and enameled in shades of violet, red and green with flowering stems heightened with gilding against a textured ground, black patinated metal hanging hooks and ceiling rose of highly stylized foliate form, cameo mark *Daum Nancy* with a Cross of Lorraine, 13in. diameter.
(Sotheby's) **$20,165**

'La Libellule', a 'marqueterie-de-verre', carved and applied glass coupe by Gallé, 1904, the milky/white, caramel colored glass superbly applied and carved with a dragonfly swooping amongst a cloud of yellow mayflies, the translucent green dragonfly's body fully speckled with silver-foil inclusions, the applied blue eyes also with inclusions, the mottled chocolate brown intercalaire wings very finely carved with veining, raised on stepped flaring 'marbled' foot, 5¾in. high.
(Christie's) **$343,115**
◄

A gilt and enamel glass coupe, by Daum, 1906, the clear glass internally marbled with yellow, the bowl etched and gilded with patterned field and cross of Lorraine and enameled with a cockerel, eagle, thistles and oak leaves, inscribed with the legend *Vigilat* and *XIIIe Concours National et International de Tir. Nancy 1906* around the rim, the foot overlaid with green and etched with thistles and the legend *Qui s'y frotte s'y pique* and enameled with the arms of Nancy, 4½in. high.
(Christie's) **$6,440**

◄ A fine and rare Venini murrina arlequino figure, designed by Fulvio Bianconi, circa 1950, the harlequin's body in blue and white murrina amidst a lavender ground with silver foil inclusions, with applied lattimo glass hands and feet, the face a slice of murrina encompassing eyes, brows, nose and mouth, unsigned, 8in. high.

(Sotheby's) **$25,300**

A chemist jar and cover, inscribed for toothbrushes, with gilt cover, the blue ground cartouche with gilt, red and green border, 19th century, 28cm. high.

(Tennants) **$1,040**

A Clichy brass-mounted faceted patterned millefiori inkwell and stopper, the base of globular form containing two interlaced garlands composed of predominantly white and claret canes with a central lilac, green, pink and white pastry-mold cane, enclosed by two circlets of assorted pink, green and white canes, set on an opaque turquoise cushion, the shoulder cut with narrow flutes forming a hexagon, the sides cut with six circular raised printies divided by vertical flutes, the conforming stopper containing five C-scrolls composed of assorted canes in shades of green, pink, claret, blue and white, enclosing a large central pink and green rose within a circlet of white, green and claret canes, set on a opaque turquoise ground, cut with top and five side printies divided by vertical flutes, brass mounts, 4³/₈in. diameter, 4½in. high.

(Christie's) **$5,520**

A rare enameled glass jug 'parlant' by Gallé, circa 1900, the body internally streaked with red and green etched and fully enameled with an exotic swimming fish with richly gilded details, 5½in. high.
(Christie's) $8,096

►

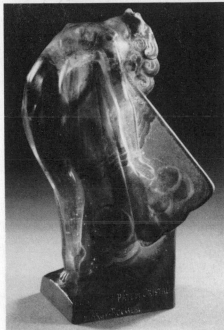

Murano Studio glass mosaic pedestal vase, attributed to Artisti Barovier, circa 1920s, large ovoid goblet-form composed of fused murrine arranged as four golden amber iris blossoms on extended leafy blue stems with red elements between and against sky blue starry background murrine; all raised upon colorless knop stem with applied blue decorative prunts and rigaree above, cupped blue platform foot, 18½in. high.
(Skinner) $28,750

Gabriel Argy-Rousseau and Bouraine, sculpture 'Papillon', 1928, pâte de cristal, clear glass internally decorated with emerald green and blue, modeled as a standing female nude, her back arched over her butterfly wings, intaglio molded mark pâte de cristal d'Argy-Rousseau and Bouraine and numbered 16, 10in. high.
(Sotheby's) $42,251

A carved and internally decorated cameo glass vase, by Ernest Leveille, 1890, the watery gray body internally decorated with patches of sandy yellow and orange, overlaid in rich brown and etched and finely wheel carved on both sides with an underwater scene incorporating a host of fish and other marine life amidst fronds of seaweed, partly fire-polished, 6⅝in. high. *(Christie's)* **$39,364**

◄

A marquetry glass vase, by Gallé, circa 1900, rectangular section, internally colored with purple from half height with milky gray/blue speckled with white at the base, inlaid in 'marqueterie sur verre' technique with layers of white, purple, gray/green, amber and yellow and finely wheel-carved with a narcissus and single bud, 8⅛in. high.
(Christie's) **$33,741**

Jutta Sika for Glasshütte Lötz Witwe, Klostermühle/Böhmen, distributed by E. Bakalowitz & Söhne, Vienna, vase circa 1905. *(Sotheby's)* **$16,496**

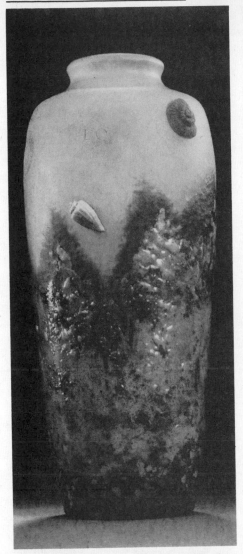

A magnificent and rare pair of gilt-bronze and opal crystal 'Medici' vases by La Compagnie des Cristalleries de Baccarat, Paris, late 19th century, each of campana form with a molded rim above a panel painted with a battle scene centered by Napoleon on horseback, with scroll mask handles, the body with gilt swags, ribbon ties and the imperial cipher on a green ground, the stand similarly decorated with an eagle, on a base cast with foliate scrolls and anthemia and on claw feet, indistinctly signed *Maxort*, 85cm. high.

Opal crystal refers to the colored glass produced by Baccarat and sometimes referred to as opaline. While in France the pure crystal was being perfected to the neglect of other methods of manufacture, Bohemian glass was becoming popular and in general their colored glass was of a higher quality than its French counterpart. In 1836, the Society for the Promotion of French Industry launched a series of contests to imitate the Bohemian pieces and eliminate threatening competition. By 1839 Mr Dumas, reporter on the glass section of the 1839 Exhibition of French Industrial Products, could write: *This exhibition has proved that we no longer have anything to learn from Bohemia. (Sotheby's)* **$71,435**

Daum 'Geologia' vase, circa 1905 clear glass internally mottled with yellow and with deep red towards the base, the lower section overlaid with a crusty surface of vitrified powders in shades of blue, turquoise, brown, green and indigo, the upper section carved with two ammonites and applied with a further ammonite and two shells, each with carved details, wheel-cut inscription *Geo..lo..gia* wheel-cut mark *Daum Nancy* with a Cross of Lorraine, 12^{7}/8in. high. *(Sotheby's)* **$27,600**

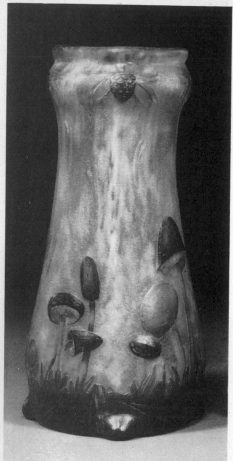

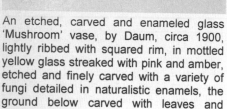

A Baccarat bud vase with close millefiori base, the vase of tear-drop form cut with honeycomb facets terminating with a clear glass knop above a close millefiori paperweight base, 2¾in. diameter, 5⅝in. high. *(Christie's)* **$5,520**

An etched, carved and enameled glass 'Mushroom' vase, by Daum, circa 1900, lightly ribbed with squared rim, in mottled yellow glass streaked with pink and amber, etched and finely carved with a variety of fungi detailed in naturalistic enamels, the ground below carved with leaves and blades of grass, 10in. high. *(Christie's)* **$20,619**

A rare Orrefors Edvin glass vase, designed by Edvin Öhrström, dated *1944*, the cylindrical vessel in turquoise blue glass overlaid in purple, cut with a gypsy palmist amidst an open palm with life lines, with linear devices and stars in the background, inscribed *orrefors Sweden 1944*, 5½in. high. *(Sotheby's)* **$20,700 ▶**

◄ Vetreria Artistica Aureliano Toso *Oriente* face vase, model no. 5299 design by Dino Martens, circa 1954, waisted vessel of brightly colored glass sections, zanfirico, mesh woven squares, gold dust and pinwheel arrangement with the face of 'Geltrude' composed abstractly with two murrine canes and six red rods, partial base label *4835/5299,* 11½in. high. *(Skinner)* **$18,400**

Webb cameo glass tricolor water lily vase, complex oval body composed of transparent ice blue overlaid at top quarter in stippled ruby red with white layer below etched and carved as pond lilies and leaf pads upon the clear blue water background, base borders center 'Webb' medallion, 7½in. high.
(Skinner) **$20,700**

Thomas Webb Old Ivory cameo glass vase, George Woodall design of double gourd body completely cut in fantastical scenes incorporating warriors on horseback, half-man half-animal figures, bird-serpents, kings and queens, all in elaborate frames and floral backgrounds, original circular mark on base *Thomas Webb & Sons Cameo*, 9in. high.
(Skinner) **$23,000**

A Régence beechwood table-globe, the Louis XVI celestial globe inscribed *PARIS / chez FORTIN Ingénieur et / Mécanicien du Roi pour les Globes / et Spheres. Rue de la Harpe. 1780*, set within a molded circular frame supported by four cabriole legs headed by stylized scrolled scallop-shells and hatched lambrequins, the cabochon-headed acanthus scroll feet joined by a baluster X-shaped stretcher carved with egg and dart, husks and stylized C-scrolls and centered by a canted bronze boss, 18in. diameter. *(Christie's)* **$17,480**

A fine mid 19th century Newton's terrestrial globe, inscribed *Newton's New Terrestrial Globe compiled from the most recent authentic surveys of British and Foreign Navigators and Travellers, Published March 25th 1853, manufactured by Newton & Son, 66 Chancery Lane*, on mahogany stand with reeded baluster column and tripod base with scroll feet, diameter of globe 60cm. *(Bearnes)* **$18,468**

◀

A pair of William IV mahogany globes, by William and Alexander Keith Johnston, Edinburgh. The 18in. terrestial globe made up of two sets of twelve chromolithographed gores, the equatorial graduated in degrees running clockwise and counter clockwise and also in hours and minutes, the ecliptic graduated in days and showing the symbols of the houses of the zodiac, Greenwich Meridian and equinoctial colure shown, the countries colored and outlined. *(Christie's)* **$52,808**

A pair of Regency mahogany terrestrial and celestial globes by Cary's. The Terrestrial Globe inscribed *Cary's/New/Terrestrial Globe/Exhibiting/The Track And Discoveries Made By/Captain Cook;/ Also Those of Captain Vancouver On The/Northwest Coast Of America;/And M. De. Laperouse, On The Coast of Tartary/Together/With Every Other Improvement Collected From/Various Navigators To The Present Time/London/Sold By R. Fidler. No. 24 Wigmore Street,* the Celestial Globe inscribed *Cary's/New And Improved/ Celestial Globe, On Which/Is Carefully Laid Down The Whole Of The Stars And Nebulae/Contained In The Astronomical Catalogue, Of The/Rev'd. Mr Wollaston, F.R.S./Compiled From The Authorities Of/Flamsteed, De La Cahle, Hevelius, Mayer/Bradley, Herschel, Maskelyne & C/With An Extensive Number From The Works Of Miss Hersschel/The Whole Adapted To The Year 1800, And The/Limits Of Each Constellation Determind/By A Boundary Line/London/Sold By R. Fidler, No.24 Wigmore Street.* The globes 20in. diameter.

John Cary in partnership with his brother William were one of the foremost London map and globe sellers of the late 18th and early 19th Centuries. They built up a thriving and prosperous business, both as instrument makers and map publishers. Their first globes were published in 1791 and they were soon producing globes of four different diameters. *(Christie's)* **$130,310**

Rules of the Perth Golfing Society with a ▶
list of members printed for the society,
1824, this rare printed pamphlet lists the
first rules and members of the Perth
Golfing Society which was established in
1824, the pamphlet contains a list of
members as at 30th April 1825, the
regulations for the internal management of
the club and details of the nineteen rules of
the game of golf to be observed by the
members of The Perth Golfing Society.
(Christie's) **$62,320**

RULES

OF THE

Perth Golfing Society,

ESTABLISHED

5TH APRIL, 1824.

TO WHICH IS PREFIXED,

A LIST OF ITS MEMBERS.

The Golfing Annual... edited by C.
Robertson Bauchope [later David S.
Duncan}, a complete run from volume one
to 22, together 22 volumes,
advertisements, original green cloth gilt,
the final volume slightly dampstained,
1888–1909.
(Sotheby's) **$13,496**

A pair of Victorian ladies leather golfing
boots, circa 1895, with hammered-in studs.
(Sotheby's) **$1,104**

A Victorian mahogany ballot box,
the molded rectangular top inlaid
with four rectangular brass panels,
inscribed *Yes* and *No*, surmounted
by turned finials and four ebonized
poles, the front fitted with two
circular cylindrical dividers, painted
with numbers *18* and *19,* above
two pairs of two short drawers,
20½in. wide; and an envelope
posted in Edinburgh in 1868 to
*Harry Hare Esq., Secretary,
Prestwick Golf Club,* postmarked
Ayr, November 1868.
(Christie's) **$14,760**

A signed postcard of Old Tom Morris 1908, ▶
from a photograph by John Patrick of
Edinburgh and inscribed in pencil to the
reverse, *Signed by (old) Tom Morris on his
87th birthday at St. Andrews*, 5 x 3¹/8in.
(Sotheby's) **$2,249**

An exceptionally rare Henry's Rifled ball,
circa 1903, invented by Alexander Henry of
Edinburgh, Patent No. 4360, with stamp to
both poles in pristine condition, unused but
with a few flakes of original paint missing.
The great rarity of these golf balls is
probably due to the fact that they did not
work very well and not many of them were
made. *(Sotheby's)* **$48,737**

William Dunn Seniors gutty ball line cutter.   *(Phillips)*   **$64,000**

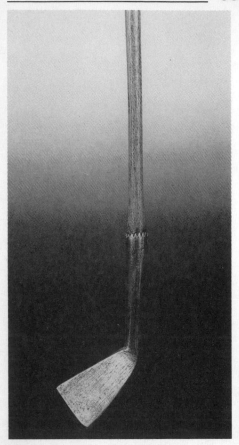

A rare feather-filled golf ball, late 18th/early 19th century, with stitched seams and painted cover, with one small hole to the leather cover, 2½in. diameter. *(Christie's)* **$14,760**

A rare blacksmith made cut-off nose track iron, late 18th/early 19th century, with slightly dished face and well-knopped hozel, the tapering hickory shaft, with suede grip and cross stringing, the hozel 4in. long. *(Christie's)* **$118,080**

A red hand hammered gutty ball, circa 1855, with what is known as the Forgan patterning, in pristine condition. *(Sotheby's)* **$12,184**

A rare blacksmith made cut-off nose track iron, late 18th/early 19th century, with dished and rounded face and long knopped hozel, with slightly bowed ash shaft with suede grip and listing, the hozel 4½in. long. *(Christie's)* **$65,600**

A Lenox Pottery tyg, with sterling silver rim, the flared body decorated with panels of male and female golfer, in shades of green, 6½in. high.
(Christie's) **$4,920**

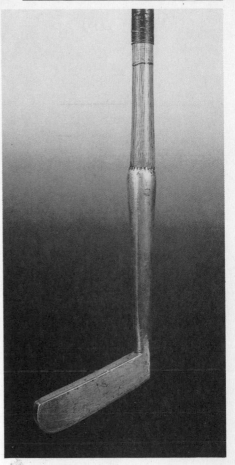

A late Victorian silver vesta case, enameled with a panel of a golfer at the top of his backswing, the reverse inscribed *Joseph Mescan,* 2¼in. high.
(Christie's) **$6,232**

A rare metal-headed blade putter, late 18th/early 19th century, with fruitwood shaft and well-knopped hozel, the shaft with a band of whipping repair and bearing a paper label inscribed in ink *Probably Simon Cossar,* with suede grip and listing, the hozel 6¼in. long.

This rare metal headed putter is one of only a few known to exist, as tradition dictated the use of wooden clubs in the era of the feather-filled golf ball and especially with putters. There is a famous portrait of Mr Henry Callender by Lemuel Francis Abbott, dedicated to the Society of Golfers at Blackheath which was painted circa 1807, beside him to his left resting against a fire surround is an almost identical club to this. *(Christie's)* **$155,800**

An H.M.V. 203 Re-entrant gramophone in mahogany case, on leafage carved turned and squared supports, 2ft.4in. wide. *(Russell, Baldwin & Bright)* **$9,600**

▲
A rare Gramophone Company de luxe gramophone, 64in. high, 1920-22. *(Christie's)* **$6,275**

An E.M. Ginn Expert Senior gramophone with papier mâché horn, gooseneck tone-arm, four-spring Expert soundbox with carton, replacement Collaro spring motor and crossbanded quarter-veneered oak cabinet on cabriole legs with claw-and-ball feet, the horn 28½in. diameter; and an Expert fiber-cutter and BCN thorn sharpener. *(Christie's)* **$7,825**

The pottery of the Han period (206BC-220AD) is the earliest really attractive Chinese ware, for it was about this time that the ornamental qualities of the medium were realised. Also, at this time there was a certain amount of contact with the Near East and even the West, which led to the general introduction of glazes, which had been in use in Egypt from ancient times.

Han pottery is usually either red or slaty gray, depending on the provenance of the clay, and varies in texture from soft earthenware to something approaching stoneware. The bulk of it is glazed, the typical glaze being a translucent greenish yellow, though this is subject to many variations. One of the characteristic features of pottery of this period is the frequent appearance of 'spur marks', usually three in number, around the mouth or base of a piece, which were made by the supports used when the ware was placed in the kiln.

Han pottery is decorated in various ways: either by pressing in molds with incuse designs, giving a low relief effect, or by the use of stamps or dies, or by applied strips or dies, or by applied strips of ornament, all of which would be covered by the glaze.

A small gilt-silver crouching bear, Han Dynasty, the animal cast hunched and supported on its forelegs, the left leg bent and the right knee raised curled beneath the well rounded body, the mouth fiercely opened, the gilding somewhat worn, traces of red pigment and green malachite encrustation, 2⅜in. high.
(Christie's) **$18,745**

A brown-glazed pottery recumbent hunting hound, Eastern Han dynasty, modelled with a long neck and raised head with alert expression, ears upright and jaws apart as if to bark, eyes and whiskers well defined, the long body resting on small paws, the left hindleg bent and the short tail curled upwards, 17¾in. wide.
(Christie's) **$13,122**

A fine Prussian Garde du Corps officer's helmet, circa 1900, polished tombac skull with nickel edges, silver-plated parade eagle with gilded crown, nickel guard star with black enamel central eagle, white enameled backing, brass chin-scales retaining cockades, gray silk lining, leather headband. *(Sotheby's)* **$7,498**

A fine and rare Italian embossed parade morion, circa 1590, probably Milanese, of so-called 'Spanish form', made in one piece, with almond shaped skull rising to a short stalk at its apex and encircled at the base by a row of lining-rivets, narrow slightly down-turned brim with plain inward-turned edge accompanied by a narrow recessed border containing a further row of later lining-rivets, and fitted with contemporary decorated iron plume holder at the rear. The scenes embossed on the helmet represent the legendary hero Horatius Cocles saving Rome from capture by the Etruscan forces of Lars Porsena. *(Sotheby's)* **$40,480**

◄

A rare and important late Western/early Spring and Autumn period Zhou Dynasty bronze helmet, (800–500 B.C.) The front and back of the helmet are almost identical, the reinforcing plates to brow and rear with border of imitation bubble rivets. The sides extend downwards to form ear protectors. At the lower corner of each of these ear protectors there are two small loops probably for the attachment of a leather chin-strap. At the top of the helmet there is a central upright oblong loop finial, probably for a plume, this partially blocked by earth and corrosion encrustation. Heavy green patination overall, possibly a battle site find with traces of iron oxide from sword or spear heads, 11¾in tall. This is an important and very early example of the 'lost wax' bronze casting technique. *(Bonhams)* **$16,250**

A rare and impressive kawari hachi, Edo period, mid 17th century, the russet iron bowl formed as a butterfly, the wings forming the crown and decorated with brass nunome, the proboscis running down the front of the bowl surmounted by large copper eyes, the brow of the helmet cusped over the eyes with small hinged flaps on each side, the sides and rear of the bowl overlaid with iron chrysanthemum leaves, each pair with a small flower.

Helmets of unusual shape were first encountered during the latter half of the 16th century. The fashion of the period was for simple helmets which could be speedily made, but men of rank needed to be recognised and so, initially, these simple helmets were decorated with extravagant crests or had elaborate shapes built on them in leather, wood and paper. Many others had the form crudely modeled in iron which was then filled, molded and finished with lacquer to obtain the required shape.

The armorer who made this fine example has taken great care with forging the metal, obviously at the direction of his patron, and has not used any lacquer to improve his modeling.

(Christie's)   **$113,610**

A fine 1843–1847 pattern heavy cavalry officer's helmet of the 3rd or Prince of Wales Dragoon Guards, complete with black horsehair mane and braided knot, red leather lining, green leather lining to the peak and tail and having a full velvet backed chin strap.
(Bearne's) **$17,280**

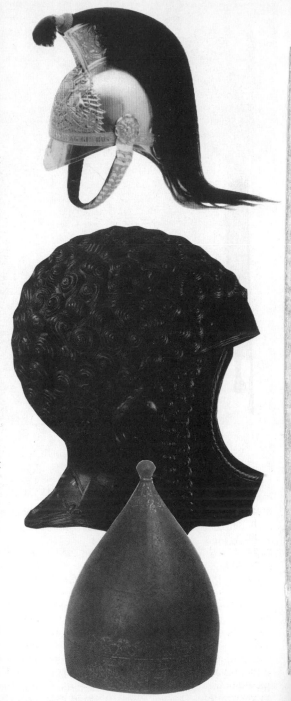

An important Italian parade helmet by Filippo Negroli of Milan, circa 1530–5, with rounded one-piece skull strongly shaped to the nape and pierced at the brow with holes for the attachment of a face-mask, hinged cheek pieces strongly shaped to the chin and fastened together there by a turning-pin, and two neck-lames at the rear, the skull superbly embossed and chased in high relief, except at the brow and nape, with curly hair extending downwards as long side burns into the cheek-pieces, each of which is embossed and chased in high relief with a naturalistically modeled pierced ear, and at its lower edge with palm-fronds extending backwards into the lowest neck-lame, 11½in. high.
Filippo Negroli (recorded 1525–51) is acknowledged as the greatest embosser of armor that ever lived. His reputation is based not only on his masterly handling of his material, but on a superb and restrained sense of design that places him among the foremost Italian sculptors of his age.
(Sotheby's) **$178,400**

A 16th century Turkish turban helmet of gently paneled conical form, from one piece, with the spherical knop with 2 bands of 'damascened' calligraphy and motifs. *(Graves Son & Pilcher)* **$8,635**

drawer all flanked by fluted quarter columns above a shaped apron centering a carved shell, on cabriole legs with rosette, pendant and acanthus-carved knees and ball-and-claw feet, the high chest of drawers 97¾in., the dressing table 30½in. high.
(Christie's) **$717,500**

The Mifflin family Chippendale carved mahogany high chest of drawers and dressing table, Philadelphia, 1750–55, the high chest in two sections: the upper section with molded swan's neck pediment terminating in rosettes and centering a pierced cartouche with cabochon motif flanked by flame-and-urn carved finials above a case fitted with a thumbmolded central shell and vine-carved drawer over three graduated thumbmolded long drawers all flanked by fluted quarter columns; the lower section with mid-molding above a brush slide over a thumbmolded long drawer above two thumbmolded short drawers centering a thumbmolded shell and vine-carved

An important Queen Anne carved, parcel-gilt, figured walnut bonnet-top high chest of drawers, Boston, Massachusetts, 1730–50, in two parts, the upper section with a swan's neck pediment surmounted by three fluted urn-and-flame finials, the scrollboard fitted with a blocked deep drawer with faux shell-and-vine decoration, flanked by two herringbone-inlaid short drawers with four graduated thumbmolded long drawers, the lower section with five short drawers.
(Sotheby's) **$937,500**

characteristics adapted from other regional centers as well as features unique to the immediate region. The Boston influence can be seen in the contour of the skirt and form of the lower case, legs and overall drawer arrangement. The Philadelphia influence is evidenced by the profile of the arched pediment.
(Christie's) **$387,500**

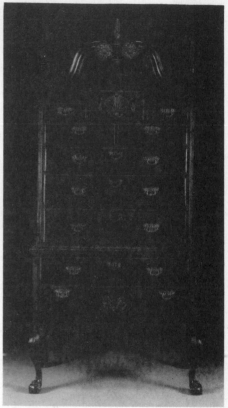

A Queen Anne carved cherrywood high chest of drawers, probably Colchester, Connecticut, 1750–1780, in two sections: the upper with a molded broken swan's-neck pediment terminating in carved pinwheels centering a carved finial above a rectangular case fitted with three short drawers; the lower section with one long thumbmolded drawer above three short thumbmolded drawers, the center with a carved fan over horizontal fluting on a shaped apron, with cabriole legs and pad-and-disk feet, 82in. high. 39in. wide

With its distinctive pediment, incised and carved decorative elements, and overall form, this high chest can be firmly placed among the finest products of New London County cabinet making. Probably made in Colchester, the chest exhibits

A Chippendale carved walnut high chest of drawers, Philadelphia, 1740–50, in two sections: the upper with molded broken swan's neck pediment terminating in carved rosettes centering and flanked by urn and leaf-carved finials above a rectangular case fitted with three short thumbmolded drawers, the center relief-carved with pierced shell, over two thumbmolded short drawers above three similar graduated long drawers.
(Christie's) **$299,500**

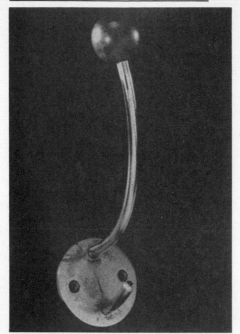

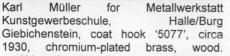

Karl Müller for Metallwerkstatt Kunstgewerbeschule, Halle/Burg Giebichenstein, coat hook '5077', circa 1930, chromium-plated brass, wood.

Although originally designed for mass production, this coat hook was not produced in series and this is the only documented example. *(Sotheby's)* **$375**

Two mixed metal bird cage hangers, the first with raised silver gourd vines inlaid to the bronze hook suspended from a circular plate cast in low relief with pine trees and gold leafed cranes, the reverse signed *XU Huaqing*, the second also of bronze, the hook section cast to simulate bamboo with gold inlaid inscription and circular bosses and suspended from a square plaque with an inscription and figural scene incised and picked out in gold leaf, 6½ and 6in. long. *(Butterfield & Butterfield)* **$1,380**

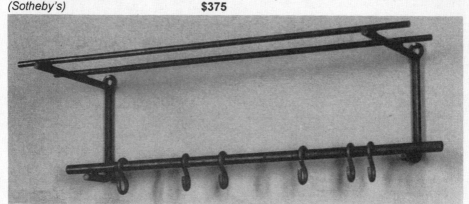

Gerrit Rietveld, wall-mounted coat rail, 1924, wrought iron, with six 'S' shaped hooks, 27½in. wide.

This design was used in the Schröder house and in a Dutch apartment block. An illustration in the Dutch publication Goed Wonen, from circa 1957, shows the coat rail in situ. *(Sotheby's)* **$5,624**

 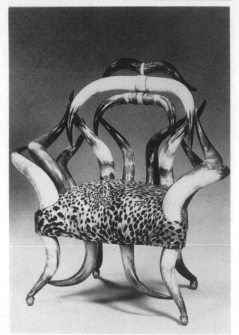

Victorian horn parlor chair, third quarter 19th century, 39½in. high. *(Skinner)* **$920**

A longhorn arm chair, attributed to Wenzel Friedrich, active circa 1860–90. *(Christie's)* **$5,175**

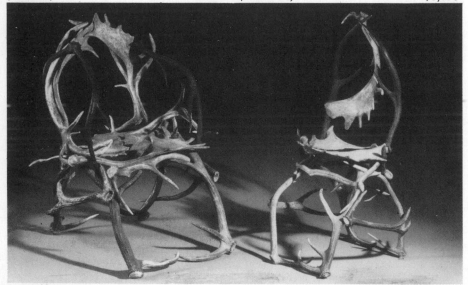

A suite of German antler seat-furniture, 20th century, comprising three armchairs and ten side chairs, each composed of various antlers with concave back and splayed legs. The two firms believed to have produced the majority of antler furniture are H.F.C. Rampendahl of Hamburg and Friedrich Böhler of Frankfurt. *(Christie's)* **$32,258**

Jean Puiforcat, ink pot and cover, circa 1930, the almost cube-shaped base with canted corners in clear and frosted glass etched with geometric motifs, with silver-colored metal collar and square section silver-colored metal cover enameled in black with conforming motifs, clear glass liner, 4¹/₈in. high.
(Christie's) **$5,185**

Ebonized wood figural inkwell, Continental, probably Italian, 19th century, in the form of a blackamoor head, with glass eyes, hinged head reveals brass inkwell, 6¼in. high. *(Skinner)* **$805**

A Regency bronze and marble inkwell, the hinged scallop-shell enclosing a removable glass well, pierced sand-well and semi-circular well, supported on a dolphin, above a black and gray-veined square plinth, with foliate molded square base, 6in. high.
(Christie's) **$4,686**

A French bronze ram's head inkstand, late 19th century, the head cast with a collar to its neck, the top hinged to the cylindrical recess, 6¹/₈in. high.
(Christie's) **$5,690**

A Symbolist bronze self portrait inkwell, cast after the model by Sarah Bernhardt, 1880.

Modeled with large bat wings feathered on the exterior, spiny reptilian tail and the clawed limbs of a mythical beast, clutching an open bowl with massive ram's horns and set with a devil's head, the inkwell concealed beneath a removable cover in the form of a pile of books, a space for a quill pen cast into her hair, on shaped bronze base, 12in. high.

Signed and dated in the maquette *Sarah Bernhardt 1880*, foundry mark for Thiebaut Frères Paris.

The strong Symbolist influence of this piece is a departure from Bernhardt's more conventional or Romantic subjects. It reflects not only certain knowledge of the work of such artists as Moreau and Doré, but also more directly her own role at the time. In 1879, Bernhardt was rehearsing for the role of Blanche de Chelles in Octave Feuillet's play 'Le Sphinx', in which the mysterious and even demonic heroine wore a poison ring in the form of a sphinx, and with whom Bernhardt may well have identified. The inkwell appears to have been conceived on one level as a celebration of her role in Feuillet's play, and on a deeper level as an evocation of what Bernhardt perceived herself to be.
(Christie's) **$34,270**

An American silver and favrile glass inkwell, Tiffany & Co., New York, 1902–1907 (the glass circa 1897), the bombé body of rich cobalt blue glass decorated with iridescent silver-blue pulled feathering, scratched *L.C.T.* and *H212* on bottom, the silver collar with horizontally-fluted ribs, the bulbous hinged repoussé chased with lobes and a spiral rosette, 5¾in. high. *(Sotheby's)* **$16,100**

An American mogul-style gold, enamel and jewel-mounted inkwell, Tiffany & Co., New York and Paris, circa 1900, the round glass body with raised bosses, overlaid with gold strapwork enameled in green with blue and red enamel flowers and cabochon rubies, around the neck a band of varicolored enameled flowers and leaves, marked on the rim *Tiffany & Co.*, 3¾in. high.
(Sotheby's) **$51,750**

Inros are slim, rectangular lacquered boxes which were used by men for carrying their family seal, any medicine they needed and their tobacco. These boxes were worn hanging from the belt beside the sword and they were in general use between the 16th and 19th centuries. Most inros were made in three or five sections which slotted neatly together. Cords were threaded through the sides of the box and each cord was secured in place by a bead called the ojime. The knot between the inro and the belt was kept in place by a netsuke.

A three case inro in the form of an armor, signed *Kakosai*, Edo period, 19th century, the suit of armor, complete with helmet and mask, displayed on an armor box, the tehen-kanemono forming the top of the silver himotoshi, a red lacquer mask, the armor and helmet in gold and black nashiji and ishime-ji and gold hiramakie on a red ground, aogai details, the armor box covered with a shippo design in aogai kirikane, silver and e-nashiji.

(Christie's) **$10,300**

A large single case inro, signed *Deme Monkon Kizamu Kajikawa Saku* and Nippon pot seal, Edo period (19th century), carved in the round in the form of a mask of Hannya wrapped around a bell, representing the Noh play 'Dojoji', decorated in various colors of gold, shibuichi, red and patinated silver, the base in muranashiji, nashiji interior, lacquer netsuke in the form of a Hannya mask, 4⁷/₈in. high.

In 'Dojoji' the priest Anchin, amorously pursued by Kiyohime, the daughter of an innkeeper at Masago, takes refuge under a large bronze bell. Kiyohime, rushing upon the bell, turns into a dragon which wraps itself around the bell, causing it to become red hot and melt. No trace of Kiyohime or the priest remain apart from a handful of white ash.

The signature implies that the carving is by a member of the Deme family of mask carvers and the lacquer by one of the Kajikawa family or that the lacquerer is pretending that such is the case.

(Christie's) **$6,561**

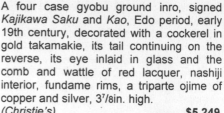

A four case gyobu ground inro, signed *Kajikawa Saku* and *Kao*, Edo period, early 19th century, decorated with a cockerel in gold takamakie, its tail continuing on the reverse, its eye inlaid in glass and the comb and wattle of red lacquer, nashiji interior, fundame rims, a triparte ojime of copper and silver, 3⁷/8in. high. *(Christie's)* **$5,249**

An inro in the form of a suit of armor with ▶ a rare attached Kabuto netsuke and stirrup ojime, signed *Shokasai*, Edo period, 19th century, the armor carved in the round decorated in black, gold and silver 'russet iron' ishime and red lacquer with hiramakie and nashiji, the armor box, upon which it is displayed, the Somada style with silver and aogai kirikane and e-nashiji, nashiji interior, fundame rims, with a boxwood ojime in the form of an abumi (stirrup) with an inlaid reden mon and a rare netsuke in the form of a Kawari kabuto with its shikuro in stained ivory, an oni mask maedate, signed *Ryuzan*. *(Christie's)* **$28,110**

A single case inro, Edo period, late 18th/early 19th century, carved in the round in the form of a Nembutsu oni carrying a gong and a subscription book, collecting donations for a temple, unusually it is divided vertically with a hinge at the lower end, thus requiring pairs of himotoshi rings, one set around the rim of each side of the container, decorated in red, gol, shibuichi and black ishime lacquer in hiramakie and sparse gyobu, with raden inlays for the subscription book and the eyes which have red lacquer irises and black pupils, the mottled black interior is scattered sparsely with gyobu, with a silver and shibuichi ojime, 4½in. high. *(Christie's)* **$4,686**

A rare mid-18th century brass Ptolemaic Armillary sphere, signed *Daniel Heckinger fecit a Augusta Vendelicorum* [sic], circa 1735, the foot is composed of four scrolled brackets that straddle a windrose below, and support a disk above. The windrose is cut with sixteen triangular points each labeled with the appropriate wind. At the edge is a pin-bearing for a magnetic compass. The edge is divided in degrees 0° to 90° in four quadrants, and the magnetic declination is marked by an arrow at 18° West of North. This value applied to Augsburg (Augusta Vindelicorum) between 1730 and 1750. Up till this time the change in the declination had been very rapid, the value being zero in 1650 and 8° in 1700.

The meridian ring is divided on one side into degrees, with half of the ring labeled from 90°–0–90°, the other from 0–90°–0°. At the top is a 24-hour circle with a arrow pointer.

(Christie's) **$224,940**

A late George II mahogany barometer by George Hallifax, Doncaster, the case in the form of a miniature longcase clock, with molded stepped top above an arched glazed dial signed *George Hallifax Doncaster fecit*, on a silvered plaque flanked by foliate mask spandrels, the barometer dial with silvered chapter ring engraved with different weather variations and calibrated 28-31, Rudian mask-and-foliate spandrels, flanked by engaged columns, the trunk centered with a brass molding chapter ring with pierced blued steel hand, square plinth with terminal moldings, 45½in. high.

(Christie's) **$94,920**

A George III mahogany invalid's ▶ chair attributed to John Joseph Merlin, the winged buttoned back, arms and padded seat upholstered in close-nailed burgundy hide on square tapering legs joined by stretchers with brass wheels. *(Christie's)* **$1,980**

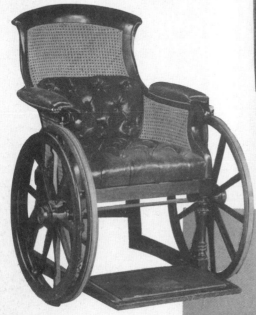

An early Victorian mahogany bergère wheelchair, with a shaped arched top-rail, caned back and sides, the brass hub caps stamped *J. Ward, Leicester Square, London*, the legs stamped *J. Ley*. *(Christie's)* **$4,125**

▶

A 19th century mahogany and brass-bound invalid's chair, the curved toprail above cane-filled back and sides, the sides with spoked wheels with screwed brass rims, the hubs inscribed *J. Ward, Leicester Square, London*, the back 37¾in. high. *(Christie's)* **$2,750**

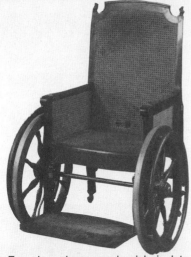

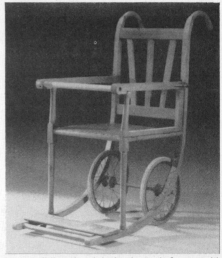

A French mahogany wheelchair, late 19th century, with caned back, sides, seat and brass bound beech wheels with turned spokes, fitted with carrying handles and a foot rest, bearing a label *Dupont, Lits et fauteuils mecaniques, 10, rue haute…Paris. (Christie's)* **$1,600**

An invalid's wheelchair, the oak frame with fold-down side, cross safety bar, foot rest, twin-tired wheels, and leatherette-covered seat, 41in. high. *(Christie's)* **$320**

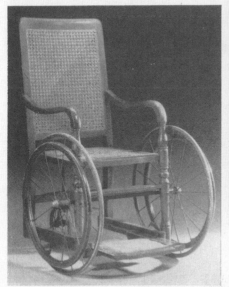

An invalid's wheel chair, with cane seat and back, iron-tired wheels with hand-driving outer rim, arm rests and adjustable foot slide, the frame with rubber-tired rear castor, 42½in. high.*(Christie's)* **$400**

A Victorian brass-mounted mahogany and satin-birch wheelchair, the caned tub bergère with padded arms, seat and foot-rest covered in close-nailed green leather, on ring-turned baluster legs above a sliding and hinged footrest, with a large wheel to each side and a small wheel to the reverse with label to the underside printed *Trapnell & Gane,/ 38,39,40 College Green, / Bristol.* *(Christie's)* **$4,800**

Pair of wrought iron pipe tongs, *Fort W.M. Henry Capt. B Williams 1756*, with incised decoration, 17¼in. long. *(Skinner)* **$9,200**

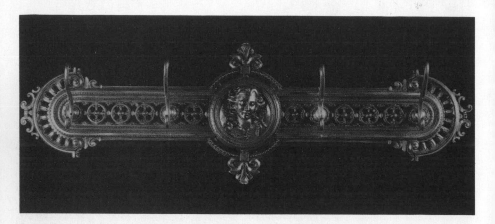

A Victorian cast iron wall hanging coat rack, the oval four hook backplate pierced with roundels and cruciform trefoils, and centered by a portrait medallion in high relief of a young woman shown wearing a diadem, within a molded frame of beaded borders, the ends modeled with protruding and pierced C scrolls, 44in. wide. *(Christie's)* **$1,385**

A rare cast-iron waffle iron depicting the Great Seal of the United States, American, circa 1800, of traditional scissor-form with loop handle catch, the circular molds decorated with wing-spread American Eagles and shields and inscribed *E. Pluribus Unum*, 27½in. long. *(Sotheby's)* **$5,462**

A German wrought iron Armada chest, the sides decorated with pierced panels with figures and masks, between foliage, the top with seven-bar lock, 16th century, 31½in. wide. *(Christie's)* **$26,240**

A cast-iron torchère, probably by Durenne of Sommevoire, circa 1865, in the form of an Egyptian boy upholding a torch, the circular column base cast with flowers and stylized acanthus foliage, 214cm. high.

The firm of A. Durenne of Haute-Marne in Sommevoire was established in 1855 and was renowned for casting a variety of highly decorative figures and groups. This particular example is a very slight variant of one exhibited at the Exposition Universelle Paris 1867 and illustrated in 'The Art Journal Catalogue' London 1867. *(Sotheby's)* **$7,498**

An American painted cast iron horse tether modeled as a jockey, late 19th/early 20th century, shown with one arm outstretched, mounted on a weighted square plinth, 48in. high. *(Christie's)* **$2,460**

A rare painted sheet metal and iron figure of an Indian, American, 19th/early 20th century, with the full length figure of an Indian wearing a yellow headdress and red and black costume shooting an arrow, 49in.high. *(Sotheby's)* **$9,775**

A cast iron side table, designed by Pierre Chareau, 1930, flat circular base, flat rectangular top set with removable brass plated ashtray in open three-legged support, 27½in. high. *(Christie's)* **$8,567**

Wrought iron snake, America, 19th century, the serpentine textured body made of conjoined pieces of pipe with flattened head showing open mouth, forked tongue and brass screws used as eyes, with a contemporary wall bracket, 66in. long. *(Skinner)* **$16,100**

A German painted iron armada chest, 17th century, bound with wrought iron straps overall, with hasps and pierced false escutcheon and twin writhen handles, painted overall with foliate bosses flanking rural scenes, the cover with escutcheon and key turning an elaborate locking mechanism, with pierced foliate engraved steel plate, shooting nine bolts to the interior, 17½in. high, 31¾in. wide.
(Christie's) **$4,550**

▲
Wrought iron snake-form holder, 19th century, with ball joint and caliper form clamp, 20¼in. high.
(Skinner) **$2,530**

A molded painted and gilded metal figure of a mermaid, 20th century, the full bodied figure of a young mermaid resting on her scrolled tail molded with scalework, arranging her long golden hair in a hand mirror, height 35in., length 42½in.
(Sotheby's) **$28,750**

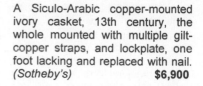

A Siculo-Arabic copper-mounted ivory casket, 13th century, the whole mounted with multiple gilt-copper straps, and lockplate, one foot lacking and replaced with nail. *(Sotheby's)* **$6,900**

▶

A South German ivory group of frolicking putti, from the Kern workshop, first half of the 17th century, six nude children holding hands and dancing in a circle, 5¼in. high. Compare both Leonhard and Johann Georg Kern's manner of carving putti, specifically the facial features, hair, and body types. Furthermore, both sculptors frequently used compositional devices such as circles of overlapping figures, figures with joined hands and masses of entangled figures. *(Sotheby's)* **$11,500**

A French or German ivory comb, 15th century, one side carved with two jousting knights, the verticals with scrolling flowering vine and rope-twist border, the other side with bathing scene and a bed to the right, the verticals ensuite to the flipside, 4⁷/8 x 5¾in. *(Sotheby's)* **$28,750**

An Anglo-Indian gold and green-decorated and carved-ivory plinth, late 18th/early 19th century, the square stepped top above a foliage-carved pinched neck with twisted border, above a gadrooned cushion frieze with foliage corners and centered on each side by a mask, on a stepped and concave-molded plinth, 12in. high. 17¾in. square.
(Christie's) $16,974

◄
A carved skeleton in coffin, the coffin with hinged lid and iron handles opening to a black fabric-lined interior containing a jointed and articulated skeleton which rests on a steel spring that pops up when the lid is opened, height 1¾in. x length 6¾in.
(Sotheby's) $9,200

A South German turned and carved ivory covered cup, second half of the 17th century, the undulating side carved with an aquatic bacchanal incorporating tritons, harpies, river gods and Neptune in his scallop shell chariot, fitted with two scroll handles in the form of harpies, the center of the well with a roundel with a profile portrait of a Roman soldier, the domed and turned lid surrounded by marsh and tall grass with rocks, snails and birds, surmounted by finial of a young triton riding a dolphin, 5in.
(Sotheby's) $40,250

An ivory cylindrical brushpot, 17th/18th century, the plain sides rising to a slightly beaded outer edge at the flat mouth rim, with pale yellowish-russet mottling, inlaid ivory base, 5½in. high.
(Christie's)   **$5,175**

A Continental carved ivory model of a mythical winged beast, on rectangular base, now mounted as a candle stick, height 15¼in.
(George Kidner)   **$41,500**

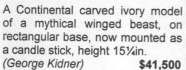

A pair of Dieppe carved ivory and paste gem set figures of Renaissance ladies, mid 19th century, both wearing dresses intricately carved with foliate designs and mounted with blue and red paste studs, 11¾in. high.
(Christie's)   **$11,997**

Two French ivory polyptych leaves, second quarter of the 14th century, the right panel depicting the Coronation of the Virgin in the upper register and the Adoration of the Magi below beneath a triple arch, the left panel depicting the Last Judgment above and the Crucifixion below also beneath triple arches, each panel surmounted by large cusped and crocketed arch, joined by one silver hinge and remainders of a latch, each panel: 7³/8 x 2⁷/8in. *(Sotheby's)* **$25,300**

◀ Fine ivory zodiac Ryusa Manju, signed *Kaigyokusai Masatsugu,* carved with a continuous depiction of the twelve zodiac animals, some accompanied by offspring and mates, each with inlaid black or red eyes and exquisite detailing, the bottom signed *Kaigyokusai Masatsugu* along the body of radish being nibbled on by many of the various creatures, 1½in. diameter. *(Butterfield & Butterfield)* **$16,100**

A French (Paris) ivory relief panel from a casket with scenes from the Hunt, circa 1330–1350, the first three compartments with scenes of lovers on horseback, some figures holding falcons, one with a horn, the fourth compartment with figures before a castle, 4³/16 x 9¾in. *(Sotheby's)* **$107,000**

Iznik, formerly the Byzantine town of Nicaea, lies in the north-western part of Anatolia, on the shores of Lake Iznik, some one hundred kilometres from Istanbul. It was most likely founded in the 4th or 3rd century BC. It played an important role in the early history of the Christian church, being the place of the First Church Council in 325 AD and again in 787 AD. It was occupied by the Ottoman Sultan Orkhan in 731 AH/AD 1331. After Timur's invasion of the city in 805 AH/AD 1402, the town began to decline. At the end of the 15th century Iznik was a town with a small population and poor mud-brick built houses, but with pleasant gardens. Its fame was due only to the beautiful pottery and tiles, which were manufactured there during the 16th century. That was the heyday of Iznik pottery. Although exquisite pottery was produced by the inhabitants of Iznik, it was not a rich town. Every traveler who visited the city during the 16th century remarked that its population was poor and the houses were neglected.

A Bamiyan monochrome pottery mouse, Persia, 11th/12th century, a bath rasp, with pointed ears, tail down the middle and all-over raised dots, decorated with a turquoise glaze with splashes of manganese. objects other than bowls and jugs from Bamiyan are rare. *(Bonhams)* **$1,755**

A fine Iznik pottery dish, Turkey, circa 1590, with sloping rim, painted in polychrome with a central medallion containing a spray of three tulips reserved on a raised ground, the medallion encircled by lotus panels, the rim with wave and rock design, 9⅝in. diameter. The design of the medallion of this compact dish is related to that of tiles such as those from the tomb of Sultan Selim II at Ayasofya, completed in 1574–5. *(Bonhams)* **$74,965**

A fine Iznik pottery jug, Turkey, 2nd half 16th century, with bulbous body, slightly waisted neck and curved handle, painted cobalt-blue, green and red with black outlines, the decoration divided by a guilloche band into two zones, each with a band of 'saz' leaves alternating with branches of oranges, 9in. high. An archetypal example of the form of jug (Bardak) that was popular in the 1560s. *(Bonhams)* **$30,305**

A rare Iznik pottery jug, Turkey, circa 1530–40, with globular body, cylindrical neck and 'S'-shaped handle, decorated in cobalt-blue, sage-green and turquoise, with some black, the body and neck each with a frieze of large rosettes alternating with smaller rosettes and further smaller rosettes above and below, the rosettes joined by vines and some of them intersected by serrated leaves, the handle with a ladder design and solid band on the sides, 7½in. high.

A rare Iznik pottery dish, Turkey, circa 1565, with sloping bracketed rim, decorated in cobalt-blue, green and black in reserve on a raised red ground with a medallion containing interlaced arabesques centered on a small medallion containing interlaced arabesques centered on a small medallion with eight small flowerheads, the rim with wave and rock design, 11³/8in. diameter. (Bonhams)   **$55,825**

This important jug belongs to Atasoy/Raby's group of wares in the 'Potter's Style' so called because up to the 1530s Iznik artists were either restricted to the court style or were heavily influenced by Chinese porcelain. By the 1530s, these artists had gained a sense of self-confidence and began experimenting with their own designs. The 'Potter's Style' was short-lived, hence the rarity of this piece, and such pieces were only produced up until the early 1540s.
(Bonhams)   **$71,775**

A fine Iznik blue and white pottery dish, Turkey, circa 1560, with sloping bracketed rim, painted in different shades of cobalt-blue, the design outlined in black on a brilliant white ground.

Wares of this type are based on Chinese prototypes from the Xuande Period (1426–35), a number of which are preserved in the Topkapi Saray Museum, Istanbul. (Bonhams)   **$146,740**

A fine white jade carving of a recumbent elephant, Qianlong, the reclining beast carved with its head sharply turned to the left, the wrinkled ears, tusks carved in high relief, the feet, eyes, tail and skin folds strongly incised, the stone of fatty appearance and of white coloration with brown streaking and faint white clouding, 5½in. wide. *(Christie's)* **$37,490**

▶

Fine and large jadeite figure of Guanyin, circa 1900, the elegant figure depicted standing with eyes downcast and both hands before her holding a double gourd vase tipped downward, all carved expertly from the evenly toned rich green matrix with small areas of pale russet utilised in the edges and folds of the deity's robes, the study mounted on a wood lotus stand in turn attached to a repoussé sterling silver base. *(Butterfield & Butterfield)* **$40,250**

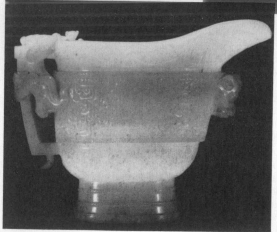

A fine pale gray jade archaistic libation vessel, probably Song Dynasty, of oval shape with a wide spout and squared loop handle, delicately carved around the exterior with a wide band of geometric motifs between two confronted dragons below the rim and ruyi lappets above the base, all divided by a lion mask in high relief below the spout and a sinuous chilong at the handle, the high slightly spreading foot with twisted rope motifs and a narrow key-scroll band, 6¾in. wide. *(Christie's)* **$41,239**

A pair of Dutch leather and brass jardinières, late 19th/early 20th century, each with pentagonal everted and stepped rim above five painted leather panels with naïve scenes depicting figures and houses surrounded by flowers and creatures, flanked by reeded tapering pilasters on a molded base and on part-gadrooned feet, 32¼in. high. (Christie's) **$21,821**

A pair of brown oak, bamboo and polychrome-decorated jardinières, 2nd half 20th century, of Regency style, each with later tin liner and molded pentagonal top, above paneled sides depicting chinoiserie scenes of birds, rocks and foliage, on five bun feet, 34in. high.

The jardinières display Chinese garden vignettes with bird-inhabited bamboo and shrubs executed in cameo-blue against a rosy pink ground, and correspond to wall-paper introduced for the exotic Chinese corridor or promenade gallery, created around 1830 at King George IV's Marine Pavilion, Brighton. Their trompe l'oeil bamboo frames, likewise correspond to the Great Corridor's beech-wood bamboo and oak furnishings. (Christie's) **$26,243**

A Continental brass oval jardinière, late 19th century, decorated with repoussé ornament, the sides with a pseudo armorial device, flanked by fleurs de lys, the obverse with a panel of clustered fruit, the ends applied with lion mask ring handles, the lower body with gadrooned ornament, on pierced cabriole legs with mask and hoof feet, 28½in. wide.
(Christie's) **$2,215**

A wooden jardinière, manufactured by J. & J. Kohn, circa 1905, circular base with four uprights, the top pierced with a double row of checkers, 34in., high, 21³/₈in. diameter.
(Christie's) **$2,999**

A parcel-gilt and biscuit porcelain jardinière, Paris, circa 1890, the border molded with cherubs and applied with rams' heads above a relief of putti with garlands of flowers, 48cm. high.
(Sotheby's) **$10,833**

A wrought iron and brass jardinière, designed by Hamesse, circa 1900, rectangular form with repoussé brass panels each decorated with fish and marine creatures on four bowed wrought iron legs joined by a central brass shelf, original lead liner, 39½in. high.
(Christie's) **$8,640**

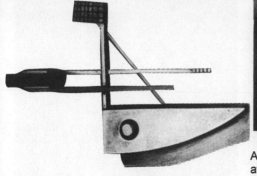

Designed and executed by Peter Macchiarini, brooch, circa 1940, steel, brass, copper, ebony, stamped on the reverse with the designer/maker's mark Macchiarini, 3¼ x 2⅛in.
(Sotheby's) **$1,593**

A small gilt belt buckle, the design attributed to Josef Hoffmann, manufactured by the Wiener Werkstätte, circa 1905/20, decorated with formalized foliate motifs and detailed with fine beading, 2³/₈in. wide, stamped *WW* monogram, Viennese poinçon and a further indistinct mark. *(Christie's)* **$4,284**

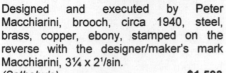

Designed and executed by Harry Bertoia, brooch, circa 1946, silver-colored metal, 2³/₈ x 1½in.
(Sotheby's) **$4,124**

Diamond, sapphire, ruby, silver-topped gold brooch, featuring singel-cut diamonds, enhanced by round-cut sapphires, accented by ruby cabochons, set in silver-topped 14ct gold.
(Butterfield & Butterfield) **$5,750**

Theodor Fahrner, Pforzheim, pendant and chain, circa 1930, silver colored metal, topaz, marcasites, the reverse stamped with maker's mark *TF*, 14½in. full length including chain. *(Sotheby's)* **$3,749**

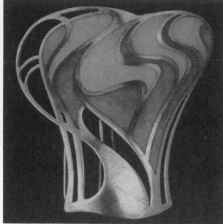

A gilt and enameled buckle, designed by Koloman Moser, manufactured by Georg Anton Scheid, circa 1900, pierced whiplash design detailed in blue and yellow enamels, 2¾ x 2½in.
(Christie's) **$6,560**

An enameled gold Baroque pearl turkey pendant, possibly Spanish, circa 1600, the body in the form of a Baroque pearl, the head, neck, wings and tail in opaque and translucent polychrome enamel and chased with cross hatching, set with seventeen table cut rubies in cusped collets, two pendants pearls, two suspension chains with three shaped enameled links each set with a similarly set ruby, scrolled suspension scrollwork cartouche set with a ruby on either side, pear shaped pearl drop, 3in. high.

Although this bird has been described as a dodo it would seem to have more in common with representations of the turkey. The turkey species 'meleagris ocellata' a central American bird, is remarkable for its splendid colorful plumage and is compared to that of a peacock. Spain in the second half of the sixteenth century had a fascination for exotic animals due to the continual contact between it and its New World Colonies.
(Sotheby's) **$28,750**

A large silver-gilt and enamel ornament by George Frampton, 1898, circular panel depicting a single tree in vibrant blue and green enamels detailed with tiny gold flowers, the broad silver-gilt surround with eight bands enclosing three wirework hoops, hung with three smaller circular pendant drops enameled with simple formalized flowers, 3³⁄₈in. diameter.
(Christie's) **$15,933**

A Wurlitzer 1080 juke box, designed by Paul Fuller, for 24 disks, with disks and in working order, 1947, 147cm. high. Because of its conservative, 'Olde Worlde' style, this juke box was nicknamed 'The Colonial'. *(Auction Team Köln)*

$9,700

▶

A Wurlitzer 750 juke box for 24 disks, with coin slots for 5, 10 and 25ct. designed by Paul Fuller, it has curved 'Bubble Tubes' to left and right, in working order and with disks, 1941, 143.5cm. high. *(Auction Team Köln)*   **$9,154**

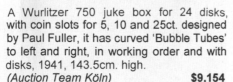

▶

A Wurlitzer 1015 juke box. This classic juke box was designed by Paul Fuller and in two years some 60,000 models were produced. It is the most glamorous box of the 'Golden Age', with eight bubble tubes, and a four-color rotating cylinder which constantly produces new color effects. This one is stocked with twenty four 78rpm disks, in working order and in original condition, 1946, 88 x 155 x 66cm. *(Auction Team Köln)*   **$9,044**

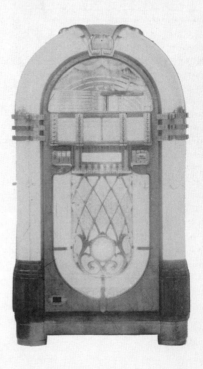

Peter Behrens for AEG, Bingwerke, Nürnberg, electric kettle and cover, 1909, nickel and chromium plated metal, ebonized wood and woven cane, the underside stamped *AEG* and numbered 8½in. high. *(Sotheby's)* **$1,593**

A rare copper tea kettle, Benjamin and/or Joseph Harbeson, Philadelphia, circa 1800, with a hinged strap handle stamped *HARBESON::* rotating on shaped tabs centering a slightly domed lid with turned knop, the bulbous shouldered body below fitted with a gooseneck spout, 11in. high. *(Sotheby's)* **$3,737**

A rare oversized copper hot water kettle-on-stand, signed *W. H. Pries, Canal Street, New York*, 19th century, of bulbous form and of impressive size with hinged bail handle and projecting spout, with domed lid and brass finial, mounted on cast-iron tripod. Marked *W.H. PRIES. 433 Canal St. NY.*, kettle 15¾in. high including handle. *(Sotheby's)* **$3,735**

Peter Behrens for AEG, Bingwerke, Nürnberg, electric kettle and cover, 1909, brass, ebonized wood and woven cane, 9in. high. *(Sotheby's)* **$1,875**

A BMW key-ring, the circular key-ring fob, decorated with the BMW motor car emblem, suspended from an oval-link chain to a key-ring fitting, signed by Fred Paris. *(Christie's)* **$300**

A Jaguar key-ring, the circular key-ring fob decorated with the Jaguar motor car emblem, suspended from an oval-link chain to key ring fitting, signed by Fred, Paris. *(Christie's)* **$187**

A Mercedes Benz key-ring, the circular key-ring fob, decorated with the Mercedes Benz motor car emblem, suspended from an oval-link chain to a key-ring fitting, with French assay marks, signed by Fred. *(Christie's)* **$280**

A Rolls Royce key-ring, the circular key-ring fob, decorated with the Rolls Royce motor car emblem, suspended from an oval-link chain to key-ring fitting, with French assay mark, signed by Fred, Paris. *(Christie's)* **$375**

KEYS

An early 18th century French iron masterpiece lantern key, 5¾in. long. *(Lyle)* **$4,850**

A North Italian key, the bow cast and chiseled with scrolls, circa 1600, 8¼in. long. *(Lyle)* **$818**

An 18th century cut steel key with a comb end, 5½in. long. *(Lyle)* **$500**

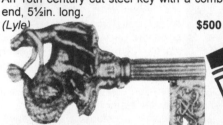

A fine Italian 18th century iron casket key, with figural head, 4¼in. long. *(Lyle)* **$6,500**

Two large Italian wrought-iron keys, 17th century, perhaps originally used for shop signs, both with elaborate openwork scroll bows, and comb-form bits, 18in. and 20¼in. long. *(Sotheby's)* **$2,300**

A rare roironuri ground lacquer violin case, late 18th/early 19th century, decorated in gold, silver and iroe hiramakie, takamakie with two pheasants with inlaid eyes, in a rocky landscape beside a flowering plum tree, the sides with a landscape of islands and boats, the interior with five small compartments depicting foliage, the kanagu with flowers and scrolling foliage, the interior is lined with ribbed purple velvet, some old wear and chipping to the lacquer, 31¹/8in. long. This seems to be the only recorded example of an export lacquer violin case. *(Christie's)* **$5,345**

A painted lacquer box, Continental, early 19th century, the cover painted with a bust-length portrait in a yellow vest, the interior with inscription, *Mr. DeWitt Clinton*, 4in. diameter. *(Christie's)* **$1,725**

A pair of large Chinese black lacquered papier mâché vases and stands, 20th century, of tapering shaped cylindrical form with waisted bases and pierced stands, decorated overall in gilt with Oriental female figures, shown on balconies overlooking landscapes, with conforming foliate and other geometric scrolls, 82in. overall. *(Christie's)* **$8,100**

A large Export lacquer casket, late 17th century, the two doored cabinet decorated in gold and red hiramakie, takamakie on a roironuri ground bordered with nashiji, depicting cranes in a rocky river landscape beneath pine, the interior with a group of various sized drawers, engraved copper kanagu, 13⁹/16 x 14⁹/16 x 11¼in.

Towards the end of the 17th century the rich shell-inlaid coffers of the Momoyama period were gradually replaced by a more restrained and elegant style with carefully placed gold lacquer decoration on a plain black lacquer ground.
(Christie's) **$15,000**

An Export silver lacquered cabinet, late 17th century, decorated in silver takamakie and iroe hiramakie with a mountainous lakeside landscape, the interior reveals two panels similarly decorated, with two secret compartments, one with a drawer, the interior in silver hirame, the kanagu engraved with scrolling foliage, 15 x 12¼ x 11⁵/8in. *(Christie's)* **$20,493**

Fine and gilt and black lacquer large fan form covered bo, Edo Period, the shape replicating a flat oblate fan with bamboo brace; the exterior surfaces finished in a black ground for mountain landscapes with huts, temples and travelers worked in gold and silver hiramakie and takamakie with togidashi and kirigane highlights, 18in. long.
(Butterfield & Butterfield) **$6,000**

A rare rectangular lacquer box, early Edo Period (circa 1650), decorated in gold hiramakie, okibirame, nashiji, kirigane and aogai inlay with a panel depicting a bird perched on rocks by a riverbank, beneath a flowering plum tree, birds flying above, the rim and the sides of the cover with a key-fret pattern, the base with swimming ducks and other birds among rocks and reeds, the inside of the cover with boats by an island with pine and other trees, the inner tray with karashishi and peony within a panel on a geometric ground, the reverse in hirame with scrolling foliage to the sides, the European gold mounts, probably German, elaborately engraved, some old wear and slight chips, 9⁷/8 x 2¼ x 4⁵/8in. *(Christie's)* **$13,280**

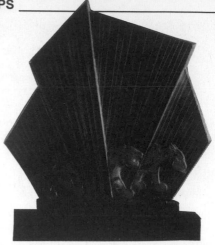

A rare pâte de verre lamp, by Gabriel Argy-Rousseau, circa 1928, flat fan-shaped panel molded with two tigers stalking through foliage, the glass detailed in pink, purple and natural tones, the animals with finely molded features, set in heavy rectangular bronze stand, 7⁷/₈in. high.
(Christie's) **$23,989**

A Paduan bronze oil lamp in the form of a negro bust, from the workshop of Severo da Ravenna, first half of the 16th century, cast with the head tilted backward and the mouth open, the tongue protruding to form the wick, his hair adorned with vine tendrils, olive-brown patina beneath reddish varnish and black lacquer, 4¹/₈in. high.

This form of oil lamp was made popular in the classical period, and Radcliffe discusses two types which developed in the Renaissance period. The bronze falls into the second category with a more modern design of the bust form incorporating draped shoulders.
(Sotheby's) **$25,300**

Poul Henningsen for Louis Poulsen, Copenhagen, table lamp 'PH', circa 1927, opalescent glass, brown enameled metal, bakelite, 42.75cm., 16¾in.
(Sotheby's) **$15,933**

A burr amboyna and ostrich shell table lamp, the design attributed to Jacques-Emile Ruhlmann, circa 1925, the gently domed faceted octagonal base raised on four small ivory ball feet, and with central ivory disk surrounding electric fitting, ostrich shell shade, 7¼in. high.
(Christie's) **$9,200**

A Paduan bronze boat-shaped double oil lamp, early 16th century, the lamp cast with acanthus circling at the ends, the lid also with acanthus and surmounted by finial in the form of a seated Neptune, the whole resting on a baluster-form stem adorned with scales, leaves and gadrooning, supported by clawed legs, 11¼in. high.
(Sotheby's) **$21,850**

Muller Frères and Chapelle, heron lamp, 1920s, wrought iron armature cast as a bird balanced on one foot, his head hunched into his shoulders, the body blown with raspberry pink glass with blue at the tail and with foil inclusions, on a square gray marble base, the glass with engraved mark *Muller Fres Lunéville*, the base marked *Chapelle Nancy*, 15³/8in. high.
(Sotheby's) **$23,046**

Dirk Van Erp copper and mica table lamp, original medium patina, broad conical shade of four mica panels set in a riveted hammered copper frame with rolled edge, supported by four curving arms riveted to trumpet neck on bulbous base with circular foot, 16½in. high.
(Skinner) **$20,700**

Fulper Pottery and leaded glass mushroom table lamp, domed shade inset with textured amber slag glass and iridescent green jewels, set into flared cylindrical base with two sockets, gray and light blue flambé glaze over mirrored, luster gunmetal, base stamped with vertical *FULPER* in box, circular *VASECRAFT* stamp, 20½in. high, shade diameter 17in.
(Skinner) **$21,850**

Daum, dragonfly lamp, circa 1905, clear glass internally mottled with powder blue and aubergine towards the base, overlaid with spring green and yellow and etched with buttercup stems, the shade applied and carved with a hovering dragonfly, the base with cameo monogram *DN* with a Cross of Lorraine, the shade with cameo mark *Daum Nancy* with a Cross of Lorraine, 18in. high.
(Sotheby's) **$57,615**

A Regency simulated-rosewood metamorphic library armchair, in the manner of Morgan and Sanders, the scrolled tablet back and seat covered in red leather flanked by scrolling arms and a paneled seat-rail, on saber legs and block feet, with brass screw, the underside stamped *I.S.*, the back-right foot spliced.

Messrs Morgan and Sanders' invention of 'two complete pieces of furniture...in one - as an elegant and truly comfortable armchair and a set of library steps' was praised in R. Ackermann's The Repository of Arts, July 1811.
(Christie's) **$11,247**

A brass-studded leather-mounted library pole ladder, with six rungs, 6ft.8in. high. *(Sotheby's)* **$1,840**

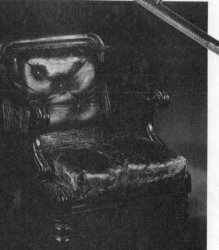

A William IV mahogany metamorphic library chair/steps, with a reeded frame, with a close studded red-leather padded back and downswept arm rests, on shaped supports decorated with lotus carvings, above a caned seat with a red-leather squab cushion, on turned and lotus lapetted tapering legs, hinged to reveal four rising steps. *(Christie's)* **$5,168**

A Regency grained-oak metamorphic armchair / library steps in the manner of Morgan and Sanders, the tablet toprail and lotus-leaf carved splat flanked by scrolling arms with patera terminals and above a caned seat, on square tapering legs, opening to reveal four steps,
(Christie's)   **$5,060**

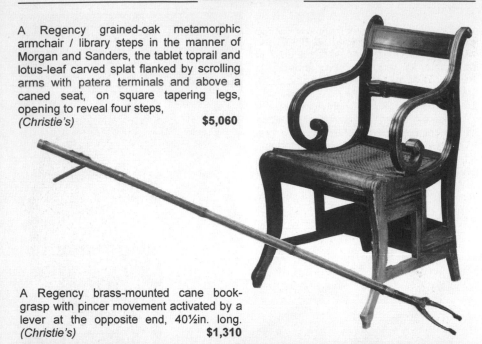

A Regency brass-mounted cane bookgrasp with pincer movement activated by a lever at the opposite end, 40½in. long.
(Christie's)   **$1,310**

A pair of mid-Victorian library armchairs, each with a rounded rectangular padded back, arms and concave seat covered in deep buttoned dark red leather, the arms terminating in lion-masks, on scrolled and acanthus-carved downswept supports, on cabriole legs with lion-paw feet. *(Christie's)*   **$35,834**

◄
A pair of carved and painted pine circus lion wagon supports, American, probably New York, circa 1880, each carved in the three-quarter round, the figure of a rearing lion with open jaws, 47in. high.
(Sotheby's) **$5,175**

A fine carved and painted pine circus tableau lion's head, attributed to Samuel Robb, New York, circa 1880, of impressive size, carved in the half-round, the stylized head of a lion with open jaws and upturned eyes, diameter 38in.
(Sotheby's) **$9,200**

A pair of carved and painted Lions-of-Judea, American, late 19th century, carved in the half-round with stylized figures of seated lions grasping Hebraic scrolls of the Ten Commandments in their paws, 45in. high. These pieces are from a Temple in Cleveland, Ohio, circa 1860–80. *(Sotheby's)* **$16,100**

Antique English oversize Liverpool pitcher, circa 1798, one side with polychrome transfer decoration of a vessel flying an American flag, with military arms and *The Merrimeck, Moses Brown, Comr.* below. Reverse with Masonic emblems. Masonic square and compass and the letter *G* below handle. Wreath enclosing initials *PB* above American eagle shield below spout, 12in. high.

This rare Liverpool jug was apparently purchased by or presented to Captain Moses Brown of Newburyport between 1799 and 1801. Moses Brown was born at Newburyport or Salisbury in 1742. At age 15 he apprenticed at sea under William Coffin of Newburyport. He married Sarah Coffin of Newburyport in 1764. He was in command of the privateers Diligent and Intrepid during the American Revolution, and commanded three more in the years 1780–83. *(Eldred's)* **$15,400**

Liverpool creamware jug, England, early 19th century, transfer printed reserves of Thomas Jefferson and James Monroe, misidentified as Hancock, with handpainted foliate gilt highlights, 9¾in. high.

The Liverpool potters were masters of the art of quickly adapting their wares to the demands of the moment, to the extent that they had no qualms about awarding different identities to the same illustration. For example, the stock portrait of Monroe, which usually titled *James Monroe, President of the United States of America,* appears also on a presentation pitcher, entitled *Philip Crandall - Born May 7th 1760.* *(Skinner)* **$20,700**

A brass and steel door lock, 18th century, in the style of an earlier period, the fascia pierced and incised with a vase issuing flowers, with the initials *L.W.* *(Christie's)* **$1,042**

A German steel lock, 17th century, of shield form and embellished with scrollwork around the edges, together with two steel keys, 17th century. *(Sotheby's)* **$2,500**

A French steel and brass masterpiece lock, 17th century, of square form and shooting five bolts, the covered plate elaborately pierced and engraved with flowerheads and foliate scrolls, with timing mechanism on reverse, 4^7/8in. square.

The dial on the reverse was used to indicate the number of times the door has been opened; each turn of the key causes the number on the dial to change. *(Sotheby's)* **$11,500**

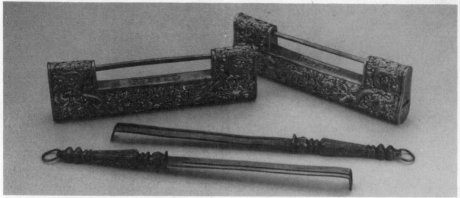

A rare pair of gilt-bronze cupboard locks and keys, locks cast with Wanli six-character marks in a line and of the Period, each lock finely cast on both sides with a pair of five-claw dragons contesting a flaming pearl amidst clouds. The nianhao cast in a line on the inner face below the bar; the long rectangular keys with shaped faceted handle terminating in a loose ring, each lock and key inscribed *wu* or *si*, corresponding to five and six, locks 11^3/8in. long. *(Christie's)* **$35,000**

An important Queen Anne block-and shell-carved figured mahogany tall case clock the dial signed *Seril Dodge, Providence, Rhode Island,* the case, Goddard-Townsend School, Newport Rhode Island, circa 1770.

The eight-day movement of this clock was manufactured by the accomplished Providence, Rhode Island clockmaker Seril Dodge. After apprenticing in Norwich, Connecticut to the clockmaker Thomas Harland, Dodge relocated to Providence and established a clockmaking business on Thomas Street, 'two doors north of the Baptist Meeting House'.
(Sotheby's) **$266,500**

The John Bringhurst Chippendale carved and figured walnut tall-case clock, Jacob Godshalk, the case attributed to the Garvan Carver, Philadelphia, Pennsylvania, circa 1765, the hood with molded swan's neck crest ending in flower-head-carved terminals centering a cabochon and C-scroll-carved cartouche flanked by a pair of urn-and-flame finials, 8ft.5in. high.
(Sotheby's) **$442,500**

A magnificent and highly important George III mahogany parcel-gilt musical and astronomical longcase clock and barometer, unsigned, circa 1770, three train movement, the going train having deadbeat escapement.
(Christie's) **$128,000**

An important Louis Philippe mahogany six month going longcase regulateur, the 10¾in. diameter silvered dial signed *Ame. Jacob*, anchor escapement planted on the backplate, stamped *souscription Aimé Jacob No. 17*, 7ft. 1in. high.
(Christie's) **$88,000**

Louis Wain (1860-1931) was an English illustrator and designer who is best remembered for his illustrations of cats engaged in human pursuits. In the early 1900s he designed a series of postcards, the A-Mewsing Write-away Series, on this theme for Raphael Tuck. These are now highly collectable, as indeed is anything by Wain.

Between 1910-20 Wain also designed pottery figures of cats. These were very much in the Cubist style, and highly coloured in, for example, green, orange and black. There is a distinct progression which can be noticed in Wain's work. From early, fairly naturalistic portrayals, his style becomes increasingly anguished – no placid, cuddly fireside moggies, these – and some of his latest models are so weird as to be hardly recognisable as cats at all. This reflects the progression of Wain's own psychological decline. He became increasingly eccentric, and died in an asylum in 1931.

A Louis Wain porcelain cat vase, decorated in white, green, russet and black, enamels, with impressed and painted marks, 15.5cm. high. *(Christie's)*   **$2,602**

'The Lucky Knight Errant Cat And His Meow Meow Notes', a Louis Wain figure, modeled in relief, painted in shades of red, blue, green, yellow and black painted signature, 14.5cm. high.
(Christie's)   **$810**

A large glazed earthenware cat, designed by Louis Wain, 1920s, modeled with typically formalized features, hollow to form a vase, 10in. high, incised signature *Louis Wain* on the body, impressed mark *Reg. No. 637128*, stamped and stenciled *Made in England. (Christie's)*   **$3,749**

A Queen Anne carved walnut lowboy, Pennsylvania, circa 1750, the rectangular thumbmolded top with notched corners above one long frieze drawer and three short drawers, the shaped apron below on delicate cabriole legs ending in trifid feet, 34¼in. wide. *(Sotheby's)* **$37,950**

A fine Queen Anne carved and figured walnut lowboy, Philadelphia, circa 1750, the rectangular thumbmolded two-board top above one long and three short overlapping drawers, the shaped spurred apron below on volute-carved cabriole legs, ending in shod trifid feet, width of top 35in. *(Sotheby's)* **$107,000**

A fine and rare William and Mary walnut veneered, inlaid and turned oak or ash lowboy, New England, circa 1730, the rectangular crossbanded and herringbone-inlaid thumbmolded top above three similarly inlaid short drawers, the tripartite apron below hung with pendant acorn finials flanked by ring-turned tapering legs joined by a shaped X-form stretcher surmounted by a similarly turned finial on ball feet, 32½in. wide. *(Sotheby's)* **$18,400**

Dame Lucie Rie was born in Vienna in 1902, where her father was a doctor and university professor, and where she studied under Powolny after the First World War. She married Hans Rie, a business man, and quickly won acclaim in her native land for her work. This mainly consisted of simple, thinly potted stoneware, sometimes polished or covered with rough textured glazes, her style influenced both by functionalist ideals and by Roman pottery. Her mark at this time was *LRG* over *Wien*.

In 1938, as the Nazis tightened their stranglehold on the country, the Rie's fled to Britain. Hans moved on to the United States, but Lucie decided to stay. She found work in a lens factory, and started making ceramic buttons in her spare time. In 1945 she was joined by another refugee, Hans Coper, and their continuing friendship and mutual support was to be a pivotal influence in both their lives.

After the war they began making domestic wares as their bread and butter, but also continued with their own pots. Most of Rie's pieces from this period were either of porcelain decorated with unglazed bands of cross hatched decoration colored with manganese oxide, or stoneware in elegant, simple shapes.

She used color sparingly, and developed a number of glazes, notably a yellow one containing uranium. Others were characterized by their rough, uneven texture.

The significance of her work was recognized when she was made a Dame of the British Empire in 1990, shortly after the first of a series of strokes had forced her retirement from active potting. She died in 1995.

A monumental stoneware covered pot, manganese with vertical sgraffito to upper body, white glazed rim and cover, impressed *LR* seal, circa 1952, 18¼in. high. *(Bonhams)* **$44,520**

An important earthenware shallow bowl, black with a golden bronze interior, painted *LRG Wien*, circa 1936, 9⅞in. diameter. *(Bonhams)* **$24,645**

A porcelain conical vase, bronze with a band below the rim, red with two white lines, the cylindrical base flaring to the wide round rim, impressed *LR* seal, circa 1966/67, 7⅜in. high. *(Bonhams)* **$11,925**

A stoneware oval bowl, off white pitted glaze with brown flecks and manganese rim, impressed LR seal, circa 1960, 5¹/₈in. *(Bonhams)* **$6,678**

A tall necked stoneware vase, spiraling glaze to flared rim and neck, white, green. pink and brown with speckles, impressed *LR* seal, circa 1967/8, 14½in. high. *(Bonhams)* **$25,440**

A porcelain footed conical bowl, interior with a yellow and brown cross meeting in the well dividing a brown grid filled with yellow and green spots, the exterior matt with a yellow cross meeting at a brown circle above the foot, impressed *LR* seal, circa 1954, 6¼in. diameter. *(Bonhams)* **$9,540**

A tall cylindrical pot, green and brown inlay decoration, impressed *LR* seal, circa 1953, 18¼in. high. *(Bonhams)* **$22,260**

Charles Rennie Mackintosh (1868-1928) was one of the Art Nouveau/Deco period. He was apprenticed as an architect in Glasgow, during which time he also studied at the Glasgow School of Art, winning a scholarship to visit France and Italy in 1890. After this, he also began to design furniture. In 1897 he won the competition to design and furnish the new Glasgow School of Art.

Mackintosh became the leading figure in what came to be known as the Glasgow School. Other members of the group were Francis Newbery, the headmaster of the School of Art, and his wife, Mackintosh's own wife Margaret MacDonald and her sister Frances who married the remaining member, the architect Herbert MacNair.

Charles Rennie Mackintosh (1868-1928), Glasgow Institute of Fine Arts, lithograph in colors. *(Christie's)* **$88,350**

A high back oak chair, the oval top rail carved with apple motif, designed by Charles Rennie Mackintosh for the Argyle Tea-rooms. *(Christie's)* **$431,200**

Mackintosh strongly influenced the Vienna Secessionist movement, and his work generally found more acclaim abroad, especially in Germany and Austria, than it ever did in his own country. The keynote of Mackintosh's designs was simplicity of form, with long straight lines complementing gentle curves. Chairs have long attenuated backs and low seats; tables have slender tapering legs. Decoration was never allowed to dominate a piece, as was often the case with Continental Art Nouveau. His color schemes tended to be light and delicate, and pieces were often painted white. He used stylized decorative motifs again and again so that they became almost a hallmark of his work.

A Charles Rennie Mackintosh ebonized mahogany writing cabinet designed for William Blackie at the Hill House, 1904. *(Christie's)* **$1,108,800**

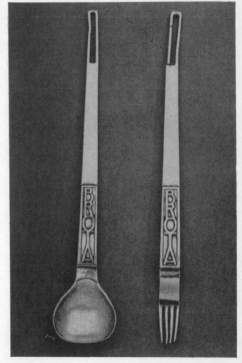

A stained oak ladder back chair, designed by Charles Rennie Mackintosh for Miss Cranston's Willow Tea Rooms, Glasgow, circa 1903, the high back with thirteen bowed slats, additional flat slat at the top, drop in rush seat with bowed back.

An order for 137 of these chairs was completed by Alex Martin, cabinet maker for a number of Mackintosh's designs, in 1903, at a cost of 17/6d per chair. The strengthening top slat was added to the majority of the Tea Room chairs at a later date to prevent the original bowed slat from breaking when the chairs were lifted and moved. *(Christie's)* **$37,490**

A Christening set given by Charles Rennie Mackintosh to his godson Dr Braccio Agnoletti, comprising silver spoon and fork and a Scottish quaich, London marks for 1903, quaich 175gr.
(Christie's) **$43,700**

A Louis XVI style ormolu-mounted rouge royal marble rotary mantel clock, late 19th century, of urn form with domed lid and foliate cast finial above a lip applied with Roman hour dial and Arabic minutes dial above bullrushes flanked by handles cast as Nereus and a nereid each holding a trident, on a spreading socle encircled by a dolphin, on a stepped square plinth, 27¾in. high. *(Christie's)* **$25,300**

An Italian white marble figure of a young girl, entitled 'Son Contenta', by F. Pugi, Florence, last quarter 19th century, of a young girl in formal dress holding a doll in her hands, on an octagonal base with arabesque pattern, with tablet inscribed *Fec Pugi Firenze*, the base front inscribed *SON CONTENTA*, 33in. high. *(Christie's)* **$10,300**

◄

A French white marble bust of Benjamin Franklin, after Jean-Antoine Houdon, 19th century, his head slightly bowed, a cravat around his neck and a partially buttoned waistcoat beneath his cloak, upon waisted socle, 25¼in. high. *(Sotheby's)* **$18,400**

A sculpted white marble model of a winged phallus, probably late 18th century, after the model of a Grecian oil lamp, with legs, one raised, later mounted on a rosso lavento marble plynth, 6¼in. long.
(Christie's) **$1,897**

A large Italian marble group of Menelaus and Patroclus, after Pietro Tacca, the helmeted Greek hero scantily clad and dragging the dying, naked youth across the rocks, 49½in. high.

This group relates directly to a classical marble in the Loggia dei Lanzi, Florence, which was brought by Cosimo I, Grand Duke of Tuscany, in Rome in 1570. In the second quarter of the sixteenth century Pietro Tacca is recorded to have made a model for the restoration of this marble group for Ferdinand II.
(Sotheby's) **$9,200**

▶

A marble figure of a putto emerging from an egg, by Emanuele Caroni, Italian, 19th century, signed *E. Caroni* and *Firenze 1888*, 25½in. high.
(Christie's) **$11,500**

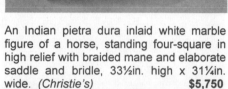

An Indian pietra dura inlaid white marble figure of a horse, standing four-square in high relief with braided mane and elaborate saddle and bridle, 33½in. high x 31¼in. wide. *(Christie's)* **$5,750**

A French ormolu-mounted brêche violette marble urn with a pedestal, by Robert, circa 1880, the urn with a molded edge, above a waisted fluted neck, the bulbous body with spirally-fluted lower bowl, flanked to each side by a scrolled handle with three playful putti, hung with flower garlands, on a stepped socle with egg-and-dart-cast edge, inscribed *ROBERT/SCULPTEUR.* The urn 28½in. high.
(Christie's) **$20,600**

▶

An Italian white marble group entitled *La Danza di Zefiro e Flora*, by Giovanni Maria Benzoni, Rome, circa 1867, Zephyr naked, Flora scantily-clad, dancing together, a 'wicker' basket of flowers behind them, on a circular base inscribed *G.M. Benzoni. Roma. 1867*, on an octagonal marble pedestal, the group 68in. high, the pedestal 27½in. high.

According to Rota the popularity of the present work entitled La Danza di Zefiro e Flora was such that it was executed no less than five times by Benzoni.
(Christie's) **$83,000**

272

This Hungarian born architect and designer joined the Bauhaus in 1920, where he specialized in interior design. In the early twenties he started designing wooden furniture, and much of his output reflected the influence of Gerrit Rietveld. He became head of the cabinet making workshop in 1925, and started to design pieces made out of tubular steel, and chairs with canvas backs. He left the Bauhaus in 1930 and lived for a while in Berlin, before coming to Britain in 1935. He designed coffee tables for Isokon and a bentwood chaise longue, with latex foam upholstery. He moved on to join Walter Gropius at Harvard in 1937, and remained in the States, where he worked as an architect and designer.

Marcel Breuer for Standard-Möbel Lengyel & Co., Berlin, adjustable swivel chair 'B7', designed 1926-1927, manufactured 1927-1928, chromium-plated tubular steel, black painted wood, 36^7/$_8$in. high. *(Sotheby's)* **$9,747**

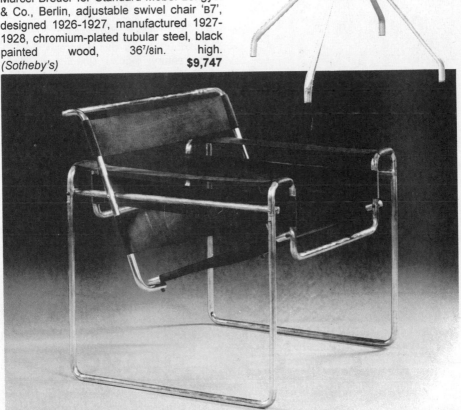

Marcel Breuer for Standard-Möbel Lengyel & Co., Berlin, 'Wassily' club chair 'B3', designed 1926, manufactured 1927-28, chromium-plated tubular steel, black canvas, 30in. high. *(Sotheby's)* **$28,118**

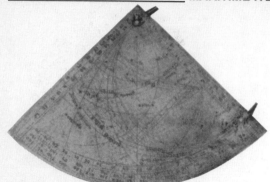

A rare medieval astronomical quadrant (quadrans novus), radius 5¾in., possibly Northern European, 14th century. *(Christie's)* **$23,750**

A souvenir plate from S.S. Normandie designed and signed R. Liftreau, by Haviland of France, 9¾in. diameter. *(Christie's)* **$560**

A Chadburn brass ship telegraph, English, 20th century, signed *Chadburns,* 80cm. *(Bonhams)* **$804**

An 18th century mahogany and brass octant by John Williamson, the frame with double 'pin hole' sight and cover, 1769, 40cm. wide. *(Phillips)* **$5,400**

A Siebe Gorman & Co., 12 bolt diving helmet, circa 1890–95, constructed in copper and brass, the hand beaten bonnet with three face plates with brass grills, spitcock valve, air inlet, pepperpot adjustable exhaust valve, blanked off early telephone(?) valve, the helmet stamped *3632,* the corselet with four straps and twelve bolts, interrupted thread, recessed neck ring, weight studs to front, stamped *3964 Devenport,* 17in. high. *(Christie's)* **$5,060**

A three-bolt Russian diving helmet, circa 1975, hand beaten with three face plates, each threaded, front with pags for removal, 19in. high.
(Christie's) **$3,310**

U-boat bell, the submarine responsible for the torpedoing of R.M.S. Lusitania in the Spring of 1915, cast in brass with raised characters for *U 20* to front, complete with clapper. The submarine U-20 was one of the four U-19 class submersibles ordered for the German Navy in 1912. Built in the Danzig Navy Yard and the first of the diesel-powered submarines in the Imperial fleet, the U-19's displaced 837 tons (submerged) and measured 210½ feet in length with a 20 foot beam. Despatched to the Irish Sea on 25th February 1915, soon after the declaration of the war-zone around the British Isles, she (in company with U-27) sank several ships between 9th and 11th March before the patrol on 7th May during which she sank the Lusitania. Early in July, she (in company with U-39) then sank another twenty vessels and scored further successes in the Channel approaches on 4th-5th September the same year. On 4th November 1916, U-20 was escorting U-30 back to Emden when both submarines ran aground on the West Coast of Jutland. U-30 was subsequently refloated but despite a massive salvage operation, U-20 could not be saved and was scuttled the following day rather than allow her to be captured and used as propaganda by the allies
(Christie's) **$22,080**

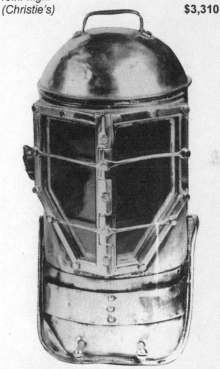

A Miller-Dunn Co. copper style II navy standard diving hood, American, 20th century, with brass angled glazed visor, arched shoulders air inlet and handle, 61cm. high. *(Bonhams)* **$1,929**

An Admiralty pattern 6-bolt diving helmet by C.E. Heinke & Co. Ltd, No. 120 (all matching), circa 1920–30, constructed in copper and bronze, the polished copper bonnet with telephone elbow, air inlet elbow, three circular ports, the front removable and stamped *120*, 19in high. *(Christie's)* **$6,440**

A fine and important carved and painted pine carving from the packet ship 'Congress' depicting Liberty with shield and eagle, Maine, circa 1840, the elegant seated figure carved in the round, wearing a blue-feathered headdress, a pink gown, a blue drapery over her legs, a gilt medallion around her neck and cuffs on her wrists, 37in. high. *(Sotheby's)* **$310,500**

◀

A carved and painted wood figure of a sailor, 20th century, the fully-carved figure of a bearded sailor wearing a black hat, a blue jacket, a white shirt, a black tie and blue pants, standing with one hand on his hip, the other holding a coiled rope, on a rectangular wood base, 76in. high. *(Sotheby's)* **$9,775**

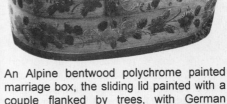

An Alpine bentwood polychrome painted marriage box, the sliding lid painted with a couple flanked by trees, with German inscription, mid 19th century, 17in. wide. *(Christie's)* **$2,584**

A late 18th century bentwood Alpine marriage box, the sliding lid painted with a couple in contemporary dress in a floral border, 48cm. wide.
(Christie's) **$3,230**

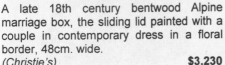

An Alpine painted bentwood marriage box of oval form, the lid painted with male and female figures in 18th century costume, their names in German script and indistinctly dated, 18th century, 19¼in. wide. *(Christie's)* **$2,018**

An Alpine bentwood polychrome painted marriage box, the sliding lid painted with a couple in formal dress within a floral border, inscribed and dated *1853*, mid 19th century, 18in. wide.
(Christie's) **$3,876**

A mid 19th century bentwood Alpine marriage box, the sliding lid painted with a man and a woman, the sides with floral decoration, 51cm. wide.
(Christie's) **$3,604**

The Martin Brothers co-operative, which set up in 1873, consisted of Robert Wallace Martin, who had worked for the Fulham pottery, and his brothers Walter & Edwin, who had previously been employed by Doulton. Walter was thrower, and Edwin decorator, while a further brother, Charles, became the business manager and ran a shop in Brownlow Street, London.

Martinware comes in a wide variety of shapes. The decoration is mainly incised, with the colors reminiscent of Doulton stoneware. The most common motifs are plants, birds, animals and grotesques, of which perhaps the most notable are R W Martin's 'wally birds'. These are often found as tobacco jars, with the heads forming the lids, and generally have a somewhat menacing air.

A large Martin Brothers stoneware bird jar and cover, the standing broad beaked creature casting a sideways glance, 1897, 29cm. high. *(Christie's)* **$14,720**

An amusing Martin Brothers stoneware model of a baby owl, the creature has a pale brown rotund body resting on a circular base above ebonized stand, with large talons, its removable head having long ears and its beak open wide expecting a tasty morsel, 27.5cm. high, signed on the neck and base Martin Bros. London & Southall and dated 10-1895.
(Phillips) **$5,000**

A Martin Brothers stoneware bird vase and cover, standing, the wise old bird modeled with a balding head, casting an upwards, knowing glance, 1902, 26cm. high. *(Christie's)* **$13,800**

A Martin Brothers stoneware face jug, modeled in relief either side with a smiling face, in shades of white and brown on a buff ground, dated *1900*, 17cm. high. *(Christie's)* **$4,048**

A large barrister bird, modeled by Martin Brothers, 1892, removable head, the finely detailed plumage crisply incised, richly colored in shades of forest green, deep blue and stone, set on ebonized wood stand, 10¾in. high.
(Christie's) **$16,324**

A large grotesque bird, modeled by Martin Brothers, 1900, removable head, modeled with finely detailed plumage richly colored in shades of gray/blue, green and stone, with touches of brilliant Prussian blue, set on original ebonized wood stand 14in. high. Interior of neck incised *R.E. Martin and Brothers London & Southall II 1900*, incised around the base *R.W. Martin London & Southall II 1900*.
(Christie's) **$20,619**

A rare somen (full face mask), Momoyama period, late 16th/early 17th century, the lower half and brow sections forged as one with the nose and upper lip riveted on after, large open eyeholes with rounded eyebrows embossed above, each cheek boldly pouched, exterior surface lacquered smooth with a red/brown lacquer, the interior lacquered brown with traces of gilding. *(Christie's)* **$17,800**

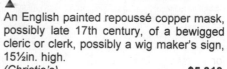

▲
An English painted repoussé copper mask, possibly late 17th century, of a bewigged cleric or clerk, possibly a wig maker's sign, 15½in. high.
(Christie's) **$5,310**

A somen (full face mask), indistinctly signed under the chin *Miochin Ki Mune...*, Edo period, 18th century, the boldly forged russet iron mask in three pieces, the brow plate embosssed with wrinkles and eyebrows, small eye holes, large yadome (standing flanges to protect the chincord) on the cheeks and large otayori-no-kugi (pegs under the chin to stop the chin cord sliding forward), red lacquered interior. *(Christie's)* **$8,435**

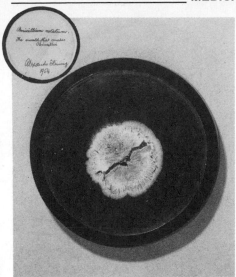

by Ernest Chain, Howard Florey and their colleagues, Fleming was duly honored for his discovery by fellowship of the Royal Society in 1943, a knighthood in 1944, and the joint-award, with Chain and Florey, of the Nobel Prize for Medicine in 1945. He further became president of the Society for General Microbiology in 1945, rector of Edinburgh University in 1951, and enjoyed the freedom of Dorval, where he had schooled, as well as that of Chelsea and Paddington. Fleming died suddenly in his Chelsea home on 11 March 1955, from a coronary thrombosis, and is buried in St. Paul's Cathedral.

(Christie's) **$13,280**

An important culture of penicillium notatum, the mold that makes penicillin (probably grown from the original mold), contained in a glazed circular mount, 2¹/8in. diameter, the underside inscribed in ink and signed *Alexander Fleming*, 1954.

Born in Lochfield, Ayrshire on 6 August 1881, Alexander Fleming followed a childhood and early education of straitened circumstances, with a scholarship award to study at St. Mary's Hospital Medical School, Paddington, in 1901. Prizes, trophies and examination honors ensued, as did promotion through assistant directorship of the Institute of Pathology and Research, the post of professor of Bacteriology at the University of London, and principalship of the Institute for the last nine years of his life.

Fleming's work on penicillin grew out of his investigation of lysozymes, bacteriolytic agents found in such diverse places as tears, turnip juice, milk and nose mucus. Fleming noticed their ability to dissolve contaminated cultures, and in 1929, his culture plate of Penicillium mold led him to write that 'penicillin may be an efficient antiseptic for application to, or injection into, areas infected with penicillin-sensitive microbes'. Whilst the long-awaited stabilisation and purification of penicillin was finally accomplished in 1940 in Oxford,

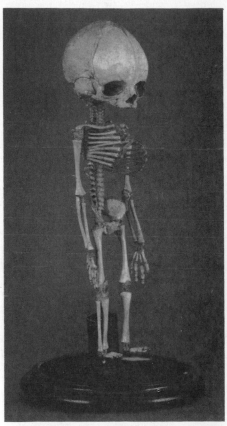

A [?] late Victorian foetal skeleton, female, approximately 6 months of age, 9¹/16in. high, on wooden plinth base with protective glass dome.

(Christie's) **$4,550**

A 19th century silver metal penis, with plunger and valve, 3¼in. long. (Christie's) **$1,563**

A beechwood and ebony stethoscope, 12¼in. long, signed, *G.F. THACKRAY LEEDS,* 12¼in. long. (Christie's) **$2,024**

A painted pine apothecary chest, American, 19th century, the rectangular molding above an arrangement of 42 graduated short drawers on bracket feet, width 5ft. 8in.(Sotheby's) **$19,550**

Instruments, books and documents from the estate of the brothers Reinhold and Friedrich Wappler.

The Wappler Brothers, born in 1870 and 1872 in Anhalt, Saxony, were pioneers in the electro-medical field. Reinhold studied physical and electrical engineering in Wittenberg and Berlin, while Friedrich was a cabinetmaker. They emigrated to America in 1891, and after working for a short time for General Electric and the Edison Co., they set up their own Wappler Electric Controller Co. in 1898. Their first product was a rheostat, which enabled the illumination of small diagnostic lamps. This was followed by a muscle stimulator, a sinusoidal current machine and an electrical surgical wave generator, but from 1899 they started designing and constructing X-Ray machines, winning a gold medal for their King model machine, the first without a Rhumkorff coil.

The collection consists of items from every phase of the company's history, together with personal documents and related literature.
(Auction Team Köln) **$9,379**

At the beginning of the 18th century the race was on in Europe to find the secret of manufacture of Chinese-type porcelain. The winner was Augustus the Strong, Elector of Saxony, thanks to his sequestration of a young alchemist, J F Böttger, whom he originally employed to turn base metal to gold. When Böttger failed at this, Frederick set him the alternative task of porcelain manufacture under the eye of Ehrenfried Walther von Tschirnhaus, a Saxon physicist who was also fascinated by this challenge. Success finally came in 1710, and a new red and white porcelain manufactory was set up in the Albrechtsburg at Meissen.

Production problems persisted, however, and it was not until 1713 that the first pieces were offered for sale, the decoration of which was largely influenced by the court silversmith Johann Irminger, and featured molded and applied vine leaf and foliage reliefs and modeled and applied rose sprays.

The king wanted color, but Böttger was never really successful in finding enamels which would withstand the firing temperatures required to fuse them into the glaze, and much of his output remained white.

Poor Böttger never enjoyed his triumph. He was still under guard until 1714, and at the mercy of a capricious ruler who refused to entertain his plans for improved kilns etc. In 1719 the factory's arcanist, Stölzel, smuggled its secrets out to Vienna enabling a rival establishment to be set up there, and when Böttger died in March of that year, at the early age of 37, the factory was in disarray.

Immediately however a turn-round occurred. The king made instant reforms, installed the new kilns he had denied Böttger, and underglaze blue was achieved. From Vienna too came the repentant Stölzel, bringing with him the enamel painter Gregorius Höroldt, who quickly perfected a superb range of overglaze enamels and used them to create fine copies of oriental wares as well as his own chinoiserie inventions.

Through Höroldt, Meissen finally came to fame and fortune, and the first marks were introduced. For 15 years painted decoration remained paramount, and was only superseded by J J Kaendler's relief molding and figurines in the late 1730s. .

From 1740 Kaendler's output was phenomenal. In addition to a constant supply of naturalistic figures, he designed new relief patterns for tablewares, and it is to him more than anyone that Meissen owes its long triumph, which started to wane only after the peace of 1763, when the victorious Frederick the Great of Prussia was successful in luring several fine modelers (though not Kaendler) to his new factory in Berlin.

A Meissen model of a snarling marten, circa 1734-1735, modeled by J.J. Kändler, the brown animal rearing up over a tree-stump with mushrooms and ferns growing at its base, 15¼in. high.

The present animal would appear to be one of only two known examples of this model. The other, marginally larger but with far less vegetation on the tree-stump, was deaccessioned from the Porzellansammlung, Dresden and sold by Rudolph Lepke, Berlin, 7-8 October 1919. *(Sotheby's)*   **$57,750**

A pair of Meissen hen teapots and covers, circa 1735, blue crossed swords marks, modeled by J.J. Kändler, one with bright iron-red, blue, purple, green and black plumage enriched in gilt and gilt with Laub-und-Bandelwerk panels on the neck and on either side of the cover emplacement, the cover modeled as a monkey; the other similarly decorated but in a slightly different pose, the cover as a recumbent black dog, 6¾high. *(Sotheby's)* **$29,900**

A Meissen ewer emblematic of 'Air', 19th century, blue crossed swords, incised and impressed marks, of baluster form with feather-molded neck and foot, the body applied with figures of Juno, Zephyr, and attendant musical putti emblematic of the Wind, 26in. high.
(Christie's) **$7,475**

A Meissen figure of a map seller from the ▶ 'Cris de Paris' series, circa 1748, faint blue crossed swords mark, modeled by J.J. Kändler, in turquoise hat, brown coat, iron-red flowered waistcoat and fawn breeches, carrying a map box on his back, an unfurled map of the World and a parcel in his hands before a tree-stump, on mound base applied with yellow flowers, 6½in. high.

The painter of the map of this example displays an idiosyncratic view of world geography, with America curiously situated to the southeast of Africa and Asia. *(Sotheby's)* **$17,250**

A Meissen figure of an articulated nodding magot, circa 1740, modeled by J.J. Kändler, the seated pagoda figure in black skull cap, iron-red kerchief, yellow-lined robe painted in Purpurmalerei with flower sprays, yellow-lined turquoise trousers and iron-red slippers with upturned pointed toes, the head, tongue and hands separately made and pinned to nod and wave, 8in. high.
(Christie's) **$19,550**

A pair of massive Meissen pot-pourri vases and covers, late 19th century, blue crossed swords marks, each domed cover with pink and green foliate-molded candleholder above similar acanthus, the rims pierced with pink Vitruvian scrolls, the shallow bowls with turquoise gadrooned rims with rams' head handles joined by berried laurel swags and painted with scattered flowers, raised on three in-curved flat legs molded with flowerheads in circlets, on tripartite base with three winged sphinxes and square plinth painted with flowers and molded with turquoise and pink rinceaux, some restoration and chips to both, 22⅝in. high. (Christie's) **$25,300**

A Meissen model of a cat, circa 1745, modeled by J.J. Kändler, seated to the right, pawing a rat grasped between its jaws, with fine gray patched fur, on a green oval mound base, 7in. high.
(Sotheby's) **$12,650**

▶

285

This world famous character was arguably the greatest creation of the legendary Walt Disney, and certainly the one which, more than any, made his fortune. Yet his name was the result of the merest chance. After much agonising, it was decided the character should be christened Mortimer. But as her husband left for the studio to start work on Mortimer, Mrs Disney called him back at the last minute with the immortal words, 'Why don't you call him Mickey?'

Mickey first hit the screen in 1928, and his popularity has lasted right up to the present day.

Mickey Mouse doll by Steiff, Germany, with original metal tag punched through the left ear, 19in. tall, black velvet body, green trousers with 4 mother of pearl buttons, yellow gloves and red shoes, all made of velvet. Original black eyes of oilcloth, few seem resewn, signs of age.
(Auction Team Köln)   **$1,492**

Mickey Mouse Drummer (Bell, Italy), approximately 1937, lithographed mechanical tin toy with rear spring powered rack. Manufactured by Bell, Milano/Italy, a family owned business company which produced an undeterminate number of small mechanical tin toys from 1919-80. Marked *Bell 278 Made in Italy*, 6½in. tall. Not listed in the appropriate literature, not to be confused with the much later and more common 'Mickey Drummer' from 'Nifty Toys'. Only 3 known worldwide!
(Auction Team Köln)   **$16,000**

A Mickey Mouse novelty openface pocket watch in plated case, with enameled dial, subsidiary seconds and keyless lever movement, dial and movement, signed *Ingersoll. (Bearnes)*   **$332**

A painted wooden rocking Mickey Mouse swinging on a stand, made by Triang, circa 1938-9, 32¼in. long.
(Christie's) **$1,000**

A fine and scarce Mickey Mouse tinplate mechanical bank, German, early 1930s, possibly made by Sehulmer and Strauss, brightly lithographed with a background of green and yellow, 6in. high.
(Christie's) **$23,000**

Rare 1947 Mickey Mouse Ingersoll watch in-store display, the only one known to exist, together with a 1947 Ingersoll Mickey Mouse watch.
(Christie's) **$23,000**

Tin plate clockwork 'Mickey Mouse' barrel organ toy, German, circa 1930, possibly Distler, 8¼in. high.
(G.E. Sworder & Sons) **$2,210**

An 18ct. gold and diamond-set 'Mickey Mouse' octagonal wristwatch with bracelet, signed *Gerald Genta, Geneve*, recent, 32mm. diameter.
(Christie's) **$10,000**

A rare officer's hallmarked silver gorget of the Honourable Artillery Company, engraved in the center with the Royal Arms and Supporters, with motto scroll below *'Honi Soit Qui Mal Y Pense'*, in the right hand corners the Prince of Wales's Feathers, on the right the badge and motto of the Company, with traces of original liner and replacement silver embroidered rosettes, hallmarked *London 1787* with maker's mark *CH* - probably Charles Hougham.
(Wallis & Wallis)   **$5,120**

A museum quality life size model of a WW1R Field Artillery gunner of the 29th Division, 1917, wearing tin helmet with painted red triangle, khaki tunic with red triangle shoulder patches, leather jerkin, breeches, puttees and boots, with leather cartridge bandolier, linen haversack, water bottle and mess tin, and carrying an 18 pounder shell.
(Wallis & Wallis)   **$1,150**

An Imperial Chemical Industries Ltd., Eley & Kynoch ammunition display case, mounted on gray card, within glazed oak display frame, 78.2 x 64cm.
(Tennants)   **$2,461**

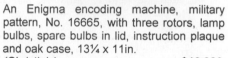

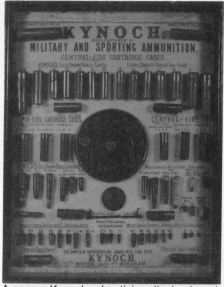

An Enigma encoding machine, military pattern, No. 16665, with three rotors, lamp bulbs, spare bulbs in lid, instruction plaque and oak case, 13¼ x 11in. *(Christie's)* **$12,330**

A scarce Kynoch advertising display board, 26¼ x 20½in. overall, entitled *Kynoch Manufacturer of Military and Sporting Ammunition Central Fire Cartridge Cases*, displaying identified cartridge cases from 4 to 20 bore in brass, and colored paper cases, various pistol and rifle ammunition, friction tubes and railway fog alarm; all identified, in wooden frame. *(Wallis & Wallis)* **$2,240**

Civil War presentation drum, sticks and a jacket, drum has a silver plaque *Presented to Samuel H. Proctor by the members of Lincoln Guard. June 12th 1865*, and sergeant's frock coat with paper label *Worn by a 14 year old drummer boy in the Civil War/S.H. Proctor*, drum 15½in. diameter. *(Skinner)* **$17,250**

An Eley Brothers Ltd., London, ammunition display case, the various cartridges, bullets and accessories mounted on crimson baize, around a central circular panel bearing the maker's name and crest, within a glazed, molded mahogany display frame, 136 x 76cm.
(Tennants) **$4,445**

A Nema – Neue Maschine Type T-D, 1947. A rare machine formerly known as a secret key machine, with ten rotors and the lowest known serial number TD 195, which escaped being scrapped by the Swiss Army. A total of 640 machines were produced, the numbers beginning at TD 100. This solidly constructed encoding and decoding machine was a successor to the legendary Enigma. When in 1943 the delivery of long awaited Enigmas was halted, the Nema was urgently developed following the Enigma principle of drums and reflectors, and was put into production even before the end of the war. It represented a considerable electrotechnical advance and offered the greatest degree of cryptological security for off-line machines which was possible at that time.
(Auction Team Köln) **$13,399**

A Holland and Holland leather-covered shotgun cartridge magazine, the top stamped *JSB*, and the front *Hon. J. Seymour Berry / 25 St. James Place / S.W.I.*, 18in. wide.
(Christie's) **$2,700**

290

A pair of Minton majolica spill vases, modeled by John Henk, one supported by a cockerel, the other a hen, each on an oval base with leaf decoration, 36.5cm. high, shape numbers *1982* and *1983*, impressed marks and date code for 1876. *(Bearne's)* **$11,880**

A life-size Mintons majolica model of a peacock, modeled by Paul Comolera, date cypher for 1876, standing proudly, tail falling behind him, atop a tree-stump modeled with trailing blackberries and wild mushrooms, inscribed at the base *P. Comolera* and impressed twice to the underside *Mintons/2045/S* and with date cypher for 1876, 62in. high.

Paul Comolera (d.1897) is recorded as a modeler specializing in life-size models of birds and animals at Mintons from 1873 until circa 1880. He was born in Paris and after completing his studies at the Rue d'Enfer, as a pupil of François Rude, he made his debut at the Salon in 1846. The majority of his works were cast in bronze but some of his models were produced in faience by H. Boulenger & Cie, at Choisy, as well as the 'majolica' wares at Mintons.

It is thought that only twelve examples of the life-size peacock exist today. *(Christie's)* **$155,800**

A Minton's majolica jardinière, the semi-globular body applied with garlands of fruit and pink ribbons, hung from flowerheads and the mouths of lions, on a low pedestal supported by three figures of men, 50.5cm. high. *(Bearne's)* **$5,064**

An important pair of 19th century Minton majolica jardinières on stands, the planters with green wreath rim, the bases fluted, 26½in. high.
(Dee Atkinson & Harrison) **$12,225**

A Minton majolica teapot and cover in the form of a seated Chinaman, holding a grotesque mask, his detachable head forming the cover, circa 1874, 7in. high.
(Christie's) **$2,000**

A Minton majolica jug, the mottled manganese and blue body molded in high relief with two pairs of peasants drinking and dancing flanking a seated figure, code for 1873, 10½in. high.
(Christie's) **$1,650**

A pair of large Minton majolica turquoise-ground jardinières, circa 1875, with six strapwork bands headed by lion mask and fixed ring handles, 17½in. high.
(Christie's) **$5,500**

A pair of Minton majolica cornucopia vases, circa 1872, modeled as putti astride cornucopiae issuing from dolphins, 27in. high. *(Christie's)* **$5,700**

A Minton stoneware encaustic bread plate, designed by A. W. N. Pugin, the rim with the text *Waste Not, Want Not*, circa 1849, 33cm. diameter. *(Christie's)* **$1,600**

A painted mirror frame, by Ben Nicholson, 1930, stained and painted with zig-zags, dots and stripes, 29 x 29in. Top of frame inscribed *BN 1930*, reverse inscribed *Ben Nicholson 15 St. Leonard's Terrace Chelsea.* (Christie's)   **$29,992**

A very fine and rare Classical giltwood and part-ebonized four-light girandole mirror, circa 1825, of impressive size, with a wingspread eagle finial above recumbent lions centering a rocky crag flanked by scrolling leafage, the circular rope-carved frame below with reeded slip and convex plate, the frame mounted with four scrolling candlearms and a shaped apron comprised of intertwined serpents with a leafy pendant, 4ft.8in. high x 34in. wide. (Sotheby's)   **$96,000**

A Queen Anne engraved pier glass, the plates reframed in a George III giltwood beaded border, the arched rectangular divided and beveled central plate within a beaded slip and outer mirrored border, engraved with stars, circles and diamonds, within an outer molding, restorations regilt, one plate cracked, originally with a further cresting, 69¾ x 38in. (Christie's)   **$23,575**

A gilt-bronze strut mirror, the plate in the form of a palette, held by an artist in 17th century dress, 71cm. high. (Sotheby's) **$5,210**

A hammered metal mirror, manufactured by the Wiener Werkstätte, circa 1925, promoting Lloyds shipping line, frame with pierced lettering above: *Österreichischer Lloyd Triest*, repoussé with typical design, the mirror etched *Triest: Egypten Dalmatien Levante Indien: China Japan*, 25¾ x 11in.
(Christie's) **$8,997**

An Italian carved giltwood pier-glass, ▶ Piedmontese, third quarter 18th century, the scrolled and shaped frame surmounted by a laurel wreath cresting supporting trophies, the sides and base carved with bullrushes and laurel garlands, the central rectangular mirror plate surrounded with shaped mirror panels, 241cm. high.
(Sotheby's) **$32,649**

A Chinese-Export Canton enamel and gilt hand mirror, 18th century, the oval mirror surrounded by a foliate border and above a scrolling foliate support and rounded handle, the reverse painted on glass with a young lady at her dressing mirror, 11½in. high. *(Christie's)* **$6,681**

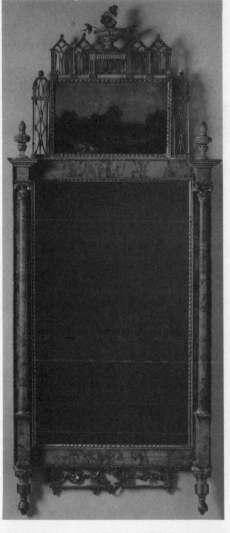

One of a pair of Dieppe mirrors, circa 1840, each with an oval beveled plate, surmounted by a coat of arms and the motto *Montoiye St. Denys*, applied with cherubs, mounted on a velvet border, 89cm. high.
(Sotheby's) (Two) **$7,222**

A marble and giltwood Bilbao mirror, Spanish or Portuguese, circa 1800, of impressive size, surmounted by a crest in the form of an urn issuing a spray of flowers with a pierced surround below centering an oil-painted panel depicting a bucolic scene with cottages and a gentleman in the foreground, 55¼in. high.

Executed in the Neoclassical style, this mirror would complement the contemporary decorations of a Federal home and serve as an exotic accessory. *(Sotheby's)* **$19,550**

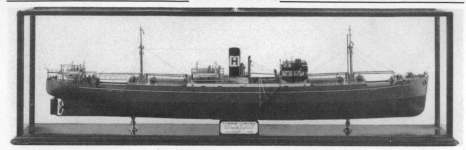

A detailed builder's model of the S.S. Harpalion and S.S. Harleden, built by R. & W. Hawthorn, Leslie & Co. Ltd., Newcastle-on-Tyne, for J. & C. Harrison Ltd., London, with masts, derricks and rigging, anchors, fairleads, bollards, winch, rope drums, ventilators, deck rails, companionways, hatches, deck winches, superstructure with wheelhouse and open bridge with mirrored windows, 18¾ x 62½in. *(Christie's)* **$11,960**

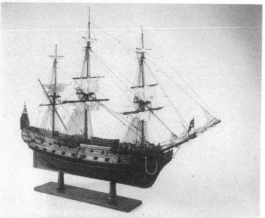

An exhibition standard 1:72 scale rigged and partially planked model of the Royal Naval 5th Rate Roebuck, a frigate of 1774 built by W.M. Brown with bound masts, yards with stun's'l booms and foot ropes, standing and running rigging with scale blocks, furled stitched linen sails with rope borders and reefing points, carved figurehead in the form of a lady holding a spear with dogs at her heels, the whole finished in matt varnish and mounted on two carved wood columns, 47 x 55in.
(Christie's) **$14,720**

A well detailed and presented display model of the steam yacht Corsair IV, with masts and rigging, anchors, winch, anchor winch, fairleads and bollards, bilge pumps, deck rails and companionways, awning stanchions, superstructure with glazed windows and wood-capped deck rails, 57 x 56in. *(Christie's)* **$11,960**

An exhibition standard 5in. gauge model of the B.R. (ex LNER) Class B1 4-6-0 locomotive and tender No 61003 'Gazelle', built by Aubrey Bentley to the design of M. Evans with brazed superheated copper boiler with water and pressure gauges, safety, blower, injector, steam brake, whistle, clack and twin blowdown valves, 14 x 65½in. *(Christie's)* **$11,904**

A 20 Volt electric Swiss-outline 'Crocodile' articulated electric locomotive, painted in dark green with yellow lining, gray roof and dark red wheels, with twin motors, external and interior lights, 62.5cm. long, 1933. *(Christie's)* **$51,520**

A finely engineered 5in. gauge model of the GWR King Class locomotive and tender No. 6009 'King Charles II' built by W. S. Baker, with brazed superheated copper boiler with fittings including water and pressure gauges, in finely lined GWR livery and lining, firing irons, Dexion trolley, 15 x 72½in. *(Christie's)* **$13,735**

A steam First Series DR 01 Pacific 2.3.1 (4-6-2) locomotive and four-axle tender, painted in lined dark green with red wheels, vaporising spirit lamp, twin double-acting cylinders, reversing from side-rod or track, lubricators and usual steam fittings, in original box and straw packing, 52cm. long overall, 1929. *(Christie's)* **$13,800**

A British-market electric 1.4.1. (2-8-2) 'Cock o' the North' locomotive and four-axle rigid-frame tender, LNER No. 2001, painted in lined green, with 20 Volt DC mechanism, with various instructions, in original box, 53cm. long overall, 1937.
(Christie's) **$25,760**

An American-market hand-painted clockwork Pennsylvania rail road pullman passenger train set, comprising 2.3.1. (4-6-2-) Pennsylvania locomotive and four-axle tender, lined in gray and black with red wheels, 62cm. long. overall, 37cm., pullman cars, two parlor cars '1903', and one smoking and baggage car 'Jefferson', in lined dark green with painted rivets, 1912. *(Christie's)* **$44,160**

An electric DR 2.3.1 (4-6-2) 'Borsig' streamlined locomotive and four-axle tender, painted in lined dark red and black, specially factory-fitted with (66) 20 Volt AC mechanism, 52.5cm. long overall, 1937. *(Christie's)* **$18,400**

An exhibition standard 4½in. scale model of the Burrell single cylinder three shaft two speed traction engine Reg. No. WTE 615 Harvey, built by A. Howarth with silver soldered copper boiler with stainless steel smokebox and firegate with fittings including water gauge with shut-off cocks, pressure gauge, safety, blower, injector, water lift, whistle, clack and blowdown valves, cylinder 2½in. bore x 4in. stroke, finished in green, maroon, red, black and polished brightwork with red and yellow lining correct to Burrell specification, 46 x 68in.
(Christie's) **$21,977**

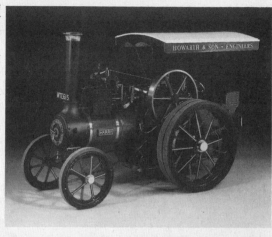

A late Victorian painted-metal, brass and silver-mounted humidor, by W. Thornhill & Co., in the form of a model coach, the central compartment with hinged lid under two of the four padded seats, enclosing a plain brass interior, with five lanterns two of which act as cigar-cutters and a stick holder, with match container to the reverse, simulating a luggage hold, the coach resting on four brass wheels, the front two articulate, with a harness with 'Comet' to the reverse, 10½in. wide.

Walter Thornhill and Co. are listed in the Kelly's Directory of 1890 as: 'Cuttlers, silver-smith, dressing case, travelling bag, writing case, and desk makers: specialties, latest novelties for wedding presents etc...by appointment to the Queen and their Royal Highnesses, the Prince and Princess of Wales.' Established in 1734 they were based at 144 New Bond Street and at 5 & 6 Little Bruton Street, Westminster.
(Christie's) **$32,453**

Most of the 19th century money banks available are made of tin or cast iron and were manufactured in America. Some of them are mechanical and seem to make money disappear. There were magician's hats, which, when money was placed beneath them, it disappeared. A Trick Dog money bank worked by a lever. The coin was placed in the dog's mouth and it jumped through a hoop and put the coin into a barrel.

A John Harper & Co. Hoop-La Bank, English, circa 1890, the clown with white face, and yellow robes, 22cm. long.
(Sotheby's) $4,700

Painted tin architectural form still bank, American, mid-19th century, in the form of a brick home with mansard roof and attached outbuilding, 7in. wide.
(Skinner) $4,025

A rare tinplate Mickey Mouse mechanical bank, German, probably by Sehulmer & Strauss, early 1930s, 7in. high.
(Bonhams) $9,450

Cast iron 'Girl Skipping Rope' mechanical bank, 19th century, 8in. high.
(Du Mouchelles) $40,000

A Shephard Hardware Co. 'Punch and Judy bank', painted cast-iron, red, yellow and blue booth with squabbling couple, 6¼in. base length.
(Christie's) $1,700

A Meissen monkey ewer and cover, circa 1750, faint blue crossed swords and incised *M* to the underside, modeled as a seated monkey wearing a puce tasseled fez and neck ruff seated and holding a cup and saucer in his left hand, the spout issuing from his left hand resting on his knee, the fez as the cover, the tail as the handle, 7½in. high.

(Christie's) **$8,625**

Painted carved wood monkey figure with tray, probably France, late 19th century, dressed in a greenish yellow smock with red cuffs, collar, belt, and hat on a green rockery base, 65in. high.

(Skinner) **$10,925**

A Copeland majolica model emblematic of 'Sloth and Mischief', after L.A. Malempré, naturalistically modeled as a brown monkey riding atop a large green and brown tortoise, the monkey using his tail as a harness, on a pale-blue mound and cobalt-blue canted rectangular base, impressed title, marks and date *1877* on base, 43.3cm. high.

(Christie's) **$16,100**

A Meissen model of a seated monkey, circa 1733, blue AR mark, modeled by J.G. Kirchner to the right and turned to the front with a pink face and ears and a black-streaked and blue-splashed coat, 10¼in. high. *(Christie's)* **$38,400**

Minton majolica garden seat modeled as a crouching monkey, 1870, 47cm. high. *(Christie's)* **$11,450**

A pair of patinated bronze monkeys, French, circa 1930, angular crouching monkeys, hands folded on feet, 29½in. high, signed in the maquette *CG*. *(Christie's)* **$13,443**

An Italian micro-mosaic panel, late 18th century, the circular panel depicting figures in front of a ruined arch, the stained and gilded frame with beaded slip and berried laurel border, the panel 10¼in. diameter. *(Christie's)* **$9,375**

An Italian micro-mosaic marble, mahogany and parcel gilt guéridon, in the manner of Percier and Fontaine, the micro-mosaic top late 18th century, the base early 19th century. The top inset with a circular arabesque micromosaic panel centered by Cupid in his chariot being drawn by two doves, in an extensive Italian landscape upon a white ground with foliate arabesques and urns to each side emblematic of the Four Seasons, the circular foliate and twisting garland border within a further giltwood acanthus-leaf border, the acanthus-leaf rim enclosing three small slides, on three griffin monopodiae supports with acanthus-leaf capital centered by an acanthus-wrapped baluster, on a fluted concave-sided triangular plinth and block feet, 43in. diameter.

This mosaic top may conceivably have been executed by Antonio Aguatti, one of the most celebrated Roman mosaicists, who signed a related mosaic tablet with Cupid-driven chariot that was later set into a Parisian snuff-box circa 1810. Interestingly, Aguatti also signed two other 'box' mosaics 'in piccolo' of spaniels, as well as a table top displaying a Cupid-driven chariot, which is now in the Hermitage. *(Christie's)* **$178,400**

An Italo-Byzantine mosaic of Saint John, probably Venetian, 16th century, decorated on a gold ground with the apostle wearing a halo, his gaze directed up, his robes in tones of red and outlined in blue, 18½ x 15in. *(Sotheby's)* **$6,900**

Ayrton Senna, JPS Lotus 1985, The original race-suit overalls worn by the driver during the British Grand Prix; special 4-layer nomex by stand 21, in black livery with yellow bands to sleeves and chest, with sponsors logos for Nacional, Olympus, JPS, Elf, Renault, GoodYear and Champion.

The British Grand Prix at Silverstone was won by Alain Prost, with Ayrton unable to finish. However he had produced a stirring drive, starting from 4th on the grid, he led for much of the race, to be sidelined by a mechanical problem in the later stages. He found this suit too restrictive, even removing the shoulder straps to ease mobility, and did not use it again thereafter, donating the overalls to his friend and former mechanic, during his Formula Ford 2000 Championship-winning year of 1982, Jonathan 'Spider' Horswell.
(Christie's)   **$33,741**

After E. Montaut, Michelin, 'Le Pneu Michelin a Vaincu le Rail' a very rare original poster for the event inscribed *Heath bat de 30 minuits 600 kilometres le train le plus rapide du monde*, facsimile signature printed, full color lithograph, linen backed, 61 x 43in.
(Christie's)   **$3,450**

Bernd Rosemeyer, a white linen racing wind-cap, given to Neubauer after a race event in 1937, it bears a wax seal stamp with initials *A.N.*, to strap base.
(Christie's)   **$6,000**

Brooklands, The Founders Gold Cup 1931; A fine 9 carat gold lidded trophy cup awarded to the entrant of the winning car driven by William Craig; of Grecian style, with fluted and hand-engraved patterning and ornamental handles to sides, height overall 10in. *(Christie's)* **$7,498**

Bernd Rosemeyer, Castrol silver helmet. A presentation helmet in continental silver, engraved and inscribed *Castrol 1934*, awarded in recognition of his racing achievements during the season; lining repaired and replaced. A unique memento of this legendary driver in German racing history, 7in. high. *(Christie's)* **$16,870**

Geo Ham, Monaco Grand Prix 1952, rare original artwork painting; the poster design for this special event run for sports-racing cars only; watercolor and gouache, with white highlights, signed with initials *G.H.*, 22 x 16in. *(Christie's)* **$15,000**

Mille Miglia 1953, a scarce commemorative printed cotton scarf; a competitor's memento for the event, decorative silkscreen design incorporating well-known Mille Miglia logo and motif. *(Christie's)* **$773**

Eleven turned and carved wood butter molds, American, 19th century, including an oval heart and tulip-decorated Pennsylvania example, three decorated with American eagles, two with cows, and five others with decorations including acorns and thistles, lengths ranging from 3½in. to 7in. (Sotheby's) **$2,300**

19th century American cookie mold roller with a strawberry and vine motif, stamped J. Conger. (Skinner) **$1,000**

A fine carved mahogany cookie board, M. Hall, probably New York, early 19th century, the square shaped mahogany board with canted corners carved in relief with the bust portraits of two officers, initialled H and P above a star flanked by cornucopia and an American gun-boat flying the American flag, signed at the base M. Hall, 12in. x 12in.
(Sotheby's) **$2,990**

A fine carved mahogany cookie board, stamped J.V. Watkins, New York and J. Conger, New York, early 19th century, the square form board carved in relief with the arms of the State of New York stamped in each four corners.
(Sotheby's) **$4,000**

It was in the early years of this century that Robert Thompson went to work in his father's joinery in Kilburn, Yorkshire, serving the needs of the local farmers.

In the local churches and abbeys, however, Robert saw the magnificent work of the medieval craftsmen in wood, and became convinced that work of similar quality and style could be made for domestic use.

Only seven miles from Kilburn is the Abbey and College of Ampleforth, and when Father Paul Nevil wanted some furniture, he commissioned Robert Thompson to make it. It was the opportunity which was to make him famous.

Thereafter Thompson worked exclusively in English oak. He insisted on natural, out-of-doors seasoning, maintaining that kiln drying would destroy its character.

His most obvious signature, however, is the mouse which can be found on all his pieces, and from which his nickname derives.

A Robert 'Mouseman' Thompson oak dressing table, with rectangular cheval mirror on rectangular, molded and chamfered top, on two pedestals each with three short drawers and eight octagonal feet, 106.7cm.
(Christie's)   **$4,000**

A pair of Robert 'Mouseman' Thompson oak armchairs, each with horseshoe arms and back, carved with two cats' heads and shaped terminals, dated *1928*.
(Christie's)   **$4,000**

A Robert 'Mouseman' Thompson oak cheese platter, elliptical form with handle, carved in relief with mouse motif, 37cm. wide. *(Christie's)*   **$862**

A Robert 'Mouseman' Thompson oak bookshelf, rectangular form with arched ends, carved with mouse motif, 45cm. wide. *(Christie's)*   **$775**

A Robert 'Mouseman' Thompson oak buffet, the rectangular top above a plain frieze, on octagonal section legs with platform shelf, 182cm. wide.
(Christie's)   **$3,700**

A fine grand format musical box by Nicole Frères, No. 32025, playing four overtures (William Tell, Barber of Seville, Semiramide, Magic Flute, Gamme No. 1235), with lever wind, instant stop, gilt tune-list and rosewood veneered case. The lid and front inlaid with brass stringing and brass, tortoiseshell-red enamel and mother of pearl inlay, 28in.
(Christie's) **$26,565**

A Lochmann's Original 24½in. disk musical box in upright case with glazed and gilt door, coin mechanism, glockenspiel, curved glass motor-cover, fretted pediment and early stand with disk storage, 89in. high. *(Christie's)* **$14,800**

A rare Symphonique Duplex cylinder musical box, No. 20867, the two cylinders playing ten airs with tune indicator, tune-sheet headed *Tirelire. Duplex. Mandoline. Zither,* zither attachments on both combs, double-spring crank-wind motor with silent ratchet, 32½in. wide.
(Christie's) **$24,665**

An extremely fine, rare and important silk embroidered picture: The Tree of Life, Morris Family, Philadelphia, late 18th century, worked with pale green, blue, yellow, rose, gold, and white silk stitches on a white moire ground with the figure of a leopard and a lion beneath a tree bearing exotic blossoms and buds with butterflies and a small bird perched in its branches, the figures standing on a series of hillocks with strawberries and blossoms, 13½ x 18in.

This masterpiece of Philadelphia girlhood art is the fourth and best preserved 'tree of life with lion and leopard' embroidery to emerge from oblivion and it represents Philadelphia's most opulent pictorial needlework of the colonial period. The fashion for exquisite silk on silk embroidery featuring flowers and foliage, and occasionally with birds and beasts, prevailed in Philadelphia when Boston girls favored pastoral scenes with a 'Fishing Lady' in canvas-work. This preference was no doubt introduced by Philadelphia's premier English-born Quaker schoolmistress Elizabeth Marsh (1683–c. 1741) who taught the daughters of the city's most prominent families from 1725 until about 1740. Under her instruction intricate band samplers were worked by girls of the Howell, Hudson, Logan, Morris, Rush, and Trotter families, and in 1738 she surely taught nine-year old Margaret Wistar who worked a floral pattern on silk for a pair of sconces that is identical to another made by Ann Marsh (1717–1797), daughter of the schoolmistress.

Ann Marsh continued her mother's school until at least 1792, and her surviving account book reveals that between 1772 and 1789 she was patronized by such families as Emlen, Head, Hilligas, Howell, Warder, Wistar and John Cadwalader. *(Sotheby's)* **$288,500**

A fine embroidered picture, anonymous, attributed to the Folwell School, Philadelphia, early 19th century, worked in green, gold, blue and white silk threads on a painted silk ground, with the figures of an amorous young lady and gentleman in a landscape with a small cottage and two reapers in the background, 19½ x 23½in.

This subject matter, patterned drawing and composition suggest that the design for this needlework picture is the work of Samuel Folwell, a Philadelphia artist who is known to have created the designs for many 18th century Philadelphia needlework pictures.
(Sotheby's) **$23,000**

A silk on silk needlework picture, designed and painted by Samuel Folwell (1764-1813), Philadelphia; possibly wrought by Eleanor Genge Hatch, circa 1810, worked in red, green, yellow, white, ivory and brown silk threads in various stitches on a blue, white and brown-painted background depicting two maidens in classical garb, one at rest leaning against a tree and the other holding a bunch of wheat in one hand and a laurel branch in the other, 20 x 27in. sight.

Samuel Folwell (1764-1813), the only American artist whose drawings for schoolgirl silk compositions and memorial miniatures on ivory have been identified, operated a school in Philadelphia with his wife Ann Elizabeth Gebler Folwell (1770-1824) in the early 19th century.

The needlework illustrated here employs many of the motifs typically associated with Folwell's work. These include the thatched cottages, distinctively drawn faces, and flipperlike hands of the figures.
(Christie's) **$21,850**

A rare needlework hunting scene, Boston, Massachusetts, 1740-1745, worked in a variety of green, blue, gold, brown, pink and yellow wool stitches, on a canvaswork ground, with the figure of a hunter astride a dark-brown horse galloping through fields with grazing sheep, leaping stags and birds flying overhead, 21in. wide.

This sprightly pastoral scene descended with the Grafton coat of arms is believed to have been worked by the same girl at a Boston boarding school, either Zerviah (1728-1750) or Elizabeth (1734-1814), the eldest daughters of William Parker (1703-1791) and Elizabeth Grafton of Portsmouth, New Hampshire. Its reclining white lamb surrounded by green is reminiscent of another white lamb against dark green ground and worked by Ann Peartree on Boston's earliest known signed and dated canvaswork picture of 1739.
(Sotheby's) **$32,200**

The traditional Japanese kimono had no pockets so any possessions had to be carried around in little purses or boxes swinging from the belt, which was a sash called the obi. The cords which attached the purses to the obi were held in place by a netsuke (pronounced netsky). The simplest netsuke were wooden toggles but adroit Japanese craftsmen soon seized the opportunity of turning the toggle into an object of beauty by carving it into the shape of birds, animals, flowers or people. It became a matter of pride to own a fine netsuke and by the end of the 18th century the elaboration of the carving reached a peak with many famous artists specializing in netsuke alone.

Netsuke were made out of wood, ivory, bone, rhino, buffalo or stag horn, jade, jet, turtle shell, amber or more rarely metal. The subjects were innumerable ranging from characters in Japanese folk tales and representations of traditional craftsmen to eroticism, which was a popular subject.

A large number of the over 3,000 craftsmen known to have made netsuke lived around Osaka, Nagoya, Kyoto and Edo but the popularity of their wares declined after 1868 when Japan was opened up to the West and foreign style clothes with pockets began being worn.

A fine ivory netsuke, signed Tomotada, Edo Period (18th Century), of a wolf, seated and holding down a frightened crab with his paw, eyes inlaid in horn, age cracks, 1¹³/₁₆in. long.
(Christie's) **$31,867**

An ivory, wood, silver and stone netsuke, signed *Tokokyu*, with Seal Ryubai, Meiji Period (19th century), well carved from ivory, various colors of wood, red and green lacquer, silver, stained ivory and brown stone inlay, of a priest showing a cat to a young boy who holds a buri-buri toy by a tasseled red cord, 2in. high.

This piece is typical of Tokoku's mature work. Born in 1846 in Edo, he had made ivory manju in his early days, having taught himself to carve without being apprenticed to an older artist. In later days he turned to pipe-cases and inro, before reverting to this type of netsuke, for which he had become so renowned. He opened his own school in 1862, and died in 1931.
(Christie's) **$10,871**

A coral and kinko netsuke, signed *Someya Chomin* on an inlaid gold plaque, Meiji period (late 19th century).

The large well-formed branched piece of coral encased in a hinged mount of silver and two colors of gold, the pierced three piece mount formed as a group of three karako and an elephant in procession beneath a pine, one of the karako carries a banner and another is blowing a trumpet, 2³/₈in. high. *(Christie's)* **$14,996**

A fine ivory netsuke, signed *Tomotada,* Edo Period (18th century), of a goat steadying a branch of loquat fruit to eat it, with horn inlay, 1⁷/₈in. long. *(Christie's)* **$26,243**

A fine stag antler netsuke of a shark, Beisai seal, Edo Period (19th century), the unusually elongated and slender body with the tail slightly curved, the eyes inlaid with horn, 4¾in. long.

Ogawa Beisai was a 19th century stag antler carver whose work is known from only one thoroughly individual documented piece illustrated in Okada's 1951 Japanese Tourist Board book Netsuke. It is an individual depiction of a stag and doe lying on the large corona of the deer antler, and it is signed *carved by Beisai at the old age of 65.* It records that Beisai used an antler which, he specified, had been naturally shed. *(Christie's)* **$8,435**

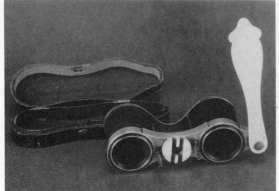

A rare 19th-century pair of silver telescopic opera glasses, signed on the eyepiece surrounds *LUNETTE BAUTAIN* and stamped *B.C.* within a lozenge, the telescopic action operated by an ingenious mechanism of folding rack and pinion guides for the silk-covered telescopic bellows with ivory adjuster, with folding ivory handle, in original silk-lined shaped leather-covered case, 4⁷/₈in. wide.
(Christie's) **$2,747**

◄

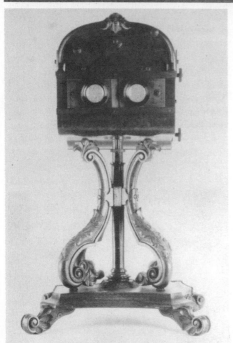

Natural stereoscope, C.H. Charlesworth, Huddersfield; the walnut-veneered case with hinged top and inset mirror, side door, base focusing knob, lacquered-brass fittings, laterally-adjusting viewing lenses, engraved brass plate with black infilling *The natural stereoscope, C.H. Charlesworth, maker, Buxton Road,* Huddersfield, internally colored blinds, raised on an adjustable brass column and four scrolling legs above a shaped base.
(Christie's) **$7,498**

A Mutoscope no. 2091, with Mutoscope, New York, trade plate, of cast iron construction, painted green, gold and red with Red Indian head and eagle emblem, with one picture roll, 'Dry swimming practice on the beach', 164cm. high.
(Auction Team Köln) **$5,873**

Kinora viewer, Bond's Ltd., London; oak body, hand-cranked, with a pair of viewing lenses for simultaneous viewing by two people, mounted on a pedestal type stand. *(Christie's)* **$2,060**

William Storer patent camera obscura, polished mahogany-body, with sliding lid fitted with brass patent arms and printed label on the underside: by the King's *Patent. The Royal-Delineator. To be had of no one but W. Storer. NB: The Royal Delineator is an optical instrument that obviates the defects of the camera obscura as it does not require the sun.*

William Storer patented a design for a reflex camera obscura in 1778, which he marketed as his 'Royal Accurate Delineator' and was granted patent no. 1183. *(Christie's)* **$4,500**

A Victorian Bi-unial lantern, in mahogany lacquered brass and japanned tin with suppliers plate, *Walker Tyler London*, complete with screen with poles and a good collection of colored lantern slides. *(Dreweatt Neate)* **$2,392**

A Powell & Lealand No. 1 stand microscope, in lacquered brass with binocular and monocular body tubes, dated *1895*, 19in. high. *(Christie's)* **$7,120**

A very fine enameled goose tureen and cover, Qianlong, finely modeled as a goose squatting on its webbed feet, the body covered with finely enameled sepia plumage, the short tail and folded wings with wings naturalistically drawn in blue, green, iron-red and sepia, all below the slightly bent neck supporting the small head with a pale breast, blue back-feathers, a red crown and plain parted bill, 14½in. high. *(Christie's)* **$127,170**

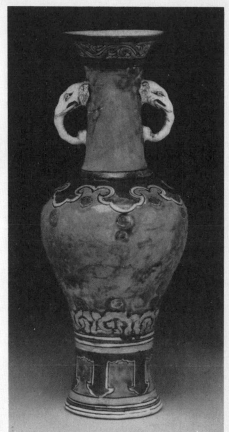

Fine 'Fahua' Pottery vase, Ming Dynasty, of slender baluster form and delicately modeled elephant head handles; painted in brilliant underglaze blue to form a ruyi lappet band around the shoulder and a lotus lappet band surrounding the waisted base, the remainder of the exterior unevenly covered in turquoise enamel enriched with green, aubergine and brilliant yellow enamel banding, 15¾in. high. *(Butterfield & Butterfield)*

◄ **$24,150**

A famille rose two-handled moon flask, painted with two seated figures holding fans before a bed, another figure at a door, the reverse with figures in a terraced garden beside rockwork, a figure playing a musical instrument at a table through a window, 13½in. high. *(Christie's)* **$28,100**

A fine large famille verte dish, Kangxi, vividly enameled in the center with two ladies in long robes with flowing sashes seated by a bench on a garden terrace beside plants and pierced rockwork, the large roundel enclosed at the rim by a richly-colored trellis-pattern band reserved with six cartouches enclosing Scholars' Objects between brackets, small rim frits and small chips, 15¼in. diameter. *(Christie's)* **$24,375**

A pair of black and white seated spaniels, Qianlong, modeled seated on their haunches and looking sharply to the right and left, each with its mouth slightly open and a bell on an iron-red collar around its neck, enameled with black patches of varying size, 6½in. high. *(Christie's)* **$8,000**

A Haniwa standing figure, Tumulus period (250-552 AD), the columnar figure of a female shaman standing with outstretched hands, her oval face surmounted by a butterfly-shaped headdress and wearing a round bead necklace and loop earrings, 35⅝in. high.

This is a figure of a female shaman (in Japanese shamanism, good and evil spirits can be influenced by the ministrations of priestesses).

Although many Haniwa figures can be identified as male by their armor and swords, more subtle clues indicate the female nature of a figure. *(Christie's)* **$18,745**

A Swiss white metal novelty timepiece, La Cloche Frères, Paris Londres, first quarter 20th century, the rectangular case with basketwork engine-turned side and top panels, modeled in low relief to the front as an owl with colored glass eyes, the hinged rear door showing the owl from behind, on green hardstone base, white enamel Roman convex dial, blued hands, the inverted movement with vertically positioned lever escapement, 5in. high. *(Christie's)* **$10,672**

A Whieldon type model of an owl, perched upon a wedge shape rusticated base, with detailed plumage and brown eyes, circa 1760, 20.5cm.
(Tennants) **$16,669**

A cast-iron figure of a perched owl, American late 19th/early 20th century, cast in two pieces, the swell-bodied figure of a standing owl with prominent wing and feather detail, mounted on a rod in a black metal base. *(Sotheby's)* **$2,185**

Austrian owl-form cookie jar, 20th century, silver plated head and collar, glass eyes, clear glass jar, 9⁷/₈in. high.
(Skinner)   **$1,092**

An impressive Austrian carved and stained wood model of a long eared owl, 19th century, shown standing on a rocky outcrop, with detailed plumage and inset glass eyes, the head opening to a recess, 20½in.high. *(Christie's)*   **$5,692**

A pair of cast iron owl andirons, Rostand Manufacturing Company, Milford, Connecticut, circa 1920, each molded in the half-round depicting a seated owl with glass eyes and articulated ears, beak, body and tail with claw feet, on an arched twig support, stamped *407 E*, on the reverse, 15¼in. high.

A 1921 trade catalog of the Rostand Manufacturing Company, 'Brass and Iron Fireplace Fixtures' (Milford, Connecticut, 1921), shows an identical pair of andirons under catalog number 407, the same number stamped on the back of this pair. Listed at $10.00, the cast iron andirons were one of the most expensive items offered. *(Christie's)*   **$4,370**

Franz Bergman Viennese patinated and gilded bronze novelty figure of a long eared owl, the base in the form of two books, the figure opening by means of a button on the base to reveal a further gilded bronze figure of a nude female, signed, 7¾in. high.

(Lawrences) **$4,185**
▶

A Staffordshire slipware owl-jug and cover, 18th century, of lead-glazed red earthenware slip-decorated in cream and brown, the cover modeled as the owl's head with dark brown eyes set in wide cream sockets edged with dot borders beneath a raised ridge crest, the oviform body with allover scrambled combed decoration, the reverse with a short protruding tail below a loop handle, modeled perched on a circular waisted socle with two three-clawed feet, 9¼in. high. (Christie's) **$30,300**

A carved and painted pine owl, American, late 19th/early 20th century, the stylized figure of an owl with carved feathers and wings, fitted with glass eyes and standing on a stylized tree trunk, 18in. high. (Sotheby's) **$47,150**

A Clichy convolvulus (morning glory) weight, the white flower of trumpet form edged in brown and green, growing from a long curved green stalk, with a large leaf issuing from the stalk, set on a ground of fine white swirling latticinio, 2½in. diameter. *(Christie's)* **$23,000**

A French pedestal weight, Clichy, mid 19th century, the six concentric rows of assorted millefiori canes in shades of pink, lilac, green, claret, blue and white, including one row of green and white moss canes, another row with eleven pink and green roses. *(Christie's)* **$17,250**

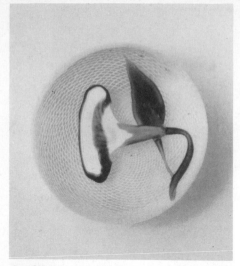

A Baccarat faceted garlanded horse weight, the clear glass set with an opaque white plaque decorated with an engraved blue horse trotting on a small blue grassy ground, with narrow blue rim, enclosed by a garland of alternating red and white and red, green and white millefiori canes, cut with top and six circular side printies, 3³/₈in. diameter. *(Christie's)* **$25,300**

A Ray Banford overlay basket weight, the clear glass set with a bouquet of shaded pink and white roses, set amongst numerous green leaf-tips growing from radiating stems about a central large pink blossom, overlaid in red and white and cut to form a basket, diamond-cut base, 3in. diameter. *(Christie's)* **$2,070**

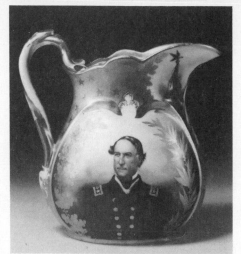

General Ulysses Simpson Grant (1822-85) captured Vicksburg, Mississippi, on July 4th, 1863, executing one of the boldest movements in modern warfare. Ten days later, Port Hudson surrendered and the Confederacy was severed in two, with the Union Army controlling the Mississippi River. When President Lincoln appointed him General-in-Chief, Grant devised a strategy to cut the Confederacy into fragments; to engage all its armies at the same time, and to destroy those armies by following them wherever they might go. On April 9th, 1865, General Robert E. Lee surrendered the Army of Northern Virginia on Grant's terms, concluding the Civil War. *(Sotheby's)* **$20,700**

A rare Paris porcelain pitcher with American portrait decoration, 1860-66, painted by Rudolph T. Lux, on one side of the baluster body with a portrait of Ulysses S. Grant and on the reverse with a portrait of Admiral David G. Farragut, each between gilt oak and laurel boughs within a gilt scroll-edged cartouche reserved on a gilt ground patterned with vermiculation and stars and further reserved on the front and spout with a three-quarter-length figure of Liberty holding a billowing American flag and below her left arm signed *LUX.*, 8³/8in. high.

Admiral David Glasgow Farragut (1801-70) was appointed to command the West Gulf Blockading Squadron in early 1862 with orders to reduce the defenses guarding New Orleans. In April 1862 he ran his ships past the forts defending the Crescent City, destroyed eleven Confederate vessels and took New Orleans. He then continued up the Mississippi River and passed the defenses of Vicksburg before returning to blockade duty in the Gulf. By the end of 1862, Farragut held the whole of the Gulf coast within the limits of his command except for Mobile. In August 1864 he led his fleet against the defenses at the entrance to Mobile Bay, forcing his way over the mines, inspiring his men with his famous cry: *Damn the torpedos*, Mobile Bay was the crowning event of Farragut's naval career.

A good pair of Napoleon III faience and gilt-bronze vases, Paris, circa 1870, each with a cover with a pineapple finial, the body painted with cherubs and female dieties, indistinctly signed *Maxant*, the foliate cast handles hung with swags of laurel leaves, on a trumpet foot, 120cm high including covers. *(Sotheby's)* **$50,554**

Pearlware was the name given in 1780 by Josiah Wedgwood to a whitened version of his celebrated creamware which he had just developed successfully.

This was made by adding a touch of blue coloring to the body. It could be just as thin as porcelain, and formed an excellent background for blue printing, enabling it to complete favorably with Chinese wares. It was quickly adopted by many other potteries, and became extremely popular in the late 18th/19th centuries.

A Staffordshire pearlware figure of a lion, one front paw resting on a ball, and picked out in iron red and black, the green glazed round base molded with leaf scrolls and picked out in blue, yellow, puce and red, 15.2cm. high.
(Dreweatt Neate)   **$1,237**

A Yorkshire pearlware figure of a spotted horse, standing four square, with turned head and black, green, blue and claret coloring, on a stepped rectangular green and blue base, 19th century, 43cm. high.
(Tennants)   **$13,940**

A pearlware group of a tiger and hind, the tiger dragging the hind by the neck in its jaws, 14½in. wide, early 19th century.
(Christie's)   **$14,168**

A rare Ralph Wood, Junior pearlware portrait bust of George Washington, circa 1800, finely modeled wearing a yellow waistcoat, open to reveal a white jabot beneath an iron-red jacket, on a marbled waisted socle base, impressed title on the back of the base, impressed *Ra.Wood/Burslem* inside base, 10in. high.
(Sotheby's)   **$1,380**

An early child's pedal car with bell in excellent original condition; wooden frame chassis with steel springs, adjustable seat height, wheels with solid tires; original red paint with gold lining, circa 1910. *(Christie's)* **$4,140**

A Mors wooden-framed, pressed tin ▶ pedal car, red livery with yellow lines, 114cm. long, circa 1907. *(Auction Team Köln)* **$2,490**

◀ A '7' early American tinplate pedal car by American National, hand painted in red and black, with cream and green trim, 114cm. long, circa 1910. *(Auction Team Köln)* **$2,587**

Bentley 4.5 liter 'Blower' – An electrically-powered model child's car by Meynell-Phillips; with metal chassis and glass fiber body, propulsion by 12 volt electric motor rear mounted; features include 4 wheel brakes, forward and reverse speeds, wire-spoke wheels, electric lamps and horn, circa 1960s, limited edition, 80in. long. *(Christie's)* **$3,562**

A George III mahogany serpentine Pembroke table, the rectangular twin-flap top above a frieze drawer and simulated drawer to the reverse, on scrolled cabriole legs headed by anthemions and joined by a serpentine X-stretcher, on scrolled feet with brass caps and leather castors, 35¼in. wide open.

The usefulness of such Pembroke tables is discussed in Messrs. A. Hepplewhite & Co's, The Cabinet-maker and Upholsterer's Guide, London, 1788, which also provided patterns for a table-top with bowed front and corners and a serpentined leg with voluted foot.

(Christie's) **$49,634**

◄

A Chippendale carved mahogany Pembroke table, labeled by John Townsend (1733-1809), Newport, 1782-1795, the rectangular top flanked by hinged leaves above a conforming frame fitted with one long drawer with printed paper label with cockbeaded surround over an applied ovolo molding above a cross-hatched frieze above pierced brackets, on stop-fluted legs, appears to retain original brasses, 36¾in. wide.

An important addition to ongoing scholarship on the work of John Townsend, this Chippendale Pembroke table is one of only two such tables bearing the label of late eighteenth-century Newport's most celebrated craftsman.

Other Pembroke tables labeled by John Townsend, indicate that the cabinetmaker used the same basic form and construction methods, but altered his decorative techniques to suit the pocketbook of his clients or to adapt to changing styles.

(Christie's) **$68,500**

Waterman's, a black hard rubber 'Smallest Pen in the World' safety pen, with small gold nib, American, circa 1920, in blue card Waterman box, the safety version of this pen is much rarer than the eyedropper version. *(Bonhams)* **$8,400**

Mont Blanc, a no. 6F safety pen with Toledo work overlay, the overlay with panels of elegantly sinuous foliate and floral designs, surrounded by a geometric linear design with square and circular 'punched' pattern columns, and Mont Blanc 'M' nib, German, circa 1920s.
(Bonhams) **$6,400**

Omas, a silver pearl celluloid colored double pen, with scissor mechanism, two pump filling reservoirs allowing the user to write with two different colors of ink, original nibs, Italian, circa 1945. *(Bonhams)* **$5,600**

A Bion-pattern fountain pen, the brass body of tapered cylindrical form decorated with red hard wax and copper foil glass, both incorporating black 'dragged' lines, the cap with central threaded pin screwing within the nib retaining tube, quill nib, the barrel retaining original cork and thread bound stopper covered by a screw-on seal terminal with intaglio lion, closed 125mm. Probably French, but possibly English or Italian, mid 18th century.

The Bion is an important and extremely rare pen. It is the earliest fountain pen where the pen itself survives (rather than just a written description alone) and was a great leap forward from the quill pen towards the fountain pen we know today.

It was made throughout most of the eighteenth century, the great age of scientific instrument making. Its inventor remains a mystery, and so this long-lasting design is named after the talented mathematical-engineer and scientific instrument maker Nicholas Bion (1652-1733). *(Bonhams)* **$3,024**

Cardeilhac, tureen and cover, circa 1925, silver-colored metal, the deep bowl ringed with silver-colored metal band joining the large shaped ivory handles and bound by four sets of two rings, set on openwork base intersected by ivory, the slightly domed cover with ivory handle bound by four rings. Underside of bowl with maker's mark and *Cardeilhac Paris*, underside of foot with maker's mark and *Made in France*, 9½in. wide.
(Christie's) **$24,006**

A rare pewter flask, Johann Christopher Heyne, Lancaster, Pennsylvania, 1715–81, the removable thimble-sized lid threaded above a circular line-incised vessel. *(Sotheby's)* **$10,350**

A Modernist cocktail shaker, designed by Silvia Stave, manufactured by Hallberg, Sweden, circa 1930, spherical with loop handle, 'T' grip on cover, inner strainer, 7¼in. high.
(Christie's) **$10,624**

A pewter creamer, attributed to William Will, 1742–98, Philadelphia, active 1742–98, baluster form, with curved and beaded spout and spurred double scroll handle, on beaded and molded plinth, 4½in. high.
(Christie's) **$6,900**

Liberty & Co. pewter owl pitcher, incised decoration with ceramic blue eyes, impressed *English Pewter Made By Liberty & Co., 035*, 8in. high.
(Skinner) **$373**

A rare pewter chalice attributed, to Johann Christopher Heyne, Lancaster, Pennsylvania, 1715-81, the molded rim above a tapering body on a bulbous ring turned support, the molded dome base below on a circular foot, 8¾in. high.
(Sotheby's) **$41,400**

◀

A rare and important pewter flagon, Johann Christopher Heyne, Lancaster, Pennsylvania, 1715–81, the domed lid with molded thumb tab and heart-shaped spout, cover above a flaring beaded body, mounted with a strap handle raised on three cherubic mask feet, height 11½in.
(Sotheby's) **$145,500**

A hand turned tinfoil phonograph with brass mandrel on steel threaded arbor, 15in. wide. *(Christie's)* **$5,630**

◀ A completely unknown and undocumented Danish tinfoil phonograph by Christian Frederik Sørensen, 1882, of very attractive design, exactly copying Thomas Edison's first recording system. After Edison's invention in 1878 some tinfoil phonographs did come on to the market in various countries, but none as well made as this. *(Auction Team Köln)*

$16,500

Edison Home phonograph, Model A, the first Edison cylinder player with the banner emblem, 1898. *(Auction Team Köln)* **$1,320**

Jacques-Henri Lartigue, 'Premier vol de Gabriel Voisin de l'Aeroplane 'Archdeacon', Merlimont', 1904, gelatin silver contact print, $2^5/16$ x 2½in., red crayon and blue ink cropping lines on recto, dated annotated and with 'sun' monogram added later in ink on verso.

This first flight by Gabriel Voisin was taken from the dunes at Merlimont. Flying was a great obsession of Lartigue and his family, especially his older brother Maurice, nicknamed 'Zissou'. Lartigue describes this great fascination in his diary: *'There is one thing all of us want to do...it's an idea we all dream and talk about...an idea that Zissou is absolutely obsessed with...to get up in the air!' (Christie's)* **$18,860**

Benjamin Brecknell Turner (1815–94), 'Scotch Firs, Hawkhurst', circa 1852, albumen print from a waxed paper negative, 11¼ x 15³/8in., mounted on two-tone card titled in pencil on mount.

Turner, an amateur photographer, was and is recognised as one of the great photographers of the 1850s, the decade in photographic history when experiment and experience coalesced to produce many of the finest photographs of the nineteenth century. He was recognised alongside Roger Fenton for his landscape and rural photographs. This picture was one of two which he exhibited at the Society of Arts in 1852 and according to family tradition it was so admired by Prince Albert that Turner presented him with a copy. *(Christie's)* **$35,834**

Jacques-Henri Lartigue, 'Renée Perle allongée sur un canapé, Paris', 1931, gelatin silver print, 2³/8 x 3½in., annotated later on verso.

Lartigue remembers how he was struck by the beauty of Renée Perle, a model at Doeillet, who was to become his mistress for a short period from 1930–32. *'She is beautiful. The small mouth with the full painted lips! The ebony black eyes!... Renée! She is tender, devoted, passionate... Renée is beautiful; she is tender; she is everything I desire. I live in a dream'.*
(Christie's) **$22,632**

Horst P. Horst, Coco Chanel, Paris, 1937, printed later, platinum palladium print, 15¼ x 14¾in., signed in pencil in margin, numbered *2/10* on verso, matted, framed.
(Christie's) **$12,259**

Gustave Le Gray (1820–62), 'Brig on the Water', 1856, albumen print, 12⁵/8 x 16¼in., the photograph's red facsimile signature stamp on recto, mounted on card, matted.

A fine print of Le Gray's masterpiece, a photograph which was the subject of great international acclaim and speculation when it was first exhibited in London at the Photographic Society's annual exhibition in December 1856, and in Paris at the second exhibition of the Société Française de Photographie in the following year.

Since the invention of the medium, photographers had bemoaned the fact that it was impossible to achieve successful views including sky detail.
(Christie's) **$93,225**

Robert Doisneau (1912-1994), 'Le Baiser de l'Hotel de Ville', 1950s, printed later, gelatin silver print, image size 9½ x 11¾in., signed in ink in margin, titled and dated in ink on verso, matted.
(Christie's) **$3,772**

Jacques-Henri Lartigue, Femme aux Renards ou Arlette Prevost dite 'Anna la Pradvina' avec ses chiens Cogo et Chichi (Avenue des Acacias), Bois de Boulogne', 1911, gelatin silver print, 2⅝ x 4⅜in., later signed, dated and annotated and with photographer's ink credit stamp on verso.

In a single image, Lartigue captures the essence of the Belle Epoque: the 'Femme aux Renards' represents all the luxuries and frivolities, the ornaments and eccentricities which soon gave way to restraint with the start of the war. The horse-carriage on the far right of the frame and the automobile coming in on the left make reference to the end of one era and the beginning of another. This image, taken at the age of seventeen, masterfully illustrates Lartigue's unique ability as a photographer. First and foremost, however, Lartigue was an observer of life: *'Women... everything about them facinates me - their dresses, their scent, the way they walk, the make-up on their faces, their hands full of rings, and, above all, their hats'. (Christie's)* **$74,620**

Jacques-Henri Lartigue, 'L'envol de ma ▶
cousine Bichonade, (40, Rue Cortambert),
Paris', 1905, gelatin silver contact print, 2¹/8
x 2⁹/16in., red crayon and blue ink cropping
lines on recto, initialed in pencil, dated and
annotated later in ink on verso.

Richard Avedon refers to this well-
known image in his afterword in Lartigue,
Diary of a Century *'And the events he
photographs...so many of them are the
result of his own invention. He
creates...And that's the secret. Bichonade
didn't just jump down the stairs like that on
her way to...the Métro. It was Lartigue
who made her do that. And he was ten
years old at the time...And his suggestions
are rarely direct. They're oblique. They
come from impulses, not ideas. I'm sure
he didn't say 'Bichonade, jump down the
steps.' I'm sure he leaped down the step
himself and she followed him but by the
time she did, he was there with his
camera.'*
(Christie's)   **$30,176**

Julia Margaret Cameron, Thomas
Carlyle, 1867, albumen print 13 x
10in. , mounted on card, trimmed
to edge of print, matted.

Carlyle (1795–1881), born in
Scotland but later living in
Chelsea, London was best known
as an essayist (for the Edinburgh
Review) and historian. This
portrait was taken the year after
the death of his wife, Jane Baillie
(née Welsh), a descendant of John
Knox. She left a diary, discovered
and read by Carlyle in which she
described her suffering and
neglect as a result of his
absorption in his work. Publicly
perceived as a genius, his
Reminiscences, written the same
year and published unedited in
1881, showed him to be subject to
bouts of nervous depression and
bursts of temper. Cameron's
portrait, while showing an artistic
and powerful man, also hints at
this inner sadness or melancholy.
(Christie's)   **$15,088**

The 'science' of phrenology sprang to prominence in the late 18th century, when one Franz Josef Gall, a Viennese doctor, expounded the theory that the brain was divided into 46 abstract qualities, such as Amativeness, Conscientiousness, Combativeness, etc., and then proceeded to site these qualities on different parts of the brain's area. He further theorized that it was possible, by measuring the size of the area and any irregularities on a given skull, to gauge the under- or overdevelopment of the brain area beneath. So a man with a well developed Amative area would be likely to be a womanizer, and so on.

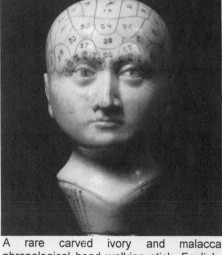

A rare carved ivory and malacca phrenological head walking stick, English, 19th century, the handle carved as a head with incised and numbered sections, over a tapered malacca shaft fitted with a metal tip. *(Sotheby's)* **$3,162**

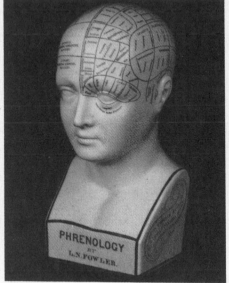

An extremely rare carved and painted wood phrenological head, American, 19th century, the head divided into sections, painted with black hair and eyebrows, red lips and flesh tones, the oval base inscribed *Phrenology.*, 15½in. high.

This is reputed to be one of only three known examples.
(Sotheby's) **$4,312**

An English pottery 'phrenology' bust developed by L. N. Fowler of Ludgate Circus, London, quarter-length, the cranium divided by black lines with printed labels, the rectangular base edged in blue, titled and inscribed, late 19th century, 30cm. high. *(Christie's)* **$825**

An unusual opaque glass phrenology head, mounted on a cast-iron ivy garland incorporating an inkwell, the inkwell and cover embossed *WASHINGTON MANUAL RASEE*, 6⁵/₈in. *(Christie's)* **$2,845**

An extremely rare painted plaster phrenological head, 19th century, a mustached man with head divided into numbered and lettered sections, wearing a bow-tie, on a stepped rectangular pedestal, 18½in. high. *(Sotheby's)* **$3,162**

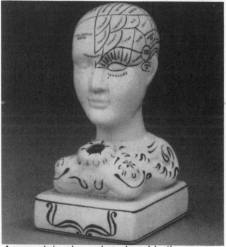

A rare molded plaster portrait bust phrenological head, stamped *Reuben W. Hoit, Boston*, 19th century, the head divided into numbered sections, the front of base inscribed *John Pallet* the back stamped *Manufactured by Reuben W. Hoit, Boston*, 13½in. high.
(Sotheby's) **$3,162**

A porcelain phrenology head in the manner of F.B. Bridges, the cranium outlined with the areas of the sentiments, on scroll and flower-form base, decorated in blue and modeled to serve as an ink and pen stand, on plinth base, 6in. high.
(Christie's) **$570**

A fine marquetry and ivory satinwood Steinway Grand Piano, circa 1904, overstrung with an 88 note compass, the case decorated with ivory inlaid oval medallions of classical figures, flanked by ribbon tied foliate swags and acanthus scrolls, the nameboard and keyboard lid inlaid with musical trophies and ribbon tied foliate swags, the stand with six square tapered legs inlaid with husk chains beneath ionic capitals and tied by solid stretchers and with a lyre shaped pedal support, 87in. long.*(Bonhams)* **$35,000**

◄
A Steinway & Sons ebonized baby grand piano, serial number 429699L, with a piano bench. *(Sotheby's)* **$14,950**

A marquetry, gilt-bronze porcelain and lapis lazuli upright piano by Declercq, Paris, circa 1865, the hinged top with a parquetry lattice ground, within thuya and bois satiné bandings, above a frieze centered by a jeweled panel, painted with lovers in landscapes, above further marquetry panels with musical emblems, ferns and birds, flanked by fluted uprights, headed by female busts, the sides with panels filled with scrolls. *(Sotheby's)* **$67,981**

A fine carved whale ivory and fruitwood pie crimper, probably American mid 19th century, having a gun pistol handle continuing to a woman's hand grasping a crimper inlaid with a band of fruitwood, 9in. long. *(Sotheby's)* **$2,500**

A fine and rare seahorse pie crimper, whale ivory, probably American, mid 19th century, the stylized figure of a seahorse with incised and painted black mane grasping a wheel in its forelegs, 6in. long. *(Sotheby's)* **$7,475**

An unusual carved whalebone and ivory pie crimper, probably American mid 19th century, having a shaped and faceted whalebone handle with contrasting dark wood spacers, fitted with a fluted wheel and a whale ivory terminus in the form of a clenched fist, 12in. long. *(Sotheby's)* **$3,000**

A fine and rare three-wheeled whale ivory pie crimper, probably American, mid 19th century, having a squared and shaped baluster handle sprouting bird's heads to which are fastened a pair of pie crimpers and a pricking wheel, the handle base incised with a rose blossom and bud stamp, 8¼in. *(Sotheby's)* **$5,175**

An unusual carved and incised pie crimper and pricker, probably American, mid 19th century, the elongated turned handle with incised red and green rings and spacers for contrasting wood continuing to a four-pronged pricker and fluted wheel, 10in. long. *(Sotheby's)* **$2,587**

An unusual inlaid and appliqued ebony and whale ivory crimper, probably American, mid 19th century, in the form of a lady's hand with frilled cuff and ebony base and fingers extended over a crimper with applied oak leaves, 8¾in. long. *(Sotheby's)* **$2,300**

◄ Figural carved wood pig-form footrest, America, 19th century, velvet covered body, felt ears, button eyes, 20in. long. *(Skinner)* **$1,265**

A fine carved and painted pine pig trade sign, American, late 19th century, fashioned from a pine plank with applied tin ears and wrought-iron corkscrew tail; painted black and white and suspended from two hangers, height of pig 29in. *(Sotheby's)* **$9,775**

►

A carved and painted pine carousel pig, attributed to Gustav Denzel, Philadelphia, third quarter 19th century, the full bodied figure of a pig with open jaws and upright ears wearing a red blanket and saddle decorated with ears of corn, 57in. long. *(Sotheby's)* **$5,175**

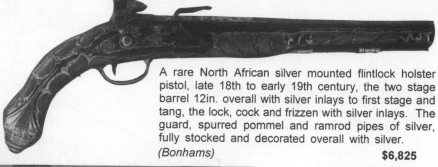

A rare North African silver mounted flintlock holster pistol, late 18th to early 19th century, the two stage barrel 12in. overall with silver inlays to first stage and tang, the lock, cock and frizzen with silver inlays. The guard, spurred pommel and ramrod pipes of silver, fully stocked and decorated overall with silver.
(Bonhams) **$6,825**

A very rare cased pair of Philadelphia style Deringer pocket pistols, the pistols and case inscribed *W.F. Cody 1866*, with .41 calibre 2¼in. rebrowned barrels.

William Frederick Cody (1846–1917) enlisted in the 7th Regiment Kansas Cavalry, in 1863. His subsequent one year contract (1867–68) with the Kansas Pacific Railway, to supply buffalo meat, earned Cody the famous soubriquet 'Buffalo Bill'.
(Sotheby's) **$17,250**

▲
A boxlock flintlock 'duck's foot' pistol, 7½in., turn off cannon type barrels 2¼in., numbered 1-4, frizzen spring sunk in breech top, throathole cock, foliate and trophy engraved frame with *Raith*, slab walnut butt with oval vacant silver escutcheons, steel trigger guard.
(Wallis & Wallis) **$3,360**

▶
A rare miniature teppo, the barrel signed *Hara Masatada*, Edo period, late 18th/early 19th century, the iron barrel well and boldly carved with two monkeys beside a silver waterfall, gold inlaid details, the black lacquered stock covered with karakusa in hiramakie, with a large Aoi mon in hiramakie and tsukegaki, silvered brass mounts with clouds in katakiri bori, the wood, ivory and iron ramrod signed *Sadayoshi*, 4¼in. long.
(Christie's) **$9,000**

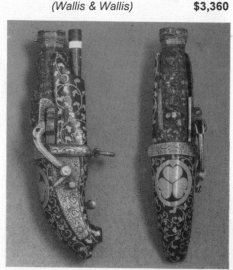

338

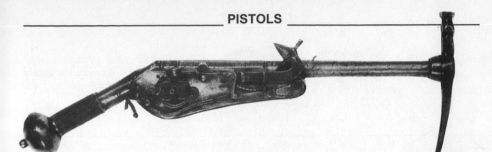

A rare German wheel-lock pistol combined with a war hammer, circa 1570–80, made entirely of steel, with two-stage barrel decorated with engraved and chiseled bands at respective ends of the faceted breech and fitted with a socketed hammer head sweated-on over the muzzle, flat rhomboid-shaped lock with boxed mechanism, external wheel retained by a pierced iron cover, safety-catch, sliding pan-cover with button release, and a rudimentary sear externally engaging the trigger carried slightly forward of the grip, the latter retaining its original wire binding, and fitted with a compressed faceted hollow pommel formed in two halves, 20½in. long. *(Sotheby's)* **$7,820**

A rare percussion box-lock 'Duck's Foot' four-shot pistol, by J. Richards, London, early 19th century, converted from flintlock, with turn-off barrels numbered from 5-8, signed brass action engraved with a martial trophy, iron trigger-guard and belt hook, vacant silver escutcheon, and rounded checkered walnut butt, Tower private proof marks. *(Bonhams)* **$2,400**

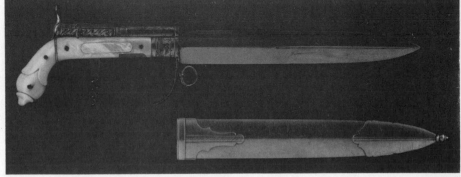

A rare European combination knife pistol, with a 9in. double edged blade, the nickel scabbard with incorporating top and lower chape, retaining an amount of original gilded finish with belt hook the single shot pistol of approximately .32 center fire caliber, with lift up breech of flute design, the pull down trigger in the form of a corkscrew, the nickel silver pistol grip with trap and mother of pearl sideplates, with singular lower knuckle guard, overall length 17½in., late 19th century. *(Bonhams)* **$7,312**

A fine carved plane, this European router in oak, 7 x 6in. is elaborately carved into the face of a ram, 17th/18th century.
(Tool Shop Auctions) **$2,393**

A significant yellow birch crown molding plane by Cesar Chelor, one of the most important, if not the most important New England plane maker. He was the black slave of Deacon Francis Nicholson (1683-1753) of Wrentham, Massachusetts, who is considered to be the first colonial planemaker.

Cesar Chelor quite possibly made many of the planes bearing the Francis Nicholson imprint. In his will recorded in 1753 Nicholson freed Chelor giving him his bedstead, bed and bedding, a variety of tools, ten acres of land and grazing and timber rights. Chelor married Judith Russell in 1758, raised a family and died intestate in 1784 leaving seventy seven pounds two shillings and sundry tools and lumber.

This magnificent plane was found twenty years ago by a furniture dealer in Natick, Massachusetts. It measures 13¹/8 x 4³/8in. it is stamped *CE:CHELOR LIVING IN WRENTHAM*. The 18th century repair to the handle using a dowel increases rather than decreases the charm of this fundamentally important representative of 18th century American planemaking.

There is a cusp on top of the handle, a feature which appears on only one other Chelor plane. Despite its obvious magnificence the astonishing feature of this plane by Chelor is its completely original condition, as though Cesar himself had only yesterday leaned across the workbench saying 'Here, try this one'.
(Tool Shop Auctions) **$13,944**

A 20½in. dovetailed Norris A1 jointer, rosewood infill. An exceptional example of this rare plane. *(Tool Shop Auctions)*
$2,623

An important 15c/early 16th century wrought iron musical-instrument maker's plane, 16th/early 17th century with toothing iron and protruding tote, 6¾ x 1½in. The correct style primitive wooden wedge appears to be original. This plane would have graced one of the luthier's' workshops of Europe, possibly even in Cremona itself. *(Tool Shop Auctions)*   **$2,021**

A rosewood handled center wheel plough plane with ivory tips by The Ohio Tool Company. *(Tool Shop Auctions)*
$10,043

A unique Stanley prototype block plane, 7⁷/₈ x 2¼in. This low angle block plane with no mouth adjustment has all of the recognisable Stanley construction features. It has 100% black japanning to the inside of the body and *STANLEY* cast into the vertical adjusting knob, similar to all early Stanley block planes.

There is strong evidence to suggest that these prototypes originated from an old R&D building that was demolished at the Stanley Tool Works in the mid 1970s.
(Tool Shop Auctions)   **$8,500**

A 16th/17th century musical-instrument maker's plane, 6 x 2³/₁₆in., complete with toothing iron and conceivably original wedge. *(Tool Shop Auctions)*   **$2,021**

A late 19th century walnut cased 'Penny-in-the-Slot' polyphon (thought to be by Nicole Freres of Leipzig) with 19.75in. diameter metal disks, twin 7.5in. steel combs with Sublime Harmony, contained in walnut case with deep molded cornice and arched glazed door with split turned columns to front, one drawer under, on associated stand of similar form, the fall-front door opening to reveal storage compartment for 21 spare disks, 27 x 67in. *(Canterbury)* **$10,000**

A late 19th century walnut cased 'Penny-in-the-Slot' polyphon (thought to be by Nicole Freres, Leipzig) with 15.5in. metal disks, twin 6.5in. steel combs with sublime harmony, contained in case with small paneled shelf above, arched glazed door with twin split turned columns to front and with conforming undertier with racks to hold 25 disks, on bun feet, 19½ x 64in. high. *(Canterbury)* **$6,000**

Jean-Théodore Perrache (1744-after 1789), Dr. Benjamin Franklin, facing right in russet-colored coat and waistcoat, frilled cravat, signed on the obverse *Perrache/fecit* and inscribed and dated on the counter enamel *Docteur/Benjamin Franklin/1786*, enamel on copper, oval, 1¾in. high.
(Christie's) **$30,912**

John Downman, A.R.A. (1750-1824), a very fine miniature of Sarah Hussey Delaval, Countess of Tyrconnel, facing left in pale gray riding habit, white waistcoat and scarf tied at corsage, black riding hat with black feather and rosette in her powdered curling hair en queue; ship and seascape background, oval 3¼in. high, silver-gilt frame.
(Christie's) **$86,700**

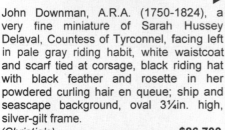

Alexander Cooper (c. 1605–1660), a fine and important portrait miniature of Lord William Craven, facing right in embroidered white doublet, wide lace collar, shoulder-length curling hair and mustache, signed with initials in gold *AC*, on vellum, oval, 1⅞in. high, silver gilt frame.

William Craven (1606–1697), eldest son of Sir William Craven, Lord Mayor of London, suceeded to his father's large fortune as a child. He was educated at Trinity College, Oxford and Middle Temple and spent much of his youth in military service abroad.
(Christie's) **$59,808**

John Smart (1742/43–1811), a very fine portrait miniature of Miss Twining, facing left in white dress with ruffled neckline, white sash, double strand of pearls in her short, curling brown hair, signed with initials and dated *JS/1801*, oval, 3¼in. high. *(Christie's)* **$50,232**

◄

Isaac Oliver (d.1617), a gentleman, facing right in embroidered white doublet with stiff white lace collar, beard and mustache; blue background within gold border, on vellum laid down on card, oval, 2in. high. *(Christie's)* **$30,912**

Moritz Michael Daffinger (1790-1849), a very fine miniature of a young lady called Princess Esterházy, facing left in long-sleeved blue riding habit with black braiding, long black scarf knotted around her neck, wearing a black silk top hat with flowing black gauze veil and white frilled muslin ribbons, parted brown hair; wooded landscape background, signed in pencil *Daffinger*, oval 3⁵/8in. high, fine gilt-bronze frame with beaded and corded borders and pierced ribbon-tie cresting.

An old inscription on the backing paper identifies the sitter as Fürstin Esterházy.

Portraits by Daffinger depicting sitters in riding habits are extremely rare.
(Christie's) **$54,740**

Jeremiah Meyer, R.A. (1735-1789), Anne Chambers, née Radcliffe (1741-1825), facing left in white dress with fichu, pink bows at corsage and wrist, large white bonnet tied with pink ribbon under her chin in her powdered curling hair, her left hand raised to her face; seated on a blue sofa, oval 3⁵/8in. high, gilt-copper mount.
(Christie's) **$43,000**

▶

John Smart (1742/43–1811), a very fine portrait miniature of a young lady, facing left in salmon pink dress, white underdress with double lace border, fichu, high-piled powdered curling hair signed with initials and dated *J S / 1788 / H*, oval, 2¼in. high, gold frame with bright cut border, the reverse with scrolling gold initials *AJ* on plaited hair ground, set in a hinged fausse-montre gold locket case.
(Christie's) **$38,640**

Richard Gibson (1615-1690), Elizabet Capell, Countess of Carnarvon, facing righ in low-cut white dress with yellow bodice diamond clasps at corsage, fur cloa draped around her shoulders, drop pea earrings and a rope of pearls entwined i her curled brown hair, signed, dated an inscribed on the reverse *Elizabeth Capell Countess of Carnarvon / 1657*, on vellun oval, 3³/16in. high, gilt-metal frame wit spiral cresting.
(Christie's) **$32,25**

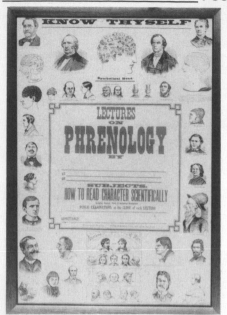

Cappiello, Leonetto (1875-1942), Le Petit Dauphinois, lithograph in colors, 1933, printed by Devambez, Paris, backed on linen, 46 x 62in. *(Christie's)* **$8,280**

Advertising poster, 19th century, the poster printed with the following information, *Lectures on Phrenology from Phrenological magazines Fowler & Wells Co. 18 E. 22 Street, New York. Know Thyself,* 29½in. x 19¾in. *(Sotheby's)* **$805**

Löffler, Berthold (1874-1960), Kunstschau, Wien 1908, lithograph in colors, 1908, printed by Alb. Berger, Wien. *(Christie's)* **$7,360**

Zero (Hans Schleger 1898-1976) Journalists, You Can Be Sure Of Shell, lithograph in colors, 1938, *printed by Waterlow & Sons, Ltd., London,* 29½ x 44½in. *(Christie's)* **$5,520**

On the Frontier, lithograph in colors, 1901 printed by Armitage and Ibbetson, England, linen backed, 86in. high. *(Christie's)* **$7,475**

O'Galop, (Marius Rossillon), Nunc est Bibendum, lithograph in colors, 1896, printed by Cornille & Serre, Paris, vertical and horizontal fold marks, backed on linen, 61 x 46in. *(Christie's)* **$10,120**

Cappiello, Leonetto, La Menthe-Pastille, lithograph in colors, circa 1929, printed by Devambez, Paris, backed on linen, 63 x 47½in. *(Christie's)* **$8,832**

J. Ringelfey, mountain skiing scene, lithograph in colors, circa 1890, backed on linen, 19½ x 15in. *(Christie's)* **$3,496**

Alphonse Mucha calendar 'Biscuits Lefevre-Utile', 1897, lithograph, laid on paper, signed in the block with *F. Champenois-Paris*, 60.5 x 44cm. *(Sotheby's)* **$5,762**

◄ A German inlaid priming-flask, circa 1580-1600, with wooden body of hemispherical section, the inner face inlaid with a circular pattern of engraved horn foliage involving large conventional flowerheads, the outer face inlaid with a close-set interlaced pattern of engraved bellflower spirals bordered by engraved horn cabling at the edge and enclosing a central horn warrior bust medallion, and fitted with blued iron arched top with standing nozzle, 4³/8in.
(Sotheby's) $3,450

A rare Dutch silver-mounted and ► tortoiseshell-veneered powder-flask, Leiden silver mark, late 18th/early 19th century, with truncated triangular body of oval section veneered over both sides with variegated tortoiseshell inset with chased and bright-cut silver plaques illustrating differing scenes from the chase, fitted with decorated silver reinforces at the edge, domed silver base chased with scrolling foliage inhabited by hounds and birds-of-prey, pierced with a central oval also veneered in tortoiseshell and inset with a chased crested silver coat-of-arms, flat silver top decorated en suite with the base and incorporating a short nozzle with long silver cap, 7¼in.
(Sotheby's) $4,000

◄ A fine and rare German ivory priming-flask incorporating a compass and sun-dial, late 17th century, with plain flat-sided circular body, the outer face inset with an ivory central roundel finely carved in high relief with a stag and a hind and faintly inscribed with a small device, probably that of the carver, the inner face with a shallow central cavity fitted with a simple compass of silver and blued iron, with engraved ivory lid incised on the inside with a graduated dial, the gnomon formed of a slender cord joined at a diagonal to the main body, and fitted with silver hinge and catch, with turned ivory nozzle, silver tap formed as a stylized bird and two silver rings for suspension, 3⁷/8in.
(Sotheby's) $4,887

An important Spanish gold-damascened iron priming-flask made for the Farnese family, Dukes of Parma and Piacenza, late 16th century, originally blued and now oxidised to russet, formed of two shallow convex halves and cut with a line of cabling over the seam, with short faceted nozzle formed with a chiseled oval molding, fitted with chiseled pivot cap and a pair of suspension rings chiseled as serpentine monsters, decorated throughout with Spanish Mannerist designs minutely and delicately drawn in the manner of Damianus De Nerve and damascened in gold on a lightly incised ground.
(Sotheby's) **$20,700**

A rare inlaid wooden powder-flask, mid 17th century, with fruitwood body strongly domed and fitted with a flat back inlaid with elaborate geometric patterns of contrasting strips of black and white horn, the back inlaid with a geometric border enclosing shaped arabesque cartouches in the middle, fitted with a chased silver plaque on the top, fruitwood nozzle with bone spout and turned plug retained by a chain fitted to a chased silver collar, 7½in.
(Sotheby's) **$3,000**

A fine German carved ivory powder-flask, third quarter of the 17th century, perhaps Schwäbisch Gmünd, of circular convex form filled on one side with a silver medallion cast in relief with a crested and mantled coat-of-arms within a laurel wreath, the reverse side filled with a flat ivory plaque finely engraved with a South German landscape incorporating a figure in contemporary dress with hounds and a shot hare, the sides delicately carved in relief with a finely drawn narrow circular frieze of bears, stags, boar, lions and wolves all entwined in combat with hounds, 4⁷/8in. The quality and delicacy of the ivory is suggestive of the Maucher workshops in Schwäbisch Gmünd.
(Sotheby's) **$6,900**

Art Deco found one of its most vivid expressions in the bronze and ivory, or chryselephantine, figures of F Preiss. Virtually nothing is known about Preiss, save that he was probably born in Vienna. Even his forename is in doubt. He is generally known as Ferdinand, though an Ideal Home Exhibition Catalog of the time refers to him as Frederick, which is probably simply an anglicization of Friedrich. His work, which appeared in the 20s and 30s, was closely copied by one Professor Otto Poerzl of Coburg, so closely in fact that there has been speculation that they may by one and the same. His figures were distributed in Britain by the Phillips and MacConnal Gallery of Arts, which published an illustrated catalog with model numbers. They chiefly featured classical and modern nudes, children, some nude and some clothed, and dancers. The ivory is always beautifully carved, and the subjects have sweet, pretty faces, and graceful arms and hands. The bronze is usually cold-painted in cool colors such as silver, blue and gray, and while the classical nudes can be somewhat stilted, the modern counterparts are lithe and vibrant.

Most lively of all are, however, the Olympic figures, a series including golfers, tennis players, skaters and javelin throwers. They glorify physical prowess and the body beautiful, enthusiasms which came to be hijacked by the Nazis in their preoccupation with the physical superiority of the Aryan master race. Preiss captured this so well that, rightly or wrongly, suspicion has always abounded that he was an adherent of the movement.

'Culotte Girl', a bronze and ivory figure, cast from the model by Ferdinand Preiss, 1930s, the young woman wearing culottes, cold-painted with metallic mauve, standing with her hands in her pockets, green onyx base, 13³/8in. high, base engraved *F. Preiss. (Christie's)* **$13,972**

'Male Tennis Player', a bronze and ivory figure, cast from the model by Ferdinand Preiss, 1930s, the male figure in cold-painted tennis attire, lunging forward to reach the ball, green and white onyx base, 9¾in. high, base engraved *F. Preiss. (Christie's)* **$21,252**

'Spring Awakening', a bronze and ivory figure cast form the model by Ferdinand Preiss, 1930s, the female figure in cold-painted wrap, with arms outstretched and head flung back, veined black marble base, 14¼in. high, signed in the maquette *F. Preiss*.

The classical appearance of this figure attests to new developments in dance in the early twentieth century, in particular the impact of Isadora Duncan's methods whose focus on freedom of movement with a deliberate return to flowing classical dress revolutionized the modern dance movement.

Also known as Invocation, Spring Awakening was marketed in the 1930s in London by the Phillips & MacConnal Gallery of Fine Arts at 16 Conduit Street where it was sold for 21 guineas. *(Christie's)* **$32,844**

◄

'Flame Leaper', a bronze and ivory figure cast form the model by Ferdinand Preiss, 1930s, the female dancer in silvered bikini costume across cold-painted flames, holding torches, black marble base, 13¾in. high, base engraved *F. Preiss*, circular foundry mark *PK*.

Flame Leaper was marketed in the 1930s in London by the Phillips & MacConnal Gallery of Fine Arts at 16 Conduit Street where it was sold for 24 guineas. *(Christie's)* **$67,200**

Paul Revere (1735–1818), The Bloody Massacre Perpetuated in King Street, Boston on March 5th 1770 by a party of the 29th Rgt, engraving with hand-coloring 1770, on laid paper, watermark Strasburg Lily with pendant initials *LVG*, a good impression of this extemely rare print, second (final) state, with a narrow margin at bottom, trimmed on or just inside the platemark on the other three sides, 10½ x 9in.

The Bloody Massacre is one of the earliest political prints in America and depicts a pivotal moment in the young country's struggle for independence. A group of British soldiers, taunted by a small mob of patriots, opened fire on the civilians in an act of confusion that was later seen as outright murder. Five men died at the scene.

Paul Revere learned the art of printmaking through his skills as a silversmith. Like the fifteenth century goldsmiths before him, who developed engraving and etching, Revere drew an easy parallel between chasing silver and engraving copper plates. His composition comes from Henry Pelham, who had asked Revere's opinion on his engraved depiction of the historical moment. Revere took the composition and proceeded to publish his own print, well ahead of Pelham's and only a few weeks after the incident. Naturally, Pelham was enraged and called Revere's actions 'dishonorable'.

Revere's engraving, based as it is on Pelham's, depicts the British soldiers as executioners: they stand stiffly in line and fire at the crumpling mass of unarmed Bostonians, their red uniforms and grim expressions suggesting devils emerging from clouds of smoke. A small dog, long the symbol of obedience and loyalty, stands ominously in the foreground, seemingly oblivious to the violent scene behind him.
(Christie's) **$57,500**

▲
Scriven and Gaugain, after Hennet, Robert Gregson, a fine and rare full-length stipple engraving, framed and glazed, 17¾ x 13¾in.

Bob Gregson, 'the Poet Laureate to Pugilism', composed lively and popular songs and poems on fighting and fighters. In the early years of the nineteenth century, he fought John Gully twice and Tom Cribb once for the title of Champion of England. He lost all three bravely.
(Sotheby's) **$712**

Steinlen, Theophile Alesandre (1859-1923), Le Journal. La Traite Des Blanches, lithograph in colors, circa 1899, printed by Charle Verneau, Paris, vertical and horizontal fold marks, 73 x 47in.
(Christie's) **$3,312**

N. Currier (Publisher), 'The Road, - winter', hand colored lithograph, a fine, fresh impression, with touches of gum arabic, on stone by Otto Knirsch, 1853, 17½ x 26¼in. *(Sotheby's)* **$36,996**

Audubon, John James, American ▶ White Pelican. *[plate CCCXI from* Birds of America. *London: J.J. Audubon, 1827-1836]*.

Broadside 38 x 25¼in. Hand-colored engraved plate with etching and aquatint by Robert Havell, Jr. after John James Audubon on J. Whatman 183[?]. *(Sotheby's)* **$74,000**

Toulouse-Lautrec, Henri de, Elles, lithograph in colors, 1896, CP. or GP monogram lower right, on linen, 25 x 19½in. *(Christie's)* **$20,240**

Cheltenham township was one of the earliest surveyed divisions in the Philadelphia area. Originally settled in 1681 by 14 pioneers from England who had been granted land by William Penn, the township was shown on Thomas Holme's map of 'The Improved Part of the Province of Pensilvania (sic) in America' published in London in 1687.
(Sotheby's) **$519,500**

The Jacob Meyers fine and rare Queen Anne carved and figured walnut open armchair, Philadelphia, Pennsylvania, circa 1750, the serpentine line-incised crest centering a scrolled leaf and ruffle-carved device flanked by volute-carved ears, the brilliantly figured vasiform splat and trapezoidal slip seat below flanked by shaped arms, with scrolled knuckle hand-holds on incurvate arm supports.

This chair was passed down in the family form Jacob Meyer who settled in Pennsylvania in the first half of the 18th century. The chair went to Jacob his son who married Margaret Castor. From that time on, the chair has been passed through the women named Margaret....The son, Jacob, served in the Revolutionary War under General George Washington and changed the spelling of the family name to Myers after the death of his father. The family was located in Cheltenham, Pennsylvania, and was intertwined with the Rowland family who began a shovel works there in 1795.

The Rowland family had come to Pennsylvania with William Penn on the ship Welcome and received a land grant.

▲

A very fine rare Queen Anne carved and figured walnut compass-seat side chair, Philadelphia, circa 1750, the serpentine shell and volute carved crest above a pierced acanthus and volute carved vasiform splat flanked by rounded stiles, the slip seat below within a conformingly-shaped frame, on ruffle, shell and leaf carved cabriole legs ending in panelled trifid feet, height of seat 16⅞in., height of crest 42½in.
(Sotheby's) **$134,500**

Pieced and appliqued quilt 'Remember the Maine', Mary Dunn Leroy, Lakewood, New York, circa 1898, the field of four American flags with appliqued letters reading '*Our heroes*', '*Dewey, Sampson and Hobson*', the outer border in concentric red and white stripes, blue center border with appliqued stars, 70 x 70in.
(Skinner) **$6,325**

A fine pieced wool and cotton ▶ Amish quilt, probably Mifflin County, Pennsylvania, late 19th/early 20th century, composed of slate blue, dusty rose, olive green and black patches arranged in a variation of the Nine Patch pattern, the field heightened with feather, cable and diagonal line quilting, 80 x 84in.
(Sotheby's) **$9,200**

A fine and important appliqued and stuffed album quilt attributed to Mary Evans, Baltimore, Maryland, 1850, centering a large square reserve with reverse appliqued red feather border enclosing a flower-filled basket surrounded by a be-ribboned floral wreath, the inner border with twelve pictorial squares including flower baskets and urns, 90 x 90in.
(Christie's) **$132,000**

A rare 1937 Emerson Cathedral radio in bright red, yellow veined imitation onyx plastic cabinet.
(Academy Auctioneers)
$7,546

Stewart Warner 1920s Model 300 radio set complete with 415 speaker, 21in. high. *(Lyle)* **$735**

◄ A green Ekco circular casing, Type AD 65, with (distorted) semi-circular dial, circular central speaker grille with three chromium-plated strips, 15½in. diameter, and a G.E.C. speaker cone.
(Christie's) **$5,265**

Emor Globe radio, circa 1947, in a chrome plated case and black metal stand, 43in. high.
(Lyle) **$1,475**

Radiosonanz Type DR12 two tube Audion receiver with RTV stamp of 8.4.25.
(Auction Team Köln)
$4,280

A Loewe OE 333 local receiver, circa 1926.
(Auction Team Köln)
$2,950

A Philco 444 radio, 15in. high.
(Lyle) **$400**

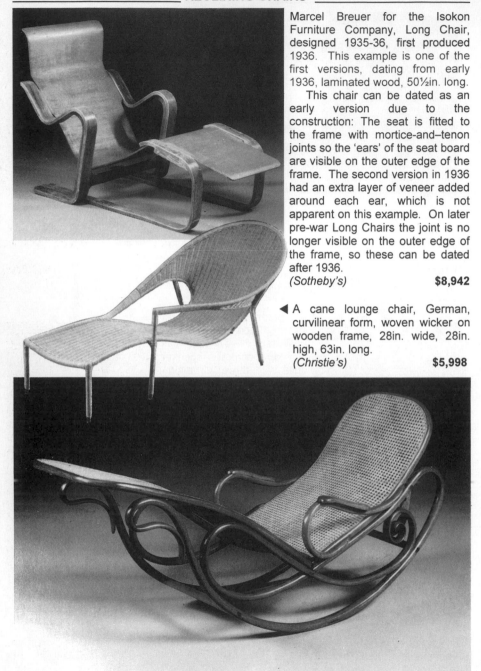

Marcel Breuer for the Isokon Furniture Company, Long Chair, designed 1935-36, first produced 1936. This example is one of the first versions, dating from early 1936, laminated wood, 50½in. long.

This chair can be dated as an early version due to the construction: The seat is fitted to the frame with mortice-and–tenon joints so the 'ears' of the seat board are visible on the outer edge of the frame. The second version in 1936 had an extra layer of veneer added around each ear, which is not apparent on this example. On later pre-war Long Chairs the joint is no longer visible on the outer edge of the frame, so these can be dated after 1936.
(Sotheby's) **$8,942**

◄ A cane lounge chair, German, curvilinear form, woven wicker on wooden frame, 28in. wide, 28in. high, 63in. long.
(Christie's) **$5,998**

A rare bentwood and cane rocking reclining chair, no. 7500, manufactured by Thonet, circa 1880. The adjustable back hinged in the center. This model was featured in the Gebrüder Thonet catalogs of 1888. *(Christie's)* **$35,983**

Redware is the original pottery of the American colonies. Its manufacture began in the early 1600s, lasting well into the 19th century, with a potshop in just about every village.

Redware was cheap and easy to make. Its basic color came from the presence of iron oxide in the clay, which, when fired produced various red tones. It could however be given various other colors by additions to the glaze. While imperfections in the clay often provided interesting natural decorations, the prevalent form of intentional decoration was the use of slip.

One of the earliest recorded potteries was at Jamestown, Virginia, which was operating in 1625.

Carolina and Georgia were other states with a strong pottery tradition. Most important of all, however, was Pennsylvania, where the Amish carried slip decoration one stage further to make intricate sgrafitto designs.

A rare slip-decorated glazed redware tray, Pennsylvania, 19th century, of rectangular form inscribed with the legend *Money Wanted*, 14½in. wide. *(Sotheby's)* **$23,000**

A very rare pair of figural red-ware lions, attributed to John Bell, Waynesboro, Pennsylvania, mid-19th century, depicting a standing figure of a male and female, each with alert expressions, perked ears and open mouths, with articulated manes, hind quarters and tails in their backs, standing on an oval floral-decorated base, glazed all over in a mottled brown and yellow color, 6½in. high. *(Sotheby's)* **$9,775**

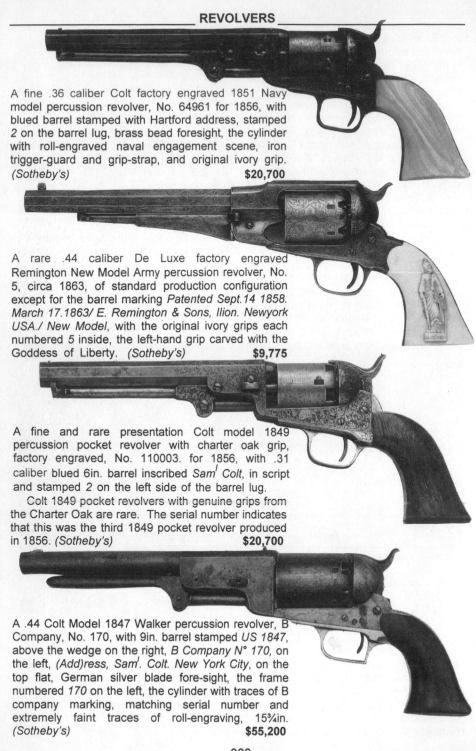

A fine .36 caliber Colt factory engraved 1851 Navy model percussion revolver, No. 64961 for 1856, with blued barrel stamped with Hartford address, stamped 2 on the barrel lug, brass bead foresight, the cylinder with roll-engraved naval engagement scene, iron trigger-guard and grip-strap, and original ivory grip. *(Sotheby's)* **$20,700**

A rare .44 caliber De Luxe factory engraved Remington New Model Army percussion revolver, No. 5, circa 1863, of standard production configuration except for the barrel marking *Patented Sept.14 1858. March 17.1863/ E. Remington & Sons, Ilion. Newyork USA./ New Model*, with the original ivory grips each numbered 5 inside, the left-hand grip carved with the Goddess of Liberty. *(Sotheby's)* **$9,775**

A fine and rare presentation Colt model 1849 percussion pocket revolver with charter oak grip, factory engraved, No. 110003. for 1856, with .31 caliber blued 6in. barrel inscribed *Sam[l] Colt*, in script and stamped 2 on the left side of the barrel lug.

Colt 1849 pocket revolvers with genuine grips from the Charter Oak are rare. The serial number indicates that this was the third 1849 pocket revolver produced in 1856. *(Sotheby's)* **$20,700**

A .44 Colt Model 1847 Walker percussion revolver, B Company, No. 170, with 9in. barrel stamped *US 1847*, above the wedge on the right, *B Company N° 170*, on the left, *(Add)ress, Sam[l]. Colt. New York City*, on the top flat, German silver blade fore-sight, the frame numbered *170* on the left, the cylinder with traces of B company marking, matching serial number and extremely faint traces of roll-engraving, 15¾in. *(Sotheby's)* **$55,200**

This is a colorless variety of quartz, crystalline silica, which from the time of the Renaissance became popular in Europe for making drinking cups, flagons, caskets and jewelry. These usually would be silver or gold mounted.
Rock crystal was also a popular material for watch cases in the 17th century.

An important Viennese Renaissance style rock crystal, silver and enamel centerpiece compôte, last quarter 19th century, attributed to Herman Ratzersdorfer, the rock crystal center bowl and cover in the form of a mythical creature having the head of a horse, the tail of a dragon, and the wings of an eagle, the mounted polychromed enamel and silver rims depicting stylized scrolls, flowers and winged creatures framing the ornately etched rock crystal body decorated with scales, scrolls and figures of eagles, all above a baluster standard and domed base, bearing similar decorations, 18¼in. high, 19in. long.

The firm of Herman Ratzersdorfer was founded in 1843, producing gold, silver, enamel and rock crystal in the Neo-Renaissance taste. He began showing his rock crystal and enamel pieces when he participated in the 1871 London Exhibition, and then went on to participate in the 1873 Exposition Universelle in Vienna, and the 1878 and 1889 Expositions de Paris.

Numerous European silversmiths were creating objets de vertu in the Renaissance Revival taste of the late nineteenth century, among them Herman Böhm, Politzer, Karl Paxrainer, B. Neresheimer, and D. Giobbe, all of whom drew upon exotic natural materials such as rock crystal, hardstones and enamels. The resurgence of the use of rock crystal among Viennese silversmiths had much to do with the unification of Germany in 1871, when the contents of the Hungarian mines became accessible.

(Christie's) **$86,100**

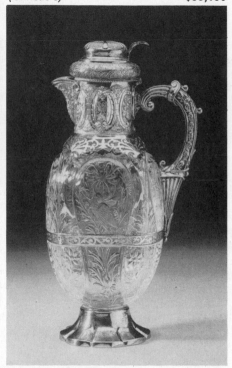

A Stevens and Williams 'rock crystal' silver-gilt mounted wine ewer, circa 1900, the mounts marked for Sheffield, 1909, with maker's marks for Walter and Charles Sissons, probably engraved by John Orchard, the slender lobed oviform body deeply cut with birds perched on flowering branches divided by flowers, the hinged domed silver-gilt cover chased with an encircling garland, on a spreading foliate foot, 12¼in. high.

(Christie's) **$7,682**

A fine and rare painted and smoke-decorated plank-seat rocking chair, Pennsylvania, circa 1820, the horizontal crest flanked by projecting 'bamboo'-turned stiles centering six similarly turned spindles, the compass-form plank-seat below, on turned flaring 'bamboo' legs joined by stretchers, on shaped rockers with scrolled terminals, painted in tones of green, red, and white on a yellow field, height of seat 16½in.
(Sotheby's) **$8,625**

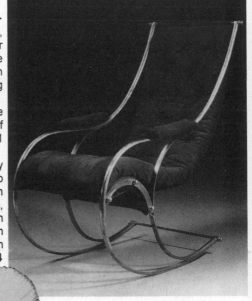

A Victorian steel and brass rocking chair, after a design by R. W. Winfield & Co. for the Great Exhibition of 1851, the serpentine frame flanking a buttoned green suede back and seat with conforming padded arms.

A rocking chair of essentially the same design was shown by Winfield and Co. of Birmingham at the Great Exhibition of 1851 as part of a large display of metal furniture.

The design may have been inspired by an even earlier model by John Porter who published a very similar chair in an advertisement for metal garden furniture, circa 1839. The simplicity of the design ensured that the chair remained in production by Winfield well into the 20th century. *(Christie's)* **$4,904**

An Italian silvered (Mecca) grotto rocking chair, 19th/20th century, the back and seat in the shape of a scallop-shell and with arms in the shape of a scrolling fish, on seahorse-shaped supports and on outstretched fish-shaped rocking rails, joined by reeded and scalloped stretchers.
(Christie's) **$6,250**

Rootwood covered incense box, tri-foot base and root-form finial, subtle depiction of a tenuki bear emerging from the left side, 8in. high. *(Eldred's)* **$300**

A tall rootwood sculpture, 18th/19th century, cut off at the very base of the stem and to be displayed upside down and seen from one side, the gnarled and knotty twisting roots with open areas, polished to a honey brown tone, the reverse carved to be flat, 17½in. high.
(Christie's) **$1,495**

A small 'four-sided' rootwood sculpture, 18th/19th century, to be displayed upside down and viewed from all sides, the gnarled roots forming a twisted shape as they grew, the polished wood of pale and darker honey tones, 10¼in. high.
(Christie's) **$3,220**

Royal Dux is the tradename of the Duxer Porzellanmanufaktur, which was established in 1860 in Dux, Bohemia, now Duchov, Czechoslovakia. It was noted at first for its portrait busts and extravagantly decorated vases, many of which were destined for the American market. From the 1920s onwards it produced Art Deco style figures, of single ladies, dancing couples etc. Marks include an *E* (for the proprietor Eichler) in an oval surrounded by *Royal Dux Bohemia* set on an embossed pink triangle.

A Royal Dux 'Bohemian' group in the form of a mounted cavalier with plumed hat, talking to a peasant girl holding water pitchers, set on an oval mound base, molded and painted with flowers, 41.5cm. high. *(Bearne's)* **$2,136**

A Royal Dux bust of a lady dressed in lace trimmed decolleté dress and wearing a ribboned hat, impressed tablet mark *454* and painted number *15*, applied pink triangle mark, height 56cm.
(Wintertons) **$2,640**

A Royal Dux large figure group, depicting an Arab astride a camel with Moorish attendant carrying baskets on oblong plinth base, stamped and printed marks, 23½in. high. *(Christie's)* **$3,250**

An American pictorial hooked rug, late 19th/early 20th century, worked in red, yellow, black and blue fabric with the figure of an ocean liner under steam, 30½ x 64in.
(Sotheby's) **$5,175**

An American pictorial hooked rug depicting a bird on a branch and a butterfly, first half 20th century, worked in brown, blue, yellow, lavender and green fabrics with a bird on a fruit tree branch and a butterfly, the whole surrounded by a cream and yellow border, 28½ x 20¼in. *(Sotheby's)* **$1,150**

An unusual American pictorial hooked rug, late 19th/early 20th century, worked in tones of blue, green, pink, brown and cream with a mountain lion crouching on a branch surrounded by foliage, 30 x 42in.
(Sotheby's) **$4,025**

An American pictorial hooked rug, 20th century, worked in tones of green, blue, violet and brown fabric with the figures of two foxes resting near a lake side with cattails in the foreground, the whole within a black border, 33½ x 55½in.
(Sotheby's) **$4,312**

Figural hooked rug depicting pointer, New England, dated *1901*, and titled in red, the charcoal dog with light brown ears and eye on a cream and light brown background with red, blue, white and cream geometric details, 30 x 35¼in. *(Skinner)* **$4,140**

A tufted rug, designed by E. ▶ McKnight Kauffer, 1930s, central design of intersecting squares and rectangles in shades of mushroom, beige and cream and mid-blue on a beige ground, 50 x 70½in., monogrammed in the weave *EMcKK*. *(Christie's)* **$5,140**

Figural hooked rug, New England, 19th century, depicting a hen and rooster with seven eggs between, worked in cream, indigo, red and black, 23¾ x 40¾in. *(Skinner)* **$9,200**

A kura and abumi (saddle and stirrups), Edo period, 19th century, the wooden saddle frame decorated in gold takamakie and hiramakie with a design of peonies and foliage on a gold nashiji ground, retaining its kagami-shihote loops for attaching the harness, with a pair of iron stirrups similarly decorated, fur and gilt leather shitagura and aori, and partially gilt black leather kurashiki (saddle pad). Saddle 14½in. long and stirrups approx. 11¾in.
(Christie's)   **$20,619**

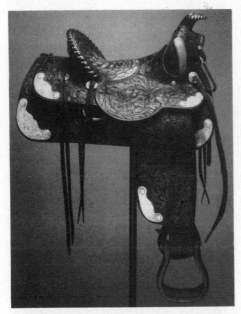

◀

A circa 1936 black leather saddle, hallmarked *N. PORTER PHOENIX* with the longhorn motif. The leather is completely tooled in a foliage design and the seat is padded and stitched. Silver lacing adorns the cantle, horn, and gullet. The back of the cantle is dated *1936* on the silver plate, with the hallmark *N. PORTER CO. ARIZONA*. Seat: 15in. Swells: 12in.
(Christie's)   **$3,680**

A kura and abumi (saddle and stirrups) Edo period, 19th century, the wooden saddle frame decorated in iroe takamakie with karashishi playing among large peonies, retaining its kagamishihote loops for attaching the harness, with a pair of iron stirrups decorated in gold takamakie with a design of a peony on a nashiji ground, leather shitagura, cloth aori and leather oname decorated in gilt with kikyo and Namiwa ni Hagikukusa mon, cloth kurashiki (saddle pad), some old damage. Saddle 14½in. long and stirrups approx. 12in. long. *(Christie's)*   **$12,184**

Samplers were originally a record of embroidery patterns which could then be copied. The earliest dated one is in fact English, made in 1586, and was worked by Jane Bostock. Early examples are rare, for they were made only by the leisured upper classes. By the mid-1700s however, sampler work was spreading to all classes. By this time too printed patterns in book form were becoming more readily available, and the original function of the sampler changed to become more and more of an apprentice piece for young girls, where they could practise and display the various stitches they could execute.

On the earliest samplers, motifs tended to be embroidered at random. By the mid 17th century however there were indications that greater attention was being paid to overall design. Horizontal border patterns of geometric floral motifs are typical of samplers dating from 1650-1720 and around the end of the 18th century the decorative aspect was obviously becoming increasingly important. Samplers became more and more a record of a child's name, age, home (with illustrations of a house, plants and animals,) together with, very often, an uplifting moral or religious verse or text.

A family record sampler, signed Rebecca C. Taggert, Salem, New Jersey, dated June 12, 1827, worked in a variety of green, blue, pink, yellow and white silk stitches on a linen ground with a depiction of the Salem Meeting House and a list of Rebecca Taggert's family members. 22½in. high x 19in. wide. *(Sotheby's)* **$8,050**

Pair of needlework samplers, Elizabeth H. Moore 1826 and Martha A. Moore 1826, Philadelphia, central reserves of pious verses surrounded by foliate sprays, butterflies and baskets of flowers above lower panels of Federal houses flanked by trees, flowering vine borders, framed, 25½ x 21in. *(Skinner)* **$19,550**

A fine and rare needlework sampler by Alice Mather, Norwich, Connecticut, 1774, worked in green, blue, rose and white silk and metal threads, on a black background with bands of alphabets and numerals embellished with a verse *Who can find a virtuous woman. For her price is far above rubies*, above a scene depicting a shepherdess with a flock of sheep. This needlework sampler is part of a small group of Norwich samplers, with solidly worked black backgrounds, Greek key bands and four petaled stylized flowers. *(Christie's)* **$49,500**

An Important needlework sampler, signed *Mary Lord, Boston, Massachusetts*, dated *1754*, worked in blue, green, yellow, ocher, brown and white silk stitches on a linen ground with Adam and Eve flanking the Tree-of-Life entwined with a serpent, surrounded by large blossoms with detached petals, and various animals including a lion, a bear, a unicorn, a frog, a rabbit and birds, 16¾ x 11½in.

Ten-year old Mary Lord's splendid work is presently the latest known example with the typical motifs that characterize Boston's earliest group of samplers.
(Sotheby's) **$100,000**

▶

A fine needlework sampler, signed *Jane Hammell, Burlington County, New Jersey*, dated *1829*, worked in green, blue, yellow, pink, beige, brown and white silk stitches on a linen ground with a brick house flanked by birds in trees, elegantly dressed couples, dogs and ducks, and below a spread-winged American eagle, inscribed with a verse and *Jane Daughter of John and Keturah Hammell wrought this in the ninth year of her age August 1829*, 17¼ x 17¾in. *(Sotheby's)* **$40,250**

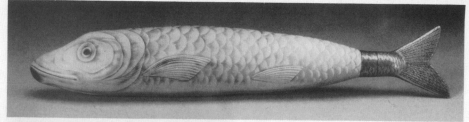

Webb cameo glass carp perfume, extraordinary large size full-bodied figural fish bottle of red glass overlaid in white, cameo carved in intricate realistic detail overall and mounted with hallmarked two-part hinged rim and tail cover enclosing original glass stopper, underside inscribed *Rd. 15711*, total length 11in. *(Skinner)* **$25,300**

An extremely rare Kelsterbach porcelain and gilt-metal mounted scent bottle and stopper, circa 1760–65, modelled by Vogelmann, with a little boy pulling the horns of a goat amongst fruiting vines, 3½in. high. *(Sotheby's)* **$3,000**

'Quatre Soleil', a Lalique amber-tinted scent bottle and stopper, 7.2cm. high. *(Christie's)* **$22,880**

A late Victorian novelty silver and cut glass scent bottle, London 1884, maker's mark of S. Mordan & Co. Ltd., realistically modeled as a snake, the screw-off top as the head, set with glass eyes, in original fitted leather box, 14in. long. *(Bonhams)* **$14,400**

◄ A small mounted iridescent glass bottle, by Tiffany studios, the lobed body with delicately feathered peacock trails, 5in. high, engraved mark *Louis C. Tiffany* on base, the stopper numbered *07109*, the mount with maker's marks.
(Christie's) **$11,040**

▶

A fine and early 19th century French gold and black enamel scent bottle, depicting Cupid holding a butterfly in one hand and a bow in the other, standing on a pedestal amongst reeds, trailing roses and fluttering butterflies, the reverse depicting Cupid shooting an arrow in similar surroundings, the knop hinged cover showing Cupid catching butterflies with a net, with split pearl borders, 3½in. high.
(Bonhams) **$3,520**

Baccarat for A. Gravier 'Voltigy', the bottle and stopper modeled in the form of a butterfly with wings displayed, the upper body enameled in translucent crimson, in fitted cream silk box and with paper label, molded *Voltigy A Gravier*, heightened in black, stenciled circle mark, 3⁵/8in. high
◄ *(Bonhams)* **$9,280**

Scholar's rocks are pieces of natural rock which have been naturally washed out and shaped, usually by water, and which are found at the bottom of lakes or rivers in China. Most are quite small, but they can measure up to 4 feet in height. Mounted, occasionally polished, but otherwise untouched, they were greatly prized in China by scholars as an adornment for their studies, which they could contemplate in their meditations.

One tends to think of them as being 17th century pieces, but they are extremely difficult to date, and many may be 18th or 19th century discoveries.

They also appeal to the Chinese taste, as seen in their gardens, for creating a representation of the world around them in miniature.

A scholar's rock, of upright aspect, the stone pierced and penetrated with a myriad of interconnecting passages and hollows and forming a jagged silhouette, the stone possibly Zhiaqing limestone of ivory and butterscotch tones, 22½in. high.
(Christie's) **$6,900**

A large upright blackish-gray scholar's rock, of yingshi type, the form reminiscent of a dancing figure, with criss-crossed texture and white veining throughout, 51¼in. high.
(Christie's) **$20,700**

Paul Etienne Saïn, four panel abstract ▶
screen, circa 1930, each panel with gold
leaf decoration on a red and brown ground,
the reverse lacquered in black, one panel
marked *B. Roger, Herbst*, each panel 68¼
x 17½in. *(Sotheby's)* **$19,205**

◀
Piero Fornasetti, 'Reflecting City' folding
screen, 1955, lacquered wood, reversible
brass hinges, castors, 81in. high, each
panel 19¾in. wide.
(Sotheby's) **$11,178**

▶
A three-fold lacquer screen by
Leonor Fini, circa 1930, decorated
with three dancing figures, against
a black ground, 57 x 15¾in.
　Leonor Fini was a follower of
the Surrealist movement in Paris
and London from 1933, and later in
New York, Brussels and Zurich.
Her first exhibition was in Milan,
closely followed by a one-woman
show in Paris in 1935.　In the
1940s and 50s she produced
some notable theater and ballet
designs, including Le Rève de
Léonor (1945) for the Ballets des
Champs Elysées, Le Palais de
Cristal (1947) for L'Opera de Paris,
and Les Demoiselles de la Nuit
(1948) for the Ballets de Paris.
(Christie's) **$14,996**

◀ A fine three-fold painted screen, probably early 18th century, the central domed fold painted with a garden scene looking out from a grotto and a courtyard with trees and classical buildings beyond, the smaller sides similarly painted, 250.5cm. wide.
(Sotheby's) **$23,920**

▶

Paul Etienne Saïn, four panel abstract screen, circa 1930, each panel with white gold leaf decoration on a black ground, the reverse lacquered in black, one panel marked *B. Roger, Desbrosses* and *Paul Etienne Saïn*, each panel 67¾ x 16½in.
(Sotheby's) **$6,914**

◀
A rare wrought iron and glass firescreen, designed by Edgar Brandt and Daum, circa 1920s, glass medallions etched with foliate patterning, inset into wrought iron rosettes entwined with twisting branches of leaves and berries, 29½ x 37¼in.

Edgar Brandt presented at the Exposition des Arts Décoratifs, Paris 1925, a large wrought iron, part-gilt screen entitled L'Oasis. Showing a stylized fountain amongst luxurious vegetation, the screen was punctuated by wrought iron medallions cast with stylised motifs which both in design and decorative usage were very similar to the wrought iron and glass medallions of the present screen.
(Christie's) **$48,737**

This strange word is thought to be derived from a surname – perhaps of a particularly artistic sailor – because it is a general term applied to the works of art or handicrafts made by seamen on long voyages. The most common application of scrimshaw was fine engraving on bone or ivory which was produced by sailors in 19th century whaling ships. They used whale's teeth or whalebone as their medium and some of their artwork was very skilled. They darkened the incised detail with black ink or soot. The usual subjects chosen for illustration were life at sea or depictions of Eskimo life, fishing and trapping, which they witnessed on their voyages. A few scrimshaw pieces have erotic carvings. Scrimshaw work either stands on its own or is incorporated into gongs, inkstands and boxes.

Engraved whale's tooth, early 20th century, decorated with a reserve of a whaling scene, flanked by various whaling implements, rope border, 9¼in. long.
(Skinner) **$2,760** ▶

Engraved whalebone jewelry casket, 19th century, the top polychrome decorated with elegant ladies and a child flanked by birds amidst trees, the sides with reserves of birds amidst foliage, the top lifts to reveal a removable tray with four covered compartments and a door, decorated with snakes, fish and foliate devices, on shaped bracket feet, 10in wide.
(Skinner) **$5,462**

A fine engraved and scrimshawed ▶ whale ivory, baleen and whale teeth watch stand, probably American, third quarter 19th century, the watch stand flanked by a pair of whales' teeth engraved with whaling ships and centering an oculus engraved with a lighthouse and trimmed with tortoise shell, the later and shaped base inlaid with baleen stars and diamonds, 7in. high.
(Sotheby's) **$14,950**

Engraved polychrome decorated whale's tooth, Edward Burdett (1805-33), obverse depicting an English whaleship with boats away involved in the chase, reverse depicts the whaleship 'Elizabeth of London, trying out, vine and dot borders, decorated with intaglio cutting and heightened in red sealing wax and black color. 6¼in. long. *(Skinner)* **$60,250**

A fine and rare engraved scrimshawed erotic sperm whale tooth, probably American, mid 19th century, the obverse engraved with the figure of a reclining nude, the reverse with two nude women with details picked out in red, blue and black ink, 6½in. high.

Though it was not uncommon for whalemen to express their longings through 'suggestive scrimshaw', these pieces are rarely seen today. Most were thrown overboard at the end of a voyage by God-fearing captains anxious to protect their reputations at home. Whalemen themselves were reluctant to have evidence of their impure thoughts in their possession when returning to wives and sweethearts. It is speculated the ocean floor is now home to hundreds of nude or naughty ladies like the one reclining on this tooth. *(Sotheby's)* **$51,750**

Federal mahogany inlaid lady's tambour desk, attributed to John and/or Thomas Seymour, Boston, 1794–1809, this two-section desk has a rectangular overhanging top with inlaid edge above a conforming case with tambour doors inlaid with swags of graduated sand-shaded three-petal husks flanked by inlaid fluted pilasters and opening to a blue painted interior of six valanced compartments above four drawers and a fold-out writing surface with inlaid edge; the lower case includes three cockbeaded, graduated drawers outlined in satinwood inlay and stringing flanked by checkerboard inlay with stringing above pierced brackets and square tapering legs which terminate in 'therm' feet and are husk-inlaid, 37½in. wide.
(Skinner) **$200,500**

▶

A Federal inlaid mahogany secretary desk, attributed to John Seymour and Son, Boston, 1794–1809, in two parts: the upper section with a rectangular top with band inlaid edge above a conforming case fitted with inlaid tambour doors punctuated by inlaid pilasters opening to reveal an interior fitted with arched pigeonholes with ivory line and oval inlay over two short drawers above a short drawer; the lower section with mid-molding and full-front lined writing surface above a case fitted with three graduated line-inlaid long drawers flanked by inlaid fluted pilasters, on square tapering legs with husk inlay and spade feet, 37½in. wide.

Introduced into the American vocabulary via English trained craftsmen and pattern books during the 1790s, the tambour desk reflects the changing tastes and demands of Boston's elite.
(Christie's) **$145,500**

A gilt metal trolley, French, circa 1950, lyre-shaped supports, three glass shelves, on castors, 28¾in. high.
(Christie's) **$1,630**

◄Ludwig Mies van der Rohe, for Bamberg Metallwerkstätten, serving trolley, designed 1927–29, manufactured circa 1930, nickel-plated steel, tubular steel, wood handle, glass, 28⁷/₈in. high.

A trolley clearly based on the earlier Bamberg model appears in the Thonet catalog from the year 1935 credited to A. Bamberg.
(Sotheby's) **$27,180**

Alvar Aalto for Oy. Huoenekalu-ja-Rakkennustyötehdas AB, Turku, Finland, tea cart, model '98' designed circa 1935–36, manufactured after 1936, retailed by Artek OY. AB, Helsinki, distributed in the U.K. by Finmar Ltd, bent laminated and solid birch, plywood, lacquered wood, the underside with Finmar Ltd label 5, 21⁷/₈ x 35½in.
(Sotheby's) **$5,624**

A Federal inlaid mahogany settee, Philadelphia, 1790-1810, the arched crestrail above an upholstered back flanked by downswept armrests terminating in inlaid handholds over inlaid tapering baluster-turned supports above an upholstered seat with bowed front, on square tapering line and oval inlaid legs, 60in. wide.
(Christie's) **$29,900**

Alessandro Mendini for Alchimia, 'Kandissi' sofa, 1979, walnut veneered wood and painted blue, yellow, pink, white, green, black, blue, upholstered seat, back and rear panel covered in blue, purple, brown, beige and cream fabric, 80in. wide.
(Sotheby's) **$20,493**

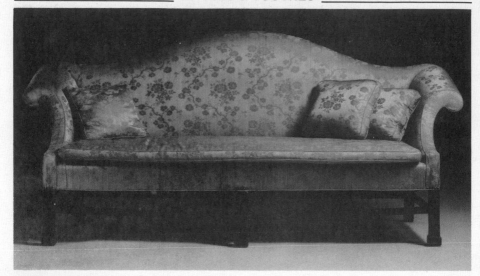

A Chippendale mahogany camelback sofa, Philadelphia, circa 1780, the serpentine crest with outscrolled arms on downswept supports centring a loose fitted cushion, the overupholstered seat below on square legs joined by stretchers on Marlborough legs, 7ft.9in. *(Sotheby's)* **$79,500**

A classical carved mahogany settee attributed to Duncan Phyfe, 1768–1854, New York, 1820-40, the tablet crestrail centering a foliate-carved panel above an upholstered back flanked by outward scrolled upholstered arms headed by dolphin carved supports with scaled body, carved eyes, mouth and teeth continuing to a tablet front rail edged with beading centering a foliate-carved panel, on carved hairy paw feet with feathered and foliate-carved and scrolled knee returns, 91½in. long.

This elegant sofa possesses the elements associated with the height of the classical style developed in New York between 1820–40: the tablet crest and seat rail, the scaled dolphin supports, feathered and acanthus carved knees, and hairy paw feet. A related example with scaled supports is located in The Metropolitan Museum of Art. *(Christie's)* **$40,250**

A silvered-wood 'Grotto' three-seater settee, of triple shell-back form, flanked by a pair of scrolled dolphin arm supports, on six shaped legs, 58in. wide. *(Christie's)* **$18,850**

A George III giltwood settee, possibly by Thomas Chippendale, the shaped back, outscrolled sides, seat and seat-cushion covered in blue foliate damask, the back with a rockwork and C-scroll cresting, the C-scroll arched apron with blind-trellis ground and rockwork border, on cabriole legs and scrolled feet, 93in. wide.

This richly carved settee has its serpentined frame embellished with Roman acanthus foliage and water-scalloped cartouches in the manner of 'French easy chairs' adopted by Thomas Chippendale (d. 1779) for his St. Martin's Lane trade label, and illustrated in his Gentleman's and Cabinet-maker's Directory of 1754. *(Christie's)* **$66,400**

Porcelain production began at Sèvres in 1756 when the Vincennes factory was moved there, and the first 14 years of its output are considered by many to be unsurpassed.

At first, a soft paste porcelain was made, with silky glazes and richly ornate decoration. It was hugely expensive to make, however, and had the further disadvantage that it could not be molded into complex shapes, which tended to fracture in the kiln.

Nevertheless, it was dear to the heart of Louis XV, who was wholly responsible for funding the operation, and his mistress Mme de Pompadour. He assisted it further by issuing several decrees granting virtual monopolies in favor of Sèvres, and even acted as salesman in chief, holding annual exhibitions at Versailles and selling off the pieces to his court.

Sèvres products are remarkable for their brilliant ground colors and chemists were constantly at work developing new tones. Honey gilding, then a virtually new technique, was also widely used, while a host of flower and figure painters (Louis engaged fan painters for this) added their designs. With regard to form, tableware shapes largely followed those of the delicate lines of contemporary silver. Sèvres was also famous for its soft-paste biscuit models, notably in the period 1757-66, when Etienne Maurice Falconet was chief modeler.

On the abolition of the monarchy Sèvres was taken over by the State in 1793. Under Napoleon's appointee Brogniart, soft paste was finally abandoned (it was revived again in the late 1840s) in favor of a new hard paste formula which was particularly suitable for tableware.

Soft paste wares are clearly marked in blue enamel with the usual crossed Ls motif and a date letter (doubled after 1777). In hard paste, a crown is placed above the blue mark from 1769-79. After 1793 a date appears instead of the letter.

A fine pair of 'Sèvres' and gilt-bronze vases, Paris, circa 1890, each of ovoid from, with a bell shaped cover painted in terracotta, orange and gold and surmounted by a pinecone, the similarly decorated neck above a body painted with elegant gentlemen and ladies in a garden in front of a chateau with lakes, temples, waterfalls and urns; the other with a Venetian wedding with the bride and groom leaving a palace accompanied by figures and saluted by women with flowers in a gondola opposed by similar figures arriving at a palace filled with oleander, all flanked by foliate cast scroll handles surmounted by female figures, on a trumpet foot and square base on paw feet terminating in foliage, 141cm. high. *(Sotheby's)* **$83,130**

Though at first sewer pipe art may seem a contradiction in terms, some very attractive objects were produced by workers in sewer pipe factories in their own time and for their own pleasure. So popular was the practice of slipping their own offerings into the kiln that those caught doing so could be 'fired' in the other sense. It was a long lived form of folk art activity as well, for the practice continued, mainly in the American midwest, from around 1890-1950.

Most of the items produced had practical applications, for example, lamp bases, bookends, doorstops, marbles, but animals, particularly lions, were also very popular subjects. Most were molded, and the workers would individualize their pieces with their own decorations or glazes. The items were highly prized, and theft and fights over ownership were not uncommon.

Some factory owners realised the merit of what the men were producing, and made the practice more official, themselves turning out pieces for advertizing and souvenir purposes. These, unlike the men's personal items, were stamped with the company's name.

Pieces can to some extent be identified geographically and historically by color and the texture of the unglazed clay, but such pointers are seldom conclusive. The attractiveness of the piece is the main factor in determining its value, and some can now fetch astonishing sums.

A fine pair of molded yellow clay recumbent lions, American, 19th century, the figures posed on molded oval bases, the mane covered in a dark brown Rockingham glaze, 9in. high. *(Sotheby's)* **$1,725**

An unusually fine and impressive sewer tile lion, probably Ohio, 19th century, the recumbent lion facing left; covered in iridescent brown glaze, 17in. high x 37in. long. *(Sotheby's)* **$10,350**

A rare pair of large sewer tile lions, probably Ohio, 19th century, the recumbent lions, facing straight ahead; covered in a black-brown glaze, 15in. high x 30in. long. *(Sotheby's)* **$12,650**

A carved and painted pine sewing ▶
box, American, late 19th/early 20th
century, the box carved on all
sides, with scroll feet, inlaid star
and applied decorative carving, and
drawer, surmounted by an
American 'Bellamy-style' eagle
perched on a shield, opening to a
well lined with red satin, 13¼in.
long. *(Sotheby's)* **$2,587**

A Continental fruitwood work-box, 19th
century, in the form of a miniature leather
trunk with simulated leather straps and
handles, the hinged sprung top with central
brass roundel enclosing a blue watered
silk-lined interior, 8in. wide, 3½in. high.
(Christie's) **$2,640**

A Regency penwork needlework
box, circa 1820, of rising square
section with domed cover depicting
a boy in a landscape, with bands of
trailing foliage and acorns to the
borders, gilt metal lion mask ring
handles, with pink papered interior
and divided frieze drawer below,
6¾in. high.
(Christie's) **$1,677**

A Regency Tunbridgeware painted ▶
wood workbox, circa 1820,
modeled as a cottage, decorated
with trees to the facades, the
hinged roof opening to reveal a
paper lined interior with lift-out tray,
6in. wide.
(Christie's) **$5,310**

A Federal birch veneered and inlaid sewing box, Boston, 1800-1815, the hinged rectangular top with lunette-inlaid edge opening to a conforming case fitted with a compartmentalized removable shelf, the case veneered with lunette-inlaid edge, appears to retain original blue paper interior, 3¾in. high, 9¾in. wide, 7in. deep.

The precise and delicate quality of the craftsmanship, use of lunette inlay, ivory escutcheon, and original blue-green paper lining the interior of this box, are features associated with the Seymour workshop.
(Christie's) **$9,775**

◀

A fine and rare inlaid whale ivory and fruitwood sewing box, signed *T. Nickerson*, probably American, mid 19th century.

The rectangular box with hinged lid opening to a deep well fitted with whale ivory thread spools, the top inlaid with stars and flowerheads and the shaped plaque inscribed *T. Nickerson,* outlined with a mica floral wreath, the front and sides inlaid with whale ivory hearts and stars along with mica trees and hearts and stars of contrasting light and dark wood, 9½in. long.
(Sotheby's) **$16,100**

◀

A fine Federal paint-decorated bird's-eye maple sewing box, New England, circa 1810, of rectangular form with a hinged lid opening to a divided well, the interior covered in pink paper, the sides fitted with brass carrying handles, the front fitted with a single drawer raised on gilt ball feet; the top painted with a winged angel and a dog, the sides and front painted with war trophies, wreaths and flowers, 6½in. high.
(Sotheby's) **$7,475**

A rare Nuremberg 'Clown' sewing machine, No. 4024, the seated cast-iron figure with nodding head and working arms operated by a porcelain-handled crank, on iron base with lion's paw feet, 8¾in. high. *(Christie's)* **$4,519**

An Anchor sewing machine, with chain-stitch mechanism, arm formed as an anchor and rectangular base, on wood plinth, 12in. wide overall. *(Christie's)* **$3,600**

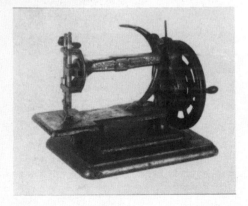

An American Florence long shuttle machine with decoration in good condition. With shuttle. Serial No. 48.346. A rare and complete example in original condition, circa 1868. *(Auction Team Köln)* **$4,690**

A rare Kimball & Morton 'Lion treadle sewing machine, the machine head formed as a standing lion, on treadle with end standards cast with heraldic beasts, 26½in. wide, with registration mark of 1868. *(Christie's)* **$7,762**

A small chain-stitch sewing machine, probably a Newton, Wilson 'Matchless', with parallel action needle arm, gilt and red decoration, wood baseboard and case, 7½in. wide.
(Christie's) **$4,600**

A burr walnut veneered davenport, ▶ sewing machine secreted in case, with carved columns, two doors to rear, drop flap bureau and false drawers to sides.
(Academy Auctioneers) **$5,250**

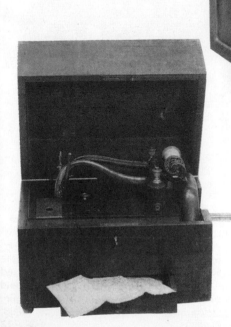

Grover & Baker's Family Box Machine, 1855, the first portable sewing machine, serial no. 7,198, with two-thread chainstitch and empty needle card and sales documentation from 1864.
(Auction Team Köln) **$2,263**

Simple, sturdy furniture and artifacts were produced in the late 18th and early 19th century by the Shaker sect in New England and New York State, originally for use by Community members. Later, however, chair-making in particular developed into quite an industry supplying neighbouring towns. The pieces were painted (usually dark red) but undecorated. Most typical items are rocking chairs and slat back chairs designed to be hung on a wall rail. Production declined after 1860.

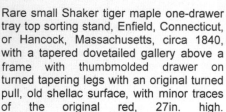

Shaker cherry and butternut sewing case, probably Enfield, Connecticut, circa 1840, the rectangular overhanging cherry top above a frame and panel constructed case of four butternut thumbnail molded half-width drawers over a full drawer with turned pulls resting on square tapering legs, the sides and back of single poplar recessed panel, darkened finish probably original, 27in. wide.
(Skinner) **$23,000**

Rare small Shaker tiger maple one-drawer tray top sorting stand, Enfield, Connecticut, or Hancock, Massachusetts, circa 1840, with a tapered dovetailed gallery above a frame with thumbmolded drawer on turned tapering legs with an original turned pull, old shellac surface, with minor traces of the original red, 27in. high.

The sides of the gallery are tapered with the wood thicker at the bottom of the gallery sides than at the top edge. This feature has been found on a number of pieces of furniture known to have been made either at Enfield, Connecticut, or Hancock, Massachusetts.
(Skinner) **$35,000**

Shaker cherry drop-leaf sewing case, probably Hancock, circa 1820, the overhanging rectangular top with a single drop leaf supported by a wrought iron 'crane-like fixture' above two thumbmolded graduated drawers with turned pulls and straight skirt joining four block-turned legs, 28in. wide.
(Skinner) **$18,400**

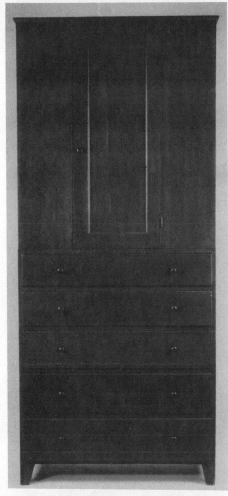

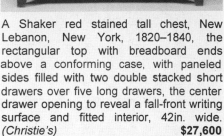

A Shaker red stained tall chest, New Lebanon, New York, 1820–1840, the rectangular top with breadboard ends above a conforming case, with paneled sides filled with two double stacked short drawers over five long drawers, the center drawer opening to reveal a fall-front writing surface and fitted interior, 42in. wide. *(Christie's)* **$27,600**

Shaker painted pine cupboard over case of drawers, Mt. Lebanon, New York, circa 1830, with quarter-round cornice molding, flat door panels with forged door latch opening to three shelves above five rounded edge graduated drawers on cut foot base, with plank sides, original finish, and faded color, 85in. high.
(Skinner) **$79,500**

▶

Shaker painted cherry candlestand, New Lebanon, New York, 1820–40, the square top above a turned tapering classic center post and tripod base, with original translucent red stain, with old varnish, 25¾ high. *(Skinner)* **$28,750**

between 1750 and 1790. He trained his three sons, John Jr. (1751-1823), Calvin (1761-1835), and Lebbeus(1763-1827), in the clockmaking business. After completing his apprenticeship in 1770, John Bailey Jr. worked as a clock maker on Curtis Street in Hanover.

(Sotheby's) **$28,750**

A very rare Chippendale brass-mounted mahogany double-case shelf clock, the dial painted and signed by J. Minott, Boston, Massachusetts, the works by John Bailey, Hanover, Massachusetts, circa 1793.

In two parts; the removable hood, surmounted by three brass ball-and-steeple finials, above a shaped crest above a glazed door opening to an enameled dial with phases of the moon, and calendar date indicator inscribed *John Bailey HANOVER*, brass stop-fluted columns flanking, with ogee bracket feet below, 47¼in. high.

This venerable shelf clock, was manufactured by the prominent Hanover, Massachusetts clockmaker John Bailey Sr. (1730-1810). John Sr., a Quaker, was established as a clockmaker in Hanover

A fine and rare Chippendale inlaid and figured mahogany shelf clock, Aaron Willard, Boston, Massachusetts, circa 1800, surmounted by a pierced crest with brass urn finial, the kidney-shaped glazed door panel opening to an enamel dial decorated with floral wreaths and inscribed *Aaron Willard Boston*, the cross-banded and crotch-figured case below on a molded base and ogee bracket feet, eight day movement, 39in. high.

(Sotheby's) **$31,050**

The Shibayama were a family of Japanese inro artists who, in the late 18th century, developed and specialized in a style of encrusted lacquer (now known as Shibayama) in which a decorative surface was covered with minute, delicately carved encrustations of materials such as ivory, mother of pearl, coral, gold, silver and metallic alloys. They were meticulously designed and executed, with realistic patterns showing human, animal and plant forms.

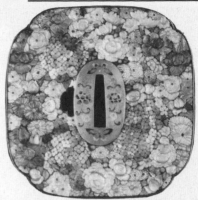

A large Shibayama style tsuba, Edo period, 19th century, decorated all over in various colored and stained aogai inlays depicting a dense profusion of flowerheads with elegant cloisonné enamel butterflies among peonies around the seppadai, mokkogata silver mounted mimi, 3⁷/8in. *(Christie's)* **$5,625**

A four case Shibayama inro, Meiji period, late 19th century, the wood cases enclosed by sheet silver on the top, bottom and sides forming a frame, enclosing a gold panel on each side, the silver frame decorated with cloisonné flowers and scrolling foliage, both panels on a kinji ground, the front with a stream in togidashi, hiramakie details, with a woman with an umbrella beneath a weeping cherry tree in a high wind, the reverse shows two vases, one with peaches and the other with chrysanthemums, suspended from a well pulley, the designs inlaid in aogai, stained ivory, tortoiseshell and wood, nashiji interiors, fundame rims, 4⁷/8in. high. *(Christie's)* **$9,373**

A Shibayama silver-mounted tusk box and cover, late 19th century, the cover surmounted with a sculpted group of an ape and her infant, the front with applied ornament depicting a parrot beside a blossoming tree, with signed mount to one side, on gadrooned hardwood plinth, 12¾in. high. *(Christie's)* **$6,480**

A Victorian grained and composition side-table, in the Adam style, the rectangular white marble top inlaid with bluejohn with a central fluted and geometrically decorated oval, the central circle surrounded by four urns, on block feet, 61in. wide.

The statuary white marble top of this 'mosaic' sideboard-table is inlaid in Derbyshire bluejohn in Roman 'pavement' fashion. Sacrificial ewers, accompanying a central flowered patera, are within a trellised and scalloped fretwork of ribbons and a flower-spandreled elliptic medallion with antique-fluted frame. The frame of the table is embellished en suite with an elliptic patera wreathed by wheat, emblematic of the harvest-goddess Ceres, and is accompanied by pastoral trophies of festive instruments. Its design and ornament reflects the antique taste promoted by The Works in Architecture by Robert and James Adam, published between 1773 and 1822. *(Christie's)* **$90,138**

A matched pair of Scottish boxwood tree tables, mid-19th century, each with two tiers and decorated on all sides with knotted pieces of wood, on four natural supports, and four conforming feet, 32in. wide. *(Christie's)* **$16,031**

An important Federal figured maple inlaid mahogany marble-top tambour-front sideboard signed *John Seymour, Boston, Massachusetts,* 1798–1805, the rectangular inlaid and crossbanded top above two frieze drawers with bottle drawers below centering tambour slides opening to a compartment, the crossbanded apron on square double-tapering legs ending in crossbanded cuffs, 45in. wide.
(Sotheby's)   **$156,500**

The Great Exhibition London 1851, a magnificent totara knot and boxwood sideboard by Johann Martin Levian, Victorian, dated *1851*, the upper part with a cresting flanked by dragons and with two further cartouches headed by masks, above a boxwood panel enclosed within a glazed frame carved with foliage, nymphs and satyrs, separated by masks, swags of fruit and flowers and flanked by carved roundels, centered by medallion portraits of Queen Victoria and Prince Albert respectively, 311cm. wide.
(Sotheby's)   **$504,485**

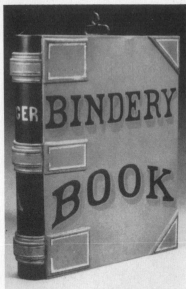

American School, 19th century, electric tattooing flash: a rare trade sign, 8¾ x 13in. (Sotheby's) **$1,380**

Painted tin 'Book Bindery' trade sign, 19th century, 19¼in. high. (Skinner) **$575**

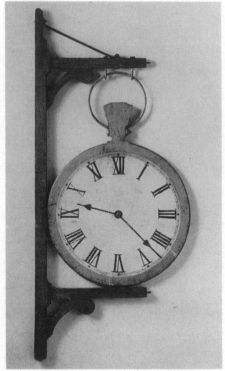

A painted metal barbershop trade sign: *Shave for a Penny, Let Blood for Nothing, Teeth Drawn With a Touch*, the top with reinforcing wrought iron band, the sign inscribed on both sides, 32½ x 26½in. (Sotheby's) **$690**

A carved and painted wood and metal pocket watch trade sign, American late 19th century, the flattened silhouetted form painted on both sides with black Roman numerals on a white face, within a gold rim, suspended between two brackets, 27in. high. (Sotheby's) **$3,450**

Painted and decorated two-sided tavern sign, *Thompson Hotel, Vernon Stiles 1831*, in gilt letters flanking a scene with men in a carriage drawn by two white horses pulling in front of early 19th century dwellings, all on a black ground, the other side is similarly painted but shows weathering, on original iron hangers, 44¼in. high.

The Vernon Stiles Inn stands in the Connecticut town of Thompson at the intersection of routes 193 and 200. The major part of the present wood frame building built about 1814 still stands. Vernon Stiles operated the Inn for many years beginning in 1831. Famous guests included the Marquis de Lafayette and his aide-de-camp, Rochambeau. The historically and architecturally significant Inn continues today.
(Skinner) **$17,250**

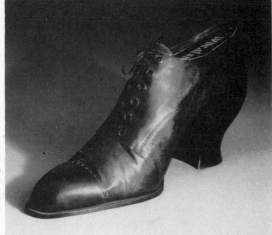

A late Victorian or Edwardian leather shoe shop display sign, late 19th or early 20th century, in the form of a ladies shoe, laced and with waisted raised heel, inset with a plaque to the top inscribed *Wheatsheaf*, 40in. long.
(Christie's) **$14,531**

A fine carved and painted pine trade sign, James L. Bufford, probably New England, circa 1850, the oval planked form inscribed in ornamental lettering *James L. Bufford Coach and Sign Painter*, the reverse with a bust portrait of George Washington, oval: height 37in. *(Sotheby's)* **$9,200**

A rare carved and painted pine trade sign: Captain Ahab, American, late 19th/early 20th century, the full length standing figure of Captain Ahab wearing a stovepipe hat and black coat, holding a harpoon, the one legged sea captain standing on a base inscribed *Ahab's Whale Oil Soap*, overall height 32¾in.
(Sotheby's) **$26,450**

An unusual painted tin umbrella trade sign, American, late 19th/early 20th century, the slightly opened umbrella held by an outstretched hand, 41in. high.
(Sotheby's) **$13,800**

William Henry Brown (1808-1883), silhouette profile of Andrew Johnson, signed, dated and inscribed *W.H. Brown/1842/Senator Andrew Johnson/ Washington, D.C.*; together with a silhouette profile portrait of Mary Anne Appleton, signed, dated and inscribed, *SAMUEL Metford/1840/Mrs. Mary Anne Appleton/Boston/1840*, ink and gouache hollow cut on paper.
(Christie's) **$2,990**

Auguste Edouart (1789–1861), two gentlemen in a furnished parlor, one seated, the other holding a document: a free-cut silhouette portrait, black paper mounted over a gouache interior ground, 13 x 9¼in. *(Sotheby's)* **$4,600**

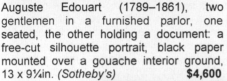

Mary Hana, circa 1784-1787, a pair of miniature silhouettes of the cabinetmaker William Savery and his wife, Mary, cut paper, 6¼ x 5¼in.

John and Mary Hana are listed in the 1793 Philadelphia Directory as living on Fifth Street, between Pine & Spruce Streets. Both were members of the Greater Meeting at Second Street.
(Christie's) **$8,625**

Lady Louisa Kerr, Maria, Countess of Carhampton; Helen Moseley; Thomas Bacon Esq. a group of three silhouettes, cut out on card with wash backgrounds, each signed and dated.
(Bearnes) **$1,760**

A Victorian claret jug modeled as a wyvern, with a hinged head, textured plumage, cast feet and a cast handle, engraved on the tail with a coronet and monogram, by Richard Sibley, 1869, 22.5cm. high, 24oz.
(Christie's) **$4,550**

An American silver jardinière and plateau, Gorham Mfg. Co., Providence, RI, 1905, Martelé, .9584 standard, the stand domed, with a rippled edge descending to form four feet and two handles, the bowl of bombé form, raised on four feet, with two scroll handles and an undulating rim, both parts chased with strawberries, cherries, hazelnuts, and leaves, the removable flower grid with a gilded pierced rosette over a wire mesh, 256 oz. gross, length over handles 23½in.

According to Samuel J. Hough, this jardinière and plateau were completed December 12, 1905. The jardinière took 120 hours to fashion, then 186 hours to chase, the plateau 50 hours and 88 hours. The chaser in both cases was George W. Sauthof, in 1905 the second most highly-paid chaser at Gorham. The net factory price for the two pieces, including the gilding of the pierced flower grid, was $895.00. *(Sotheby's)* **$123,500**

◄

A pair of silver candlesticks, designed by The Silver Studio, maker's mark of *Liberty & Co., Birmingham, 1902*, stamped *CYMRIC*.

Each on shallow spreading circular foot embossed with leaf motifs, the tapering stem applied with elongated straps headed with stylized flower heads, with spherical sockets and plain detachable wax pans, 7¾in. high. *(Christie's)* **$11,316**

Two important silver sideboard dishes, one probably Francis Garthorne, 1691, the other maker's mark *H*.? date letter overstruck by *Garthorne*, circa 1675, both London, scalloped circular, engraved in the center with a crest within crossed plumes below the eighteen lobed sides, 17in. diameter, 116oz. 17dwt.
(Sotheby's)   **$94,355**

A rare silver cream-jug, maker's mark of Paul Revere, Boston, circa 1765, pyriform, with double scroll handle, on three trefid feet, the body repoussé and chased with flowers and scrolls, the knees also flat-chased with rocaille, the cartouche with later monogram, marked under base *.REVERE*, 4in. high, 4oz.
(Christie's)   **$63,000**

A rare, small medieval, silver-gilt hardstone set chalice, the hemispherical bowl with a slightly everting lip, on a circular trumpet foot with flared rim and a compressed circular knop, flanked above and below with beaded wirework bands, the knop and foot both decorated with blind filigree scrollwork bands, both cabochon set with irregular shaped stones and pearls, the bowl engraved on one side with the figure of a bishop proffering a symbolic model of a church or cathedral to the figure of a saint with raised open hands, 8.1cm high, 2.75oz.

A precise dating of the chalice is very difficult, however the shape, proportions and particularly the engraving: the Romanesque architecture, the style of costume and bishop's miter and the rendering of the face, hands and feet, point strongly to the pre-Gothic era and are consistent with other items from the 11th–13th centuries. The engraved figures may be portraying the Saints Dunstan and Peter, respectively.
(Christie's)   **$45,500**

A silver and mixed metal tray, maker's mark of Tiffany & Co., New York, 1873–91, shaped rectangular, on four scroll feet, with spot-hammered surface and molded rim, the field applied with a mixed metal dragon-fly and a branch, marked under base *5546/685*, 11¾in. long; gross weight 19oz.

(Christie's) **$20,700**

A rare American silver matching octagonal pepper and mustard pot, John Burt, Boston, circa 1730, with projecting base band, applied with two molded bands near the base and two at the lip, matched on detachable domed cover, with an urn finial and scroll handle, the bases engraved *Mary + Cutt*, one stamped twice with a swan, the other with fleurs de lys as an aid in aligning covers to bodies, each marked *I. Burt* in a rectangle, 5oz., 3¾in. high.

(Sotheby's) **$31,050**

An American parcel-gilt silver and other metals Japanese-style tray, Gorham Mfg., Providence, RI, 1882, in the form of a trompe l'oeil still life, comprising a plain silver-gilt dish engraved with foliate monogram, resting on a ruffled, chased napkin, applied with a branch of apples with gilt leaves and red patinated copper apples and a spray of darker patinated cherries, one leaf applied with a bug, marked on the base and stamped with number *E77*, 29 oz. 10dwt. gross. 11in. wide.

The Gorham code E77 indicates that this was an individually made piece and not a production item.

(Sotheby's) **$16,100**

A rare early Irish chocolate pot, maker's mark *?R* below a fleur-de lys, Dublin, 1694, the tapered cylindrical body engraved with armorials, curved spout at right angles to the handle with cut card decoration at the terminals, similarly cut-card decorated lid with swivel acorn finial, 8¾in. high, 23oz. 3dwt. in all.

The arms are probably those of Gordon quartering Badenoch for a lateral descendant of the Earls and Marquesses of Huntly. This would appear to be one of the earliest known Irish chocolate pots. *(Sotheby's)* **$40,330**

A Japanese silver and gilt kogo, surmounted by a sleeping rooster and decorated throughout with chrysanthemums and foliage, signed *Setsuho Hidetomo*, Meiji, 7cm. diameter. *(Bearne's)* **$8,862**

Designed and executed by Christian Dell at the Metallwerkstatt Bauhaus Weimar, wine jug and cover, 1922, alpaca with hammered finish, ebony, the underside with designer/maker's monogram *CD*, 7⁷/8in.

This wine jug can be regarded with justification as a landmark piece in the story of design at the Bauhaus. Dating as it does from 1922 it is earlier than any other recorded example of the fully eleborated geometric contructions which have come to be associated with the school, principally through the work of Dell and Marianne Brandt.
(Sotheby's) **$163,815**

◀ A fine Dutch silver-gilt beaker stamped *O* the date mark for 1665 or perhaps maker's mark Dirk Jans Filensis, the tapered cylindrical body finely engraved with three ovals depicting Joseph's Dream above a further three depicting the story of the Good Samaritan between birds on fruit pendants, all framed and entwined by auricular straps concealing masks, monsters and figures, further engraved and inscribed below with caricatures of the three estates, a nobleman, cleric and peasant, 6in. high, 7oz 12dwt.

Such caricatures are typically after engravings by Abraham Bosse, in particular the nobleman can be related to one on the title page of Bosse's Le Jardin de la Noblesse Française, 1629. *(Sotheby's)* **$57,615**

A fine Charles II silver-gilt beaker, maker's mark *TH* crowned above a pellet, London, 1674, the tapered cylindrical body of exceptional gauge and decorated with a broad band of matting, 4in. high, 15oz 2dwt. *(Sotheby's)* **$57,615**

A parcel gilt silver beaker, marked with the cyrillic initials of Boris Gavrilov, Moscow, 1741, tapering cylindrical, the body chased and engraved with three allegorical ovals within covered drape, foliate and scallop cartouches, with mask and scroll decoration at intervals, the rim and spreading foot gilt, 5⁵/₈in. high, 246gr. *(Christie's)* **$2,263**

The magnificent American silver punch bowl and ladle from the Mackay service, maker's mark of Tiffany & Co., New York, 1878, shaped circular, with a lobed and serpentine rim with stylized foliage, the bowl with spiral lobes, each with grapes and leaves against an engraved and chased ground, one side applied with the Hungerford coat-of-arms, crest and motto, the other side with a monogram MLM, the shaped circular base pierced and applied with foliage, the feet formed as stylized elephants' heads, the matching ladle with a parcel-gilt stem in varicolored gilding, the gilt circular bowl with a spout, 23¼in. diameter, ladle 21½in. long, 478oz.

In 1873, John W. Mackay discovered one of the largest silver veins in America, the Comstock Lode near Virginia City, Nevada, for which he was dubbed the the 'Bonanza King'. According to legend, when his wife, Marie Louise Hungerford Mackay, visited the mine, she decided to have a half ton of silver shipped to Tiffany's with instructions to make an elaborate dinner service for twenty-four. Two hundred silversmiths worked for two years on the service, producing 1,223 pieces of which 305 were holloware items. The set was completed in 1878 at which time it was sent to the Tiffany & Co., exhibit at the Exposition Universelle in Paris where it received a great deal of attention from the press. The Mackays moved to Paris where they entertained distinguished guests on a lavish scale, including the former United States President, Ulysses S. Grant.

(Christie's) **$222,500**

An American silver sugar bowl and cover, John Burt, Boston, circa 1735, of hemispherical form with contemporary arms in baroque cartouche, the domed cover with matching crest, marked on center of base and cover JOHN BURT in rounded rectangle, 7oz. 15dwt.

(Sotheby's) **$107,000**

A James I parcel-gilt wine bowl, London, 1607, maker's mark RS with heart below and flower between, the bowl chased with four fleurs-de-lys on a broad band of punched diaper ornament, the interior with raised central boss, later engraved with two coats-of-arms, marked on rim, 4in. diameter, 3oz.

(Christie's) **$46,092**

A fine silver coffee pot, maker's mark of Philip Syng Jr., Philadelphia, circa 1760, baluster form, on cast circular foot, with scroll spout and wood handle, the domed cover with large bud finial, engraved under base with monogram *MPP*, marked twice under base with *PS* and leaf pseudo-hallmark, 11½in. high; gross weight 38oz. 10dwt. *(Christie's)* **$90,500**

A George III silver coffee pot, maker's mark of Thomas Whipham and Charles Wright, London, 1762, part-spirally fluted pear-shaped and on spreading circular foot, with fluted leaf-capped spout and hinged domed cover with baluster finial, engraved beneath the foot with the initials *E.B.* and dated *1762*, 10½in. high, gross 25oz. *(Christie's)* **$5,280**

◀

A coffee pot, designed by Jean Tetard 1935, manufactured by Tetard Frères, 1936, of streamlined form, macassar profiled handle, 6¼in. high, French poinçon, maker's mark on body and lid. *(Christie's)* **$21,125**

An important silver and mixed metal pitcher, maker's mark of Tiffany & Co., New York, circa 1880, baluster form, the base spreading to imitate water, the spot-hammered sides and handle applied with copper and gold dragonflies, irises and carp in a pond with openwork leaves joining handle; 9in. high, gross weight 35oz. 10dwt.

This pitcher was made to one of Tiffany's most important designs in the Japanesque style, exhibited at the Paris Exposition of 1878.
(Christie's) **$46,000**

A silver and mixed-metal pitcher, Tiffany & Co., New York, circa 1880, globular, the spot-hammered surface applied with butterflies amid branches with gold and copper leaves, the curved handle with reeded insulators; marked under base 4706/1932, 8in. high, gross weight 30oz.
(Christie's) **$25,300**

▶

A large and unusual silver Art Nouveau pitcher, maker's mark of Gorham Mfg. Co., Providence, circa 1897; Martelé, baluster with flaring body and elongated neck, on circular stepped base, the body repoussé and chased with peacock feathers and scrolls, with curving handle shaped as feather, with engraved inscription *Thayer* under base; marked under base, 17½in. high, 126oz.
(Christie's) **$19,550**

A George II Scottish silver bullet teapot, maker's mark of Coline Allan, Aberdeen, circa 1750, on stepped spreading circular foot, the body of plain slightly compressed spherical form, with part fluted curved spout, single scroll fruitwood handle issuing from acanthus capped sockets, the hinged cover with baluster finial, 6½in. high. 20oz. gross.
(Christie's) **$22,908**

A fine silver teapot and stand by Paul Revere II, Boston, circa 1790, with a tapering cylindrical spout, a carved wood handle and an oval cover with a bud finial, the sides bright-cut engraved with floral swags centering oval shields, the conforming stand with a molded rim and four feet, gross weight 24oz.*(Christie's)* **$165,000** ▶

◀ A German silver-gilt teapot, stand and lamp, Stuttgart, circa 1815, 14½in. long x 11¾in. high., 87oz. *(Christie's)* **$6,498**

A George I Irish silver teapot apparently without maker's mark, Dublin, 1714, octagonal and later initialed *MP* below a baron's coronet and molded girdle, the underside with scratch weight 13oz 12d, height 4¼in.
(Sotheby's) **$38,410**

and secondly Winthrop Atwill, at some time after her first husband's death in 1854. Cornelia Atwill's will was dated October 30, 1895, and the two codicils of 1898 describe numerous gifts to the Metropolitan Museum of Art. *(Christie's)*   **$85,000**

An important silver and enamel exposition vase, maker's mark of Tiffany & Co., New York, 1893, made for the Columbian Exposition, 1893; design attributed to John T. Curran, formed as a bouquet of daisies, the stylized stems ending at the base in spiraling scrolls, the pierced rim with daisy buds, the flowers painted with matte-finished and shaded enamel, the interior gilt, the base etched with monogram *CAA* amidst daisies; marked under base, 14⁵/₈in. high, gross weight 56oz. 10dwt.

Cornelia A. Atwill, donor of The Magnolia Vase to the Metropolitan of New York, in 1899.

Cornelia A. Atwill was the daughter of John and Sarah Talman of New York. She married, firstly, Seward Barculo in 1834,

'The Large Water Vase' an enormous and monumental Victorian silver four-handled vase, Edward Barnard & Sons, London 1855, 1710oz., 42in. high.

The original order describes a vase and cover holding thirty gallons, weighing together 1798 oz. 6dwt. The vase was accompanied by a ladle, two feet ten inches long, with a capacity of about three pints and weighing forty-six ounces. The items were supplied with a *wainscott cupboard... with folding doors, lined with purple cloth, two swan's down bags for the vase, for body and foot... and a deal packing case.* The total cost came to £33 6s 3d. *(Sotheby's)*   **$750,500**

407

Francisco Tamagno (1851–?), Chamonix, Mont-Blanc, PLM, lithograph in colors, circa 1900, printed by Emile Pecaud & Cie., Paris, 39 x 24in. *(Christie's)* **$8,464**

Anonymous, Winter Sports in Switzerland, American Express, lithograph in colors, circa 1908, 39½ x 25in. *(Christie's)* **$10,120**

Anonymous, St. Moritz, photography and lithography in colors, circa 1950 printed by Orell Füssli, Zürich, 49 x 35½in. *(Christie's)* **$10,672**

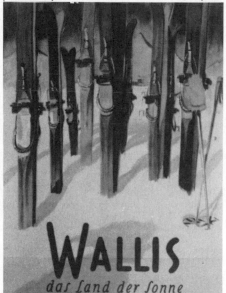

Herbert Libiszewski, (1897–1985), Wallis, lithograph in colors, 1949, printed by Sauberlin & Pfeiffer S.A., Vevey, 50 x 35½in. *(Christie's)* **$11,408**

Emil Cardinaux, (1877–1936), Zermatt, lithograph in colors, 1908, printed by J.E. Wolfensberger, Zürich, 40 x 27½in. *(Christie's)* **$10,120**

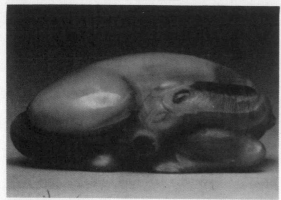

Rare Hornbill snuff bottle, in the form of a recumbent horse, gracefully posed with head resting on curled front legs, the removable tail functioning as the stopper, well hollowed out and finished, 2¾in. long. *(Butterfield & Butterfield)* **$5,750**

Important porcelain snuff bottle in the form of a Manchu official, Guangxu mark and period, the figure captured in mid-stride wearing a belted and medallioned tunic, his hat finial forming the stopper, four character Guangxu mark at the base of the robe, 4in.
(Butterfield & Butterfield) **$9,775**

A carved ivory snuff bottle, Qianlong seal mark and possibly of the period, carved as twin boys representing the spirits of mirth and harmony, wearing loose hanging robes with colorfully painted hems, one holding a peach, the other a leaf-shaped fan, both with hat-shaped stoppers, 3in. high. *(Christie's)* **$5,998**

A Louis XVI gold and enamel presentation snuff box, set with a miniature of Benjamin Franklin, the box, Paris, 1786, the miniature by François Dumont, circa 1786, the miniature signed, the box circular with panels on the sides and base of purple enamel on an engine-turned ground, the gold mounts with bell-flowers and beads on granular ground, the inside of the box of tortoiseshell inscribed on the top *Franklin a La Fayette*, the cover set with a miniature of Franklin three quarters sinister and waist length in gray jacket and waistcoat, diameter of box 3¹/8in.
(Sotheby's) **$68,500**

A Meissen gold-mounted Royal portrait rectangular snuff-box, circa 1750-55, the exterior painted with episodes from the labors of Hercules, the sides with Hercules and the Nemean lion, the Cretan Bull, Cerberus and the infant Hercules strangling Juno's snakes, the base with the 'Daughters of Evening' in the garden of the Hesperides, the interior finely stippled with a bust-length portrait of Augustus III by Johann Heinrici in armor and wearing the breast star of the Order of the White Eagle, a cannon being fired in the middle distance before distant buildings, 3½in. wide.

Frederick Augustus III King of Poland and Elector (Augustus II) of Saxony, was the son of 'Augustus the Strong' who had nominated himself for election to the Polish crown when John Sobieski, King of Poland, died in 1696.
(Christie's) **$26,887**
◄

A gilt-metal mounted Meissen bombé snuff box and cover, circa 1740, painted with several views of gallants and companions promenading in the gardens of an Italian palazzo, reserved within gilt ombrierte rocaille trellis cartouches enriched with iron-red and purple scrolls, the interior of the cover with a similar view of the Villa Borghese, Rome, the underside with figures in a rustic Italian landscape, the interior of the box gilt, 2⁷/8in. wide.
(Christie's) **$40,250**

411

A Scottish silver mounted ram's head table snuff mull, maker's mark *J.K.*, Edinburgh, 1860, the full ram's head on three brass-mounted wood castors, the horns with silver thistle and foliage chased mounts, set with foiled-back purple-stained quartz, the top fitted with a humidor, the hinged cover richly chased with thistles and foliage and cast shell-shaped thumbpiece, enclosing an oval snuff compartment, hinged cover engraved with similar thistles and foliage and with presentation inscription and surmounted with a foiled-back amber-stained oval quartz, complete with accoutrements, including snuff rake, snuff spoon, spike and ivory hammer, all on suspension chains issuing from a cast silver ram's head, 16in. wide. *(Christie's)* **$8,280**

A rare Scottish Provincial silver snuff mull, maker's mark of Hugh Ross, Tain, circa 1740, of oval capstan form, with hinged slightly domed cover, the body applied with bands of reeding to the foot, waist and rim, the cover chased with an escallop shell and stylized scrolling foliage on a matted ground, within a border of similar chased foliage alternating with trellis-work, the base inscribed *William Munro / of Achanie his box / 1744,* the interior gilt, 2¹/8in. high.

William Munro of Achanie, Co. of Sutherland, (d. 1748), eldest son of Hugh Munro, married in 1713 Isobel, daughter of the Rev. John Macpherson, minister of Farr. *(Christie's)* **$44,700**

412

A Victorian mahogany collector's cabinet, mid 19th century, with ebonized inlay and molding to the door, opening to sixteen velvet-lined slide drawers, on turned legs with brass castors, 37in. high, 26¼in. wide. *(Christie's)* **$4,745**

A Victorian walnut breakfront specimen cabinet, fitted with eight graduated drawers between paneled locking stiles, on a plinth base, 20¼in. wide x 28¼in. high. *(Christie's)* **$3,726**

A Victorian mahogany specimen cabinet, fitted with a glazed door enclosing fourteen drawers, each with a lift-off glass top, on plinth base, with an ivorine label *J.T.Crockett & Sons, Practical Cabinet Maker and Naturalists, Princes Street. Cavendish Sq. London.* W. 23½in. wide. x 38in. high x 22½in. deep. *(Christie's)* **$3,167**

An early Victorian floor standing mahogany specimen cabinet, second quarter 19th century, the rectangular cabinet with retractable door with molded border, the interior with eighteen trays fitted with an extensive collection of shell specimens and some minerals, the majority mounted on card with Latin names, 45in. high, 25¾in. wide. *(Christie's)* **$12,350**

A rare American 17th century silver spoon, maker's mark *IB*, attributed to Jurian Blanck, Jr., New York, circa 1680, in Dutch style, oval bowl with rat-tail cast handle, diamond-shaped in section, engraved initials *AVS*, ending in a realistically-modeled horse's hoof, marked on reverse of bowl *IB* in a conforming punch, 1oz. 10dwts., 6⁵/₈in. long.
(Sotheby's) **$8,625**

A rare Charles II ascribed West Country decorated Puritan spoon, with a flared stem, truncated at the end and stamped on the front side in low relief with a flowering plant motif and pricked *IH IS 1670* on the back of the bowl, by John Peard (I), Barnstaple 1670, 17.75cm. long, 1.25oz.
(Christie's) **$13,282**

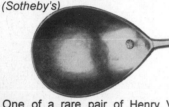

One of a rare pair of Henry VII slip-top spoons, with deeply curved fig-shaped bowls and tapering hexagonal stems swelling towards the ends, with traces of gilding on the terminals, 14.75cm. and 14.6cm. long respectively, 2oz.
(Christie's) (Pair) **$49,335**

A 15th century silver lion sejant guardant spoon, unmarked, circa 1450, 6½in. long, 28gr., 19dwt.
(Sotheby's) **$46,092**

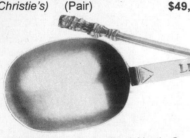

A rare Charles II ascribed North Country, death's head, disk-end spoon with a ribbed rat-tail bowl, engraved on the disk with a death's head or skull and hatched engraving, inscribed on the front of the stem *Live to Die*, the back of the disk engraved with the arms of Strickland of Boynton, Yorkshire and inscribed *Die to Live*, down the back of the stem, flanked by hatched engraving, (traces of gilding) stamped with town mark, date letter and maker's mark, by Thomas Mangy, York 1670, 19.25cm. long, 1.75oz.
(Christie's) **$13,282**

The Walter lion sejant: an extremely rare, 14th century lion sejant spoon; the long tapering hexagonal spoon terminating in the gilt figure of a lion sejant affronté on a flared pediment with tail curled around his trunk, the fig-shaped bowl deeply curved and stamped with a 'Syrian' leopard's head mark, the stem crudely scratched with two initials on the reverse *NH* or *HN*, probably second half of the 14th century, 18.9cm. long, 1.5oz.
(Christie's) **$41,745**

Devotees of Arnold Bennett's novels about the Five Towns will be aware of the names Fenton, Longton, Hanley, Burslem, Tunstall and Burmantofts – Bennett left one out – which were the center of the great pottery industry of the 19th century. It was there that Staffordshire figures were produced in their thousands and bought with eagerness to adorn chest tops and mantlepieces in homes all over the world. At one time there were over 400 factories going full blast in the area around Stoke on Trent to satisfy the demand.

Staffordshire figures were unsophisticated in their modeling and cast in the shape of popular heroes or characters from stories, plays and poetry. There was an especially popular line in politicians and heroes like Wellington and Nelson. They were press molded and decorated in underglaze blue and black with touches of color in overglaze enamel and gilding. Early examples have closed bases or a small hole in the base while 20th century pieces are usually slip cast in Plaster of Paris molds and are open ended.

A Staffordshire pottery figure of Benjamin Franklin, second half 19th century, wearing a cobalt coat and lilac-striped waistcoat, standing on a circular base inscribed, incorrectly, G. *Washington* in gilt script, holding a black tricorn hat in his left hand and the Declaration of Independence in his right, 15¼in. high.
(Sotheby's) **$2,760**

A pair of 19th century Staffordshire pottery spaniels standing on leaf capped green and rustic arched bases, in pink, 8in. high.
(Andrew Hartley) **$3,840**

▶

A black and white Staffordshire rabbit eating a lettuce leaf.
(Academy Auctioneers)
$2,550

◄ A Staffordshire creamware arbor group, circa 1765, modeled as two ladies in fashionable dress of panniered skirts and bonnets seated in a covered arbor, a pigeon perched on the rooftop above them, the figures enriched in yellow and brown streaked glazes, the arbor and pigeon in green.
(Christie's)   **$33,000**

A pair of Staffordshire pottery cat figures, ► primitively modeled in seated poses with sponged ocher markings and blue collars, 19th century, 21cm.
(Tennants)   **$800**

A pair of fine early 19th century recumbent Staffordshire lions with curly white manes, each with a lamb nestling before them on shaped and gilded base, 4¼in. high.
(Dee Atkinson & Harrison)   **$5,280**

Hansel and Gretel leaded glass window, scene of a boy and girl in peasant clothing in a wooded area with distant mountains and two birds, and a rabbit, with vining flowered border, in slag glass, some textured, stained glass faces, 62 x 42¼in.
(Skinner) **$2,990**

A leaded glass panel, designed by David Gauld for McCulloch & Co., Glasgow, 1891, the rectangular panel depicting a full-length female figure with auburn hair, in green robe, playing a stringed instrument, with stylized laurel tree, verdant landscape and flash of evening twilight beyond, formed from varying shades of blue, green, turquoise and amber antique glass, stained and painted, framed by a textured daylight border, 31½ x 18½in.
(Christie's) **$26,404**

▶

John La Farge leaded glass doorlight, symmetrical floral and foliate design in shades of blue and turquoise, central urn form with flowering branches and ribbon on a ground of rippled colorless and opalescent glass, all surrounded by 'jewel' and egg and dart borders, mounted in wood with metal rod reinforcement, 82½in. high x 36½in. wide.
(Skinner) **$27,600**

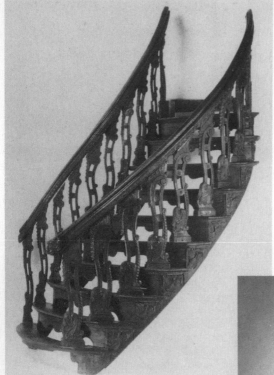

A Continental walnut and oak library staircase, 19th century, of curved form, the molded handrails terminating in scrolls, the pierced shaped spindles with stylized foliate carving and each step with shaped open risers, 124in. high x 28in. wide. *(Sotheby's)* **$7,475**

A set of Regency mahogany four-tread metamorphic library steps, by Gillows, the beige material-lined rectangular top above paneled sides, opening to reveal four beige material-lined treads, 35¾in. wide. *(Christie's)* **$15,628**

Large Step Tansu, Meiji Period, the stair treads of thick cypress planks joined to the case by wood dowels, 82⅝ x 60 x 35⅞in. *(Butterfield & Butterfield)* **$2,185**

A Federal birch-veneered and mahogany stand, Portsmouth, New Hampshire, 1790-1815, the rectangular veneered top with band inlaid top and edge above a case fitted with three graduated drawers each with three flame-birch reserves with crossbanded framing, on square tapering legs with veneered panels and socket castors, appears to retain original brasses stamped *II.J.*, 30¼in. high, 16¾in. wide.

The contrasting birch and mahogany veneers arranged in neat, linear patterns, embellished with brightly-finished brass hardware is characteristic of the finest neoclassical case forms made in Portsmouth during the Federal era.

Brass hardware, imported by American merchants from English brass foundries, supplied the bulk of hardware utilized by American craftsmen. Stamped *HJ* on the back of the bail handles, the hardware on this stand is the work of the Birmingham, England brass workers Thomas Hands and William Jenkins. Working from 1791 to 1803, Hands and William Jenkins are listed together in Birmingham city directories as 'manufacturers of commode handles, cloak pins, picture frames, looking glasses &c.' *(Christie's)* **$48,300**

A pair of mahogany luggage stands, second quarter 19th century, each with rectangular slatted tops, raised on ringed tapering legs and castors, 48cm. high, 74cm. wide. *(Sotheby's)* **$5,377**

419

A pair of George II mahogany tripod torchères, each with a dished circular top with gadrooned edge on a ring-turned spirally-fluted and acanthus wrapped baluster column and three cabriole legs headed by acanthus and C-scrolls, with paw feet, previously with castors, 14¼in. diameter, 42in. high. A pair of related tray-rimmed mahogany stands, also with serpentined and acanthus-wrapped 'claws' terminating in bacchic lion paws, were supplied in 1741 for Lyonel Tollemache, 4th Earl of Dysart's banqueting hall at Ham House, Surrey. They were described by the cabinet-maker Peter Hasert as 'high' stands, but may later have had their pedestals reduced in height from beneath their acanthus-wrapped bulbs.
(Christie's) **$139,440**

A Bavarian carved wood hall stand, late 19th century, in the form of a bear and a cub seated on a branch, on a naturalistic base fitted with a drip pan, 78in. high.
(Christie's) **$11,040**

The Arts and Crafts movement found one of its greatest exponents in the U.S.A. in Gustav Stickley (1857-1942). He was the eldest of six brothers and although he trained as a stone mason he became a famous furniture designer. In his youth he designed mainly chairs in the American Colonial style, but in 1898 he founded the firm of Gustav Stickley of Syracuse, New York which specialized in the Arts & Crafts or Mission style of furniture (from the furniture supposedly housed in the old Franciscan missions of California). He also published a magazine 'The Craftsman', which popularized this new style.

Like Art Nouveau, of which this was an offshoot, the style was seen as being a return to the simple, functional style of the medieval period. Oak was the most popular wood, and construction was simple, often with obvious signs of handwork, such as exposed mortice and tenon joints. Chairbacks were usually constructed as a series of flat vertical or horizontal boards.

Interestingly five of the brothers went into the same line of business, and the relationship between them seems to have been a highly political one. George and Albert worked in Grand Rapids, Michigan from 1891, and formed the firm of Stickley Bros. Co. around 1901. Their furniture is similar to the Craftsman style, often characterized by through tenons, but it was generally inferior in quality in terms of wood, design and finish. It was marketed as Quaint Furniture. The also produced independent designs similar to English cottage furniture.

The other two brothers, Leopold and J. George, were at first employed by Gustav but left his employment to found L.&J.G. Stickley at Fayetteville, in 1900. They too based their designs on Craftsman furniture, sometimes using veneers and laminated members, and their pieces are identifiable by the name L. & J.G. Stickley in red.

When one refers to 'Stickley' it is undoubtedly Gustav who springs most readily to mind. Certainly he was the most original designer of the family, he was also the purist, and his pieces are often austere in their unadorned simplicity.

Gustav Stickley No. 815 china cabinet, three stationery shelves, through tenons top and bottom sides, 41½in. wide. *(Skinner)* **$14,950**

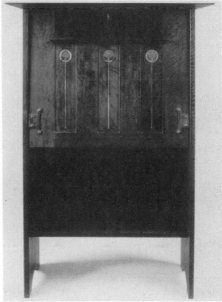

Fine and rare Gustav Stickley inlaid desk, No. 706, original dark chocolate finish with three inlaid foliate designs in exotic wood, 30¼in. wide. *(Skinner)* **$23,000**

Fine and rare Gustav Stickley child's bed, original deep brown finish, Gustav red decal, leather mattress on rope foundation, 42¾in. high.
(Skinner) **$8,050**

Rare and early Gustav Stickley bow arm Morris chair, no 336, original deep chocolate finish, original pegs and washers, original seat cushion and rope seat foundation, 30¼in. wide. *(Skinner)* **$16,100**

Gustav Stickley table with twelve Grueby tiles, circa 1902-04, with four flat rails framing twelve four-inch green tiles, signed, 24in. wide.
(Skinner) **$29,000**

Fine L. & J.G. Stickley two-door china cabinet, original dark brown finish, 48in. wide. *(Skinner)* **$4,312**

Henry van de Velde for Reinhold Hanke, Höhr-Grenzhausen, vase, circa 1903, stoneware, the underside with impressed designer's monogram and maker's mark, 10⁵/8in. wide across handles.
(Sotheby's) **$6,561**

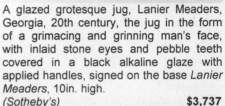

A glazed grotesque jug, Lanier Meaders, Georgia, 20th century, the jug in the form of a grimacing and grinning man's face, with inlaid stone eyes and pebble teeth covered in a black alkaline glaze with applied handles, signed on the base *Lanier Meaders*, 10in. high.
(Sotheby's) **$3,737**

Incised cobalt decorated salt glazed stoneware jug, New York, circa 1810–16, the ovoid form is decorated with a figure of a girl bent over peering between her legs, two horseshoe shaped marks are located on her backside, 17in. high.
(Skinner) **$10,350**

A rare cobalt blue-decorated salt-glazed stoneware double-jug, New Haven, Connecticut, circa 1820, each jug with a flared lip and rounded shoulder stamped two times *New Haven*, centering a molded strap handle, 7in. high.
(Sotheby's) **$1,092**

Stoneware salt glazed sculptured brown and cobalt blue decorated jug or cooler, probably Ohio or Missouri, circa 1860-70, the jug with brown glazed lizards or salamanders applied to the shoulders flanking the sculptured face of a black man, his features in high relief with coleslaw eyebrows and mustache and his eyes with cobalt blue glazed pupils, 25in. high. *(Skinner)* **$80,600**

A brown stoneware Bartmannkrug, Cologne or Frechen, circa 1550, of stout bulbous form, with bearded mask to neck of the body with the motto: *Wer: Wes: Ref: Est: Var: Ist: Wer: Wes [reversed]: Aef*, with applied portrait medallions and acanthus leaves, 8½in. *(Sotheby's)* **$1,536**

◄

Incised cobalt decorated salt glazed stoneware double jug, attributed to Stedman & Seymour, New Haven or Hartford, Connecticut, circa 1830, two ovoid form vessels joined in the middle with a reeded strap handle, decorated with pecking chickens below stylized trees, 10⅝in. high. *(Skinner)* **$17,250**

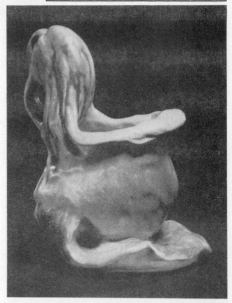

A rare glazed stoneware vase, by Georges Hoentschel, circa 1894, naturalistically modeled as an open gourd set on a leaf, a flower arching to form the handle, subtle cream and gray/blue glaze streaked with amber and speckled brown.

This piece dates from the same year as the death of Hoentschel's close friend and mentor, Jean Carriès, and the form of the piece is evocative of Carriès more naturalistic pieces, perhaps in homage to the two artists' association.
(Christie's) **$12,851**

Important Devil's face jug, Javan or Davis Brown, circa 1940, stamped signature *Brown Pottery Arden, NC, Hand Made*, the jug of unglazed stoneware depicting a devil's face with applied facial features, horns, mustache, and beard, and porcelain teeth, inscribed *Graham's Furniture and Hardware Store, Bakersvlle. NC, 19in. high.*

This unusually large jug is one of two known advertising jugs made by Brown's pottery. It was commissioned for the opening of Graham's Hardware Store.
(Skinner) **$24,150**

▶

Theodor Bogler for the Keramikwerkstatt Bauhaus Weimar, Dornburg, pitcher, circa 1922, glazed stoneware, 8½in. high.
(Sotheby's) **$6,748**

A giltwood footstool, the padded rectangular seat covered in floral petit-point needlework with a woven silk border, above four splayed eagle supports, the feet incised *I, II, III, 4* respectively, the underside with paper label inscribed *364B*, 7in. high x 27in. wide.
(Christie's) **$5,888**

One of a pair of Egyptian ivory-inlaid mahogany stools, early 20th century, inlaid overall with mother-of-pearl, boxwood and amaranth, each in the shape of a leopard, with rectangular padded seat covered in simulated leopard-skin, the heads with a geometric necklace, above a triangular tooth-shaped frieze, on naturalistic carved legs, with curled leopard-skin tails, 19in. high.
(Christie's) (Two) **$11,385**

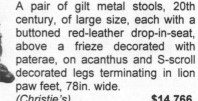

A pair of gilt metal stools, 20th century, of large size, each with a buttoned red-leather drop-in-seat, above a frieze decorated with paterae, on acanthus and S-scroll decorated legs terminating in lion paw feet, 78in. wide.
(Christie's) **$14,766**

A rare pair of green-painted turned birchwood upholstered stools, American, probably New England, 1720–1750, each having a rectangular seat on vase-and-ring-turned splayed legs, joined by turned stretchers ending in vasiform feet.
(Sotheby's) **$8,050**

A small painted stool, French, early 19th century, the hinged top in the form of four volumes, painted base with turned feet, 46cm. high, 43cm. wide.
(Sotheby's) **$3,749**

A Provincial walnut and rootwood stool, 18th/19th century, the rounded rectangular dished on three branch legs, 19in. high, the seat 13in. wide.
(Christie's) **$5,727**

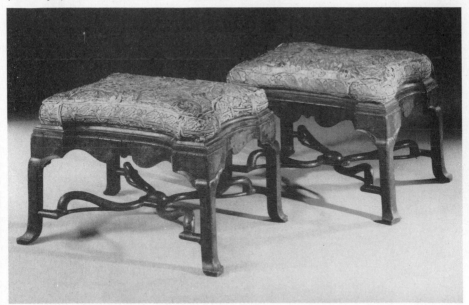

A pair of Queen Anne black and gilt-japanned stools, possibly by Philip Guibert, the rounded rectangular padded drop-in seat, with eared corners, covered in an associated late 17th century floral and foliate needlework covering for the top section and with associated early 17th century yellow and green entwined-vine needlework borders to the sides, the stool decorated overall with foliage, with a waved apron and square legs joined by a waved X-shaped stretcher, on pad feet, 18½in. high, 28½in. wide.
(Christie's) **$200,900**

A pouffe, 19th century, of circular form, the top worked with gros point flowers, 67cm. wide. *(Sotheby's)* **$1,780**

A George IV oak and brown oak stool, designed by A.W.N. Pugin, made by Morel and Seddon, the drop-in seat with its original covering of red repp with central embroidered floral motif, above a Gothic-arched paneled and molded frieze, the eared corners carved with geometric flowers within quatrefoils, above an arched apron carved with foliage to one side and stylized fruit with berries to the other, on gothic arch paneled legs and molded feet, the underside of the seat stamped *Windsor Castle 1866 Room 223* and with the *VR* flanking a crown and with paper label printed with *VR* flanking a crown and *1866*, 17½in. high, 17¼in. square. *(Christie's)* **$43,907**

A rare huanghuali folding stool, Jiaoyi, late 17th/early 18th century, the two halves of the frame of the slatted seat sharing a central member terminating in hammered iron and silver reinforcements suspending a central support locking over the hinges when opened, the seat frame with curvilinear side members, the legs of round section all the way to the base stretchers and pivoting through iron hinges with extended trefoil-terminal washers, the front stretcher with a pivoting footrest protected at the corners with metal hardware, the iron fittings decorated with beaten silver lotus designs, 20½in. high.

To date, only four huanghuali examples of this type of stool have been recorded, including the present example.

'1', a sycamore stool, designed by Pierre Chareau, circa 1925, M-shaped form, branded *PC*.
(Christie's) **$9,200**

(Christie's) **$85,000**

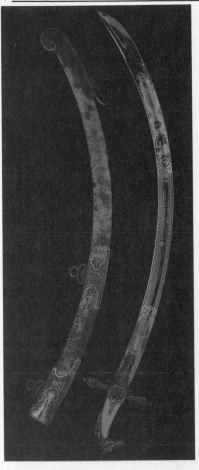

A composite cup-hilt rapier, Spanish or Italian, circa 1670-80, with very slender blade of flattened hexagonal section stamped with the Brescian name 'Caino' within the very narrow short fuller on both sides, and the name repeated, together with a crowned vacant rectangular mark, on both sides of the ricasso, iron hilt of rounded slender bars decorated with panels of entwined fluting and chiseled leaf ornament. Blade 41¾in.

(Sotheby's) **$5,750**

A very fine German silver-encrusted swept-hilt rapier, circa 1610-30, with long slender blade of flattened hexagonal section stamped *Sebastian* within the narrow fuller on one side at the forte and *Hernantes* on the other, rectangular hollow-ground ricasso, and struck with a decorative cross mark ahead of the fuller, octagonal grip retaining its original patterned binding of iron and silver wire retained by 'Turk's Heads', the blade: 42¼in.

(Sotheby's) **$13,800**

A fine Georgian presentation cavalry saber by Osborn and Gunby, dated *1804*, curved single-edged blade, with blued and gilt decoration comprising crowned *G.R.*, Neptune, Britannia, Trophy of Arms, Royal Arms, Justice, mounted cavalryman, *C.H.* monogram, foliate scrolls, floral sprays etc. and presentation inscription '*The Light Horse Volunteers of London and Westminster to Chas. John Herries Esq. in testimony of his zeal and ability in the service of the Regiment, and especially in the promotion of its discipline as assistant Adjutant in the year 1804*, gilded brass cruciform hilt, cast with tapered foliate langets, ivory grip and horse's head pommel, 30in. blade.

(Sotheby's) **$31,867**

The Symphonion was a trade make of the polyphon, which was a development of the musical box and was invented by Paul Lochmann at the time that the first gramophones and phonographs were beginning to appear. He founded the Symphonion Company in Leipzig in 1885, and, in partnership with Gustav Brachausen, started producing these machines.

Like music boxes, the sound was produced by projecting metal pegs in a disk pinging against the teeth of a metal comb. The disk was set in such a way that when it was revolved it reproduced the music or operas or songs from music halls.

A very rare Symphonion Model 25 GS in the form of a wine barrel, for 30cm. tin disks with 84-tone double comb, with wall attachment. This model differs from documented examples, in that none of them have a Bacchus figure.

Unrestored and in working order, circa 1895. *(Auction Team Köln)* **$7,114**

A German oak longcase clock/symphonion, the clock with 6.5in. silvered dial to the eight-day striking movement, by Lenzkirch, the symphonion with twin 4.5in. steel comb, to play 11.75in. metal disks, contained in ornate case of architectural design with turned cresting and finials and turned and carved columns to case with gilt brass twin scroll candle branches, conforming cupboard base, on turned and lobed supports and molded plinth base with bun feet, 78in. high.
(Canterbury Auctions) **$12,375**

A wrought iron and marble console table, designed by Edgar Brandt, circa 1925, four scrolling straps supporting marble top with pierced foliate apron, mottled gray marble top, 59in. wide, stamped *E. Brandt,* underside of marble with stenciled mark. *(Christie's)* **$46,862**

A George II mahogany, brass and mother-of-pearl inlaid supper table attributed to Frederick Hintz, the decagonal lobed dished snap top with raised center and cinquefoil center inlaid with engraved brass shell palmette and dolphin mask, scroll cartouches and mother-of-pearl trefoils centered by a foliate five petaled flower, on a baluster turned column and tripod splayed legs with brass engraved grotesque mask and shell pendant inlaid knees and pad feet with shell inlay, 70cm. diameter.

The engraved brass shells emblematic of Venus by the addition of eyes are metamorphosed into dolphin masks. ◀ *(Phillips)* **$139,400**

Painted pine and maple stretcher base table, New England, 1770–80, the scrubbed pine top with bread board ends overhangs a base in original red paint with a molded edge on the single drawer and the skirt, above four molded square legs joined by an X-stretcher also with molded edges, 49in. wide. *(Skinner)* **$34,500**

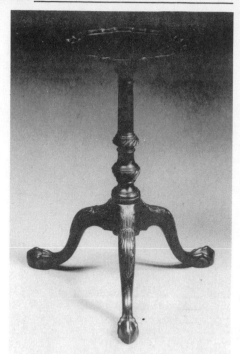

An important and very rare huanghuali altar table on stand, Gongzhuo, 15th/16th century, the two-panel rectangular top set in a mitered frame with 'water-stopping' molding and 'ice-plate' edge, the long sides of the high waist decorated with three inset panels with raised begonia-shaped centers, the short sides with one similar panel and an incense stick drawer extending almost the entire length, 38¼in. high, 41¼in. long.

This is a very fine example of a true altar table made specifically to be used in a temple for a wealthy member of refined social elite. It is made from large pieces of the best huanghuali and the workmanship is of the highest quality.
(Christie's) **$107,000**

A George II mahogany tripod table, the later circular piecrust top on a ring-turned and spirally-reeded baluster column and cabriole legs with acanthus-carved knees, on claw feet, 23in. high.
(Christie's) **$15,088**

▶
A rare Classical carved and figured mahogany and birchwood work table, Boston, Massachusetts, circa 1815, the rectangular molded top above four frieze drawers and a sliding sewing bag flanked by birchwood-inlaid dies and turned reeded-lyre-form supports joined by reeded stretchers on downswept reeded legs ending in brass paw caps and casters, 27½in. high. *(Sotheby's)* **$71,250**

432

A Regency brass-mounted rosewood cheval writing-table, by John McLean, inlaid overall with boxwood and ebonized lines, the crossbanded hinged rectangular top on an adjustable ratcheted support and with dark-red leather lined writing-surface, above a paneled frieze with a dark red leather-lined slide.

The cabinet-maker John McLean (d. 1815) acquired additional premises in Upper Marylebone Street in 1790. The label on this writing-table was in use from circa 1799 to 1805 and records his partnership with his son William (d.1825). McLean subscribed to Thomas Sheraton's The Cabinet Dictionary, London, 1803 in which he is mentioned in the text for a pouch work table... *'The design...was taken from one executed by Mr M'Lean in Mary-le-bone street, near Tottenham court road'.*
(Christie's)   **$57,270**

An oak six-leg refectory table, English late 16th/early 17th century, of large size, the top adapted to have a single drop-flap to the reverse, the cleated plank top above a facing arcaded frieze with gadrooned edge, the bulbous reeded bases with block feet joined by square section stretchers, the top variously initialed *T.M., R.T., R.W.,* and *T.A.,* and with shove ha'penny lines to one corner, 12in. 9ft. long, 31½in. wide.
(Christie's)   **$45,500**

The ancient custom of burying the dead alongside many of the items which surrounded them in life has contributed greatly to our understanding of earlier times, and most of the pottery which survives from the Tang period (618-906 AD) does in fact come from such burial sites.

These show that Tang potters were able to carve figures with skill and refinement form bodies ranging from soft earthenware to a hard porcelain-like stoneware, which varies in color from light gray and rosy buff to white.

They are usually covered with a thin, finely crackled glaze, either pale yellow or green in color, though some are more richly coated with amber brown or leaf green glazes. Splashing, streaking and mottling are all characteristics of Tang pieces, which presage the Staffordshire Whieldon and agate ware of 1000 years later. Marbling of the ware by blending light and dark clays in the body was also achieved, and again this was to be reproduced much later in the 'solid agate' ware of Staffordshire.

Of all the figures found in Tang pottery, the horse is conspicuous both for its frequency and for the spirit and character with which it is portrayed.

A rare and large painted red pottery court lady holding a dog, Tang Dynasty, mid 8th century, the lady in a delicate curved pose with right leg turned out, her hands underneath her long sleeves supporting a small dog, a lightly incised scarf falling to each side of her arms, her hair tied in a bun falling forward and to one side, her face with delicate features and touches of rouge, 20in. high.
(Christie's) **$123,500**

A rare Sancai-glazed equestrienne, Tang Dynasty, 1st half 8th century, the straw-glazed horse with delicate green-glaze to the mane and tail, the female rider poised, as though leaning forward concentrating on her game of polo, wearing a wide-lapeled jacket tied back off one shoulder and coiling around the rider's slim waist, 14in. high. *(Christie's)* **$43,700**

A Berlin chinoiserie tapestry, by Jean Barraband or Jean II Barraband, early 18th century, after designs by Guy-Louis Vernansal, Jean-Baptiste Belin de Fontenay and Jean-Baptiste Monnoyer, woven in wools and silks, the Audienz from the Grossmogulenfolge, depicting the Chinese Emperor sitting on a throne in an alcove flanked by winged grotesque figures and with an elephant emerging to the right, 141½in x 214in.

The first notable tapestry manufactories in Germany were founded around the revocation of the Edict of Nantes in 1685. Pierre Mercier, from Aubusson in the Marche, is recorded as having produced a sample tapestry for the Elector Friedrich III in Berlin in 1686. He was consequently entrusted with the establishment of a tapestry manufactory and received a grant from the Elector, but had to close it in 1713 upon the death of Friedrich III. Jean Barraband, Mercier's brother-in-law and also from Aubusson, joined Mercier in 1669. He established his own tapestry manufactory, which he ran until his death in 1709, in the Lustgarten, when his son Jean II Barraband succeeded him.
(Christie's) **$211,200**

A Tournai Renaissance allegorical tapestry, circa 1510-1530, with the winged figure of Philosophy seated on an arched architectural throne raising her left hand and holding in her right a ribbon inscribed *Felix qui potuit rerv[m] cognoscere cavsas* (happy is he who can understand the causes of things), to her left with an allegory of Nature, holding in her left arm a fruit tree and a dragon and in her right a salver with a seated youth, to her right with Plato, Pythagoras, Socrates, Homer and Aristotle conferring, possibly Bruges, 142 x 153½in. *(Christie's)* **$456,225**

A Paris allegorical tapestry, second half 17th century, woven in wools and silks, depicting Summer from the series The Seasons of Lucas, with a man shearing wheat in a wheatfield to the center, to the left with a woman bundling the wheat and being offered a jug of wine by a man and an apple by a woman, to the right with a further man shearing wheat, 10ft.3in. x 15ft6in. *(Christie's)* **$167,400**

A Brussels tapestry depicting the 'Triumph of Bacchus and Ariadne', attributed to the workshop of Jan van der Borcht, circa 1700, the two figures sitting in a golden chariot drawn by leopards, putti and bacchic revelers following behind, a scene of drunken Silenus on an ass in the left background, 17ft.8in. x 11ft.5in.*(Sotheby's)* **$46,000**

Ralph Cahoon (American 1910–1982), antique tea bin decorated with a gentleman toasting a lady, oil in wood, 24¹/8in. high. *(Skinner)* **$2,530**

A George III fruitwood tea caddy, late 18th century, modeled as a pear, with oval steel escutcheon, 6in. high. *(Christie's)* **$5,704**

Designed and executed by Hans Przyrembel, tea caddy, circa 1932, part-textured brass, the underside stamped with designer/maker's monogram *HP*, *B* and *Hand-arbeit*, 4½in. *(Sotheby's)* **$1,687**

Fine Doucai enameled bamboo decorated tea caddy, Kangxi period, of cylindrical form with horizontal ribs molded to suggest a bamboo branch, its leaves and tiny nodes outlined in underglaze blue and highlighted in two colors of green enamel and the six-character mark inscribed within a double ring to the base, 6¹/8in. high. *(Butterfield & Butterfield)* **$28,750**

◄

A rare and unusual Victorian mahogany tea caddy, circa 1840, in the form of a miniature pedestal sideboard, the galleried back above a frieze with a drawer and mock cupboards flanked by acanthus carved corbels, the interior with three lidded compartments, 13in. wide.
(Bonhams) **$3,840**

A silver champlevé enamel chinoiserie tea-caddy, marked *P. Ovchinnikov* with Imperial warrant, Moscow, 1878, with later French import mark.

Oblong, the sides with a palanquin with bearers and attendants, the ends with a seated man and woman, each with younger attendant, all within shaped border of geometric motifs with stylized floral cornerpieces, the sliding cover with a seated man and standing woman in an interior within border of geometric motifs with stylized dragon cornerpieces, 6^7/8in. long, 1,554 gr. gross.
(Christie's) **$45,264**

◄

A George II brass-mounted walnut tea-caddy, inlaid overall with boxwood and ebony checker-banding, the stepped rectangular top, with foliate-wrapped handle, enclosing a green velvet lined lid and fitted interior with shallow tray, the sides with canted corners, on claw feet, 7¾in. high, 11in. wide.
(Christie's) **$9,807**

438

A Chippendale mahogany tea table, attributed to John Townsend (1733–1809), Newport, 1765–1785, the rectangular top with molded edge above a conforming apron with central shaped drops, on stop-fluted square legs with shaped brackets, 27in. high, 82in. wide.

The molded overhanging top together with the cyma-shaped brackets, pendants and stop-fluted legs create a bold, architectonic design reflecting the design preferences of Rhode Island.
(Christie's) **$79,500**

A Chippendale carved mahogany tea table, Philadelphia, 1765–85, the circular top with molded scalloped edge tilting and turning above a birdcage support over a fluted columnar pedestal with compressed ball carved with mid-band base on a tripod base with acanthus leaf and C-scroll carved cabriole legs and ball-and-claw feet, 28in. high, 35½in. diameter.

With its scalloped edge, fluted pedestal centering a compressed ball, symmetrical C-scrolled trailing foliate carved knees and elongated ball-and-claw feet, this table exhibits the superb characteristics of eighteenth century Philadelphian Rococo; with its short fluted pedestal, bold compressed ball and molded plinth, it also shows variations within the standard Rococo vocabulary.

Known in the eighteenth century as a pillar-and-claw table, claw table, or round-top table, this form, in comparison to tray-top tables, could be placed upright against a wall when its use was finished.
(Christie's) **$121,300**

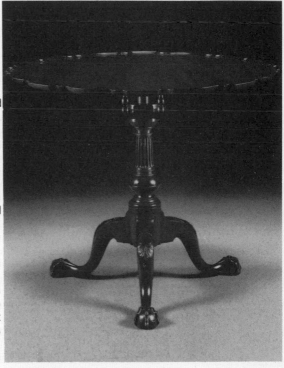

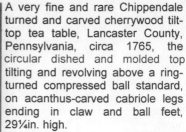

A very fine and rare Chippendale turned and carved cherrywood tilt-top tea table, Lancaster County, Pennsylvania, circa 1765, the circular dished and molded top tilting and revolving above a ring-turned compressed ball standard, on acanthus-carved cabriole legs ending in claw and ball feet, 29¼in. high.
(Sotheby's) **$288,500**

A Chippendale mahogany tray-top tea table, probably New York, 1750–1770, the rectangular dished top with cusped corners above a conforming plain apron, on four cabriole legs with shell-carved knees and ball-and-claw feet, 32in. wide.

This table, with its tray top, cusped corners, shell-carved knees, tapering cabriole legs, and diminutive sculptured ball and claw feet, reflects the transition from the grace and simplicity of the Queen Anne style to the drama and flamboyance of the Chippendale style. This table employs design characteristics found in both Boston and New York, and delineates the close mercantile relationship between these colonial port cities. Not only was the square tray-top the most popular form for a tea table among Boston patrons and craftsmen, but also the similarities of this example to earlier Boston Queen Anne tray-top forms and the use of white pine as the secondary wood, are Boston features. In comparison, New York tray-top tea tables exhibit a thicker molded edge, highly foliate carved knees, and larger ball and claw feet.
(Christie's) **$63,000**

The most widely accepted account of how the Teddy bear got its name is the one which tells how, while on a hunting trip in 1902, President Theodore 'Teddy' Roosevelt could not bring himself to shoot a bear cub which he had in his sights. It was, after all, conveniently tethered to a post by some well-meaning aide. Such fore'bear'ance on the part of the notable hunter captured the attention of the popular press, and the incident was recreated in a cartoon of the day. It certainly did no harm to the Presidential image, and Roosevelt adopted the image of a cuddly little bear as his own. When his daughter married in 1906, the wedding breakfast tables were decorated with tiny bears made by the Steiff Toy Company.

It was thus that the greatest name in bear-making came onto the stage. Margarete Steiff, a crippled German toymaker, had been making toy bears since about 1900, but it was the new craze for cuddly plush bears that was to make her fortune. The style of her early models is perhaps not the most appealing to modern taste, for she designed them with humped backs, long muzzles, elongated arms and legs and long bodies. They were stuffed with wood shavings and covered in plush, and most had a growler. All Steiff bears made before 1910 are very valuable, and if the growler still works the price rockets.

A rare black Steiff center seam teddy bear, with black shoe button eyes backed with red felt, pronounced clipped snout, black stitched nose, mouth and claws, swivel head, jointed shaped limbs, cream felt pads, hump and button in ear, 21in. tall, circa 1912.

It is believed that as little as twenty-one black bears were produced with the desirable center seam.
(Christie's) **$17,370**

'Bechico', a white Steiff teddy bear with brown and black glass eyes, pronounced snout, brown stitched nose, mouth and claws, swivel head, jointed shaped limbs, 'spoon' shaped paws and feet, felt pads, hump, growler and button in ear, 24in. tall, circa 1929.

'Bechico' was brought for a small child living in Italy in 1929. The Granbiulli he wears was made by the child's nanny, an exact replica of what a young child would wear at school. Blue for the boys and pink for the girls. 'Bechico' has spent all his life in Italy with the same family.
(Christie's) **$14,509**

◀ A dual plush Steiff teddy bear, German, circa 1920, bought by Jack Wilson, Chairman of the House of Nisbit, teddy bear manufacturers, on behalf of a private friend in the USA.
(Sotheby's)   **$88,000**

A very rare short red plush teddy bear, ▶ called Alfonzo, with button eyes, excelsior stuffing and felt pads dressed as a Russian, having belonged to Xenia Georgievna, Princess of Russia and second cousin to Tsar Nicholas II. Xenia was stranded in England following a summer holiday at Buckingham Palace when war broke out in 1914. 13in. high with Steiff button (voice box inoperative, front paws recovered in chamois leather), 1906-1909. (Christie's)   **$12,100**

◀ Teddy Girl, a Steiff cinnamon center-seam teddy bear, with large 'spoon' shape feet and hump, circa 1904, 18in. high.
    This bear was the centerpiece in the collection of the leading arctophile, Colonel T R Henderson. When his collection was sold in 1994, she set the record price ever fetched at auction for a teddy bear, which remains unbroken. Teddy Girl went to Japan, to become the main attraction of a new teddy bear museum there.
(Christie's)   **$177,100**

A very early Marconi Model 703 combined radio, record player and television, one of only eight models said to have been produced. *(Auction Team Köln)*

$2,328

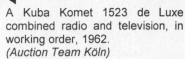

◄ A Kuba Komet 1523 de Luxe combined radio and television, in working order, 1962. *(Auction Team Köln)*

$8,408

Philippe Charbonneaux for Teléavia, television P111, 1950s, dark purple and cream wood and metal, brass, purple tinted plastic front, 54½in. high. *(Sotheby's)* ▶

$3,167

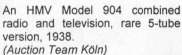

An HMV Model 904 combined radio and television, rare 5-tube version, 1938. *(Auction Team Köln)* ◄

$2,455

A French terracotta bust, entitled 'Le Chinois', after the model by Jean-Baptiste Carpeaux, last quarter 19th century, looking to his right, with long pigtail, inscribed *J. Bte Carpeaux* and with the Susse foundry stamp and cachet, on square spreading socle, 25⁵/8in. high.
(Christie's) **$12,180**

A pair of Austrian patinated terracotta busts of Omphale and a Merovingian Queen, by Goldscheider, after models by Albert-Ernest Carrier-Belleuse, late 19th/early 20th century, each with long hair, Omphale wearing a bearskin, the Merovingian Queen wearing an eagle skin, each on a square spreading socle, each inscribed *Carrier-Belleuse*, with Goldscheider stamp and numbers and impressed *REPRODUCTION RESERVEE*, 28in. and 29¼in. high. *(Christie's)* **$9,780**

An Austrian gilt and patinated terracotta figure entitled 'Chianti', by Friedrich Goldscheider, Vienna, late 19th century, of a young woman in summer dress and bonnet, helping with the vine harvest, on a circular naturalistic base modeled with a trailing vine branch, with raised title to the front, impressed *Friedrich Goldscheider /1764/23/22*, 42¾in. high.
(Christie's) **$5,623**

A North Italian terracotta figure of St. John, 16th century, the seated figure clad in a tunic and turned to the left, an inscribed tablet in his left arm and his right hand pointing to it: *Inprincipio Erat Verbu*, the eagle by his side, on shaped base, 16½in. high.
(Sotheby's) **$34,500**

An Austrian bronzed terracotta group of three schoolboys, by Hanniroff, produced by Friedrich Goldscheider, Vienna, late 19th century.

Seated on a brick wall, wearing jacket and shorts, inscribed to the side *Haniroff* and impressed to the back *Friedrich Goldscheider* and with the numbers *35/1190/2061*, 22¼in. high.
(Christie's) **$6,600**

A French terracotta group of a lion savaging a wild boar, by Edme Dumont, signed and dated *1768*, the fierce beast baring his teeth, his front paws tearing at the struggling boar, inscribed on the reverse: *E. Dumont F'.1768*, 14½in. high.

Remarkably few sculptures exist by Edme Dumont (1719-1775) who was a pupil of Bouchardon and was elected to the Academie Royale in 1768 with his well-known marble sculpture of Milo of Croton, now in the Louvre.

This terracotta group reflects the French fascination with the hunt which appears from the seventeenth century onwards, as evidenced by such paintings as Oudry's 'Combat between Lions and Wild Boars' (1745) illustrating a similar scene.
(Sotheby's) **$28,750**

A terracotta verniciata bust of St. John the Baptist, circa 1580, Della Robbia workshop, modeled as a youth, slightly to the right wearing a Roman cobalt-blue mantle fastened at the shoulders over a camel-skin vest, 13½in. high. *(Christie's)* **$17,284**

Otto Lindig for Staatliche Majolika-Manufaktur Karlsruhe, cocoa pot and cover, circa 1923, glazed terracotta, the underside with factory mark and impressed *Made in Germany*, 7³/₈in. high. *(Sotheby's)* **$11,622**

A French terracotta bust of a young girl, attributed to Jean-Baptiste Pigalle (1714–1785), circa 1770, the head slightly inclined to sinister with soft rounded features and deep incised eyes, her hair swept up at the back and coifed with tight ringlets on the sides, the bodice of her dress edged with lace and modeled with a flower, on red marble socle, 14in. high.

Trained in the Paris studios of Robert Le Lorrain and then of Jean-Baptiste Lemoyne, Pigalle later shared a studio in Rome with Guillaume Coustou II. Upon his return to Paris, in 1744, he became a member of the Academy with his marble figure of 'Mercury attaching his heel wings.' A number of important commissions followed including the marble bust of Madame de Pompadour in 1751 and the Louis XV monument for Reims which established his reputation. *(Sotheby's)* **$11,500**

A 17th century stumpwork embroidery, in silk colored threads and beads, depicting The Judgement of Solomon, dated *1654*, 9 x 13in. *(G.E. Sworder)* **$32,800**

An early southwest wearing blanket, possibly New Mexico, Rio Grande area, circa 1800–50, woven in a classic style, composed of two slightly asymmetrical panels joined at the center, woven in natural and indigo-dyed handspun wool, with a pattern of fine stripes flanking rows of tiny rectangles, one area stretched showing signs of use.

The use of fine-spun cotton warps in pairs rather than plied and twisted is an unusual feature of this blanket. Fine plied cotton warps were commonly used in Saltillo sarape weaving and in the few known Rio Grande cotton blankets all but one appear to have plied cotton warps.

The use of cotton in New Mexico weaving continued past the mid 1800s so that the use of cotton, as such, does not automatically indicate an early date.

The weft is very finely spun for Rio Grande textiles and shows the use of pure Churro wool, for there is no grease to indicate a crossing with the Merinos which came in 1859 and increased sharply after that time.

The basic color combination of indigo blue, in two shades, and white is rare in southwestern weaving. The pale beige in some areas of the white suggest a native yellow-producing dye.
(Sotheby's) **$18,400**

An Italian armorial embroidery, second quarter 18th century, with metal-thread and silk embroidered on red velvet ground, depicting a central armorial shield, almost certainly that of Francesco Maria Pasini, surmounted by a Bishop's hat, framed by a scrolling ribbon and a floral and foliate band with flowerheads to the angles, 134 x 96in.

The coat-of-arms of this embroidery is that of the Pasini family.
(Christie's) **$15,180**

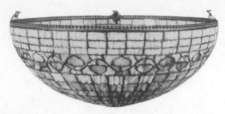

Tiffany acorn ceiling lamp shade, leaded yellow amber and opal white rippled glass domed shade with decorative belt of green acorn-shaped leaf and vine motif, beaded rim with four integrated hanging hooks, unsigned. *(Skinner)* **$6,325**

Tiffany Studios Laburnum table lamp, broad domed favrile glass segments leaded as yellow cluster blossoms pendant from brown branches with green leaves against a sky-blue background, two tags *Tiffany Studios, New York 1539,* mounted on reticulated bronze doré six-socket adjustable base, impressed *Tiffany Studios/New York 397,* shade diameter 21in. *(Skinner)* **$129,000**

Tiffany bronze tulip lamp on turtleback base, domed leaded glass shade with multicolored upright tulip blossoms and buds against rare favrile fractured transparent glass background rim impressed *Tiffany Studios N.Y., 1456-11,* raised on urn-form bronze base with twelve inset green favrile turtleback tiles below pierced rim for heat dispersal of interior lighting device, 23in. high. *(Skinner)* **$34,500**

Tiffany bronze and favrile glass chandelier, striated amber glass segments arranged in large conical brickwork shade with 5in. drop apron centering Arts and Crafts decorative circle-and-bar medial border motic, rim impressed *Tiffany Studios New York,* supported by six bronze chains suspended from conforming ceiling mount with six-light socket wheel at center, total height 54in. *(Skinner)* **$14,950**

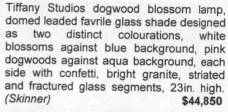

Tiffany Studios dogwood blossom lamp, domed leaded favrile glass shade designed as two distinct colourations, white blossoms against blue background, pink dogwoods against aqua background, each side with confetti, bright granite, striated and fractured glass segments, 23in. high. *(Skinner)* **$44,850**

Tiffany nasturtium double tiered chandelier, brilliant hued conical leaded glass shade depicting nasturtium blossoms of opal white, red, yellow, orange, blue, green, and brilliant royal purple among striated and mottled green leaves and stems with gray green trelliswork interspersed, beaded rim impressed *Tiffany Studios New York*, total height 48in., diameter 29in. *(Skinner)* **$225,000**

Tiffany wild rose border lamp, green and gold favrile glass segments in unusual geometric design above wide belt of red, pink and green striated glass rose blossoms and leaves impressed *Tiffany Studios New York 1997*, mounted on three-socket base with flared shaft and pedestal foot impressed Tiffany Studios New York, 22½in. diameter. *(Skinner)* **$33,350**

'Dante', a Morris & Co. two tile panel, designed by Burne-Jones, painted in shades of blue with Dante holding a book, inside a scrolling foliage border, scroll title to base, in original frame, 33cm. high. *(Christie's)* **$1,553**

Important Marblehead tile in original frame, decoration attributed to Arthur Baggs, landscape scenes with three shades of matte greens, trees with brown trunks and a speckled mustard sky and foreground, Marblehead frame in original finish with label *9.50*, impressed Marblehead marks, 9¾in. high. *(Skinner)* **$13,800**

An enameled tile panel, English, circa 1880, comprising three tiles showing two musician angels surrounding the Virgin, Renaissance architectural surround 4½ x 3in. each tile, enameled signature *DH* on each tile. *(Christie's)* **$2,062**

Minstrel, a Morris & Co. two tile panel, painted in shades of blue with a Minstrel figure playing two pipes before a fruiting foliage, in original frame, 27cm. high.

By about 1865 William Morris had designed twelve Minstrel Angels for schemes of decoration. In 1866 six figures were used for the tiled reredos at Findon church in Sussex and six were painted on the wooden organ case at Beddington church in Surrey. Over several decades the designs were re-used many times for stained-glass in numerous churches. During the early 1870s Charles Fairfax Murray, a protégé of Burne-Jones and an assistant at Morris, Marshall Faulkner & Company, adapted at least seven of these designs for pairs of six inch tiles. Their earliest recorded execution in this form was as blue monochrome tiles for the music shop of Novello & Company in 1872. Some of the figures were repeated in blue and in polychrome during the 1870s and 1880s and finally in deeper inky blue or in a limited polychrome, probably after 1900. *(Christie's)* **$3,795**

Exceptional Chelsea Keramic Art Works, Robertson & Sons tile, ceramic tile with a copper covered relief of a figure holding two rearing stallions, deep rich patina, inscribed on front *Sketched from Century Mag. HCR*, impressed on back *Chelsea Keramic Art Works, Robertson & Sons*, 10½in. square. *(Skinner)* **$5,750**

One of two William de Morgan luster tiles, decorated in various colored lusters with a Dodo and an exotic bird, both 6in. diameter, bears seal mark to back with date '98.
(Canterbury Auctions)(Two) **$2,550**

A Regency japanned metal oval tray, circa 1830, the red ground with a gilt heightened border of trailing vines, centred by an oval reserve depicting figures by a lake, the gallery with twin pierced handles, 30in. wide.
(Christie's) **$3,353**

Whimsical Victorian painted tin candle screen, 19th century, depicting girls with cats, 10in. high.
(Skinner) **$1,610**

Painted and galvanized tin birdbath, America, 19th century, the square recessed top with cove molded sides above the square recessed paneled pedestal on a stepped plinth, old weathered green painted surface, 32in. high. *(Skinner)* **$2,990**

◄ A Victorian polychrome-painted tôle bucket, the pierced oval gallery with shaped handle, the waisted body decorated with green, yellow and red flowers, on an oval spreading base, 15in. high. *(Christie's)* **$1,600**

White Star Line 'Olympic' & 'Titanic' Largest Steamers In The World, a publicity booklet entitled Notes and Illustrations of the First and Second Class Passenger Accomodation on the New White Star Line Triple-Screw Royal Mail Steamers 'Olympic' & 'Titanic'. Each 45,000 Tons, sixteen color plates including folding frontispiece of dining saloon, others for the reception room, reading and writing room, smoke room, restaurant, main staircase, verandah café, turkish bath-cooling room, swimming bath, deck state room, single berth state room, sitting room of parlor suite, second class dining saloon, second class library, second class promenade deck, cover color plate by Sam M Brown, 32pp, 12 x 18cm, bound with red ribbon, 1912. *(Onslow's)*   **$8,000**

White Star Line Fleet includes 'Olympic' 45,000 Tons 'Titanic' 45,000 Tons Largest Steamers In The World, a hanging calendar on card for 1912 with illustration of liner by Montague B Black, the tear-away calendar showing February 1912, on blue background, published by Ismay Imrie & Co London Southampton and Liverpool. *(Onslow's)*   **$3,680**

S.S. Carpathia Post-Disaster messages, 17th April, 1912, messages sent by survivors of the Titanic to New York, one initialed *HB*, Marconi headed paper stamped *CARPATHIA 17 APR 1942*, the signals secured to two album pages, 5½ x 8½in.

Harold Bride, the second Wireless Officer aboard Titanic assisted the Carpathia's with the mamouth task of transmitting signals to New York which they could not complete before they arrived. *(Christie's)*   **$2,576**

White Star Line Olympic & Titanic Third Class Accommodation The Largest Steamers In The World, a publicity booklet entitled 'Interesting Illustrations and Facts Relating to the White Star Line Triple Screw Royal Mail Steamers 'Olympic' & 'Titanic' Each 45,000 Tons', five color plates showing third class dining room, general room, two berth cabin, smoke room and four berth cabin, seven black and white photographic plates showing underneath view during construction, in Belfast dry dock April 1st 1911, 10 x 15cm., 1912. *(Onslow's)*   **$4,800**

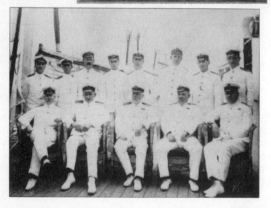

Captain Smith, a rare sepia photograph showing Smith as a member of a group of thirteen officers in White Star line Mediterranean Day Dress, Smith is shown seated center front, also shown (front right) is Hugh McElroy who lost his life with Smith when he served as Chief Purser aboard 'Titanic', 10 x 13in. *(Christie's)*   **$2,576**

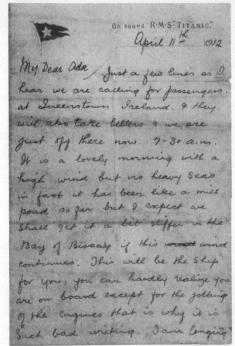

On Board RMS Titanic, an autographed signed letter on four sides on official writing paper with embossed company burgee and white Star Line watermark, letter dirty and detatched on some folds;
April 11th 1912 My Dear Ada, just a few lines as I hear we are calling for passengers at Queenstown Ireland & they will also take letters & we are just off there now 7.30am It is a lovely morning with high wind but no heavy seas in fact it has been like a mill pond so far but I expect we shall get it a bit stiffer in the Bay of Biscay if this wind continues This will be the ship for you, you can hardly realise you are on board except for the jolting of the engines that is why it is such bad writing I am longing when you can come out... I turned in at ten o'clock last night but could get no sleep owing to the rattle of water bottles, glasses and other things too numerous to mention so I was glad to get up at six o'clock...Already for you to have a trip I wish it had been possible for us to have all come together It would have been a treat I have fallen in with young couple on Liskeard named Chapman He has been home for six months holiday and got married and they are now going out together He like myself worked for his father but could not get on with him.... In fact you don't meet anyone rough second class I have a bunk to myself which is pretty lovely but still would rather be alone than have a foreigner who I could not talk to There are two beds in a bunk and a couch...I must draw to a close as we are getting pretty close to Queenstown and I'm afraid of missing the post... Your ever loving husband Jim. Everybody tells me I shall not regret the step I have taken so buck up and we shan't be long.

Jim Hocking was a second class passenger going out to America to start a new life. His wife and two children were due to travel with him but the children were too ill so he went on ahead alone and perished in the disaster.
(Onslow's) **$4,480**

A memorial picture of the 'Titanic' musicians, the eight musicians photographed with the title *The Heroic Musicians Of The Titanic* who died at their posts like men, *April 15th 1912* and a verse from 'Nearer, my God, to Thee' at the bottom, 15¹/5 x 11in.
(Christie's) **$2,576**

▶

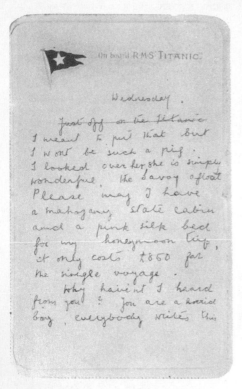

On Board RMS Titanic, an autograph signed letter on two sides on official letter card with printed burgee and reverse with White Star Line and showing burgee, from Eileen Gessney addressed to Irvine Aitchison Esq, Sherwood, Beckenham, Kent;

Wednesday – Just off on the Titanic (this crossed out) I meant to put that but I won't be such a pig I looked over her she is simply wonderful the Savoy afloat ! Please may I have a mahogany state cabin and pink bed for my honeymoon trip, it only costs £850 for the single voyage Why haven't I heard from you… If I write any more I shall say silly things than ever Eileen. Postmarked *Southampton 2.30pm April.*

Miss Eileen Gessney managed to get aboard Titanic prior to sailing to look around. She wrote this letter card whilst on board for a bit of fun and sent it to her then fiance. *(Onslow's)* **$3,360**

S.S. Virginian: Titanic Disaster and Post-Disaster messages, 14th April 1912 twelve messages starting *(11.15pm) Hear MGY call CQD SOS has struck iceberg pos 41.46N 50.14W (11.35pm) We are putting passengers and – off in small boats – weather clear. Titanic; including messages from Titanic (MGY), other vessels and Cape Race, seeking the nearest ship for assistance: (11.40pm) The MKC is making all speed for MGY but his position is 40.32N 61.18 You are much nearer to him. He is already putting women off in boats and he says weather is clear and calm Cape Race. (12.10am.) Hear MGY very faintly power greatly reduced…(12.20am) Hear 'V' faint in spark similar to MGY's Hear High tune spark probably MGY dg MBC spark died away abruptly (2.19am.) same spark called..[?].. and broke away and finally (12.27am) MGY calls unable to make out his signal Ended very abruptly as if power suddenly switched off – His spark somewhat blurred,* an out-lined footnote written vertically on the left side: *Carpathia says MGY has gone down with all hands as far as we know with the exception of 20 boatloads which they have picked Can't see anymore boats now.*

And Post-Disaster messages, mainly post-sinking 'conversation' with Carpathia: noting *Carpathia says Our Skipper is leaving here with all on board about 800 passengers chiefly third class*

William James Cotter (1885–1955) was the Marconi wireless operator from Virginian between March and August 1912.

MGY is the call-sign for Titanic, the identity of MKC is Olympic (Captain Haddock) who was certainly further away than Virginian, Carpathia (Captain A.H. Rostron) was MPA and MBC was the Baltic (Captain R.B. Ranson).

The sheet with the Disaster Messages contains the last recorded call from Titanic, believed to have been received by the Virginian alone. This is the letter 'V', a Marconi test signal which Cotter said was faint in spark and similar to MGY's. As Titanic sank, her aerial, which was suspended between the fore and aft masts, changed position, forcing the Titanic

11.15 Hear mgy calling cqd sos has struck iceberg
41.46 N   50.14 W

mgy — mgy has struck an iceberg and requires
immediate assistance His position 41.46 N
50.14 W ask your Captain to go to his assistance
Cape Race

11.35 pm

3.45 mst

mkc de mgy — sinking.
We are putting passengers and — off in
small boats — weather clear
11.35   Titanic

12.27am mgy calls unable make out his signal
Ended very abruptly as if power suddenly
switched off. — His spark somewhat blurred.

mgy mgy. Here is a confirmation msg for you of what we
have already said

mBc   about 200 miles east of us / 15am
Baltic

7.15am Russian liner Birma bound Rotterdam
55 miles from Titanic Cannot hear anything
of him. Things are serious.

2.17am Hear High tune spark probably mgy cq mBc
Him died away abruptly
2.19am Jam spark called mBc and broke away

(left margin handwritten note) Carpathia says mgy has gone down with all hands as far as we know with the exception of the lifeboats which Carpathia has picked up

operator (probably Jack Phillips), to retune and send test signals to see if there was anyone still with him, which Virginian's operator was able to pick up. Minutes later the Titanic's generators crashed through her bulkheads and she slipped beneath the Atlantic. Cotter appears to have used both Ship Time and New York Time variously throughout the messages; Ship Time is one hour fifty minutes ahead of New York Time. This explains why the last messages were received at 2.19am and finally at 12.27; this time 12.27(Ship's time 2.17am) coincides with the approximate time that Harold Bride reported his and Phillips' leaving the wireless cabin, shortly before the ship foundered.

(Christie's)   **$18,400**

White Star Line TSS Titanic color art postcard, Tuck's Oilette Celebrated Liners Series No. 9898 from Thomas Mudd to his mother Mrs Thomas Mudd, The Street, Hunting Field, Halesworth, Suffolk; *Dear Mother, Arrived at Southampton safe The Titanic is a splendid boat + you hardly know you are moving*

Tom Mudd, a young man of 19, was emigrating to the United States to start a career. He was sailing as a second class passenger and perished in the disaster.
(Onslow's) **$5,760**

A relic from the RMS Titanic, comprising a pair of ivory and brass opera glasses in case, inscribed, together with a framed manuscript letter and a volume 'Nicholls's Seamanship Guide'.

The letter states *These opera glasses were found in the fur lined coat pocket worn by Mr T Beattie the Chicago Millionaire after his body was found drifting in a lost boat from the Titanic on 13 May 1912 twenty eight days after the disaster. I was on the Oceanic at the time and were given to me as a souvenir. Alf Churchill Master, Barge Star Southwick.*

The volume is autographed by Alf Churchill and profusely annotated.
(Andrew Hartley) **$3,200**

Toasters are a comparatively new collectible, dating from the early years of this century. Many ingenious designs were patented, including one which had the toast moving through the machine like a car through a car wash! Some are very decorative, in particular those with ceramic mounting, which could of course be suitably adorned and painted.

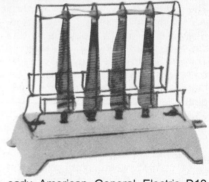

An early American General Electric D12 ceramic toaster with two-sided toasting fork, white ceramic base with gold decoration, original flex with metal plug, circa 1910. *(Auction Team Köln)* **$772**

The Eclipse, an example of the first known electric toaster, made in England, 1893. *(Auction Team Köln)* **$2,100**

An American Toastrite ceramic toaster by Pan Electric Mfg. Co., Ohio. *(Auction Team Köln)* **$1,155**

Universal E 9410 heart shaped push-button toaster with unusual flip mechanism, circa 1929.
(Auction Team Köln) **$850**

A Toastrite Blue Willow luxury American ceramic toaster, prototype, thus without electric connection.
(Auction Team Köln) **$1,694**

The name 'Toby' has long associations with conviviality and it was used by Shakespeare in his Toby Belch and by Laurence Sterne in his character Uncle Toby in 'Tristram Shandy'. Today it has come to signify a jug made like a seated male figure in a tricorn hat with a pipe or a mug of beer on his knee. This is particularly due to the creations of Doulton who took up and developed the long history of the Toby jug and made it beloved by a vast collecting public.

From 1815, when John Doulton first set up his business, the firm made Toby jugs but the earliest examples were only brown salt glazed as they had been for centuries. In 1925 however colored Toby Jugs were added to the range by Harry Simeon and their potential was immediately recognised by Charles J. Noke who made their colors even more vivid and developed them into one of the company's best selling lines.

The Best Is Not Too Good D6107 Toby jug, designer H. Fenton, 4½in. high, issued 1939-1960. *(Lyle)* **$392**

Huntsman, a Royal Doulton Kingsware Toby jug, 7½in. high. *(Lyle)* **$616**

Charlie Chaplin Toby jug, designer unknown, 11in. high, issued circa 1918. *(Lyle)* **$3,600**

Cliff Cornell (Blue Suit) Toby jug, designer unknown, 9¼in. high, issued 1956 in a limited edition of 500. *(Lyle)* **$440**

Old Charley D6030 Toby jug, designer H. Fenton, 8¾in. high, issued 1939-1960. *(Lyle)* **$296**

Squire D6319 Toby jug, designer H. Fenton, 6in. high, issued 1950-1969. *(Lyle)* **$392**

George Robey Toby jug, designer unknown, 10½in. high, issued circa 1925. *(Lyle)* **$4,000**

Tôleware is essentially painted tin, and is akin to bargeware inasmuch as the original purpose was to make basic, functional items such as coffee pots more decorative. As in so many cases however, what started as something relatively simple became much more sophisticated . Some tôleware items, such as a coalscuttles became very florid and ornate and worthy of a place in the most elegant drawing room.

A Victorian black japanned tôle purdonium of oval form, painted in gilt and enamels with foliage, with cast side handles raised on a socle base, 67cm. high.
(Cheffins Grain & Comins) **$1,600**

A painted tôle log bin, circa 1850, of oval form with pierced borders, swags and rosettes, the painted lemon-yellow ground decorated in dark green, brown and gold, flanked by two handles, the shaped cover with a spherical handle, on four feet, 66cm. high. *(Sotheby's)* **$7,873**

▶

A rare wriggle-work decorated tôleware coffeepot, Pennsylvania, 19th century, of ovoid diamond form with strap handle and conical lid, each side decorated with an American eagle and shield and tulips; the handle decorated with a serpent, raised on a flared and perforated base, 13¾in. high. *(Sotheby's)* **$1,495**

A Regency tôle ware tea tray, of canted rectangular shape, the angled gallery borders japanned in scarlet and gilded with bands of leafy swags, lunettes, guilloche and vermicular motifs, forming a frame to the central reserve painted with a still life of fruits, woodbine and a pot of auriculas on a gloomy ledge, 76cm. wide. *(Tennants)* **$13,600**

A fine painted tôleware tray, English, early 19th century, painted with a depiction of the death of General Wolfe, after the painting Benjamin West, the oval borders with handholds decorated with a meandering grape cluster and leaf motif, 23¼in. high x 30in. long.

The death of General Wolfe (1770) was Benjamin West's masterpiece. Wolfe was mortally wounded while commanding the British Forces against the French on the Heights of Abraham outside Quebec on September 13, 1759. From its first conception, West rejected literalism and embraced rhetoric in this fabricated scene. The bizarre notion that Wolfe would have tolerated the presence of Indian auxiliaries of the French, whom he considered cruel and depraved barbarians, at the moment of his apotheosis was a near bitter jest, but West had seen the Mohawks as allies of the British in Pennsylvania and idealized them as embodiments of the native noble savage. *(Sotheby's)* **$7,475**

A fine painted tôle tray depicting Aurora in her chariot, Boston School, circa 1810-1830, depicting the goddess of dawn, Aurora, driving her chariot through cloudy skies, heightened in gilt, 15½in. high x 20¼in. long.

This scene of Aurora was favored on the eglomisé panels of a number of banjo clocks by Aaron Willard and Aaron Willard, Jr. *(Sotheby's)* **$3,105**

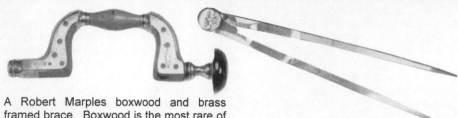

A Robert Marples boxwood and brass framed brace. Boxwood is the most rare of all fillings and this is the only example known. Although the brace is not named it bears the *ROBt. MARPLES* stamp of the 'Ultimatum Brass Framed Brace'. *(Tool Shop Auctions)* **$3,320**

A pair of 9in. German silver dividers with the face of the moon on both sides of the hinge. *(Tool Shop Auctions)* **$842**

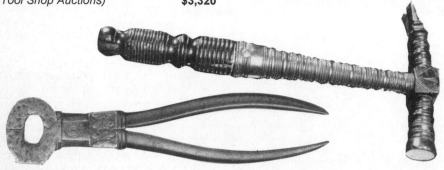

A pair of farrier's pliers, 10 x 2in. exhibiting the form that would have graced the smithies of Louis XIV when he visited his hunting lodge at Chambord. Beautifully proportioned and decorated and dated 1706. *(Tool Shop Auctions)* **$5,727**

18th century socketed hammer of superb style, 9in. overall, wooden handle elaborately turned in a series of flamboyant rings and circular reeds, 1769. *(Tool Shop Auctions)* **$4,290**

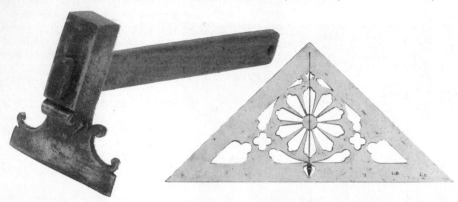

An 18c French veneer hammer with such style and elegance that only the photograph can do it justice! *(Tool Shop Auctions)* **$2,025**

A tremendous brass plumb square, 15in. wide with exotic fretworked plumb bobs forming the central design, probably 18th century. *(Tool Shop Auctions)* **$647**

A rare set of Steiff skittles, comprising king bear standing on turned wooden base, in red felt tail coat, red felt crown, black shoe button eyes and nose, pink felt inner ear with remains of white label, 10in. tall; a cream felt rabbit, with pink felt inner ears, black shoe button eyes, pink stitched nose and mouth, original ribbon and bell and button in ear, seated on turned wooden base, 8in. tall; a cream felt elephant, with black bead eyes, white felt tusks, original ribbon and button in ear, seated on turned wooden base, 7in; a gray felt cat, with black shoe button eyes, pink stitched nose, and mouth, original ribbon and bell, button in ear, seated on turned wooden base, 8in. tall; a cream felt cat, with black shoe button eyes, pink stitched nose and mouth.

For the European market nine skittles comprised a set, whereas the sets intended for America had ten skittles.

Velvet skittles were available as early as 1892. A similar set of nine skittles first appeared in the Steiff catalog of 1897. (Christie's)   **$5,119**

An unusual carved and painted primitive man on horseback pull-toy, American late 19th or early 20th century, stylized figure of a man wearing a top hat, astride a horse with leather ears, glass button eyes and hide mane and tail; mounted on a shaped wooden base with yellow wheels, 15in. wide. (Sotheby's)   **$10,350**

A 1940s metal model pedal aeroplane.
(G.E.Sworder)　　　**$660**

Painted wood spring horse, American, late 19th century, in the form of a dapple gray horse, 43¼in. high.
(Skinner)　　　**$3,450**

◄ An amusing painted and lithographed wood toy sailor puppet, probably English, mid 19th century, the jointed and articulated figure of Jack Tar suspended by strings from a balance bar, the puppet dances when the bar is moved.
(Sotheby's)　　　**$690**

A carved and painted wood Noah's Ark toy, 19th century, probably German, the vessel with a removable side panel, painted in tones of yellow ocher, red and steel-blue with black details, the gabled roof painted in thick impasto with a dove in flight, including four figures of Noah, his wife and two children, and eighty-five pairs of carved and painted wood animals, including birds and insects, cats, flies, pigs, gulls, elephants, deer, beavers and wolves, length of ark 22¾in.
(Sotheby's)　　　**$5,462**

TOYS

A hand made and hand-painted model clockwork tin car by Jouets Français, the Richard Brasier, driven by Léon Théry who won the famous Gordon Bennett Cup in 1904 and 1905, with spoked wheels and original rubber tires, spare tire on rear, leather drive belts, linen upholstery, two brass headlamps and brass horn, original driver in handpainted plaster, on wire base, 15in. long. *(Auction Team Köln)* **$10,000**

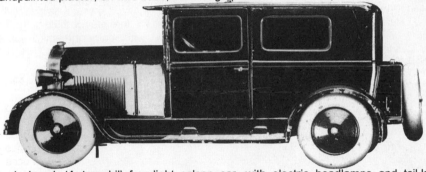

A clockwork 'Automobil' four-light saloon car, with electric headlamps and tail-lamp, painted dark blue with pale blue lining, black roof and wings, ocher window frames, silver running boards, spare wheel, operating steering, two opening doors, 42cm. long, 1928-1933, with a key. *(Christie's)* **$16,560**

A French clockwork automatic rowing boat toy, possibly by Scientific Toy Mfg., with wooden hull, and handpainted composition oarsman in original fabric clothing. The mechanism can be set to cover a certain distance before a change in direction by adjusting screw levers on the stern section. Stern cover made of tin with wooden lining, circa 1910, 57cm. long. *(Auction Team Köln)* **$3,684**

A Louis Vuitton trunk, covered in LV fabric and bound in leather and brass with wooden banding, monogramed at either end *J.O.H.P.*, the lid with white ribbon lattice, labeled *Louis Vuitton Paris London Nice Cannes Vichy*, 35½ x 21 x 13in. *(Christie's)* **$4,040**

A Louis Vuitton trunk, covered in LV fabric and bound in leather and brass with wooden banding, monogramed G.L.B. at either end, with red owner's stripes with a zigzag pattern, the interior fitted with three trays, two with compartments, labeled *Louis Vuitton Paris London Nice Lille 771678*, 35 x 19½ x 19in. *(Christie's)* **$5,152**

A fine and very rare incised and gilt-lacquered leather traveling pannier, Liao dynasty, incised through a black lacquer layer and gold-filled on four sides with pairs of phoenix, exotic birds and fantastic animals amidst leafy floral sprays and within a scrolling foliage border, the sides stitched and with brass corners and side mounts, four leather straps attached to the front and rear, 16½ x 20½in. *(Christie's)* **$33,741**

A Louis Vuitton trunk, covered in LV fabric and bound in black painted leather and brass, with wooden banding, the lid with white ribbon lattice, labeled *Louis Vuitton Paris London 180750*, 24 x 20½ x 16in. *(Christie's)* **$4,040**

A mid late Regency papier mâché tray by Clay, of rectangular form with canted angles, the black ground painted with a vase of flowers and a trailing foliate border, stamped to the underside *Clay, London*, 30½ x 21in. *(Christie's)* **$5,888**

A Victorian mahogany butler's tray on X-framed stand, the tray with hinged sides, pierced with carrying handles, on a ring-turned X-frame stand joined by similar stretchers, the tray, with sides down, the stand stamped *Moriso...Edinburgh*, 37in. wide. *(Christie's)* **$2,030**

A Louis-Philippe polychrome-decorated tôle tray, of oval shape with pierced Gothic gallery and carrying-handles, decorated with arabesques of monkeys on a cream ground with green border, on a modern ebonized and parcel-gilt stand with square tapering legs joined by an X-shaped stretcher, 23in. wide.
(Christie's) **$5,092**

An unusual Victorian painted and mother-of-pearl inlaid tray, mid 19th century, of oval outline, the ground decorated with a scene of the Crumlin viaduct with a steam train crossing, with painted and mother-of-pearl houses below and figures and sheep in the foreground, inscribed *Crumlin Viaduct*, the black painted gallery with gilt-heightened decoration, 29½in. wide. *(Christie's)* **$1,890**

A pair of Victorian lignum vitae candlesticks, the baluster knopped stems supporting flared candle sockets, on circular stepped bases, 8in. high. *(Christie's)* **$3,415**

A turned lignum vitae wassail bowl on stand, the slightly tapering ring-turned and reeded circular bowl, on a ring-turned baluster column and stepped circular base 16½in. high, 14in. diameter. *(Christie's)* **$8,018**

A 17th century hardwood caster of baluster form, the base with an ivory rim, the lid with an ivory button at the top, 6¾in. high. *(David Lay)* **$4,396**

A fine lignum vitae mortar of large size, second quarter 18th century, of baluster form, with bladed bands below the reeded flaring rim and rounded foot, 8½in. high, and a matching contemporary lignum vitae pestle, 15in. long. *(Christie's)* **$5,690**

Clear etched blown glass tumbler, John Frederick Amelung, New Bremen Glass Manufactory, near present day Frederick, Maryland, circa 1788-89, brilliant grayish color, open pontil on base, decorated with copper-wheel engraved floral and vine wreath encircling the word *Federal*, 6¹/8in. high.

This tumbler, and another with similar decoration and the word *Liberty,* were made to commemorate the ratification of the Constitution in 1788. *(Skinner)* **$83,900**

▶

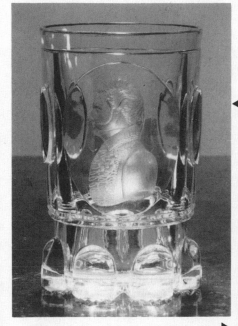

◀ A North Bohemian (Harrach) beaker engraved by Dominik Biemann with a portrait of Heinrich LXXII Prince of Reuß (1797-1853), signed *Biman*, the reverse with his coat-of-arms, circa 1830, 5¼in. high. *(Christie's)* **$191,520**

▶

A German dated thick-walled tumbler, dated *1663*, of dark emerald-green tint and cylindrical form with slightly inverted rim, the upper part inscribed in diamond-point *Trinckh mich auss und würff mich Nider/Heb mich auss so vill mich wider 16.63.* and embellished with a flowerhead above a milled band, the lower section applied with three rows of raspberry-prunts on an everted foot ring, 5¹/8in. high. These tumblers, known as 'unbreakable', all carry the same inscription and bear dates in the 1650s and 1660s. *(Christie's)* **$50,000**

It was as far back as 1714 that an Englishman, Henry Mill, first took out a patent for 'An Artificial Machine or Method for the Impression or Transcribing of Letters Singly or Progressively one after another, as in writing, whereby all Writing whatever may by Engrossed in Paper or Parchment so Neat and Exact as not to be distinguished from Print'. His design never went into production however, and it was not until nearly 130 years later, in 1843, that the American Charles Thurber in turn patented his idea of a mechanical typewriter. From then on the concept really caught the imagination of inventors and there were numerous attempts to produce readable copy. None were successful however until, in 1867, the first practical typewriter was invented by three Americans, Sholes, Glidden and Soule. Their machine worked on a shift key mechanism, which forms the basis of modern machines today.

There are plenty of early typewriters still to be found, mainly because of the enormous output of early manufacturers to cope with the immediate demand. In the 1870s alone, the companies of Remington, Oliver, Smith, Underwood and Yost sold over 50,000 models.

A North's typewriter, for the French market, with French keyboard and gilt title Le Nord on top and front frames, downstroke-from-rear type-bars and japanned cover marked *North's Typewriter.*
(Christie's) **$5,520**

A Crandall typewriter, with original tin hood, 1879, one of the most decorative typewriters of all time, with mother of pearl inlay and gilt decoration.
◄ *(Auction Team Köln)* **$4,850**

A rare Discret 'secret and universal ► typewriter', by Friedrich Rehmann, Karlsruhe, with single pointer and second adjustable scale for composing coded texts, with original wooden case, 1899.
(Auction Team Köln) **$8,814**

The Victor Index pointer typewriter, complete with ink pad, 1889. This American machine marked a milestone in typewriter history. It was already equipped with a typewheel and back hammer action, which was re-invented some 75 years later in the computer age as the daisy wheel. *(Auction Team Köln)* **$6,102**

A Columbia No 2 typewriter, with ▶ large typewheel for large and small script and with two differently designed pointers, 1884.

This is one of the most attractive early typewriters, devised by the New York clockmaker Charles Spiro, who later also developed the bar lock. It is the first recorded machine to have proportional type. *(Auction Team Köln)* **$6,102**

◀ An early Berlin Graphic pointer typewriter with a stunningly simple type system. The pointer resembles that of the 'Hall' machines, but is very robustly constructed, the Graphic is a successor to the Kneist. The imprint and carriage movement occur simultaneously by pressing the lever at the lower left stanchion, 1895. *(Auction Team Köln)*
$7,114

An unusual and attractive American Burnett typewriter with oblique typebasket, and 'streamlined' case, 1907.

Only six examples are known to exist worldwide, with very low serial numbers (this one is 786). According to Martin, the machine was only in production for a few months, and in comparison to other known models, this one is in excellent condition.
(Auction Team Köln) **$9,700**

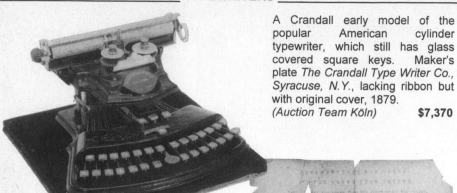

A Crandall early model of the popular American cylinder typewriter, which still has glass covered square keys. Maker's plate *The Crandall Type Writer Co., Syracuse, N.Y.*, lacking ribbon but with original cover, 1879.
(Auction Team Köln) **$7,370**

The Crown, 1894 – the first model ▶ of the famous American pointer typewriter by the pioneer Byron A. Brooks of New York. With three row typewheel, colored inking pads and the straight front which was typical of the first model. The lowest known serial number no. 209. With original wooden case and original instructions.
(Auction Team Köln) **$10,049**

◀
A very rare American Morris typewriter dating from 1885 of which only four are known.
(Auction Team Köln)

$21,600

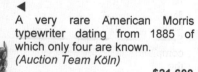

A Kosmopolit typewriter, with three typefaces and indices, on cast iron base with scrolling feet and large zinc nameplate, in walnut case.
(Christie's) **$10,120**

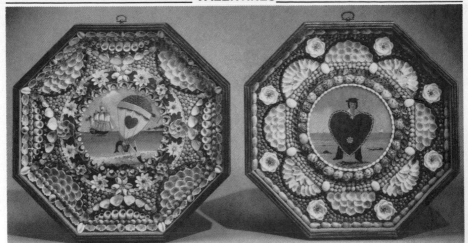

Ralph and Martha Cahoon and Bernard A. Woodman: two sailor's valentines, 20th century, the first painted with two mermaids leaping into a hot air balloon and a sailing ship in the distance, signed *R. Cahoon*, the second painted with a sailor standing on the shoreline holding a large red heart inscribed *Be My Valentine*, signed *Martha Cahoon,* each surrounded by pastel shells worked in geometric designs and set in an octagonal wood shadowbox frame, signed *B. Woodman*, overall diameter 15in.

Ralph Eugene Cahoon, Jr. was born in Chatham, Massachusetts on September 2, 1910. One of his favorite pastimes was sketching which was encouraged by his family and resulted in his entering the School of Practical Art in Boston. Upon completion of his schooling, he returned to the Cape and met and married Martha Farham in 1932. She was the daughter of Swedish immigrant parents and was a painter in her own right. Her father, Axel Farham, had been a painter for several decorating firms in Boston before he moved to Harwich to set up his own shop. Martha trained under her father, learning the art of decorative painting which included a mixture of Swedish folk painting called Rosemaling, a free-hand method of using scrolls and flowers and early American stencil design. Ralph Cahoon learned these techniques as well as observing both Martha and her father in their studio.

In 1935, the Cahoons moved to Osterville, Massachusetts and lived there for ten years decorating and selling furniture and antiques. In 1945, they moved to Santuit, a historic section of Contuit, and this became their home, studio and shop until Ralph's death in 1982. Ralph turned to easel painting full time in the 1950s and tried various surfaces to capture his primitive style of painting. He discovered that Swedish masonite was the surface that most resembled the smooth, firm surface of furniture and best exhibited his technique of incorporating the use of stencils, the play of light and dark with combinations of bold colors and smooth brush strokes to give a feeling of a captured moment in time.

Bernard A. Woodman of Marstons Mills, Massachusetts, became fascinated at an early age with a sailor's valentine belonging to his mother. He was crippled with arthritis as a child, and as the disease progressed, was declared totally disabled and unemployable. After spending some time in several occupations that left him dissatisfied, he turned his talents toward creating sailor's valentines. Woodman showed his valentines to Ralph Cahoon who proceeded to encourage and assist him in his work. Woodman and Cahoon worked together on numerous works that combined painting with shell-work borders. *(Sotheby's)* **$19,550**

Also known as matchholders or fusee boxes, these consisted of a small container with a striking surface for holding and lighting matches. They were made from about 1830 onwards in two forms, a small portable variety and a larger type for standing on a desk or table. The basic form had a hinged lid at one end and a striking surface, sometimes concealed, of parallel ridges or, later, of glass paper, at the other. As the century progressed designs became more fanciful and elaborate and many novelty forms were produced.

The Grouse Moor, silver vesta case, rectangular, the front decorated with an enameled scene of a grouse hunt featuring two guns, a dog and a beater in a heather strewn moor, J. Millward Banks, Chester 1900, 5.5cm. *(Christie's)* **$9,000**

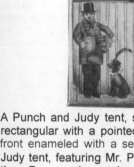

A Punch and Judy tent, silver vesta case, rectangular with a pointed domed top, the front enameled with a seaside Punch and Judy tent, featuring Mr. Punch, Judy, Toby the Dog and a drummer, Sampson Mordan, London 1887, 5.4cm. *(Christie's)* **$13,500**

Nude on shoreline, silver vesta case, rounded rectangular, the front enameled with a reclining nude female seated on a shoreline, waves and skyline beyond, London import marks, 5cm. *(Christie's)* **$1,405**

An owl, silver vesta case, realistically chased with plumage and with applied boot button eyes, probably Sampson Mordan, London 1894, 5.7cm. *(Christie's)* **$1,685**

A rare California gold match safe, probably San Francisco, circa 1855, the front inlaid with gold quartz centering an enameled reserve with a monogram *PC* or *CP* against a leaf, the reverse engraved *Souvenir of California* above a harbor scene, the hinged cover set with an agate panel, 2¼in. long. *(Christie's)* **$5.175**

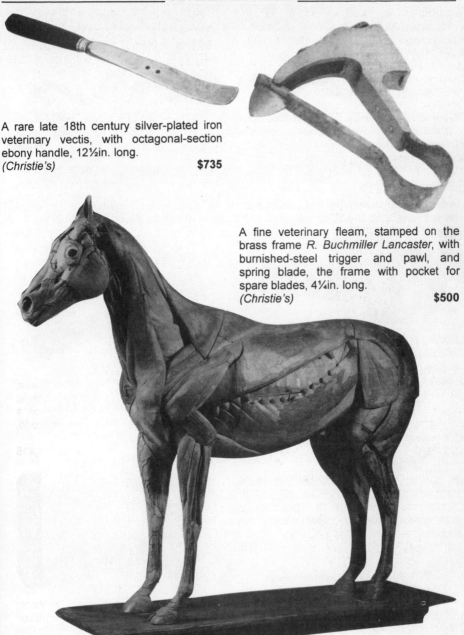

A rare late 18th century silver-plated iron veterinary vectis, with octagonal-section ebony handle, 12½in. long.
(Christie's) **$735**

A fine veterinary fleam, stamped on the brass frame *R. Buchmiller Lancaster*, with burnished-steel trigger and pawl, and spring blade, the frame with pocket for spare blades, 4¼in. long.
(Christie's) **$500**

A rare 19th-century papier mâché, plaster and wood veterinary anatomical model of a standing horse, constructed of many removable components, delicately colored to show the organs, veins, muscles and bone structure, on wood plinth base with castors, 70½in. high. *(Christie's)* **$47,840**

A narwhal tusk walking stick, the naturally tapered and writhen tusk with floral decorated silver top cap, 36¼in. long. *(Christie's)* **$3,219**

Carved wood walking stick, America, 19th century, in the form of a snake, highly stylized, intricately sculpted with each scale individually carved, with a benign face, original patina, 32in. long. *(Skinner)* **$10,350**

A fine carved whale ivory and panbone cane, mid 19th century, having a whale ivory fist handle continuing to a panbone barley shaft with relief carved diamonds and spirals, 36in. long. *(Sotheby's)* **$2,185**

Carved polychrome wood walking stick, the knob in the form of a black man's head, original surface, 39½in. long. *(Skinner)* **$6,000**

A fine and rare carved whale ivory, horn and wood cane, 19th century, having a handle carved in horn in the form of a right whale lying across the top of a carved horn whale oil keg; the tail fashioned from whale ivory, 34½in. long. *(Sotheby's)* **$4,312**

A gemset silver-gilt mounted hardstone cane-handle, in the Fabergé style, humorously carved as the head of a bulldog, with cabochon sapphire eyes, the mount as a spiked collar, 2in. wide. *(Christie's)* **$3,770**

Carved whale ivory and whalebone walking stick, 19th century, ivory Turk's head knot knob above alternating carved and paneled baleen spacers and intricately carved geometric and spiral carved panels continuing to a reeded, spiral twist then tapering shaft, ivory tip, 34in. long. *(Skinner)* **$8,050**

A jeweled gold-mounted nephrite cane handle by Fabergé, workmaster's initials unclear, St. Petersburg, circa 1890. Tau-shaped, the scroll hardstone handle with gold ropework mount with cabochon ruby finials, marked indistinctly inside mount, with original tipped cane, 4in. wide. *(Christie's)* **$5,658**

A pair of French carved giltwood wall brackets, late 19th century, each modeled with putto supporting platforms with tasseled drapery, 17¼in. high.
(Christie's) **$3,600**

One of a pair of Rococo giltwood phoenix wall brackets, probably English, circa 1760, each having a scalloped platform supported by a spread-wing phoenix perched on a C-scroll with fruit and flowers below, 16 x 12½in. high.
(Sotheby's) **$16,100**

A Régence style carved giltwood and painted wall bracket, 19th century, the breakfront platform with geometric frieze on a tapering support modeled with foliate scrolls and male mask terminal, 19¼in. high. (Christie's) **$2,650**

A cream-painted and parcel-gilt bracket, the rectangular top with gadrooned edge, the front centered by a female mask below three feathers and flanked by scrolls, with lambrequin boss, 17½in. wide.
(Christie's) **$21,250**

A George III mahogany wardrobe, after a design by John Vardy, originally an organ case, the molded cornice with breakfront center and angles above concave-cut dentils and a pair of long doors, the sides and uprights headed by acanthus and rockwork-carved volutes suspending drapery, the panels applied with foliate blind fretwork with central columns and scroll arches, the lower part of each door with quatrefoil scroll motifs within angles of rockwork clasps, 95in. high.

(Christie's) **$31,860**

An oak and cork wardrobe, designed by Eileen Gray, 1932–34, tall narrow framework with long side door, three hinged drawers and one lower compartment, 64in. high, 20¾in. wide.

(Christie's) **$55,694**

A Peter Waals calamander wardrobe, with rectangular top above a pair of cushioned panel doors, enclosing hanging space, with chamfered latch, and similarly paneled sides, on shaped feet, 47in. wide.

(Christie's) **$17,250**

An oak wastebasket, by Gustav Stickley, 1907, 14in. high, 12in. diameter. *(Skinner)* **$1,650**

A mahogany paper bin, 20th century, of cylindrical form, the exterior modeled as book spines decorated in gilt, 14in. high. *(Christie's)* **$6,375**

A mahogany octagonal waste-paper basket with sides pierced with Chinese fretwork and handles, on bracket feet, 13¾in. high. *(Christie's)* **$2,000**

A white painted waste paper basket, attributed to Josef Hoffmann and the Wiener Werkstätte, circa 1905, hexagonal, pierced with checkers and with four larger squares at the top, 24in. high. *(Christie's)* **$2,437**

◄ Breguet No. 4405 sold to Lord Willoughby on the 12th July 1830 for the sum of 5000 Francs, a fine unusually dialed première class lever watch with moonphase and calendar, finely silvered and engine turned dial with eccentric chapter ring Roman with numeral reserves, central engraved sun motif with matching hands, the moonphase with aperture at 12 o' clock flanked by day and date sectors, signed *Breguet* at 10 o' clock and opposite regulation indicator, the gilt movement jeweled to the center with 5 spoke wheels, brass escapewheel with tooth oil holes and endstone jewel, jeweled steel poised pallets, two arm bimetallic balance wheel with overcoil spring and parachute suspension, the finely engine turned case with rear shutter female winding hole and regulation square in the case band together with setting push pieces for the calendar.
(Bonhams) **$47,700**

A gentleman's fine and rare 24 hour and world time wristwatch with two crowns, signed *Patek Philippe & Co.*, 1954, the nickel plated movement jeweled to the center with gold alloy balance and micrometer regulation, adjusted to heat, cold, isochronism and to five positions, caliber 12-400 and Geneva quality seal, the engine-turned silver dial plate with raised gold baton numerals and gold hands, inner rotating 24-hour ring shaded to represent day and night, rotating once in 24 hours and adjusted by the winding crown, outer silvered rotating ring with 41 cities of the world adjusted by the second crown, in circular case with faceted lugs and snap on back, maker's leather strap and gold buckle, 36mm. diam.

Louis Cottier invented this complicated fully adjustable world time system and production of a small series of this model began in 1953. The principle of the mechanism is that the 24 hour ring rotates anti-clockwise once in 24 hours so that the time indicated on the dial face, for example, 2.00p.m. is indicated as 1400 hours at 12 o' clock on the 24 hour ring. The wearer adjusts the outer ring until his location is shown at 12 o' clock. The current time at all the other locations is then set correctly.
(Christie's) **$489,310**

A rare gold minute repeating perpetual calendar and moonphase keyless hunter pocketwatch, signed *Patek Philppe & Co.*, movement to the hammers with bimetallic balance, micrometer regulation, 31 jewels, adjusted to heat, cold, isochronism and to five positions, wolf-tooth winding, repeating on two gongs by operating a slide in the band, the matt silvered dial with applied gold Breguet numerals, subsidiary dials for day, date and month with sector for the moon at 12, gold hands, in plain heavy gold case with five piece hinges, double springs and hinged cuvette, the front cover with an engraved design of a fish within a geometrical pattern, 56mm. diameter. *(Christie's)* **$87,007**

An early 18th century German silver verge form watch, modeled as a book, each cover engraved with wheatear borders, and centered by a flower with additional foliate decoration, the spine with three wheatear bands, the page edges gilt, with a mock central clasp opening to reveal a one piece silver dial signed in the center *Planck Gratz*, with single hand and champlevé chapter ring within a chased foliate scroll surround, the rectangular movement with pierced and engraved cock with large shaped foot, and Egyptian pillars, signed *Johan Planck, Gratz*, 45 x 54 x 19mm. *(Phillips)* **$8,096**

◀

A rare Swiss double sided lever with seven world time dials and half perpetual calendar in a silver ball clock, keyless gilt bar movement with going barrel, plain cock with polished steel regulator, club foot lever escapement, compensation balance with blue steel hairspring. Roman numerals, blue steel hands, seven small chapters with Roman numerals marked *Paris - New York - St. Petersburg - Calcutta - Melbourne - Vienna - Berlin*. Substantial plain silver case with two hemispheres of lightly colored glass, one with a flat to allow the clock to stand, thumb sets for the time and calendar in the band, signed *Lawson & Son, Brighton*, circa 1890. *(Pieces of Time)* **$6,240**

Horse and sulky gilt molded copper weathervane, attributed to J. W. Fiske & Co., late 19th century, 'St. Julian', 45¼in. long. *(Skinner)* **$28,750**

Small cast iron horse weather vane, Rochester Iron Works, circa 1890, vibrant patina of rust bleeding through mustard colored sizing, 18½ x 14½in. *(Skinner)* **$31,050**

A fine molded and gilded copper leaping horse weathervane, A.L. Jewell & Co., Waltham, Massachusetts, third quarter 19th century, the swell-bodied figure of a leaping horse with applied mane and tail, mounted on an orb, overall height 26½in., 35½in. long. (Sotheby's) **$46,000**

► Rare steeplechase horse weathervane, New England, circa 1885, maker unknown, patinated copper with verdigris surface, the fully sculpted body with applied ears and eyes and applied repoussé mane and tail, 26 x 34in. (Skinner) **$86,100**

Bull molded and applied copper weathervane, possibly A.L. Jewell & Co., Waltham, Massachusetts, last quarter 19th century, fine verdigris, (bullet holes), 30¹/8 in. high, 42in. long. (Skinner) **$34,500**

485

Large cast iron horse weathervane, Rochester Iron Works, circa 1890, found in Vermont, 26 x 34in. *(Skinner)* **$48,300**

An extremely rare American locomotive and tender copper weathervane, circa 1882, the locomotive reproduced in fine detail is mounted on track with two ball finials at track end, and attached ball counterweight, in fine original condition with verdigris surface, 17in. high, 61in. long, 8in. deep. *(Skinner)* **$185,000**

Merino ram, 'Ethan Allen' molded and gilded copper weather vane, attributed to J.W. Fiske & Co., New York, late 19th century, the full bodied figure of a Merino ram with molded zinc head and sheet copper repoussé horns and ears, with weathered gilding and verdigris surface.

This weathervane stood on one of the buildings of the Abbot Worsted Company, organized in 1855 and producing wool and mohair yarns for upholstery and knitting until 1956. This manufacturer began in Graniteville, Massachusetts, and in 1879 expanded to Forge Village. *(Skinner)* **$68,500**

A large Welsh lacquered sycamore love spoon, late 19th century, the wide tapering handle pierced overall with various symbols and motifs, within chip-carved borders, with triangular-section bowl, 24½in. long, 10in. at widest point. *(Christie's)* **$4,550**

A George IV Welsh treen love spoon, dated 1825, with three integral spoons, the fret-cut handle pierced with rosettes and chip carved with zigzag borders flanking a mirror panel, carved with the initials and date *M.J. 1825 E.J.*, 15¼ x 5½in. *(Christie's)* **$7,210**

An exceptionally large Welsh lacquered sycamore love spoon, late 19th century, the wide tapering handle in two sections, hinged with two oval loops at the center, pierced overall with symbols and motifs within chip-carved borders, the bowl of triangular section, 35in. long, 10½in. at widest point. *(Christie's)* **$4,745**

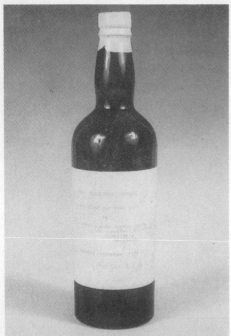

Rare 19th century Glenlivet single malt, The Glenlivet, 48 year old, distilled 19th May 1883, bottled December 1931. Distilled and bottled by George & John Gordon Smith, The Glenlivet Distillery, Glenlivet, Scotland. Plain typed label, rubber stamped and indistinctly signed in ink, *For Geo. & J. G. Smith.* Brown colored glass bottle, driven cork, plain cream colored lead capsule. Level: into neck, 1 bottle.

The above is a very rare example of 19th century Glenlivet single malt, the overall appearance of the bottle is excellent, as is the level of the spirit which is very clear and also has a good appearance.

(Christie's) **$4,890**

Very finest 50 year-old Macallan, The Macallan, 50 year old, bottle number 11 of 500, distilled 1928, bottled 1983. Distilled and bottled by Macallan-Glenlivet PLC, Craigellachie. Accompanied by a letter of authenticity signed by Allan G Shiach, Chairman. In leather bound wooden presentation case. Under strength, natural cask strength, single malt, 38.6% vol., one bottle.

The letter which accompanies the above lot states that the 50 year old is a result of bottling three barrels of spirit distilled between 1926 and 1928. Only the finest of malt whiskies can live for 50 unbroken years in the same cask. During this period both the volume and spirit strength evaporate through the oak as a natural part of the maturing process. Unlike lesser quality whiskies, the spirit content of The Macallan-50 years old is reduced naturally, and bottled at natural cask strength, exposing only a round and mellow eminence. This strength of 38.6% vol., a couple of degrees below normal bottling strength has not been diluted by anything but time.

(Christie's) **$7,335**

The Wiener Werkstätte or Vienna Workshops, were, as the name suggests, an association of Austrian artists and craftsmen after the style of C.R. Ashbee's Guild of Handicraft. Their commercial director was F. Warndörfer, and such notables as Koloman Moser and Josef Hoffmann were the first art directors. The aim of the association was to apply artistic principles and designs to the widest possible range of items, from textiles to architecture, and they became, in the succeeding decades, a driving force in European design.

They are perhaps particularly known for their metalwork, in silver and base metals. Much of their output was designed by Hoffmann in geometric, formalized Jugendstil form, though they also produced the famous 'whiplash' pieces, referred to by Charles Rennie Mackintosh in uncomplimentary fashion as resembling 'strained spaghetti'. Later, they adopted starkly Cubist, stepped forms, in which they made such items as coffee sets, samovars and lamps.

Their ceramics are notable for their stark simplicity of design. Many of their designs were produced by the Wiener Keramik workshop, which was established in 1905 under Michael Powolny and Bertold Löffler.

The Wiener Werkstätte themselves finally closed in 1932, mainly because of their inability to compete commercially with mass production.

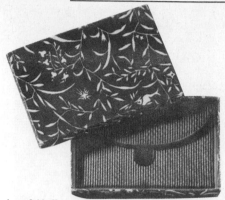

Josef Hoffman for the Wiener Werkstätte, purse, circa 1910–11, gilt tooled leather, original cardboard box, the purse stamped in gilt *Wiener Werkstätte*, 9.25 x 14.75cm. *(Sotheby's)* **$1,875**

A napkin ring, designed by Josef Hoffmann, manufactured by the Wiener Werkstätte, circa 1905/10, pierced with formalized flowers, 2³⁄₈in. wide, stamped *WW* monogram and Viennese poinçon. *(Christie's)* **$1,713**

'Spring', glazed ceramic figure of a putto, designed by Michael Powolny, manufactured by Wiener Keramik, 1907, standing holding a garland of colorful flowers, 15in. high, impressed designer's monogram and Wiener Keramik mark. *(Christie's)* **$12,184**

Josef Hoffmann for the Wiener Werkstätte, candlestick, 1925, silver-colored metal, stamped with designer's monogram *JH* and with *WW* monogram, 8⁵⁄₈in. high. *(Sotheby's)* **$6,748**

▲

A printed silk costume, textile produced by the Wiener Werkstätte, 1915/20, in the form of simple coat with central ribbon tie, inset with plain black silk panel above and below the tie, deep black silk border, patch pockets, printed with geometric design incorporating tulips and sprigs of flowers, selvedge printed *Wiener Werkstätte*. *(Christie's)* **$6,560**

A glazed terracotta frame, designed by Vally Wieselthier, manufactured by the Wiener Werkstätte, circa 1928. Rectangular with ribbon details above and at one side, modeled with three stylized heads with scattered fruit and leaves, 11¼in. maximum width. Impressed artist's and *WW* monogram, stamped *Made in Austria 489 1*. *(Christie's)* **$7,710**

An individual eggstand, designed by Josef Hoffmann, manufactured by the Wiener Werkstätte, circa 1905/10, ring base with four straps pierced with formalized flowers supporting the eggcup, 3in. high. Stamped designer's monogram, *WW* monogram and registration mark, stamped monogram *JW* for Josef Wagner, silversmith, Viennese poinçon. *(Christie's)* **$8,910**

A small chrysoprase-set vase, designed by Koloman Moser, executed by the Wiener Werkstätte, circa 1903, set with four sets of four cabochon-set chrysoprase, applied and pierced monogram and date *H 1903 B,* 4½in. high. *(Christie's)* **$11,622**

Josef Hoffmann for the Wiener Werkstätte, executed by Alfred Mayer, coffee service, 1913, comprising; coffee pot, milk jug, sugar basin and cover and tray, silver colored metal, ebony, malachite cabochons, the coffee pot, milk jug and sugar basin stamped on the underside with designer's and maker's monograms, *WW* monogram and rose trademark, the tray stamped with designer's monogram, *WW* monogram and rose trademark, coffee pot 6⁵/8in. high. *(Sotheby's)* **$33,741**

A George II mahogany wine cooler, the oval top edged with gilt-lacquered brass chain-and-rosette border, 27¾in. wide.
(Christie's) **$165,000**

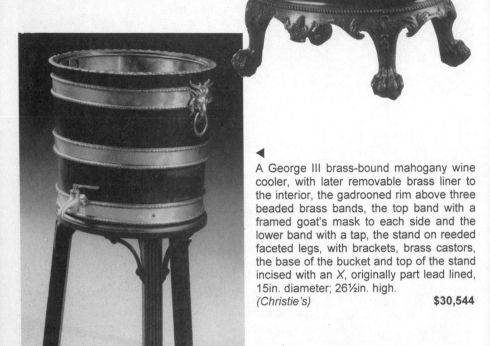

◄

A George III brass-bound mahogany wine cooler, with later removable brass liner to the interior, the gadrooned rim above three beaded brass bands, the top band with a framed goat's mask to each side and the lower band with a tap, the stand on reeded faceted legs, with brackets, brass castors, the base of the bucket and top of the stand incised with an *X*, originally part lead lined, 15in. diameter; 26½in. high.
(Christie's) **$30,544**

A carved and stained wood cellaret, late 19th century, probably Anglo-Indian, of tapering rectangular form, on claw feet, the rising cover with lozenge pattern, the side carved in high relief with trailing fruiting vines and further foliage, 25in. high, 28in. wide. *(Christie's)* **$11,385**

The 'Ker' Amen glass, circa 1745–50, the massive drawn-trumpet goblet with a plain stem enclosing an elongated tear above a folded conical foot, the bowl engraved in diamond-point with a crown above a mirror-monogram of the letters *JR* direct and reverse to form the Royal cypher of King James VIII, the figure *8* worked into the monogram at the base, flanked by the last four lines of the first verse of the Jacobite Anthem:
Send Him Victorious
Happy and Glorious
Soon to Reign Over Us
God Save The King
11½in. high.

According to family tradition James Ker of Blackshiels, a hamlet in the parish of Humbie, East Lothian, some fifteen miles south-east of Edinburgh, and the original owner of the goblet, acted as one of the bankers to Charles Edward Stuart, The Young Pretender (1720–88), a position which led to his financial ruin after the Battle of Culloden in 1746. The goblet passed from his son James Ker of Blackshiels (1750–1819) through his son James, to his son John Archibald Ker (1818–1915), his elder brother Captain James Ker (1817–1856) having been killed at the Battle of Inkerman. The glass then passed through the female line to Brigadier Thomas Farquharson Ker Howard (1899–1964) from whom it has descended to the present owner.
(Christie's) **$56,925**

A fine diamond-point engraved façon de Venise goblet, Dutch, dated *1706*, the funnel bowl engraved with a continuous scene of a stag chased by two hounds flanked by trees, inscribed *T Welvaren Van Het Vaderlant 1706*, set on a hollow ball knop flanked by mereses over a wide conical foot with folded rim, 8¹/₈in. high.
(Sotheby's) **$7,298**

Two cut glass hock glasses, designed by Otto Prutscher, circa 1910, overlaid in blue, the square stems with checkers, 8¼in. high. *(Christie's)* **$16,278**

A façon de Venise polychrome armorial goblet, first third of the 16th century, Venice or South Germany, the flared bowl enameled in iron-red, ocher, black, white and blue with the arms of Haller vom Hallerstein and Imhoff linked and suspended by ocher scrolling tendrils from a triple gilt line band, the reverse with two Haller crested helmets, on a conical foot with folded rim enriched in gilding and with a gilt band between the bowl and foot, 5³⁄₈in. high.

This goblet was most probably made to celebrate a marriage between the Von Imhoff and Haller families; perhaps the second marriage of Ulrich Haller to Magdalena Imhoff (daughter of Hans Imhoff IV), the exact date of which is not known but thought to have taken place early in the 16th century. During the 15th and 16th centuries members of the Imhoff family were affluent and influential merchants from Nuremberg, patronizing artists such as Titian and Dürer, with strong trading connections with Venice. *(Christie's)* **$75,000**

Five hock glasses, designed by Koloman Moser, manufactured by Meyr's Neffe for E. Bakalowits Söhne, 1901, each with small bowl with dappled dot effect, supported on tall slender stem, in the following colors: two green stems with clear bowls, one amber stem with clear bowl, one purple stem with clear bowl, one purple stem with amber bowl, 12½in. high. *(Christie's)* **$49,691**

A Chippendale carved mahogany easy chair, Philadelphia, 1760–1780, the arched crestrail above an upholstered back flanked by shaped wings continuing to outward C-scroll scrolled arms enclosing a compass seat, on short cabriole legs with shell-carved knees and ball-and-claw feet, 45½in. high.

Related in function to baroque style hinged-wing 'invalid' chairs, the easy chair, as it evolved in the 18th century, was an expression of greater affluence and luxury on a more substantial form. Often constructed with frames to hold chamber pots, recent scholarship indicates that these forms were located on the upper level floors of the household and used principally by men and women whose ailment required they sleep upright. The disappearance of this form in the 19th century coincides with the increase of hospitals and clinics and attests to its primary function as aiding and comforting the sick.

(Christie's) **$244,500**

A fine and rare Chippendale carved and figured mahogany easy chair, Philadelphia, circa 1770, the arched crest flanked by ogival wings and downswept arms on C-scrolled supports centering a loose-fitted cushion and overupholstered seat on cabriole legs ending in claw-and-ball feet, height to top of seat cushion 18¼in.

With its horizontally rolled arms with accompanying C-scrolls, dramatically raked-back rear legs, generous, compassed-shaped seat and substantial cabriole legs ending in ball and claw feet, this chair offers a classic Philadelphia take on the easy chair form. As the product of a combined effort by an upholsterer and chairmaker, fully upholstered chairs with protective coves or wings projecting from the sides of the back above the arms were one of the costliest forms of colonial furniture. Although the form fell out of vogue in England with the introduction of Chippendale style in the 1740s, in America it remained popular, almost without alterations, until the Federal period.

(Sotheby's) **$310,500**

A fine Queen Anne carved and turned walnut easy chair, Boston, Massachusetts, 1740-60, the arched crest flanked by ogival wings continuing to conical supports, centering a loose-fitted cushion and overupholstered bowfronted seat, on cabriole legs joined by turned block-and-vase-form stretchers and ending in pad feet. *(Sotheby's)* **$79,500**

◄ A Queen Anne mahogany easy chair, Boston area, 1730–60, the shaped crestrail above an upholstered canted back flanked by shaped wings over outscrolling arms above an over-upholstered seat with bowed front rail, on cabriole legs with pad-and-disk feet joined by baluster-turned H stretchers, 47in. high. *(Christie's)* **$55,200**

A William and Mary turned maple easy-chair, Boston, 1700–25, the arched outscrolling crest above a canted back flanked by shaped wings over outscrolling arms continuing to similar arm supports above a trapezoidal seat frame with double-ogee shaped skirt, on vasiform and ring-turned legs joined by baluster, vasiform and ring-turned H-stretchers with Spanish feet, 51in. high. *(Christie's)* **$250,000**

A George I walnut ratchet-back wing armchair, the slightly arched top, outscrolled arms, bowed seat and squab cushion covered in contemporary florally-patterned petit and gros point needlework, the cabriole legs headed by a scallop-shell and shaped brackets and terminating in pad feet, previously with castors, one leg with peg holes for strengthening.

This remarkable wing armchair has the unusual distinction of having been owned by two of the greatest and pioneering collectors of English Furniture. The celebrated connoisseur Sir George Donaldson (d. 1924) formed a 'Private Museum' at Hove, Sussex in the early 20th century. Arranged by period with a Jacobean Room, a Chippendale Room, and a Queen Anne Room, the Museum exhibited a wide range of the arts dating from antiquity to the 18th century.

The collection formed by Percival D. Griffiths under the wise counsel of R. W. Symonds is considered to be arguably the greatest collection of English Furniture formed this century. Indeed, it was Griffiths' collection that provided the content for Symond's seminal work English Furniture from Charles II to George II.

In form, this ratchet-back chair is inspired by the 'sleeping chairs' of the 17th century, such as that supplied to John Maitland, Duke of Lauderdale, (1682) for Ham House, Surrey.

However, with its 'moreen' covered back and hooks to the seat-rail, it is similarly upholstered to much of the contemporary seat-furniture supplied to Sir Robert Walpole (d. 1745) for Houghton Hall, Norfolk. The original needlework of this wing armchair has, however, been reattached and restuffed since the 1929 publication of English Furniture from Charles II to George II, and originally had needlework sides. *(Christie's)* **$166,830**

Polychrome painted and stencil decorated wood valance, America, circa 1860–80, the green painted rectangular valance with central cartouche in ivory, salmon and mustard showing farmhouse with horse, mountains and sailboats, with gilt decorated foliate spandrels, 41³/8in. wide. *(Skinner)* **$3,735**

A Swiss carved wood casket, circa 1880, by C.V. Bergen & Co., modeled in the form of a wicker basket containing a litter of six kittens, the interior of the casket button upholstered in bleu celeste sateen, the casket modeled to the front with a label held with cord, stamped *C.V. Bergen & Co., Interlaken.*, 19in. wide., 15¾in. high. *(Christie's)* **$17,075**

A carved and painted pine coiled rattlesnake, American, late 19th/early 20th century, the coiled snake with incised skin and extended rattler painted in tones of brown, olive green, black and red, 12in high.
(Sotheby's) **$9,200**

A giltwood and painted model of an Egyptian sphinx, after George John Vulliamy, possibly late 19th century, 38in. long.

The original sphinx, labeled 'Tuthmosis', was designed by George John Vulliamy, architect to the London Metropolitan Board of Works, to accompany the Egyptian granite obelisk, known as 'Cleopatra's Needle', when it was erected on the Thames Embankment in 1880.
(Christie's) **$3,036**

A Netherlandish oak figure of a reclining dragon, 16th century, probably from a Saint George group, the beast baring his fangs and with head turned back and gazing upward, 11⅝ x 18⅛in.
(Sotheby's) **$7,475**

A carved and painted pine bust of General Grant, American, 19th century, the full bodied figure with a mustache and long beard, wearing a black uniform with yellow detail, on a stepped base, 6⅝in. high. *(Sotheby's)* **$3,450**

An Augsburg polychrome limewood relief of Henry VIII, after Hans Holbein, mid-16th century, showing the King bearded, in three-quarter view looking to his left; wearing black bonnet with jewels, pearls and feather, jacket tied at the neck with gilt embroidered band, two gold chains around his neck, one jeweled, inscribed in ink on the reverse, 16½ x 14³/8in.

The image is closest to Holbein's portrait of Henry VIII of circa 1536 and to the figure of the King in the Royal group wall-painting formerly in the Privy Chamber at Whitehall Palace. The latter was finished in 1537, destroyed by fire in 1689 and is now known from the cartoon in the National Portrait Gallery.

These both date from the mid-1530s during Holbein's second sojourn in England. *(Sotheby's)* **$24,150**

A Continental polychrome-painted wood figure, late 19th century, modeled as a seated and bewigged gentleman holding a cane, with secret compartment to his back, 31¾in. high. *(Christie's)* **$2,944**

An oak carving of sleeping faun by William Simmonds, 1935, carved in three quarter relief with fine detailing, the face inset with ebony eye, stained wood plinth, 5½in. length of faun. *(Christie's)* **$13,120**

A fine carved and painted pine and gesso figure of a poodle with a basket, Wilhelm Schimmel, Cumberland Valley, Pennsylvania, circa 1880, the stylized figure of a poodle standing foursquare with tail extended back, 7½in. long.
(Sotheby's) **$35,650**

Rare carved wood and painted figure of a black man, 19th century, the figure wearing carved and painted overalls and collared shirt, looking slightly to his right, resting his hands on the end of a hoe or shovel, his right leg crossed over his left, used outdoors, appears to have been carved for a specific niche, approx. 31in. high.

At some point in his history, someone attempted to make him white by painting his face white and his hair red.
(Skinner) **$29,900**

A South German (probably Ulm) painted wood relief of 'Noli me tangere' circa 1500, the Magdalene on the right kneeling before Christ standing to the left, the Saviour holding a spade, within associated painted wood framework with tracery above, 32½ x 22½in. *(Sotheby's)* **$19,550**

Paint decorated carved wood pig, 20th century, with glass eyes, leather ears and metal tail, 20¼in. long.
(Skinner) **$862**

A German architectural fragment, the wood partially gilt painted in polychrome, in the form of an urn issuing flowers and foliage, early 18th century, 124.5cm. high.
(Christie's) **$9,570**

A Netherlandish oak group of Saint Martin on horseback, last quarter of the 15th century, the figure cutting his cloak for the beggar, on naturalistic base, 33¾ x 26in.
(Sotheby's) **$25,300**

A carved and painted pine circus figure: The Pugilist, American, circa 1870, the free-standing full-length figure carved in the round with arms extended, wearing red-and-white striped shorts, on a rectangular rolling stand, overall height 64in.
(Sotheby's) **$4,600**

An Austrian (Salzburg school) ▶ painted wood Pieta, circa 1430, the veiled figure with her left hand at her chest, her right hand supporting the neck of Christ, on integrally carved shaped base, 21½in. high.
(Sotheby's)   **$23,000**

◀ Pair of Black Forest carved figural bear-form armchairs, third quarter 19th century, 44in. high.
(Skinner)   **$12,075**

Fine lacquered wood wrestling group, Meiji period, the smooth but realistically modeled surfaces painted in tones of brown lacquer with silver lacquer highlighting the grimacing eyes of each combatant, 13¾in. high.
(Butterfield & Butterfield)
                    $5,500 ▶

Two fish and a frog, signed *L. A. Plummer 1904*, polychrome wood carving, 25 x 40¼in. *(Skinner)* **$17,250**

Carved and painted wood figural towel holder, 20th century, in the form of a woman with outstretched arms holding a bar, blue dress with applied black leather strips and foil covered belt buckle and buttons, 14in. wide. *(Skinner)* **$9,775**

Index

INDEX

INDEX

511

INDEX